The Parallel Philosophies of Sartre and Nietzsche

Also available from Bloomsbury

Lacan Contra Foucault, edited by Nadia Bou Ali and Rohit Goel
Nietzsche and Friendship, by Willow Verkerk
Sartre and Magic, by Daniel O'Shiel
'The Gift' in Nietzsche's Zarathustra, by Emilio Carlo Corriero

The Parallel Philosophies of Sartre and Nietzsche

Ethics, Ontology and the Self

Nik Farrell Fox

BLOOMSBURY ACADEMIC
LONDON • NEW YORK • OXFORD • NEW DELHI • SYDNEY

BLOOMSBURY ACADEMIC
Bloomsbury Publishing Plc
50 Bedford Square, London, WC1B 3DP, UK
1385 Broadway, New York, NY 10018, USA
29 Earlsfort Terrace, Dublin 2, Ireland

BLOOMSBURY, BLOOMSBURY ACADEMIC and the Diana logo are trademarks of Bloomsbury Publishing Plc

First published in Great Britain 2022
This paperback edition published 2023

Copyright © Nik Farrell Fox, 2022

Nik Farrell Fox has asserted his right under the Copyright, Designs and Patents Act, 1988, to be identified as Author of this work.

For legal purposes the Acknowledgements on p. xii constitute an extension of this copyright page.

Cover design by Charlotte Daniels
Cover image: Waves rolling onto a black sand beach seen from a drone point of view, Vik, Iceland (©Abstract Aerial Art / Getty Images)

All rights reserved. No part of this publication may be reproduced or transmitted in any form or by any means, electronic or mechanical, including photocopying, recording, or any information storage or retrieval system, without prior permission in writing from the publishers.

Bloomsbury Publishing Plc does not have any control over, or responsibility for, any third-party websites referred to or in this book. All internet addresses given in this book were correct at the time of going to press. The author and publisher regret any inconvenience caused if addresses have changed or sites have ceased to exist, but can accept no responsibility for any such changes.

A catalogue record for this book is available from the British Library.

A catalog record for this book is available from the Library of Congress.

ISBN: HB: 978-1-3502-4816-8
PB: 978-1-3502-4820-5
ePDF: 978-1-3502-4817-5
eBook: 978-1-3502-4818-2

Typeset by Deanta Global Publishing Services, Chennai, India

To find out more about our authors and books visit www.bloomsbury.com and sign up for our newsletters.

You ask me which of the philosophers' traits are really idiosyncrasies? For example, their lack of an historical sense, their hatred of the very idea of becoming, their Egypticism. They think that they show their respect *for a thing when they dehistoricize it,* sub specie aeterni – *when they turn it into a mummy. All that philosophers have handled for thousands of years have been concept-mummies; nothing real escaped their grasp alive. Whenever these venerable concept-idolaters revere something, they kill it and stuff it; they threaten the life of everything they worship.*
(Nietzsche, Twilight of the Idols 3.1)

An anti-metaphysical view of the world – yes, but an artistic one.
(Nietzsche, The Will to Power 1048)

This dual *series of experiences, this access to apparently separate worlds, is repeated in my nature in every respect: I am a* Doppelgänger, *I have a 'second' face in addition to the first.* And *perhaps also a third.*
(Nietzsche, Ecce Homo 1.3)

Remain faithful to the earth.
(Nietzsche, Zarathustra 1.22.3)

'Lord Contingency' – that is the oldest nobility of the world, which I restored to all things when I redeemed them from their bondage under Purpose.
(Nietzsche, Zarathustra 3.4)

Free spirit a relative concept. – He is called a free spirit who thinks differently from what, on the basis of his origin, environment, his class and profession, or on the basis of the dominant views of the age, would have been expected of him.
(Nietzsche, Human, All Too Human 225)

Now I bid you lose me and find yourselves.
(Nietzsche, Zarathustra 1.22.3)

I know of no other way of associating with great tasks than play: as a sign of greatness, this is an essential presupposition.
(Nietzsche, Ecce Homo 2.10)

Without music, life would be a mistake.
(Nietzsche, Twilight of the Idols 1.33)

Do I dare to suggest that I know *women? This is part of my Dionysian dowry. Who knows? Perhaps I am the first psychologist of the eternal-feminine.*
(Nietzsche, Ecce Homo 3.5)

This book is dedicated to my (Sartrean) mother, Anne, and my (Nietzschean) father, Terence.

Content

Preface	xi
Acknowledgements	xii
List of abbreviations	xiii
Introduction: The Nietzsche–Sartre connection	1
An imaginary contamination	1
Associative and dissociative accounts	5
A synthesizing project: Existentialism and poststructuralism	8
1 Reading Nietzsche and Sartre	11
Literary phenomenology	11
Good reading/bad reading	13
A playful reading	17
The New Nietzsche and New Sartre	19
Philosophers of paradox	27
Thinkers of three phases	32
2 Heidegger, Derrida and the metaphysical charge	39
The 'grand metaphysicians': Heidegger's verdict	39
Saints and sinners in Nietzsche's France	43
Divisive Derrida	46
In the name of the father	47
Phenomenology and perspectivism	49
3 The decentred self	55
The bewitched ego	56
The three ecologies of the self	61
A playful wisdom: *Homo Ludens*	82
The posthuman self: A Nietzschean/Sartrean hybrid	86
4 Smooth ontology	91
Smooth and striated	91
The will to power: Nietzsche's relational ontology	92
Sartre's dialectic with holes: A ternary logic	96

	Nietzsche's gay science	103
	Sartre's dialectical science	105
	Assimilation and hodological space	110
5	A creative ethics and agonistic politics	115
	Sartre's unfinished Nietzschean ethics	115
	Nietzsche's revaluation of values	117
	Sartre's three ethics: Authenticity, reciprocity and the gift	121
	Nietzsche's grand politics	124
	Positive agonism	128
	Self and Other: A dialectical exchange	131
	Anarchism, freedom and plurality	138
6	Posthuman progenitors	147
	Posthumanism and transhumanism	147
	Nietzsche's nature	151
	Sartre *in Naturabilis*	159
	Eco-phenomenologists	165
	Vibrant matter	168
	A pair of posthumanist humanists	171
7	*Lebensphilosophie*	175
	Religious atheists	176
	Gentle Nietzsche and feminine Sartre	186
	Playful pianists	196
	Madness and epiphany: Turin and Billancourt	202
Conclusion: Twin ternary thinkers		211
Notes		215
Bibliography		235
Index		249

Preface

This book is in several respects an outgrowth of my earlier *The New Sartre* and what seemed like a natural extension of its primary argument. If the 'New Sartre' was a pioneer of key poststructuralist themes, as was the 'French Nietzsche', then surely there is a strong compatibility to be found between Sartre and Nietzsche if interpreted along these lines. Once placed under a microscope, the parallel thinking of their philosophical works soon became apparent and irresistible. Suffice to say, it was the findings of others whose digging has uncovered many bones in the Sartre–Nietzsche skeleton and confirmed my suspicions of a firm DNA match. My task, as I saw it, was to piece together these different parts and assemble the whole skeleton of their connection through a systematic comparison of the full range of their philosophy and an analysis of some of the significant aspects of their lives.

First of all, this book was inspired by Christine Daigle, Robert Solomon and François Noudelmann for bringing into clear view a Nietzsche–Sartre comparison. Without their insights, this work would have proved a whole lot more difficult to conceive *ab ovo*. This project has also benefitted from fresh interpretations of Sartre's ontology (e.g. Matthew C. Eshleman (2011), Christina Howells (1992), Matthew C. Ally (2017)) that bring his *dialectical view of self and world* in line with Nietzsche's relational ontology of the will to power as well as the studies of Guillermine de Lacoste (1999) and Jean-Pierre Boulé (2005) in elucidating the 'feminine' dimension of Sartre's thinking. In the field of Nietzsche Studies, I acknowledge a significant scholarly debt to Gary Shapiro (2016) and Henk Manschot (2021) for their illuminating ecological readings of Nietzsche, to John Richardson (2020) for a clear 'dialectical' understanding of Nietzsche and to Alan D. Schrift for his adept elucidation of the French reception of Nietzsche's work. Also, thanks to all the biographers I cite (Ronald Hayman, Rüdiger Safranski, Thomas R. Flynn, Daniel Blue, Annie Cohen-Solal and Gary Cox) for bringing Sartre and Nietzsche vividly to life for me. Finally, the task of connecting Nietzsche and Sartre to posthumanism was made significantly easier by the impressive work of Francesca Ferrando (2020) and Rosi Braidotti (2013) in bringing together the disparate strands of posthumanism into an edifying and easily comprehensible form.

In general terms, I view this project as a 'Universal Singular', that is to say, as a synthetic composite of all the insights of others filtered through my singular lens of interpretation, direction and narration. Any deficiencies in the text are, suffice to say, entirely down to me. Developing the 'New Nietzsche' and 'New Sartre' in tandem, my firm hope is to gain a fresh perspective on them, both individually and collectively, and to stimulate further comparative studies (associative or dissociative) in areas I wasn't able to explore here.

Acknowledgements

Thanks to Matt Eshleman, Christina Howells, Christine Daigle and Ashley Woodward (and two anonymous reviewers) for their salient and very useful observations in regard to various aspects of this project. My gratitude also goes to Mike Neary and Benedict O' Donohoe for their academic friendship as well as to Alfred Betschart for his encyclopaedic knowledge of all things Sartre and his kindness in sharing some of them with me.

A significant mention, of course, extends to Jade Grogan, Dhanuja Ravi, Suzie Nash and Liza Thompson at Bloomsbury for their help and enthusiasm in pursuing this project and their expertise in bringing it to print.

Finally, thanks to Jonathan Webber at the *UK Sartre Society*, to John Gillespie at *Sartre Studies International*, to Elizabeth Butterfield at the *US Sartre Society* and to Urs Sommer and Paul Stephan at the *German Nietzsche Society* for keeping me well and truly in the Sartre–Nietzsche loop.

On a personal note, this book would have floundered considerably without the glowing presence (real or felt) of Willow, Søren and Raphael, but most of all and incomparably, without the support of Rachel and her bottomless sack of talents.

Abbreviations

The following abbreviations are used in the text for key works:

Nietzsche

A	*The Antichrist*
BGE	*Beyond Good and Evil*
BT	*The Birth of Tragedy*
CW	*The Case of Wagner*
D	*Daybreak*
EH	*Ecce Homo*
GM	*On the Genealogy of Morals*
GS	*The Gay Science*
G.S	*The Greek State*
HH	*Human, All Too Human, vol. 1.*
HH 2	*Human, All Too Human, vol. 2.*
KSB	*Sämtliche Briefe, Kritische Studienausgabe*
KSW	*Sämtliche Werke, Kritische Studienausgabe*
LN	*Writings from the Late Notebooks*
PP	*The Pre-Platonic Philosophers*
PTAG	*Philosophy in the Tragic Age of the Greeks*
TI	*Twilight of the Idols*
WP	*The Will to Power*
WS	*The Wanderer and His Shadow*
UM	*Untimely Meditations*
Z	*Thus Spoke Zarathustra*

Sartre

BN	*Being and Nothingness*
CDR	*Critique of Dialectical Reason, vol. 1*

CDR 2	*Critique of Dialectical Reason, vol. 2*
EH	*Existentialism Is a Humanism*
EJ	*Ecrits de jeunesse*
EM	*L'espoir maintenant*
FI	*The Family Idiot, vol. 1*
FI 2	*The Family Idiot, vol. 2*
HN	*Hope Now*
I	*The Imagination*
IF 3	*L'Idiot de la famille, vol. 3*
IM	*The Imaginary*
N	*Nausea*
NE	*Notebooks for an Ethics*
SG	*Saint Genet*
SM	*Search for a Method*
STE	*Sketch for a Theory of the Emotions*
TE	*The Transcendence of the Ego*
W	*Words*
WD	*The War Diaries*
WL	*What Is Literature?*

For simplicity of referencing, I have used the following conventions in the text:

Nietzsche's works are numbered by part/section/subsection

BT 13	*The Birth of Tragedy*, section 13
Z 3.12.2	*Thus Spoke Zarathustra*, part 3, 'Of Old and New Law-Tables', section 2
EH 3Z4	*Ecce Homo*, 'Why I write Such Good Books', 'Thus Spoke Zarathustra', section 4
Z P4	*Thus Spoke Zarathustra*, 'Prologue', section 4
GM P6	*On the Genealogy of Morals*, 'Preface', section 6
UM 3.1	*Untimely Meditations*, 'Schopenhauer as Educator', section 1

Sartre's works are numbered by volume and page

CDR 2:100	*Critique of Dialectical Reason, vol. 2*, page 100
W 66	*Words*, page 66

Introduction

The Nietzsche–Sartre connection

We were friends and have grown distant from one another. But it is right that we should be so; let us not dissemble and obscure it, as if it were something to be ashamed of. We are two ships, each of which has its destination and its course; our paths can cross and we can celebrate a feast together, as we did – and then the brave ships lay so peacefully in one *harbour and under* one *sun that it might seem they had already reached their destination and both had* one *destination. But then the almighty power of our task again drove us apart, to different seas and different climes, and perhaps we shall never see one another again – or perhaps if we do we shall not recognize one another: different seas and sun have changed us! That we had to grow distant from one another is the law* over *us [. . .] There is probably a tremendous invisible curve and star orbit within which our so different paths and destinations may be* included *as tiny stretches of the way – let us raise ourselves to this thought! But our life is too short and our power of vision too weak for us to be more than friends in the sense of that exalted possibility. – And so let us* believe *in our friendship in the stars, even if we did have to be enemies on earth.*

(Nietzsche, *The Gay Science* 279)

What is the Nietzsche–Sartre connection? This is a question that has been alluded to or touched upon on many occasions but, for some reason, rarely addressed in terms of a systematic study. This book attempts to break this relative silence and address the full range of their philosophical interconnections, presenting these two iconic existentialist philosophers in broad terms as parallel anti-metaphysical thinkers and as precursors of many themes in contemporary posthumanist thinking.

An imaginary contamination

It is fair to say that Sartre was ambivalent about what he thought of Nietzsche, wavering between adulation, emulation, indifference and guarded suspicion. It is well documented that the prankster Sartre used to throw urine-filled condoms at his foes at the École Normale Supérieure (ENS), shouting, 'Thus pissed Zarathustra', as was his intense aversion to moustaches, of which Nietzsche's was, of course, a more than immodest specimen.[1] In 1924, Sartre describes Nietzsche in his notebooks as more a poet than a philosopher, whose form of thought is better than his actual thought himself: 'Nietzsche. He is a poet who had the misfortune of being taken for a philosopher . . . he will always have success with those who prefer the form of ideas to their exchange' (EJ 471). It is likely Sartre was acquainted with Nietzsche's writings through Charles Andler's six-volume biography. Contat and Rybalka believed he had read at least to volume two, as well as the biography by Daniel Halévy. He may also have come across a selection of aphorisms published by Jean Bolle in 1934 and by Geneviève Bianquis in the late 1930s.[2] In his *Ecrits de Jeunesse*, he claims to have read Nietzsche but does not specify which texts he has read, but Cohen-Solal (1999: 146) states he did read *Ecce Homo* around the time of writing *A Defeat*.

Sartre's direct comments about Nietzsche in his texts and interviews are variable, expressing both negativity and positivity. He criticizes Nietzsche's vitalism and the idea of will to power (which he understands as a brute will to dominate others), and he dismisses the *Übermensch* as the culmination of evolution in which only the strongest survive. In *Nausea*, Roquentin's description of 'the general frailty and feebleness of existence' can be viewed as an early critique of Nietzsche's Romantic vitalism: 'There were those idiots who came to tell you about will-power and struggle for life. Hadn't they ever seen a beast or a tree?' (N 133). In *Saint Genet*, he rejects the idea of eternal return, which he understands in a literal fashion and regards as a form of nihilism. Given the prevalence of the 'Nazified Nietzsche' in Germany in the 1930s and 1940s, it is little wonder that Sartre would be reluctant to openly embrace his philosophy without reservation or some distancing. In interview in the 1970s with John Gerassi, he recalls that in his youth he took a dislike to Nietzsche's elitist jargon and viewed him as not particularly important: 'I hated him. I think his crap about the elite, his übermensch [*sic*], radicalized us a lot' (Gerassi 2009: 53). In an interview in 1975, he was more conciliatory but somewhat opaque, commenting how at the ENS he 'interested me like many others' but ultimately 'never stood for anything in particular in my eyes' (1981b: 9).

Despite this, Sartre would openly identify with Nietzschean aspirations.[3] Although, as Noudelmann (2012: 46) remarks, '[e]verything would seem to oppose the aristocratic thinker Nietzsche to the anti-elitist philosopher Sartre', Sartre's closeness to Nietzsche nonetheless 'involves foremost an imaginary contamination based on admiration and parody'. His dismissals of Nietzsche tell only a partial story, for Nietzsche was wholly important to him. As Noudelmann (2012: 45) observes, Nietzsche is a thinker 'whom we can indeed find smuggled into Sartre's work' at every corner to the point of imaginary identification and deep contamination. Daigle (2009: 57) echoes this, describing Sartre as the 'Unaware Nietzschean' and Nietzsche, despite Sartre's misunderstandings of his philosophy, as being 'very present in Sartre's intellectual universe', sharing together the project of an affirmative creative ethics as a response to a crisis of nihilism in the wake of the death of God.

This is strongly evidenced by the fact that Nietzsche didn't really leave Sartre's philosophical brain from beginning to end. His first published essay, 'The History of Truth', written as a young student and published in a French Lycée review in 1925, was a typical Nietzschean study. Towards the end of his life, he was still working on a long text of Nietzsche's ethics that he began around the time of his *Notebooks* (1947/8) as part of his ethical research, which Simone de Beauvoir described as 'a very fine study' (1984: 180). From the period 1929 to 1937, as Flynn (2014: 149, 27) observes, Sartre is very much 'under the spell of a Nietzschean exuberance'. His literary compositions, 'A Defeat' (1927), 'Er the Armenian' (1928) and 'The Legend of Truth' (1931), all reveal 'a proto-existentialist, quasi-Nietzschean character' with a valorization of freedom that runs through his entire work.

As a means of seduction for his 'first love', the actress Simone Jollivet, Sartre wrote a semi-autobiographical novel in 1927–8 as a modern retelling of the 'Tribschen Triangle' involving Richard Wagner, Cosima Wagner and Nietzsche. In *A Defeat* (*Une défaite*), Sartre foregrounds a series of Nietzschean themes, such as power, autonomy, nature and embodiment. The main protagonist, Frédéric (Nietzsche), is an ambitious young man, inspired by the will to power, who wishes to write a book about the writer and composer, Richard Organte (Wagner). He gets invited to the composer's house and falls in love with his wife, Cosima, eventually becoming a tutor to their children. Soon, however, the young philosopher of the future becomes disillusioned with Richard who is more a skilful practitioner than he is a genius and eventually the couple breaks off their relationship with him. In this tale, Sartre clearly identifies himself with Frédéric, grafting some of his own qualities onto the narrator and taking the side of Nietzsche over that of Wagner (Richard), who is presented unfavourably as arrogant and not the genius he imagines himself to be.[4] In 1928, Sartre worked on another Nietzschean novel project *Er the Armenian* in which he relates his theory of radical contingency to ethical values. Reworking Plato's Myth of Er which appears in the conclusion to *The Republic* and is used to demonstrate how the moral ultimately prosper over the immoral, Sartre shows how Good and Evil are absent from the world itself, which is morally indifferent. Echoing Nietzsche's remark that 'Good and Evil are the prejudices of God' (GS 150), Sartre has Prometheus declare, 'When the Gods will be vanquished, there will be no more Evil on earth' (EJ 322).

In 'The Legend of Truth', published in 1931 in the journal *Bifur*, Sartre set out to show the inadequacy of science and ideology as collective representations of belief against the individual judgement of exceptional artists, philosophers and writers. The published fragment deals with the levelling effect of scientific and philosophic agreement in a tone like that of 'a muted and more reasonable Nietzsche' (Caws 1984: 10). In many ways, *Legend of Truth* is a variation on Nietzsche's posthumously published essay 'On Truth and Lie in an Extra-Moral Sense' and reiterates his swingeing criticisms of scientific rationality, abstract philosophy and the egalitarian ideals of the herd, showing the genealogical and ignoble origins of truth which is neither impersonal, timeless or universal. Following Nietzsche's argument in *On the Genealogy of Morals*, Sartre argues that truth originates in commerce. The function of 'the mythical daughter of commerce' is to serve as a regulator or 'measure' in barter – over time this measure is internalized and its origins as human creation are forgotten. Truth colonizes common sense in which it becomes configured as a correspondence between subject and object. Sartre critiques the downward spiral of truth into Socratic reason through the metaphysical principle of identity and the principles of non-contradiction and excluded middle. This fixes truth as rigid and static and marginalizes the paradoxes of change, motion and becoming. In this process of Socratic reasoning, things become perceived metaphysically as 'mummified concepts' and historical explanation is nullified.[5]

In these early writings, Sartre triumphs the 'solitary man' who stands apart from the common crowd and creates his own measure and values, a model he later realizes in the literary form of Roquentin and Orestes and in the philosophical form of the 'authentic individual'. His solitary man is typically Nietzschean in his 'inverted Platonism', a human whose physical truths are not the product of universality and metaphysical reason but merely 'the systematic impoverishment of spontaneous thoughts'.[6] As Beauvoir records:

> He kept his sympathy for those thaumaturgic characters who, shut off from the City with its logic and mathematics, wandered alone in the wilderness and only trusted the evidence of their own eyes as a guide toward knowledge. Thus it was only to the artist, the writer, or the philosopher – those whom he termed the 'solitaries' – that he granted the privilege of grasping living reality. (1983: 50)

The central motif of Sartre's early Nietzschean preoccupation is the theme of *contingency*: 'Being is without reason, without cause and without necessity; the very definition of being presents us with its original contingency' (BN 801). Sartre's 'factum on contingency', a collection of notes and passages, grew eventually into *Nausea* and *Childhood of a Leader* which complement each other through their exploration of contingency. The two protagonists, Roquentin and Fleurier, are both traumatized by issues of self-identity, and each becomes what the other despises. Where Roquentin embraces contingency, Fleurier rejects it, seeking a 'necessary existence', but in wanting to 'be something', he becomes a narrow-minded racist steeped in bourgeois values like the *salauds* of bad faith. By clearly valorizing the contingency-embracing Roquentin over the 'sincere' and racist Fleurier, Sartre follows Zarathustra's injunction to welcome 'Lord Contingency' (Z 3.4) and make of it 'the perfect free gift' (N 188), thereby connecting it with his realist thirst for personal and political authenticity. A view of existence as contingent, after all, is conceived in opposition to the notion that there is (or ought to be) a necessary order of things serving as the ultimate justification for maintaining the status quo, since other configurations or paths are always possible. As Beauvoir commented:

> Sartre went to unheard of extremes in his total rejection of universals. To him, general laws and concepts and all such abstractions were nothing but hot air: people, he maintained, all agreed to accept them because they effectively masked a reality which men found alarming. He, on the other hand, wanted to grapple with this living reality. (1983: 31)

Although allusions to Nietzsche's work recede after these early writings, Nietzsche is the first philosopher Sartre mentions in *Being and Nothingness*, commenting favourably on his atheism and supporting his critique of 'the illusion of backworlds' (BN 2).[7] Following Nietzsche, he takes a view of humans as 'the evaluating animal' and siding with Heraclitus, he adopts a Nietzschean dynamic of becoming in which change more than permanence is the foundation of temporality for the *pour-soi*. Later, in the Rome and Cornell Lectures of 1964–5, he describes the 'integral man' as the worker who cultivates self-growth and follows the sense of Nietzsche's counsel to 'Become what you are'.[8]

Associative and dissociative accounts

When addressing the Nietzsche–Sartre connection, scholars take a variety of approaches. Daigle (2009) and Noudelmann (2012) offer the most associative accounts. Daigle draws a strong parallel between their creative ethics (as a response to nihilism) and the close similarity of their ethical ideals (the *Übermensch* and authenticity) but draws a line at their political thinking where Nietzsche's 'closure to the Other' sends him down the path of aristocratic elitism inimical to Sartre's democratic ethos. Noudelmann concentrates more on their aesthetic concerns and similarities, particularly their shared love of music and piano playing as an expression of their aesthetic ethic of play. Others take a mixed view of the relation between Nietzsche and Sartre, stressing the 'deep Nietzschean concerns' of Sartre's thinking but the 'ambivalent attitude towards the influence of Nietzsche's philosophy on him'.[9] In Churchill's (2013: 52–3) view, despite the 'prescient similarities' regarding Sartre and Nietzsche's early views regarding the illusion of apparently 'necessary' states of affairs concerning the absurdity of the underlying contingency of existence, 'Roquentin is no Dionysian disciple in the mould of the young Nietzsche' since he does not find respite from his nausea (let alone ecstatic life affirmation) in supreme artistic struggle and expression. Whereas Nietzsche offered a vision of communal salvation from contingency in the form of therapeutic art, Sartre held that contingency could not be overcome, or even placated, by an affirmative force (whether artistic or otherwise), 'because such a power was simply *absent* from a truly contingent world'. For Churchill, Sartre contrasts his view of contingency with the vitalist Romantic Nietzschean view of the Will since his account stresses the frailty and feebleness of existence in which everything is too weak to be underpinned by a surging and affirmative force covering all existence.

As I hope to show in the following chapters, this is a hasty conclusion to reach in regard not only to *Nausea* itself but also to the wider arc of Sartre's philosophy that dovetails ontologically with Nietzsche's will to power and ethically with his revaluation of values. First, Sartre doesn't just describe the frailty of existence in *Nausea* but also its surging power, force, vibrancy and efflorescence. This finds expression in philosophical form in his concept of 'hodological' space (BN 415) and his affective phenomenology that underpins it. Furthermore, the conclusion of *Nausea* is ambiguous and left open to interpretation – we are not sure just how redemptive art actually is for Roquentin who leaves us with only 'a tentative sort of hope' (Kirkpatrick 2017a: 126–7). Sartre later renounced hope as 'youthful folly' (W 56), echoed in his declaration in *What Is Literature?* that 'we could never be saved by art' (WL 161). But while it is true that Sartre doesn't ground art *metaphysically* as a form of salvation, this is not to say that he disregards art *juridically* as an integral part of a system of values that works towards human freedom and avoids bad faith. His project to escape the dead end of moral nihilism rests on the distinction, also made by Nietzsche, between decadent or illusory art (art for art's sake) and committed or physiological art (the tragic art of rapture and engagement). Although *What Is Literature?* warns against bourgeois art that wraps the audience in mystification and diversion, it proposes a 'committed art' that leads to reflection and change by disclosing the images and articulating the truths that society tries to hide from itself (WL 75). In *Existentialism Is a Humanism*, Sartre also follows Nietzsche's lead by conceiving authenticity as a process of creating oneself as a work of art (EH 45). There is consequently no real contrast to be found if we look at the wider arc of their work for Nietzsche's middle and later phases of thinking display the same doubts, ambiguities and ethical distinctions about the redemptive powers of art as Sartre does. Moreover, as we will see in Chapter 7, Sartre was no anti-Dionysian but, like Nietzsche, made *affect* a central element in his ethics of play, his 'eco-phenomenology' and his aesthetic theory.

Alongside associative and mixed accounts, dissociative narratives also abound. The most extreme, bizarre and puzzling of these is probably Beam (1998) who, while exonerating Nietzsche from Heidegger's reading of the will to power as a metaphysical Platonic construct, does a thoroughly 'Heideggerian job' on Sartre in order to mark out fundamental differences between them. Using *Nausea* as evidence, Beam accuses Sartre of desecrating nature in his negative depiction of the root of a chestnut tree in the park as a 'black, knotty mass, entirely beastly'. Extrapolating from this, he attributes to Sartre a Platonic worldview in which nature, existence and the senses are cast as inferior to the intellect and the insensible essences of timeless truths. Furthermore, he charges Sartre with revealing a contempt for human beings that surpasses his contempt for nature and 'rivals the misanthropy of Schopenhauer', speaking of living creatures as 'flabby masses which move spontaneously' and displaying 'an aversion for fleshy, overweight people'.

In his criticisms of Sartre, Beam makes a number of common errors that are trotted out in popular vulgarizations. First, as Davis (2011: 140) warns, it is dangerous to read Sartre's literary hyperbole uncomplicatedly as 'his settled philosophical view' as it is to make a direct ascription of Sartre to Roquentin.[10] Second, it is simply wrong to attribute 'Platonic aspirations' to Sartre, for, like Nietzsche, Sartre clearly espouses an 'inverted Platonism' (Flynn 2014: 45) in which 'existence precedes essence' and '[e]xistence is a plenitude that man cannot escape' (1981: 1807). This is vividly illustrated in *Nausea*'s central epiphany where Roquentin apprehends the 'brute existence' of the chestnut tree in the municipal garden and the inability of words and concepts to capture its living reality. Indeed, Sartre's anti-Platonic 'dynamic of becoming', as I intend to show in the following chapters, is the central axis upon which his ontology, ethics and affirmative politics squarely rest and run in parallel with Nietzsche's own Heraclitean 'philosophy of becoming' in the form of the will to power. Finally, Beam grossly overstates Sartre's pessimism and his Platonic 'resentment of being', charging him with misanthropy and 'contempt for human beings'. Not only is this a hasty and misleading conclusion to reach in regard to Sartre's early work, but it actually runs counter to the whole momentum of his later thinking and his 'ethics of reciprocity' worked out in depth in his major philosophical and ethical treatises. As we will see in subsequent chapters, Sartre's ethical vision is deeply affirmative and intersubjective, and his idea of 'integral humanity' is far removed from any misanthropic projections. Like other dissociative doubters, Beam does not fully realize the potential fruits of his comparison of the similarities in the philosophy of Nietzsche and Sartre through an uneven-handed treatment of them, as was the case with Derrida and Foucault in the 1960s, granting a positive deconstructionist reading to Nietzsche but at the same time condemning Sartre to a narrow and inapposite Cartesianism (an interpretation of Sartre's philosophy they would later confess was unfair and short-sighted). While he is quick to rescue Nietzsche from a Heideggerian reading of the will to power, he completely disregards those elements in Sartre's philosophy, pronounced and ever-present, that are anti-Platonic to the core. As I hope to show, Beam's claims that his ontology 'retains many elements of Platonism that Nietzsche rejects', including a denigration of nature and the world of becoming and 'the Platonic elevation of the intelligible (masculine) over the sensible (feminine)', do scant justice to Sartre's 'smooth ontology' (Chapter 4) and to a much more complex and multifaceted perspective on nature, the sensible, and the 'feminine' than scholars often ascribe to him (Chapters 6 and 7).

Another scholar who has toyed with the question of the Nietzsche–Sartre connection, but wavers in ascribing a full association, is Solomon (2003, 1988, 1987). Although he provides no systematic study of this question, his various allusions to their compatibility show a sensitivity to the ambiguity of their thinking and to possible interconnections. Both philosophers, Solomon (2003: 59) argues, offer a compatibilist or paradoxical version of freedom that rejects the Kantian notion of 'will as causality' and the 'noumenal self' while believing that we are responsible for our behaviour and the cultivation of our virtues. Although fatalism appealed to Nietzsche in his admiration for the Ancient Greeks and their acceptance of life and fate in the face of absurdity and suffering, he is 'very much in league with Sartre' in the belief that we bear responsibility for the consequences of our actions (2003: 162). Elsewhere, Solomon (1982) also draws some comparisons between the 'phenomenological' approach both philosophers undertake, identifying the similarities in their theory of 'affect' and the emotions that elide simple Platonic distinctions between emotion and reason. However, what holds back Solomon's account, despite his recognition of some philosophical similarities, is the individualism and Cartesianism[11] that he too readily ascribes to Sartre. This means that he senses ambiguity but explains it metaphysically in Sartre but not in Nietzsche, commenting, for instance, that Sartre 'sustains a full-blooded determinism in his philosophy, untouched by his adamant insistence that we must, even ontologically, consider consciousness as free and free from causation' (2003: 225, n.29). As we will see, it is as simplistic to view *Being and Nothingness* as a treatise of 'absolute freedom' as it is to read the *Critique* as one of 'full-blooded determinism' for in both these texts, Sartre clearly presents a mediated or 'compatibilist' view in which freedom and necessity are dialectically coextensive. With this caveat, Solomon (2003: 206) suggests it is right to view them as parallel thinkers if it can be shown that Sartre is not 'the bootstrapper' he is taken to be, which his emphasis on 'the limitations on action by way of "the situation"' strongly implies. Although he tends towards an associative view, Solomon lags behind the curve in his assessment of Sartre, still stuck in the habit of disassociation by viewing Nietzsche from the inside (as cognizing and surpassing ambiguity) but Sartre from the outside (as metaphysically encoding ambiguity). As we will see, once we release Sartre from false ascriptions of Cartesianism, the strands of association between himself and Nietzsche become ever stronger and tightly interwoven.

A synthesizing project: Existentialism and poststructuralism

In this book, I endeavour to provide a creative disclosure and extended analysis of the Nietzsche–Sartre connection, examining the constellation of their thinking and attempting to confront head-on the points of consonance and dissonance, attraction and divergence, between them. In the process I try sedulously to clear away some of the ambiguity, 'noise' and uncertainty that continue to mark their relation, presenting their philosophy as twin complementary perspectives that offer unique and singular insights but which converge strongly around a unified philosophical vision. The key defining concepts that form the nucleus of this convergence are those of *contingency*, *freedom*, *ambiguity*, *creativity*, *becoming*, *the unity of opposites*, *play*, *plurality* and *affect*, and I set out to show how these concepts infuse their philosophy across their ontology and their theory of the self, as well as their ethical and political thinking.

This synthesizing project may seem to contravene Nietzsche's warning *against mediators*: '[t]hose who wish to be mediators between two resolute thinkers are marked as mediocre: they lack eyes to see the unparalleled; seeing things as similar and making them the same is the mark of weak eyes' (GS 228). Against this injunction, however, my hope is neither to view them with 'weak eyes' nor mark them as 'mediocre' but, by contrast, to bring a closer scrutiny and a higher reflexive resolution to their extraordinary thinking. Two recurrent philosophical descriptors that feature throughout this study are those of 'monistic pluralism' and 'Universal Singular', and these are useful concepts, I suggest, to characterize the Nietzsche–Sartre connection. Their thinking, one might say, is monistically of the same kind but their individual philosophies can be configured as different modalities or inflections of it. Equally, their philosophizing has universal or common touchpoints but incarnates singular perspectives within them. Indeed, using them together, my hope is to gain a wider purchase on them both, by bringing the critical lens of one to a comparative assessment of the other. In Deleuzian/Guattarian terms (1994), this can be viewed as a process of 'adsorbsion' – a gathering of elements in a way that both forms a coalition and yet preserves something of the agential impetus of each element.

This book argues that the main factors in their (continuing) separation are those of *distortion* and *misinterpretation*, disseminated initially by Martin Heidegger and the 'French Nietzscheans', especially Jacques Derrida and Michel Foucault in the 1960s and 1970s. Heidegger's simplistic characterization of them both as 'Cartesian philosophers' was not in itself divisive, but when Derrida and Foucault absolved Nietzsche of his Cartesian connections while cementing Sartre firmly to his, Nietzsche and Sartre were forced apart and posited as divergent thinkers. Describing the European and global reception of Sartre's philosophy, Betschart (2020: 7) utilizes the methodology of communication theory to explain the distortions that took place in pigeonholing and ultimately vulgarizing Sartre's philosophy in its dissemination. Since a work can contain several messages and the same message can appear in different works, not all messages are equally received and 'there can be significant differences in content between the messages encoded by the senders and the messages decoded by the receivers'. On the way to receivers, messages are forwarded by repeaters and partly jammed by noise, which, in Sartre's case, resulted in a certain caricaturing of his work (especially *Being and Nothingness*) as dualist, Cartesian and idealist, a humanist oeuvre of 'absolute freedom'. In terms of his ethico-political outlook, this was often summarized with his slogan from *Huis Clos* that 'hell is other people', leading to an ascribed social ontology of alienation, conflict and a Hobbesian 'war of all against all'. As long as this Cartesian noise continues to reverberate in the common ear, a Nietzsche–Sartre rapprochement is unlikely and doomed to frustration (although some may see a parallel between Sartre's 'hell is other people' and Nietzsche's 'will-to-power as domination').

My aim in this book is to replace the 'noise' that crowds out Sartre's philosophy (and Nietzsche's) with a more 'musical' reading that does justice to the rhythms, complexities, contradictions, leitmotifs and nuanced resolutions of their thinking, eschewing in the process simplification, caricature, distortion or vulgarization. I set out to show, for example, that Sartre's prime accusers, the French poststructuralists, stole many of Sartre's clothes, even though they professed to dress in a different fashion and were guilty of an 'anxiety of influence' towards him in their attempt to usurp and go beyond him by using Nietzschean fire to set alight a straw man Sartre. By showing the parallel thinking of Nietzsche and Sartre, my hope is to bring the French philosopher in from obscurity in relation to current debates and contemporary posthumanist theory. Indeed, I position Sartre squarely alongside Nietzsche as a forerunner and progenitor of philosophical posthumanism, a methodological approach which is an outgrowth of the poststructuralist thinking of Derrida, Foucault, Deleuze and Guattari. Ferrando (2020: 3) defines this as 'a praxis, as well as a philosophy of mediation, which manifests post-dualistic, post-centralizing' thinking. I identify Nietzsche and Sartre as proto-deconstructionists who use paradox and contradiction in the service of a 'ternary logic' to disassemble, overturn and surpass the dualistic metaphysical thinking of the Western philosophical tradition. This is not to say, however, that they completely broke free from the subliminal influences of the metaphysical tradition in which they were inured (a point they both acknowledge at certain points in their work). Such a complete severance would of course be impossible, for, in Sartrean terms, one is always a 'Universal Singular' carrying the weight of history in one's thoughts even as one singularly seeks to dispense with customary thinking. Where metaphysical assumptions burst through the cracks of their thinking from time to time, I attempt to expose them and use a reflexive method ('Nietzsche against Nietzsche' and 'Sartre against Sartre') to bring their underlying deconstructionist logic to its fullest expression. In Nietzsche's case this means questioning some of the assumptions of the elitism of his later ethical thinking where he effects an ethical 'closure of the Other' as inconsistent with his wider genealogical critique of power and subjectivity in general, while for Sartre this involves challenging some of his 'anthropometric' and 'exclusivist' views concerning the 'human' and 'non-human' that surface throughout his writings that contravene his wider dialectical method.

By recasting the Nietzsche–Sartre image in this way, a further aim of this study is to clear away some misconceptions that surround the narrative of post-war French philosophy. Instead of viewing existentialism and poststructuralism as adversarial (as is usually the case), my aim is filter out some of the 'noise' that amplifies their incompatibility and cast them more as continuous and complementary. If we look beyond standard tropes and take a closer view of their philosophy, we soon see that the criticisms levelled at existentialists like Sartre, Beauvoir, Marcel and Merleau-Ponty – *an abstract theory of freedom, a centred metaphysical subject, an uncomplicated humanism, methodological and political individualism* – really do miss their target. Moreover, existentialism anticipates and prefigures many of the themes – *the deconstructed self* as a synthetic construct of unconscious, conscious and historical forces, *a contingent or 'detotalized' view of history, a pluralistic ethics* – that poststructuralists later assimilated to their own philosophical projects.[12] This means, for instance, that there is no complication in labelling Nietzsche as a postmodernist *and* as an existentialist as scholars sometimes wonder,[13] for, behind all the bluster and noise, there is actually no major dissonance between them. As we shall see throughout the subsequent chapters, many of the key developments in poststructuralist and posthumanist thinking can be traced back in gestate form to Nietzschean *and* Sartrean existential insights. Nietzsche, Sartre and poststructuralism are deeply philosophically entangled and, in Merleau-Ponty's (1962: viii) phrase, share a 'manner or style of thinking' that expresses diversity while working towards a common meaning.

1

Reading Nietzsche and Sartre

> *When I imagine a perfect reader, I always think of a monster of courage and curiosity who is always supple, cunning, cautious, a born adventurer and discoverer.*
>
> (Nietzsche, *Ecce Homo* 3.3)

Literary phenomenology

Writing was an obsession to Nietzsche and Sartre, a daily necessity, as Nietzsche remarked, like relieving oneself (GS 93). What perhaps characterizes their shared style most of all is the magical fusion of philosophy and literature in their writing. Sartre's *Nausea* is a *tableau vivant* of conceptual imagery and literary description bound together in a lived dynamic of 'literary phenomenology' (Inkpin 2017: 16), while Nietzsche's *Zarathustra* articulates philosophical ideas through the literary medium of 'a phantasmatic and hallucinatory landscape poem' (Shapiro 2016: 84). *Nausea* expresses Sartre's wish 'to be both Spinoza and Stendhal'[1] and takes the form of a 'phenomenological novel', exhibiting osmosis between the literary and the philosophical by virtue of the status of consciousness it establishes in Roquentin. In the words of Contat and Rybalka,

> by the dissolution of the subject that it effects; by its refusal of psychology: Roquentin has no 'character', no substantial ego; he is pure consciousness *of* the world; his experience is not a voyage into the depths of interiority; on the contrary, it is a bursting out toward things. Everything is outside: Nausea is not *in* Roquentin; he's the one who is dissolved in it. (1981: 1664)

As Sartre remarked, a writer has to be a philosopher: 'From the moment that I knew what philosophy was, it seemed normal to require it of a writer. . . . I preferred that the philosophy I believed in, the truths that I relied on, be expressed in my novel' (Beauvoir 1981: 178, 184).[2]

Replacing 'proposition by demonstration' (as Beauvoir (1983: 50) described Sartre's literary writing) doubtlessly brought to life their ideas in a literary form of glorious Technicolor, but it also contributes to the proliferating play of interpretation in understanding them. In their autobiographies, they blur the lines between fact and fiction, embarking on what Nietzsche called *mnemotechnics* – the retrospective investment of past material by later experience in which the future shapes the past. Sartre discovered, when recalling his own childhood, that the nature of autobiographical reflection is a dynamic selective process in which past experiences are appropriated to current needs, interests and projects to produce a narrative which is simultaneously fictional and true.[3] Sartre ambiguously classifies his autobiography in this manner as 'a true work of fiction' and, in equal measure, his biography of Flaubert as 'a work of fiction that I believe' (1977: 10:146).

Despite their fine writing style, the ambiguity that runs through the core of their works means that Nietzsche and Sartre are difficult thinkers to understand comprehensively without cliché or simplification. Wandering along the complex and winding highways and byways that comprise their philosophy, a feeling of disorientation soon strikes with a confusion of signposts that seem to point discrepantly in opposite directions. As Katsafanas (2018: 93) observes of Nietzsche, there is a distinct lack of systematicity in his work in which he rarely presents clear defences of his central concepts and arguments: 'Some of his claims seem mutually contradictory, to the extent that readers . . . present his texts as "booby trapped" against articulation of philosophical theory.' Caws (1984: 1) identifies a similar trait in Sartre: 'If by "argument" is understood a sequence of propositions, beginning from premises laid down with some plausible warrant and proceeding by way of intermediate steps, each accompanied by a justifying reason, to a conclusion firmly established, the discovery of arguments in Sartre's work is not easy.' His 'dual allegiance' to philosophy and literature means that although he starts out in his works to be 'lucid' and 'rigorous' like a philosopher, the writer gradually takes over with the result that 'the distance from conception to expression is progressively reduced, critical restraint yields to enthusiasm and the whole enterprise gathers momentum' (1984: 3).

'The characters an artist creates', Nietzsche wrote, 'are not the artist himself, but obviously the series of characters to which he devotes himself with innermost love does indeed say something about the artist himself' (UM 4.2). We must thus be wary in unproblematically taking Sartre's fiction as his definitive philosophical view without weighing the ambiguity in his thinking. Just as it is simplistic to take Garcin's proclamation of 'hell is other people' in *Huis Clos* as Sartre's settled philosophical view of intersubjectivity, it is also hasty to directly assimilate Roquentin to Sartre.[4] Sartre's fulfilment of his original project to be a writer gives him a level of productivity and a cheerful disposition absent in Roquentin. As he writes, for instance, '[t]he essential difference between Antoine Roquentin and me is that, for my part, I write the story of Antoine Roquentin' (WD 338). He also alludes to the gloominess of Roquentin that is contrary to his own disposition – like himself but '*stripped of the living principle*' (WD 338). In his novels, by his own admission, structures such as sadness and melancholia begin to take on a life of their own: 'That's what I did: I stripped my characters of my obsessive passion for writing, my pride, my faith in my destiny, my metaphysical optimism – and thereby provoked in them a gloomy pullulation. They are myself beheaded' (WD 339). Like Hilbert in 'Erostrate' and other characters that populate Sartre's fictional universe, Roquentin is not a double of Sartre but more 'a nightmarish deformation' of him in which only certain traits remain: 'I fool people . . . I haven't felt Nausea, I'm not authentic' (WD 62).

To pin down these two freewheeling philosophers is thus no straightforward task. Their freedom from institution and place as itinerant philosophers offers a biographical parallel to the freedom that characterized their thinking. As Hayman (1982, 1986) remarks, what exemplifies them is their continual process of 'writing against' themselves, always evolving their perspective and resisting philosophical stasis. In the 1886 preface to the second part of *Human, All Too Human*, Nietzsche, for instance, declares how, after his turn from Wagner and Schopenhauer, 'I now took sides *against* myself and *for* everything that would hurt *me* – me especially – and come hard to me'. It is impossible, in this respect, as Foucault (1988: 32) commented, to identify a single authoritative 'Nietzscheanism' since Nietzsche was a self-declared anarchist who held no regard for textual fidelity. Ambiguity can be found in the very question of whether or not there is even a Nietzschean system to speak of. In *Daybreak*, for instance, Nietzsche warns passionately against system builders – '*Beware of systematizers!*' (D 318) – and roundly condemns the 'will to a system' in *Twilight of the Idols*: 'I distrust all systematizers and avoid them. The will to a system is a lack of integrity' (TI 1.26). Many of his interpreters, however, view him as a thoroughly systematic thinker including, among others, Heidegger, Kaufmann, Danto and Deleuze. The notes of the *Nachlass* are commonly seen as Nietzsche's own will to a system in which his main philosophical concepts – the *will to power, eternal return* and the *Übermensch* – receive their fullest articulation. As I present them, Nietzsche and Sartre are *twin thinkers of contradiction and ambiguity* who bequeath us a number of interpretative puzzles, but it is within the productive play of contradiction and ambiguity that, I hope to show, the wellspring of their 'sublimated thinking' most readily flows and a greater logic of deconstruction unravels.

Good reading/bad reading

Hear me! For I am such and such a person. Above all, do not mistake me for someone else.

(Nietzsche, *Ecce Homo* P1)

Nietzsche has firm expectations of his readers who must acknowledge the temporal quality of 'the art of reading' (GM P8). It is essential to slowly digest his texts: 'read slowly, deeply, looking cautiously before and aft, with reservations, with doors left open, with delicate eyes and figures . . . My patient friends, this book desires for itself only perfect readers and philologists: learn to read me well!' (D P5). Philology, he tells us, is to be understood as 'the art of reading well' – to be able to read off a fact 'without falsifying it by interpretation, without losing caution, patience, subtlety in the desire for understanding' (A 52). But how should we read the writings of Nietzsche and Sartre? As texts with a life and meaning of their own or as texts imprinted with the 'existential signatures' of their authors?

There appears to be a paradox in Nietzsche's recommendations on how we should understand him. The philosopher who stamps personality onto his writings warns against any Cult of Personality in discerning the true meaning of the text. In his debates over the 'Homer Question', for instance, he argues that it doesn't matter who or how many wrote the work since 'the composer of the *Iliad* and the *Odyssey* is an "*aesthetic* judgment"' (KGW 2.1.263). Once the text has been written, it acquires a life of its own independent of the author's subjective meaning and intention (HH 208). Elsewhere, however, the novel and powerful method of critical inquiry that Nietzsche develops is irreducibly *ad hominem*. This *ad hominem* approach involves the interlacing of *bios* and mind and points back to the author, as well as the meaning, profundity and effect of an argument, and is consistent with his own idea of the importance of perspective.[5] He wonders, for instance, if his own and other philosophies are no more than 'intellectual detours for . . . personal drives?' (D 553), and writes of the 'great love' he has for conveying his truthfulness to his readers through which he 'has a personal relationship to his problems, and finds in them his destiny, his distress, and his greatest happiness' (GS 345). In the preface to the second edition of *The Gay Science*, Nietzsche makes an indissoluble link between his own autobiographical situation and the themes of 'convalescence', 'health' and 'sickness' in his philosophy. The great pain he suffered 'compels us philosophers to descend into our ultimate depths and to put aside all trust, everything good-natured, everything that would interpose a veil, that is mild, that is medium – things in which formerly we have found our humanity. I doubt that such pain makes us "better", but I know that it makes us more profound' (GS P3). Conscious of 'the advantages that my fickle health gives me over all robust squares' (GS P3), there is, he emphasizes, a direct relation between psychology and philosophy:

> In some it is their deprivations that philosophize; in others, their riches and strengths – those who philosophize through their deprivations need their philosophy, whether it be as a prop, a sedative, medicine, redemption, elevation, or self-alienation. (GS P2)

Nietzsche strongly reiterates this linkage in *Beyond Good and Evil*, declaring that there is 'absolutely nothing impersonal about the philosopher'; every philosophy is 'a confession on the part of its author and a kind of involuntary and unconscious memoir'. A philosopher's psychological dispositions and drives are, he maintains, 'the real germ of life out of which the entire plant has grown' (BGE 6). Thus, in every philosophy there is always 'a point at which the philosopher's "conviction" appears on the scene' (BGE 8).

As Salomé (1988) first suggested, the trajectory of Nietzsche's thinking correlates closely to the material circumstances of his life. His aphoristic style of writing, for instance, was a consequence largely of his nomadic lifestyle and the fact that he had short periods to write in between his chronic troughs of bad health. Because of this, he purposely approaches deep problems like cold baths: 'quickly into them and quickly out again' (GS 381). His aphorisms require exegesis in order to decipher them and a higher level of engagement to be understood (GM P8). They are necessarily incomplete (HH 178, 207) and serve as tests for the reader (Z 1.7). This gives Nietzsche's philosophy, as Deleuze (1983: 31) argued, a kind of magnetic and interactive quality. The use of aphorisms, along with the use of paradox, wordplay, metaphor and masks, invites evaluation and interpretation through its very form and constitution. One has no choice but to interpret and evaluate what Nietzsche actually means.[6]

Sartre's writings similarly bear the trace of environment and his unique circumstance. One cannot ignore, for instance, the narcotic influence on the *Critique*. On reading its long meandering paragraphs and interweaving interminable sentences one is struck by a certain imposition of rhythm, a kind of fuelled effort to render its writing as rapid as the movement of thinking. It was not a case of writing in the ordinary sense, as Beauvoir (1977: 385) recounted, in the way of pausing to think, making corrections and rewriting certain sentences or passages: 'for hours at a stretch he raced across sheet after sheet without rereading them, as though absorbed by ideas that his pen, even at that speed, couldn't keep up with.' Cohen-Solal (1991: 374) records,

> This is how he wrote *The Critique of Dialectical Reason*: a wild rush of words and juxtaposed ideas, pouring forth during crises of hyper-excitement, under the effect of contradictory drugs, that would zing him up, knock him down, or halt him in between . . . Heavy doses for a tough man, hyperlucid and nearly impervious to pain, who, however, would occasionally lapse into moments of absence, from which he then promptly re-emerged, ready to assume control, with vivacity and pride.

Just like Nietzsche's, Sartre's philological recommendations of 'good reading' are polysemous, often balancing on a tightrope of humanist and anti-humanist equivocation. In reference to his biographies of Baudelaire, Genet and Flaubert, Ireland (2020: 451) observes how 'Sartre is both a humanist and an anti-humanist', his analysis residing in the ambiguous space between the two. While stating in an interview, for instance, that 'the life of people who write is projected in the writing in one way or another' (1979b: 26), Sartre maintains elsewhere that 'the text towers above its author' (WL 34). Mueller (2019: 36) echoes Ireland on this point of tergiversation, showing how, as we move from *What Is Literature?* to *The Family Idiot*, Sartre's literary theory 'accords more and more importance to the figure of the reader and seeks to elucidate the possibility of the reader's freedom with increasing precision'. The implicit association of Sartre with an unqualified adherence to 'a conception of the author as a coherent, indivisible, and authoritative entity' is as false as is 'the assumption of a supposedly unproblematic and "whole" Sartrean subject'. *What Is Literature?* is often associated with the notion of the committed author but views the writer in a dual reality with the reader: 'It is the joint effort of author and reader which brings upon the scene that concrete and imaginary object which is the work of the mind. There is no art except for and by others' (WL 50). Sartre questions Kant's notion of disinterested pleasure on the grounds that it does not explain the relationship between the work of art and its viewer (WL 42). The collaboration between author and reader in an undertaking of collective freedom elicits the feeling of 'aesthetic joy' attained through the reader's contribution through which the work 'undergoes an increase in being' (WL 29). Reading is not the simple reception of a message in an act of communication but an active creation characterized by freedom. Without the reader the text would 'remain only a collection of signs' (WL 52). In *The Family Idiot*, as Mueller (2019: 44) notes, Sartre moves further still towards a more decentred reading of the author and how, in a rather 'Foucauldian move', Sartre reduces the author to a specific function in the process of reading. Where the writer leads the reader through the text in *What Is Literature?*, the reader now takes over completely.[7]

As Nietzsche and Sartre move in their analysis to a more decentred view of the subject, they very much anticipate Derrida's critique of the 'metaphysics of presence'. Derrida follows Nietzsche in decentring the subject as a privileged centre by dispersing it within the system of textual relations that is writing: 'The "subject" of writing does not exist if we mean by that some sovereign solitude of the author. The subject of writing is a system of relations between strata: the Mystic Pad, the psyche, society, the world' (1978: 226–7). For Derrida (1978: 292), it is Nietzsche's 'joyous affirmation of the play of the world' that points the way to an affirmation of the decentred play of writing that disrupts the metaphysics of presence which guides the logocentric tradition. 'Nietzsche' himself as a proper name must be placed in quotation marks and the question of the 'truth of Nietzsche' or the 'totality of Nietzsche's text' must be suspended for he writes in the various masks of Zarathustra, the free spirit, the disciple of Dionysus, the new philosopher and the Antichrist.[8]

Although my approach is highly sympathetic to the 'French Nietzsche' and to the Derridean play of interpretation, the attempt to erase Nietzsche altogether from his work – to 'write with no face' (1972: 17) as Foucault professed to – is itself, to my mind, a false move towards metaphysical closure. Although Nietzsche stresses the 'masks' and differing narrative identities of his writing, it is hard to think of an author who is more consciously a writing self connected to a real flesh and blood person and whose personality is projected so unmistakably onto the pages of his books. As Safranski (2003: 28) observes, '[d]espite his philosophical attack on the "I", there is no other philosopher, with the possible exception of Montaigne, who employs the pronoun "I" more than Nietzsche did.' In *Ecce Homo*, Nietzsche makes the link explicit between his life and his philosophy: 'I speak only of what I have lived through, not merely of what I have thought through; the opposition of thinking and life is lacking in my case. My "theory" grows from my "practice"' (EH, part of a discarded draft for Section 3).

Like Nietzsche, Sartre recognizes that reading is always subject to many interpretations: 'I know that other readers appropriate the idea at the same moment [as I do] who surpass the same material toward nearly the same, but *sensibly different* meanings' (IF 3.52). What one reads is 'enriched in my eyes by a thousand interpretations that escape me' (IF 3.52). A form of homology can be discerned between Sartre and Derrida, as Martinot (1999: 55) observes, on the question of the generation of meaning. In Sartrean reading, we can recognize the operation of Derridean différance in the notion that meaning always lies elsewhere to be decided at a later date 'the thought [read], in the instant I make it mine, remains definitively other, an other's thought that commands me to resuscitate it' (IF 3.51). But where both agree that meaning is a trace within worked matter left by another, the Sartrean trace, unlike the Derridean trace, contains Sartre's refusal to erase the person who writes or reads. For Sartre, although words take on a life of their own when 'language presents itself, in effect as an autonomous system' (1966c: 88) and where 'structures express or constitute intentions that determine me without being mine' (1977: 10.97), nonetheless they still bear 'the trace of man' (1966c: 88) as they are taken up and used by speaking subjects. The subject is always entangled within her own texts, 'projected in the writing in one way or another' (1979b: 29). This is a view that becomes obscured in his later texts but never fully relinquished, and one expressed poignantly in the following passage from *Words* as he considers the idea of posterity through writing:

> My bones are leather and cardboard, my parchment flesh smells of glue and mildew, and I strut my ease across a hundredweight or so of paper. I am reborn, I have at last become a complete man, thinking, speaking, singing, thundering, and asserting himself with the peremptory inertia of matter. I am taken up, opened out, spread on the table, smoothed with the flat of the hand and sometimes made to crack. I let it happen and then suddenly I flash, dazzle, impose myself from a distance; my powers traverse space and time, strike down the wicked and protect the good. No one can forget me or pass me over in silence: I am a large, manageable and terrible fetish. My consciousness is in fragments: all the better. Other consciousnesses have taken charge of me. They read *me* and I leap to their eyes; they talk about *me* and I am on everyone's lips, a universal and singular language; I have made myself a prospective interest for millions of glances. For anyone who knows how to like me, I am his most intimate disquiet: but if he wants to touch me, I draw aside and vanish: I exist nowhere but I *am*, at last! I am everywhere: a parasite on humanity, by my good deeds I prey on it and force it endlessly to revive my absence. (W 122)

A playful reading

It is absolutely unnecessary, and not even desirable, *for you to argue in my favour; on the contrary, a dose of curiosity, as if you were looking at an alien plant with ironic distance, would strike me as an incomparably more* intelligent *attitude toward me.*

(Nietzsche, *Letter to Carl Fuchs, July 1888*)

Attempts to fix the interpretative process in the direction exclusively of the subject or object serve only to obscure the dynamic of interpretation and put an end to its proliferating play. To avoid metaphysical closure, 'good' interpretation lies in 'the between'. This also applies to the 'truth' and 'meaning' of Nietzsche's and Sartre's texts. Although they give philosophical licence to the proliferation of perspectives in reading their work, they both refuse to issue a total carte blanche. While, according to Nietzsche, there are 'no eternal horizons or perspectives' (GS 143) and '[t]he same text allows countless interpretations . . . there is no "correct" interpretation' (KGW 8.1), he contrasts the 'art of reading rightly' (HH 270) with the 'art of reading well' (A 52). 'Reading well', he argues, properly articulates the text's 'double sense' (HH 8) that accounts for the rich ambiguity and multiplicity of textual meanings. In spite of his perspectivism, Nietzsche identifies 'bad modes of interpretation' (BGE 22) that lead to a narrowing of interpretation and dogmatism, denying 'the basic condition of all life' (BGE P): 'every such *exaggeration* of a *single* viewpoint is in itself already a sign of sickness' (WP 1020). The same is true of Sartre who states in *What Is Literature?*, 'for the reader all is to do', and yet maintains in *The Family Idiot* that elements of reading can encourage a 'mystifying' or 'demystifying' interpretation.[9]

To get beyond the horns of this dilemma, Schrift and Picard offer a third mode of interpretation based on a 'playful' method of reading. As we will see, *play* is a key element in the philosophy of Nietzsche and Sartre, forming the cornerstone of their creative ethics and ontology. Playfulness signifies a way of rearranging the world, an activity in which we recycle the elements of our lives in creative and experimental ways and transform ourselves in the process, a surrendering as well as an expression of individuality involving an openness to the world of becoming. Schrift's method of 'interpretive pluralism' (1990: 7, 180) aims for a middle ground between the 'dogmatic tendency' of Heidegger and the 'relativistic tendency' of Derrida, occupying 'a space between the interpretive demands of philological attention and perspectival creativity'. This follows Nietzsche who likens good philology to the expert art of *goldsmithing* applied to words (D P5). Goldsmiths know the limit of the material they work with and yet forge and craft this into ever new and creative forms 'between the lines'. This accords with Picard's (1986: 52) view of reading as both 'play' and 'game' whereby the reader invests her own history into the text and thereby produces it creatively. It is play that mobilizes the form of the imagination but also a game that is subject to rules and codes that have been established and intersubjectively determined. Like any in any game, Picard (1986: 169) asserts, there are inevitably 'cheats' who destroy the 'hermeneutic code' of the text by skipping passages, jumping to the end or falsely isolating passages from the context in which they occur. Picard's 'cheats' are thus akin to what Nietzsche calls his 'worst readers' who behave like 'plundering troops' and 'take away a few things they can use, dirty and confound the remainder, and revile the whole' (HH 2.137).

The texts of Nietzsche call out for playful interpretation just as Nietzsche did himself in giving positive value to 'the spontaneous, aggressive, expansive, form-giving forces that give new interpretations and directions':

> whatever exists, having somehow come into being, is again and again reinterpreted to new ends, taken over, transformed, and redirected by some power ... all events in the organic world are a subduing, become master, and all subduing and becoming master involves a fresh interpretation, an adaptation through which any previous 'meaning' and 'purpose' are necessarily obscured or even obliterated. (GM 2.12)

In *Daybreak*, he presents the image of creatures in flight, '*aeronauts of the spirit*', who fly higher and further away with all of our 'great mentors and precursors' who cannot fly any further. There still remains a 'vast and prodigious trajectory' to explore, and despite the fatigue of some including ourselves, we can take comfort in the knowledge that '[o]ther birds will fly further!' (D 573). 'A philosophy remains efficacious', Sartre wrote in a similar vein, only 'so long as the praxis which has engendered it, which supports it, and which is clarified by it, is still alive' (SM 5–6). Both philosophers share Derrida's view of reading as a 'transformational' activity, developing a multiplicity of interpretations from the fundamental polysemy of linguistic signs and giving assent to the creative projections of the reader while avoiding an unqualified relativism by implicitly recognizing acceptable 'protocols of reading'. Although interpretation is never absolutely decidable as there will always be more than one plausible interpretation, in Derrida's transformational writing interpretations are nevertheless constrained by their context and some are hence more plausible than others.

In my 'playful reading' of Nietzsche and Sartre, I situate their core insights within the development of contemporary posthumanist thinking, taking them out of the conceptual assemblages of the nineteenth century (where many scholars pigeonhole them) and projecting them into the twenty-first. In so doing, I not only mine the main seams of their thinking but also bring into the foreground those elements or emergent concepts that lurk between the lines which have been suppressed, ignored and given scant attention in common readings of them or just left latent and undeveloped in their texts. As Cox (2013: 6) writes of Sartre, for instance, the longer we study his 'myriad insights', the more territories and horizons appear. Where Sartre did not explore a territory so thoroughly as to make it his own, he pointed the way towards it, 'either promising to reach it himself in due course or inviting others to investigate his sketchy insights'. This is fundamentally a task, as Visker (2007: 3–4) avers, of perceiving the 'cracks' in his philosophy or the 'turns of argumentation' where conceptual possibilities that glimmer through have been left unconsidered or undeveloped. I offer my interpretation of Nietzsche and Sartre in this vein as a kind of *palimpsest*, an overwriting of original texts that still clearly bear the strong imprint of their original authors but which harbour new propositions and directions.[10] My hope is to find an Ariadnean thread of philological rigour and conceptual understanding that makes sense of how their many perspectives follow the walls of their labyrinthine texts. Moreover, by conjoining their philosophy to their lives, I hope to bring back into it, in Deleuze's (1987: 119) words, 'a little of that joy, that force, that amorous and political life that they both knew how to give and invent'.

The New Nietzsche and New Sartre

This tremendous event is still on its way, still wandering; it has not yet reached the ears of men. Lightning and thunder require time; the light of the stars requires time; deeds, though done, still require time to be seen and heard.
(Nietzsche, *The Gay Science* 125)

In death, as Sartre claimed, we become 'prey to the living' (BN 706) and there has certainly been no shortage of scholars who have interpreted the deceased Nietzschean and Sartrean mind. The appropriation of Nietzsche, as Strong (1996: 129) remarks, 'has become a kind of paralyzed and paralyzing text' which could only be taken care of just like his body after the onset of insanity: 'Nietzsche in the asylum, Nietzsche in the care of his sister, Nietzsche in the hands of his readers: Nietzsche under control.' From the onset of his terminal madness in 1890, his sister, Elisabeth Förster-Nietzsche, and his one-time lover, Lou Salomé, presented two very different faces of Nietzsche. Salomé's *Friedrich Nietzsche: The Man in His Work* (1894) highlighted the importance of style in his thinking (aphorism, multiple voices, different forms of narrative perspective) and the relationship between physical and mental vitality (or decline) to the production of ideas. Her overall image of Nietzsche was that of a neurotic and decadent genius whose three 'transitions' in his thought ('early', 'middle' and 'late') were expressive of changes in the situation and circumstances of his life. By contrast, Förster-Nietzsche's two-volume *The Life of Friedrich Nietzsche* (1895 and 1897) contested this view, presenting her brother as a healthy, sane and adventurous thinker who was developing the framework of a coherent and systematic philosophy. She assumed the literary rights to her brother's estate in 1895 and creatively rearranged his unpublished notes into a new work *The Will to Power* (1901, reissued in an expanded edition in 1906) with selected focus on 'will' and 'power', which exerted an influence on his reputation as a thinker of force, domination and violence. She argued that Nietzsche had hidden his 'true philosophy' in his published texts but revealed it in all fullness in the pages of *The Will to Power*.

After the 'Nazification' of Nietzsche's philosophy by philosophers such as Baumler, Rosenberg and Oehler in Germany in the 1930s, who seized upon Förster-Nietzsche's identification of the 'Bloody' Nietzsche as a philosopher of domination, Nietzsche's first American commentators reined in his stylistic and political excesses and presented him as a systematic philosopher. For Danto (2005: 13), he emerges 'as a systematic as well as an original and analytic thinker' while in Kaufmann's (1974: viii, 84) view, rather than 'a great stylist', he is primarily 'a great thinker', whose many 'all-too-human judgments' should be viewed as 'philosophically irrelevant'. As would have been his innermost wish (EH 6), Nietzsche came to the fore in France in the 1960s and 1970s when the three Hs (Hegel, Heidegger and Husserl) were displaced in French academic circles by the three 'Masters of Suspicion', Nietzsche, Freud and Marx. Two important conferences that crystallized Nietzsche's importance in France were the colloquium at Royaumont in 1964 and the 'Nietzsche aujourd'hui' conference at Cérisy-la-Salle in 1972 where, in reaction to Heidegger's reading of Nietzsche as a grand metaphysician, the 'French Nietzsche' or 'New Nietzsche' was born. Building on the work of Bataille and Klossowski, Derrida (*Spurs*, 1978), Deleuze (*Nietzsche and Philosophy*, 1962), Foucault (*Nietzsche, Genealogy, History*, 1971) and Kofman (*Nietzsche and Metaphor*, 1978) focused on the more literary and stylistic aspects of his work that worked against conceptual thinking. They argued that Nietzsche's influence extends well beyond the explicit themes of his work and prompts radical questions on thought itself in determining the direction of modernity, what it is to be 'human', and the relation between self and world.

Bataille's *On Nietzsche*, published in 1945, is the origin of what we now know as the 'French Nietzsche', arguing that the Nazi appropriation of Nietzsche ran contrary to his manifold separation between politics and cultural vitality. Bataille also pitted Nietzsche (who valorized the untotalizable, anti-systematic fragmentary embrace of excess epitomized by Dionysus) against Hegel (who subordinated all opposites to a rational synthesized totality), giving philosophical weight to the irrational and paradoxical in Nietzsche (the body, the unconscious, instinct). In tune with Bataille,

Klossowski emphasizes the role of the body and nervous system in Nietzsche's thinking by observing the relation between the body's impulses and conscious thought. The paradoxical nature of Nietzsche's thinking is refracted through his concept of the eternal return that is viewed by Klossowski (2005: 43–57) as primarily a *lived experience*. It is a 'divine vicious circle' (*circulus vitiosus deus*), a paradoxical argument that undermines the traditional categories of Western metaphysics, such as the principle of identity and the law of non-contradiction, making the singularity of every instant opaque and unintelligible (e.g. linear and cyclical). It also undermines the unified subject in that we have to cycle through all our past selves and future selves in the cycle of returning to our current self. Since we change so radically over time, there are elements of our past selves that cannot be incorporated into our current self-identity, so the process of remembering ('anamnesis') overflows our sense of self-identity. The paradox of eternal return is thus felt as a lived experience that undermines the identity of the experiencer who has the experience.

Deleuze's *Nietzsche and Philosophy* was a seminal text in the emergence of the 'New Nietzsche' and was heavily influenced by Bataille and Klossowski. Deleuze develops Bataille's critique of Hegelianism but portrays Nietzsche as a systematic philosopher who conceives the will to power primarily in terms of active and reactive forces. As primary constituents of reality, forces come together through chance in a relation through which both are mutually affected. The will to power is fundamentally a creative and bountiful force but becomes a desire for domination when sublimated only in its slavish, reactive form: 'When nihilism triumphs, then and only then does the will to power stop meaning "to create" and start to signify instead "to want power", "to want to dominate"' (2001: 76–7). 'Power, as will to power', according to Deleuze, 'is not *that which* the will wants, but that which wants in the will' (2001: 73). In his critique of Hegel, he contrasts Nietzsche's *Übermensch* (which breaks with the values of the past) with Hegel's dialectic (which is weighed down by the 'heaviness' of the past as it preserves what it overcomes, including nihilism). Furthermore, Deleuze replaces Hegelian *opposition* and *negation* at the centre of the dialectic with *difference* and *affirmation* that he finds at the centre of Nietzsche's thought. For Deleuze (1983: 8), 'Anti-Hegelianism runs through Nietzsche's work as its cutting edge'. Hegel's opposition thinking is a type of thought characteristic of the slave who defines himself by negating and opposing the master. It effaces difference and ignores the subtle gradations between poles and the complex continuous plane from which antithetical concepts and values are forged.

Despite writing little directly about Nietzsche, Foucault locates Nietzsche at the centre of his own thinking, declaring at one point, 'I am simply a Nietzschean' (1989: 327). In his essay 'Nietzsche, Genealogy, History' (1971), he contrasts traditional history (metaphysical assumption that things have an eternal, unchanging essence at their core, a unified story as the 'truth' of history) with Nietzsche's 'effective' genealogical history (the arbitrariness of history, discontinuities, accidents, multiplicities). Placing contingency at the heart of Nietzsche's thinking and developing the Deleuzian critique of Hegel's dialectic, Foucault uses Nietzsche's genealogical history to identify 'the accidents, the minute deviations – or conversely, the complete reversals – the errors, the false appraisals, and the faulty calculations that gave birth to those things that continue to exist and have value for us' (1977a: 146). In Foucault's view, Nietzsche's genealogical analysis of power shows how the constitution of 'psyche, subjectivity, personality, consciousness' is the result of definite 'methods of punishment, supervision and constraint' (1977a: 29). In Nietzsche we can thus find the first dissolution of man:

> by means of a philological critique, by means of a certain form of biologism, Nietzsche rediscovered the point at which man and God belong to one another, at which the death of the second is synonymous with the disappearance of the first, and at which the promise of the superman signifies first and foremost the imminence of the death of man. (1970: 342)

Nietzsche's deconstruction of the subject emerges as the first decisive break from modernity: 'What Nietzsche's thought heralds', according to Foucault (1970: 385), is not so much the 'death of God' but 'the end of his murderer'. This casts 'man' not as any kind of essence that expresses itself irresistibly through history but as a configuration of historical and linguistic determinations linked to the circulation of power: 'the development of humanity is a series of interpretations' (1977: 152).

Most of all, it was Derrida who built the image of the 'New Nietzsche' as a *master of deconstruction*. In some later writings, such as 'Otobiographies' (1986) and *The Politics of Friendship* (1997), he analyses Nietzsche in relation to political questions (such as his culpability for his appropriation by Nazi ideologues), but in his early work he confronts Nietzsche as a playful stylist. For Derrida (1978: 292), 'Nietzsche' appears as the proper name for thinking otherwise, 'a shorthand marker for the other of logocentrism', signifying play, interpretation, textuality. Derrida uses Deleuze's idea of opposing forces to show that forces have no identity in themselves but only in relation to how they relate to and differ from other forces 'force itself is never present; it is only a play of different quantities' (1973: 148). Differential forces give rise to what appears to be stable systems of oppositional terms:

> We could thus take up all the coupled oppositions on which philosophy is constructed, and from which our language lives, not in order to see opposition vanish but to see the emergence of a necessity such that one of the terms appears as the difference of the other, the other as 'differed' within the systematic ordering of the same. (1973: 148–9).

Nietzsche's critique of the metaphysician's *'faith in antithetical values'* (BGE 2) forms the basis of Derrida's deconstructionist method that unravels the binary conceptual hierarchies in which one term is privileged as present and the other excluded term as absent by problematizing the distinction. This involves the dual process of inversion (overturning the traditional hierarchy of a binary opposition by showing that the traditionally subordinate term is actually the dominant one) and displacement (creating new terms or 'undecidables' that cannot be reduced to the traditional hierarchical opposition). As we will see in the next chapter, it was Nietzsche's deconstructionist method that, in Derrida's view, placed him well beyond Heidegger's charge of metaphysical humanism. Pre-empting Derrida's own double procedure of inversion and displacement, Nietzsche deconstructs the truth/falsity opposition, initially inverting the relation by suggesting that untruth might be more conducive to human well-being than truth (it protects us against the harsh realities of existence), not by simply asserting the authority of untruth over truth but by displacing the grounds for their opposition by reading them in terms of their value for life: 'The falseness of a judgement is to us not necessarily an objection to a judgement.... The question is to what extent it is life-advancing, life-preserving, species-preserving, perhaps even species-breeding' (BGE 4). Similarly, in his move beyond good and evil, Nietzsche does not simply invert the good/evil hierarchy but displaces these in the favour of a revaluation of all values.[11]

Just as the 'New Nietzsche' was reborn in France sixty years or so after his death, a 'New Sartre' has emerged four decades on from his death in 1980 by a growing number of scholars who have viewed his work, and particularly his relation to postmodernism, with a fresh perspective. The old Vintage Sartre we are familiar enough with – classical, Cartesian, humanist, nihilist philosopher of conflict and grand metaphysician. This is the Sartre, anointed and flagellated in equal measure, of 'hell is other people', the 'last of the Cartesians' (Grene 1993: 232), the historian of reason (Dobson 1993) and the bourgeois champion of absolute freedom (Marcuse 1983). The old Sartreans place Sartre squarely under the influence of classical modernist thinking in the shadow of Descartes and Kant. In Solomon's (1988: 173) view, 'the structure of his philosophy is undeniably Cartesian', while, for Marcuse (1983), it is Sartre's concept of the gaze, where the other 'appears as the one who usurps, appropriates and appraises my world, as the "thief" of my possibilities', that inclines his social ontology towards an atomistic bourgeois individualism: 'Behind the nihilistic language [of *Being and Nothingness*] lurks the ideology of free competition, free initiative and equal opportunity'. Although Dobson (1993: 187, 5, 174) recognizes that 'Sartre cannot easily be appropriated as the last bastion of a discredited humanism', he insists that Sartre is a philosopher of reason who 'cannot realistically be viewed as anticipating postmodern themes' and is far away from being 'the harbinger of post-humanist trends'. This Vintage Sartre is, in many ways, a regressive, abstract and vulgarized Sartre marooned in the nineteenth century – a relic, as Foucault (2001: 541) stated, of a bygone era.

The 'New Sartre' as *un homme postmoderne* is perhaps a less familiar figure to some but one who has crept out from the shadows and into full critical view in recent times. Jameson (1995: 1) was one of the first to argue that Sartre is 'a hidden origin' of many elements of postmodernist thinking and is, in many respects, akin to the figure of Captain Dreyfus at the turn of the twentieth century. All the charges (especially his supposed incongruity with poststructuralism) are understood to be false, 'yet the victim's honour has yet to be publicly rehabilitated'. In Howells' (1992: 1) words, this idea of 'the new Sartre' presents him 'as a figure whose diversity was far from being mastered, who could not, without distortion or impoverishment, be identified with the "classical existentialism" of the 1940s, and whose relationship to Structuralism and Post-Structuralism, as well as to psychoanalysis, Marxism, and literary theory, was far more complex than ha[s] generally been supposed'. In this respect, traditional accounts of post-war intellectual history in France can be said to have pitted Sartre as a theoretical adversary to (post)structuralists such as Foucault,

Lacan, Deleuze and Derrida far too readily. Moreover, standard interpretations of Sartre's work can be seen to rely too heavily on certain themes or on particular passages in his 'classical existentialist' works of the 1940s to the serious neglect of other elements in his work of this period, and indeed, in the wider trajectory of his work as a whole. Howells makes the further claim that since Sartre's two main works of philosophy, *Being and Nothingness* and the *Critique*, predate the main wave of poststructuralist texts in the 1960s, 1970s and 1980s, they can be seen in effect to prefigure many key poststructuralist themes, such as 'the decentred subject, the rejection of a metaphysics of presence, the critique of bourgeois humanism and individualism, the concept of the reader as producer of the text's multiple meanings, the recognition of language and thought structures as masters rather than mastered in most acts of discourse and thinking, [and] a materialist philosophy of history as detotalized and fragmented' (1992: 2). These themes, she argues, are not 'the inventions of Lacan, Foucault, Lévi-Strauss and Derrida' but can 'be found in Sartre's later works' and are 'present from the outset' in even his early work which dates from *The Transcendence of the Ego* in 1936 (1992: 2). Taken together, they serve to contradict the simple identification of Sartre with the usual image of a classical intellectual steeped in a Cartesian tradition of modern philosophy which is, by implication, a form of philosophy diametrically opposed to the postmodernizing strategies of the poststructuralists.

Since Howells' rereading of post-war French philosophy, a stream of scholars, including Sawyer (2015), Mueller (2019), Baugh (1999), Martinot (1999), Chambers (2019), Flynn (2004, 2010), Butterfield (2012), Richards (2019), Reynolds and Woodward (2011), Charbonneau (1999), Rozeghy (2002) and Farrell Fox (2003, 2009, 2020) have all traced the connections of Sartre's thinking to key themes in the work of poststructuralists, such as Derrida, Lacan, Foucault and Deleuze. Sarah Richmond's newly appeared translation of *Being and Nothingness* (2018), correcting some of the inadequacies and infelicitous locutions in Hazel Barnes' original translation into English in 1956, is symbolic of a wider move to 'update' Sartre and has paved the way to a more nuanced interpretation of this endlessly discussed philosophical text. This has been aided significantly by Eshleman's (2011, 2020a) detailed analysis of the structure and methodology of Sartre's *Essay in Phenomenological Ontology* that shows how it was never Sartre's intention to separate *pour-soi* and *en-soi* in a Cartesian way, but on the contrary, to demonstrate their irreducible entanglement within an immanent unity of 'lived experience'. O'Shiel (2018) and Heldt (2020) have recently shown the way to a 'revaluation of Sartre's ontology' in *Being and Nothingness*, an ontology the interpretation of which, in Heldt's (2020: v) words, 'has become platitudinous in its orthodoxy'.

A similar renewal in understanding the *Critique*(s) has been undertaken by Flynn (2010) and Ally (2020). Flynn demonstrates how Sartre's relational ontology (which he terms 'Dialectical Nominalism') offers a *via media* between the inadequacies of methodological individualism and holism, both of which Sartre heavily critiques. He also differentiates Sartre's 'Decapitated Dialectic' (based on contingency, difference, incompletion and detotalization) from the Hegelian Dialectic (based on resolution, linearity, identity, teleology and eschatology), thus paving the way for a theoretical rapprochement between Sartre's dialectical method and postmodernist thinking. Ally (2020: 365) highlights the way in which Sartre relentlessly dissolves binarisms, employing a deconstructionist method in his 'ternary' post-metaphysical thinking: 'We might call this the *immanent imminence of the ternary*, both immanent and imminent. The third is *always coming* and *always nearby* and *always already there*. When we think with Sartre, if we look for a Third, we will find one.' For Ally (2020: 365, 372), Sartre's 'index of complementarity' between opposing pairs and his 'sensitivity to parts and wholes' puts him on the cusp of a new direction in thinking as we pass from a Holocene to an Anthropocene phase in human and natural history and places him far from Cartesian vulgarizations.

Recognizing the impetus of a palpable resurgence of new interpretations of Sartre's work, in 2013 Cohen-Solal declared that we are witnessing 'une renaissance sartrienne'. As I write this, Noudelmann's new book *Un Tout Autre Sartre* (2021) has just been published, calling us to reappraise Sartre's life and work and to bring to the fore neglected or overlooked aspects of his thinking in traditional accounts of the 'old Sartre'. This involves not only rethinking Sartre's connection to postmodernism and to currents in contemporary philosophy but also viewing his works with a fresh glance, particularly with regard to the relative play of rational and irrational elements within them. In Kirkpatrick's view (2017a), for instance, Sartre's early work comprises a 'morganatic marriage' of phenomenology and mysticism in which the influence of the latter was downplayed by Sartre (and others) because of its perceived inferiority in terms of academic and methodological respectability. The formative influence on Sartre of other sources, such as theological writers, *moralistes* and Christian mystics like Baruzi, Delacroix and Theresa of Avila, has been obscured by the shadow of the three Hs (Hegel, Husserl, Heidegger) which has formed the dominant theoretical filter through which his thinking has been understood (2017a: 5). Heldt (2020: 1, xx) adds to this view, pointing to the proclivity in Sartrean scholarship 'to render judgment on Sartre as some sort of passive disciple of Heidegger' and thus obscure his 'largely forgotten Bergsonian heritage'. After all, Sartre did not directly replicate 'the three H's' since one has to remember that his understanding was mediated by their French interpreters – Levinas (Husserl), Wahl (Hegel, Heidegger), Lefebvre (Hegel and Marx). Sartre was no mere interpreter or commentator in this respect but more a raider of texts to procure what is useful and leave the rest behind, rearticulating and reforging useful concepts while abandoning theoretical cul-de-sacs. Heidegger, Husserl and Hegel 'merely serve as grist for the Sartrean mill' (Baugh 2020: 31), and it is misleading therefore to view his work as simply deriving from his German influences.

There has been a growing analytical interest in the importance of *pre-reflective thinking* and *magic* in Sartre's philosophy. Sartre was heavily influenced by French anthropology of the 1930s that had magic as the central core of its study. Unlike Mauss, Durkheim and Lévy-Bruhl, however, whose idea of a 'pre-logical mentality' they restricted to primitive societies and certain elements of children's behaviour, Sartre sought to extend magic to a universal human dynamic, following Bergson who criticized this anthropology for contrasting too starkly between so-called primitive and civilized society. Above all, Alain (Emile-Auguste Chartier) stands out as a major influence on Sartre's early thinking, emphasizing in his *Propos sur le bonheur* (1928) the centrality of the lived body and its passions, magic, incantation and the powerful role of the imagination. These themes persist throughout Sartre's writings but peak in his early and final phases of thinking. As O'Shiel (2019: 3) demonstrates, magic is the conceptual cornerstone of his early work on the ego (1936), the emotions (1938) and the imagination (1940) but, though discussed less explicitly, also in *Being and Nothingness*, 'a work borne out of Sartre's intense preoccupation with the magical being that we are'. In his interviews after 1973, Sartre returns to a more magical or 'enchanted' viewpoint in his ontological speculations that expands upon his early affective phenomenology of consciousness and world and gives a strong posthumanist coloration to his philosophy. The role of the imagination, which was centre stage in his early writings on freedom, also becomes axiomatic to his later ethical writings and his affirmative vision of a creative ethics. Sartre confirms this in a late interview where he emphasizes the continuity of his thinking on the centrality of the imagination for envisaging a new kind of 'ethical being'. When questioned by Rybalka in 1975 about his early work, he remarked that his perspective hadn't significantly changed through the years and that '[i]t seems to me that if I had to write on the imaginary, I would write what I wrote previously' (1981: 14).

In relating an author to their epoch, there is often a 'diachronic time-lag', Sartre recognized, that operates both prospectively and respectively so that 'the author cannot be the contemporary of his contemporaries unless he is, on the whole, behind them and ahead of them' (IF 3.424). Nietzsche compares the comprehension of his writing to the light that emanates from a star – it may take a long time for what exists to be actually perceived (GS 125). As it was for Nietzsche with the French poststructuralists in the 1960s, the emergence of the 'New Sartre' in the present time, propelled by Howells, has caused us to rethink Sartre's position in twentieth-century French philosophy. Maybe, after all of the white noise, existentialism and poststructuralism were parallel philosophies rather than antithetical ones, certainly in the case of Sartre, Beauvoir, Merleau-Ponty and Heidegger. This means we can unproblematically understand Nietzsche, as is suggested by Ansell-Pearson (2011: 298), as *both* a poststructuralist *and* as 'a thinker of authenticity' who paved the way for some radical currents in existentialist thought since there is no essential chasm of difference between the two. Despite the fact that the 'New Sartre' has become a living paradigm of interpretation within Sartrean scholarship, however, it has still not seeped fully into the academic mainstream. This is reflected in Sartre's often glaring absence from the pantheon of posthuman precursors or pioneers. In Lechte's book *Fifty Key Contemporary Thinkers – from Structuralism to Posthumanism*, for example, Nietzsche and a number of phenomenologists are listed – Heidegger, Husserl, Levinas and Merleau-Ponty – but not Sartre. This is a typical oversight often repeated by chroniclers of the 'posthuman' or 'postmodern' condition. One may conclude from this that the brightest light from Sartre's star has yet to reach the eyes of many perceivers and, as such, there is a kind of time lapse that exists between Nietzsche and Sartre, one that this book seeks to rebalance by linking the New Nietzsche to the New Sartre and showing the full extent and depth of their parallel philosophies.

Philosophers of paradox

This dual *series of experiences, this access to apparently separate worlds, is repeated in my nature in every respect: I am a* Doppelgänger, *I have a 'second' face in addition to the first.* And *perhaps also a third.*

(Nietzsche, Ecce Homo 1.3)

Nietzsche's thinking can be seen as a swinging pendulum between opposites. Not only does he regularly contradict himself but even seems to enjoy doing so: 'Does the good historian not, at bottom, constantly *contradict*?' (D P2). 'This thinker', he wrote, 'needs nobody to refute him: for that he suffices himself' (WS 249). Moreover, he believed that you can make a virtue of contradiction as it is essentially a sign of spiritual abundance. He saw the inability to tolerate contradiction – to contain or negotiate opposites in the right way – as an aspect of cultural illness (GM 3.2, GS 297). Contradiction, or Nietzsche's 'dual optic' (Solomon 2003: 9), abounds at every corner of his work. *Zarathustra*, Nietzsche's favourite work of his own, his literary gift of a joyful, agonistic and bestowing friendship to his readers, is after all a book offered in contradictory fashion as a book 'for all and none'. In *Ecce Homo*, he declares, 'I contradict as has never been contradicted before' (EH 4.1) and presents his earthly prophet Zarathustra as a paragon of contradiction: 'The ladder he climbs up and down is enormous; he has seen further, willed further, had further abilities than anyone else. This most affirmative of all spirits contradicts with every word he speaks; all oppositions are combined into a new unity in him' (EH 3Z6). In *Human, All Too Human*, Nietzsche talks of a divided bicamerality in the human mind, 'two chambers of the brain, as it were, one to experience science and the other nonscience' (HH 251). He was also fond of making much of his *mixed blood*, projecting his Germanic inheritance in *The Birth of Tragedy*, and channelling it through Schopenhauer and Wagner, before repressing it in his later life.[12] '*Il Polacco*' (as he became known when he stayed at Marienbad and Sorrento during his nomadic years) associated in his imagination Polish blood with rebellion and freethinking that valorized individuality and genius over received opinion and herd behaviour. Nicolas Copernicus, the Pole, is a prefiguration of Zarathustra, 'a freethinker who effects transmutations of knowledge' (Safranski 2003: 63), while another Polish genius, Fredric Chopin, supplanted the Teuton Wagner as Nietzsche's favourite composer.

Negotiating contradiction, in Nietzsche's view, is a fundamental requirement for any form of anti-metaphysical thinking that seeks to overcome '*the faith in antithetical values*' (BGE 2). He contrasts his own 'Historical philosophy' with the binarist thinking of 'metaphysical philosophy':

> How can something originate in its antithesis, for example rationality in irrationality, the sentient in the dead, logic in unlogic, disinterested contemplation in covetous willing, living for others in egoism, truth in error? Metaphysical philosophy has hitherto surmounted this difficulty by denying that the one originates in the other and assuming for the more highly valued thing a miraculous source in the very

kernel and being of the 'thing in itself'. Historical philosophy, on the other hand ... has discovered ... that there are no opposites ... and that a mistake in reasoning lies at the bottom of this antithesis: in this interpretation there exists, strictly speaking, neither an unegoistic action nor completely disinterested contemplation; both are only sublimations, in which the basic element seems almost to have dispersed and reveals itself only under the most painstaking observation. (HH 1)

As we will see in Chapter 4, the idea that two seemingly antithetical things are really one thing at different stages of sublimation is the foundation of Nietzsche's psychology and of his philosophical monism, both of which would have been impossible without the concept of 'sublimated will to power'. In his Heraclitean conception of the absolute flow of becoming and fading away (just as in Sartre's philosophical monism and 'Dialectical Nominalism'), there are no dialectical antitheses but only fluid transitions.[13]

Unsurprisingly, many scholars have highlighted the ambiguous or contradictory nature of Nietzsche's thinking. Jaspers situates Nietzsche in an ambiguous space between the aphoristic and the systematic, as well as between the philosophical and the literary. He reveals the astonishing newness and originality of his thought, 'symbolic of the destiny of humanity itself as it presses onwards towards its limits and its sources', a case, Jaspers (1965: viii–xiv) writes, of 'modernity somersaulting itself'. However, he also looks at the 'aberrations' in Nietzsche that are 'on the verge of insanity' and involve 'mistaken naturalistic and extremist pronouncements', dismissing many of his celebrated philosophical ideas, like the will to power and the eternal return. The most important feature of Nietzsche's work is that it is replete with *contradictions*, and this is why the attempt to construct a philosophical whole in the way of a Nietzschean system often falls apart – at first '[o]ne finds it insufferable that Nietzsche says first this, then that, and then something entirely different' (1965: xi). For any proposition in Nietzsche one can usually find its opposite somewhere else in his work: '*Self-contradiction* is the fundamental ingredient in Nietzsche's thought' (1965: 10).

Several others follow Jaspers in identifying the contradictory features that make up the 'two faces of Nietzsche' (Magnus and Higgins 1996: 3). For Blanchot (1969: 244), 'Nietzsche thinks or, more precisely, writes ... under a double suspicion that inclines him to a double refusal: refusal of the immediate, refusal of mediation'. In the duplicity of Nietzsche's position, immediacy is unattainable, but desirable, while concepts are undesirable but necessary. Nietzsche practices '*une ècriture fragmentaire*' that delights in the play of language for its own sake, subverts the 'spirit of gravity' and undermines his philosophical discourse, the other side of his texts. Caught in a no man's land between the impossibility of immediacy and the ineluctability of mediation, Nietzsche opts for style, artistic play and the different masks of his texts. Where Woodward highlights the bicameral form of Nietzsche's thinking as navigating his way 'between a veneration of the tragic mythologies of the past and a projective identification with the future' (2011: 241), Ansell-Pearson reads Nietzsche's paradoxical thinking along political lines:

> There are contradictory, perhaps even irreconcilable, aspects to Nietzsche's thinking. On the one hand, one finds authoritarian strands in his work, primarily

reflected in his views on the state, on men and women, and on the necessity for hierarchy and inequality in the social structure. On the other hand, however, his thinking is characterised by libertarian dimensions which are profoundly liberating; such as, for example, his Dionysian conception of life as perpetual self-overcoming which implies the necessity of overcoming fixed boundaries divisions, and orders of rank, his notion of joyful knowledge or science (*Wissenschaft*), and his celebration of laughter. (1994: 55)

There is 'a real ambiguity at the heart of Nietzsche's thinking' which is that it often finds itself caught in a tension between two quite different kinds of libidinal economy – 'an economy of the proper' (denoting property, possession, mastery, self-aggrandizement) and an 'economy of the gift' ('squandering' or 'letting be'). This brings to light the ambiguity of will to power as mastery and domination versus a will to let be and let go (1994: 191). But, Ansell-Pearson (1994: 192) warns, even his gift-giving can be read in masculine terms as a self-originating, autonomous force. His desire to give birth to himself expresses a resentment towards his past and towards maternal birth since the subject is posited as proud and independent, a *causa sui*, expressing 'the original evasion of an unbearable origin'.

Solomon (2003: 82) also telescopes the contradictory impulses in Nietzsche's work, observing that 'Nietzsche, despite his high reputation with the poststructuralists, seemed to thrill in divisive polarities'. His views on freedom, for instance, are 'complex and confusing', bringing into play a 'paradox of fatalism and self-creation'. But this, in Solomon's (2003: 172, 181, 184) view, ties in with the essence of his perspectivism – they are two perspectives on ourselves like a Kantian antinomy in which what appears to have two contradictory appearances turns out to be the expressions of two different standpoints. We often take up one or the other of these perspectives sequentially. This duality applied equally to his conflicted and often contradictory personality: 'megalomania mixed with shyness, free spirit mixing with a love of military discipline, a thirst for solitude combined with a hunger for intimate friends.' The laughter that Nietzsche alludes to is very often hollow and forced, the 'cheerfulness the reach of a desperate man' who 'cuts a not very convincing gay figure' (2003: 161, 117). Thus, a kind of 'dual optic' defines Nietzsche's philosophy from his earliest writings on the recognition of the world's awfulness on the one hand and the affirmation of life on the other. There is also a certain irony, as Solomon notes, which pertains to his final years. The philosopher who railed against pity tragically spent his last ten years in a vegetative state, the object of pity cared for by a sister whom he despised. All in all, as an example, 'Nietzsche is more plausibly viewed as a play of opposites, like Rousseau, who cannot be understood either in terms of his work or his life alone'. It is '[o]ut of this impossible cauldron of personality Nietzsche creates himself' (2003: 32, 161).

Nietzsche's biographers also bring out the contradictory impulses in his thinking. Safranski (2003: 349) shows the tensions between the Bloody and the Gentle Nietzsche, revealing the 'traces of benevolence in Nietzsche's sometimes cruel philosophy'. This is reflected in his concept of the *Übermensch* which he imbues with ambiguity, as he does of his self-characterization as 'Caesar with Christ's Soul' (WP 983). In *Zarathustra*, he hints at the *biologistic* contents of the *Übermensch* and in his notebooks he is more forthright – his 'goal' was the 'evolution of the entire body and not just of the brain' (KSW 10.506). But in *Ecce Homo*, he is keen to strip the *Übermensch* of any Darwinian or idealist conceptions (EH 3.1). Even if, by his aristocratic radicalism, the masses should be annihilated should they become a hindrance to the production of the higher type, this must be a voluntary sacrifice – 'in his fantasies of annihilation . . . Nietzsche was still a highly sensitive soul and hence more amenable to the option that the "misfits" could offer to "sacrifice" themselves willingly' (2003: 269). This connects to the ambivalence in Nietzsche's wider orientation towards the human species – on the one hand, sharing Renaissance ideals of the 'dignity of man' and the human adventure to fly to ever greater heights (D 573) while also confounding anthropocentric arrogance: 'man as a species does not represent any progress compared with any other animal' (WP 684). In his more self-reflexive modes, Nietzsche calls into question his own pretensions as a philosopher-legislator, disclosing his identity grandiosely as a historical 'destiny' but reminding his readers that this 'little piece of dynamite' may turn out to be a buffoon (EH 4.1).

Nietzsche's avatar for his '*penchant* for discontinuity' (Hayman 1982: 360) is the figure of Dionysus, who was the God of masks. Nietzsche presented himself as a philosopher of masks who, in line with his philosophy of becoming, did not particularly want to be fully understood, pinned down and thereby exhausted of future possibilities: 'Every profound thinker is more afraid of being understood than of being misunderstood' (BGE 290). We should always wonder, Nietzsche warns, 'whether, behind each cave, there is not another deeper cave. . . . Each philosophy *conceals* another philosophy; each opinion is also a hiding-place, each word also a mask' (BGE 289). The productive play of contradiction prevents a philosopher from stagnating in an illusion of certitude and immutability. Logic, he states, is a clumsy tool that can 'handle only formulas for what remains the same' (WP 517), whereas the world of becoming is self-contradictory: 'The conceptual ban on contradiction proceeds from the assumption . . . that the concept not only designates the essence of a thing but comprehends it. . . . Logic is an attempt to comprehend actuality by means of a scheme of being we have ourselves proposed' (WP 516). Contradiction and paradox are, in this sense, modalities of Nietzsche's perspectivism – although the twin poles of deconstruction and reconstruction seem to run at odds with one another in his thinking, they constantly work in tandem. It is only through a forensic examination of the forces that determine us that we can go beyond their strict control and refashion ourselves through authenticity or by 'giving style to ourselves'. As Sartre asserts throughout his work, comprehension and praxis are always linked – because we are made, we can be unmade, assuming we know how we were made. To this end, as Hayman (1982: 361) suggests, Nietzsche's main influence was 'towards unmasking, demystification' while being 'one of the great liberators'. The poles of freedom and determinism do not exclude each other in Nietzschean and Sartrean existentialism as in metaphysical thinking but mutually reinforce.

Hayman (1986: 8) locates the same 'penchant for discontinuity' in Sartre: '[l]ike Nietzsche, Sartre took an almost religious pleasure in the sense of battling against himself.' In Boulé's (2005: 2–3) assessment, there are 'multiple, fragmented and contradictory Sartrean selves . . . Sartre was a chameleon . . . a different person to different people' who sheds his past selves like an old skin: 'Each moment of my life detaches itself from me like a dead leaf' (1995: 126).¹⁴ There are, in the main, two discernibly different Sartres – one who exhibits a more 'inclusive' sense of self as opposed to the 'compromised' sense of self that marked his early and middle years. In fact, Boulé (2005: 3) argues that it is after 1973, namely, in the last seven years of his life, that Sartre overcame his more aggressive, 'masculinist' tendencies and began to recognize and own his vulnerabilities and the feminine aspects of his personality.¹⁵ Davis (2011: 142) reinforces this appraisement of Sartre, arguing that 'contradiction and self-contestation are essential to Sartre's thought', a fact 'which endangers any unproblematized presentation of him as, say, humanist, anti-humanist or not humanist'. As we will see, this oscillation between humanist, anti-humanist and posthumanist positions is a recurring feature of his thinking that spreads through his ethics, politics, ontology and *Lebensphilosophie*, confirming the view of Barthes who, in interview with Jacques Chancel in 1976, put forward the idea that Sartre is the exemplary intellectual of his period due to the fact that he was situated at the crossroads of two cultures – at the point of division between the disintegration of the old and the birth of the new. For Barthes, the special value of Sartre's work can be located in its 'divided' or 'transitional' nature, which gives us a dynamic critical perspective that bridges both modern and postmodern outlooks. This is well summed up by Mészáros in his description of 'Sartre the adventurer':

> He is a man who perceives the contradictions of the world around him in the form of dilemmas, antinomies and paradoxes. His praise of the 'adventurer' is not a temporary lapse but an expression of his inner tensions which remain a permanent dimension of his lifework. He is the man who 'keeps together the unbearable tension' of the perceived contradictions as insuperable antinomies. For the unresolved tension – through all its transformations – drives him forward and produces the lasting validity of his major works. (1979: 88)

With this in mind, the task of my 'playful reading' is to bring to the surface the internal tensions within Sartre's thinking and the dialectical resolutions that emerge from this. Although postmodern readings see Nietzsche as speaking in several voices and from different perspectives, it is also the case that several voices can sing in unison and converge on a single set of targets and principles. One of the tasks that Nietzsche sets for himself in his philosophy of self-transformation is to harmonize or reconcile multiple voices. He views self-creation as the configuration of a subset of selves into a coherent whole – from the many emerges a singular one. In *The Wanderer and His Shadow*, he continues in the same vein, emphasizing the development but also the continuity in his thinking: 'However forcefully a man develops and seems to leap from one contradiction to the next, close observation will reveal the dovetailing, where the new building grows out of the old' (WS 198). Sartre applies this same logic to his philosophy: 'I myself think that my contradictions mattered little, that despite everything I have always remained on a continuous line' (1980: 92).¹⁶ Like Nietzsche, Sartre attacks the dichotomous logic of Western metaphysics and in places commits himself to the necessity of logical contradiction in his thought. In the introduction to *Being and Nothingness*, he asserts that the 'principle of identity' has only 'regional validity' for the *en-soi* but not the *pour-soi*:

This formulation appears to be strictly analytical. In fact, a great distance separates it from the principle of identity, regarded as the unconditional principle of all analytical judgments. For a start, it refers to a particular region of being, that of *being-in-itself*. We shall see that the being of for-itself is defined, on the contrary, as being what it is not and not being what it is. (BN 27)

Paradox is for Sartre woven into the ambiguities of existence, but his thinking very much aims towards the overcoming or sublimation of contradiction conceived non-metaphysically – the truth of an act as 'a complex movement of contradictions which are posited and surpassed' (SM 98–9n.4). He seeks dialectical intelligibility in the place of metaphysical closure by exploring the 'paradox' of concrete singularity and concrete universality. The laws of dialectical intelligibility are 'individualized universals' (CDR 49) where singularity and universality blend together and in which it is otiose to ask which is primary. Every singular act is thus part of a gestural whole. In Deleuzian terms, we might say Sartre approaches paradox interrogatively through an *index of equivocity* (1986: 166) where two contradictory elements generate a tension that allows us, in a movement of comprehension and sublimation, 'to be present at the genesis of the contradiction' (2004: 74).

Thinkers of three phases

> That *I still cleave to the ideas that I take up again in the present treatises today . . . that they have become in the meantime more and more firmly attached to one another, indeed intertwined and interlaced with one another, strengthens my joyful assurance that they might have arisen in me from the first not as isolated, capricious, or sporadic things but from a common root, from a* fundamental will *of knowledge, pointing imperiously into the depths, speaking more and more precisely, demanding greater and greater precision. For this alone is fitting for a philosopher.*
>
> (Nietzsche, *On the Genealogy of Morals* P2)

Both Nietzsche and Sartre, as Schacht (1996: 158, 178) observes, employ a procedure that may be likened to what Sartre described in *Search for a Method* as a 'progressive-regressive method' – the strategy of 'describing the present situation in its complexity, examining its history, and then conjoining these accounts in an informed analysis of the present' that serves as a 'prelude to a philosophy of the future'. True to this critical method of inquiry, I arrange my reading axiomatically around the 'double movement' of *deconstruction* and *reconstruction* in their philosophy. The deconstructive axis attends closely to the points of continuity and discontinuity that run through Nietzsche's and Sartre's texts. The reconstructive pole of inquiry offers a creative synthesis of the 'New Nietzsche' and the 'New Sartre' in the domains of ontology, ethics, politics, and brings to the fore the philosophical elements and themes, sometimes explicit, sometimes subdued or hitherto neglected aspects of their philosophy, upon which the logic of their twin thinking converges. As has often been the case with these two thinkers, many interpreters have lost sight of the evolution of their thinking by focusing too narrowly on one text or passage in isolation from the others, thereby breaking the rules of Picard's view of good hermeneutical reading. With Nietzsche, scholars often fixate upon his 'later period' (at the relative expense of his earlier works), while, for Sartre, the reverse is true, with interpreters isolating the themes of his early phenomenological period from his later 'Marxist' phase. In this book, my approach to the texts of Nietzsche and Sartre is to present them as containing a discernible line of development and unity, a kind of 'living entelechy' (Hutter 2006: 4), in which later stages recuperate earlier ones and earlier ones hold in themselves all grounds of future unfolding.

Jaspers (1965: 3) remarked how Nietzsche's books seem so readily comprehensible if single essays or aphorisms are taken in isolation, but it is only when we read the entirety of his works in a comparative way, experiencing 'both the systematic possibilities' of his thinking as well as the likely possibility of 'their collapse' that we can properly assemble a holistic view of Nietzsche: 'it is as though a mountain wall had been dynamited; the rocks, already more or less shaped, convey the idea of the whole.' The task is to reassemble the pieces while conceding that the image formed is not an objective philosophical system or set of inflexible doctrinal truths. A proper exploration of Nietzsche requires that we distinguish between the different phases of his writings in order to gain a holistic diachronic viewpoint. We must avoid, on the one hand, the view that his writings constitute a purely random 'collection of atoms', and, on the other, the view that they ought to be seen in terms of a single, coherent philosophy. Both views are insufficient since both obscure our perception of what is constant and what changes in Nietzsche's standpoint.

Salomé (1988: 31) was the first to introduce the idea that we should read Nietzsche in terms of periods as a practical way of connecting his personal development and the diversity of his reflections, formulating the division of his philosophical trajectory into three periods as 'Nietzsche's transitions' – the early (Romantic) Nietzsche (1872–76), middle ('positivistic') Nietzsche (1878–82) and mature (aristocratic) Nietzsche (1883–88). The early Nietzsche, comprising *The Birth of Tragedy* and *Untimely Meditations*, is very much under the spell of Schopenhauer and Wagner, putting in place important aspects of his mature philosophy, such as myth, tragic culture, aestheticism and Dionysianism, but not entirely sure of the intellectual terrain he inhabits. In his second phase of writings or 'middle works' (*Human, All Too Human, Daybreak, The Gay Science*), he becomes more a critic and analyst than the purveyor of a new Dionysian art. As he remarks in *Human, All Too Human*, this phase of his thinking represents a 'spiritual cure' against 'a temporary illness occasioned by the most dangerous form of Romanticism', namely that of Wagner (HH 2P2). The Nietzsche who emerges in these works is a harder and sterner, post-Romantic Nietzsche, but his open embrace of science did not signal the abandonment of his early hostility to Socratic theoreticism, with its cold, visual apprehension of the world. These middle writings represent a confusing paradoxical period of continuity (creative ethics) and discontinuity (democracy and science). Alongside a much more sympathetic view of democracy, Nietzsche embarks in these texts upon a peculiar reshuffling of art and science. Art 'makes heavy the heart of the thinker', he now states, and induces a longing for religion and metaphysics (HH 153). Artists are 'always of necessity *epigoni*', temporarily lifting the burden of life while discouraging men 'from working toward a genuine improvement in their conditions' (HH 148). Unlike the truth-seeking scientist, their backward childish condition leads to a belief in gods and daemons, the spiritualization of nature and a hatred of knowledge. The artist, Nietzsche claims in a mood shift from his earlier writings, is a habitual practitioner of deception who 'has a weaker morality than the thinker' (HH 146).

Nietzsche's mature period (*Thus Spoke Zarathustra*,[17] *On the Genealogy of Morals, Beyond Good and Evil, Ecce Homo, Twilight of the Idols, The Antichrist*) is the period many Anglophone scholars consider to be the 'quintessential Nietzsche', for it is in these later works (along with his unpublished notes from this period, the *Nachlass*) that his main philosophical concepts – *will to power, the eternal return, the revaluation of values* and the *Übermensch* – are articulated. In terms of Nietzsche's political thought, the 'third phase' marks the arrival of the 'bloody Nietzsche', the phase of his radical aristocratic individualism in which he purges himself of the more democratic sensibilities that came to the surface in his middle works. Scholars have, of course, reacted differently to this third provocative transition in his thinking. Tönnies (1987: 25) greatly admired his first two periods (aesthetic/critical) but dismissed the third 'as a witches' Sabbath of thoughts, exclamations and declamations, outbursts of anger, and contradictory statements' in spite of 'many luminous and brilliant appearances of wit'. Salomé (1988: 148) did not share this aversion but saw them as texts that plunged towards the excessive and exuberant, filling her with awe and fear, expressing more and more radical demands, such as the *Übermensch*, eternal recurrence and the revaluation of all values. His entire line of thought assumes a self-destructive course for which madness was the outcome. In his assessment of Nietzsche, Thomas Mann (1959: 144) did not wish to 'devaluate the creative achievements of a thinker, psychologist, and master of language who revolutionized the whole atmosphere of his era'. Nietzsche's early affliction with syphilis was a type of fateful predestination of his intellectual life that displayed 'the heartbreaking spectacle of self-crucifixion' (1959: 146). His early and middle phases show his genius as 'a great critic and philosopher of culture', but his dissolution begins with *Zarathustra* where his tone and ambition becomes poetic, religious and prophetic:

> This faceless and bodiless monstrosity, this drum major Zarathustra with laughter's crown and roses upon his disfigured head, his 'Become hard!' and his dancer's legs, is not a character; he is rhetoric, wild verbiage and puns, a tormented voice and dubious prophecy, a phantom of pitiable grandezza, often touching and usually embarrassing, an abortion bordering on the verge of the ludicrous. (1959: 149)

His style, in Mann's (1959: 151) view, is a process of gradual deterioration. It remains 'musical' but degenerates into 'unhealthy sophisticated and feverishly gay super-journalism, which in the end he adorned with the cap and bells of a comic jester'. Nietzsche's life was a combination of 'inebriation and suffering', in mythological terms, the 'union of Dionysus with the Crucified One' (1959: 159). His attitude becomes steadily more frenzied, a 'maenadic rage against truth, morality, religion, humanitarianism, against everything that might effect a reasonable taming of life's savagery' (1959: 161). When Nietzsche predicts 'monstrous wars and cataclysms' or begins his paean to the 'blond beast' of prey, we are filled with alarm 'for the sanity of the noble mind which is here raging so lustfully against itself' (1959: 165).

Unsurprisingly, Nietzsche's own estimation of *Zarathustra* was somewhat different to Mann's. In *Ecce Homo*, he positively enthuses about it as a 'work [that] stands altogether apart. Leaving aside the poets: perhaps nothing has ever been done from an equal excess of strength' (EH 3Z6). His unbridled enthusiasm for *Zarathustra* is in contrast to his attitude towards his first book *The Birth of Tragedy* which was a deeply ambivalent one. He considered it 'badly written, ponderous, embarrassing, image-mad and image-confused, sentimental . . . a book for initiates' but also revealing of 'new secret paths and dancing places'. Beneath the 'dialectical ill-humour of the German' and its 'bad manners of a Wagnerian', however, we can still find 'a *strange* voice' and 'the disciple of a still "unknown God"' – Dionysus and the life-affirming activities of art as antidotes to life's cruelty (BT A3, 5).

The relative merits of Nietzsche's different works in the eyes of his commentators have given rise to a division in Nietzschean scholarship between those who make a sharp distinction (or not) between his published and unpublished works – between the 'Lumpers' and the 'Splitters'.[18] Splitters, like Schlechta, argue that no new central thought is to be found in the *Nachlass*, only variations on established themes, and so generally disregard *The Will to Power*. Heidegger, by contrast, is an 'inverse splitter' who prioritizes the unpublished over the published works. The *Nachlass*, he argues, contains Nietzsche's 'main structure', a master text to which all his published texts stand as an entrance way: 'His philosophy proper was left behind as posthumous, unpublished work' (1987: 1:9). The common approach among scholars, however, tends to be that of the 'moderate Lumper', treating his different works 'relationally' as forming a whole but giving priority to the published works and using the *Nachlass* as secondary references.[19] My own approach is one of a Strong Lumper, following Jaspers in assigning no particular primacy to any of Nietzsche's texts: 'it must be realized that none of Nietzsche's forms of communication has a privileged character. . . . Nowhere is Nietzsche's work truly centralized: there is no *magnum opus*' (1965: 5). While one could question whether Lumpers do justice to the due stylistic care Nietzsche gave to his published writings and provide an answer as to why the *Nachlass* were left unpublished, the *Nachlass* do more than simply provide variations on pre-established themes but expand and develop them in a more systematic and illustrative way. If anything, Nietzsche's stylistic excesses in the published works could be seen alternatively as a form of 'mask-wearing' or writerly embellishment that can obscure or inflate his core philosophical insights. In determining Nietzsche's ontology and politics, I draw upon two of his unpublished works (*The Will to Power* and *Philosophy in the Tragic Age of the Greeks*) that expand upon themes (e.g. agonism and relationism), sketched out but not fully drawn, in his published texts.

Similar controversies and differences in approach relate to Sartre's oeuvre (putting to one side the question of the isomorphism between his philosophy and literature). Generally speaking, his unfinished works – *Notebooks for an Ethics*, *The Critique of Dialectical Reason, Vol. 2* and *The Family Idiot, Vol. 4* – are not really questioned by Sartrean scholars despite the fact they were incomplete, whereas *Existentialism Is a*

Humanism (1945) and *Hope Now* (1996) have, for different reasons, courted some scepticism among Sartre scholars. *Existentialism Is a Humanism*, a hastily delivered lecture at the Club Maintenant in 1946 in response to the growing popularity of existentialism as a rising cultural phenomenon, has become the *locus classicus* of existentialism and, along with *Being and Nothingness*, is the text many associate most readily with Sartre. While roughly consistent with *Being and Nothingness*, it has been described as 'imprecise, frequently vague and intentionally rhetorical' (Eshleman 2020a: 13), a text 'full of crudities, misstatements and wilful exaggerations for effect' (Moran 2018: xiii). Significantly, it was the only one of Sartre's texts that he personally regretted publishing and a work with Kantian, Cartesian, idealist and universalist overtones that obscured the 'immanence of being' in his early work and splintered his existentialism away from the poststructuralist philosophy of Deleuze, Foucault, Derrida and Lyotard. *Hope Now* is a series of interviews edited and published by Benny Lévy in 1991 in which he and Sartre embark on 'plural thinking' in the domain of ethics and politics. The Lévy interviews were renounced by the 'old Sartreans' (the *Temps Modernes* group of Beauvoir, Lanzmann, Bost and Pouillon) who tried to block their publication. Beauvoir regarded the interviews with horror, calling them the 'abduction of an old man' by his young secretary and countered them with a publication of her own interviews conducted in 1974, which she included in her last book, *Adieux: A Farewell to Sartre*. Sartre responded in turn that the interviews were a genuine reciprocal exchange of ideas that opened up new directions of thinking for him, declaring: '[t]he itinerary of my thought eludes them all, including Simone de Beauvoir.'

Scholars often divide Sartre's work into two periods – the early 'phenomenologist Sartre' (1936–45) and the later 'Marxist' Sartre (1949–80), but some add a third, qualitatively different period of Sartre's thinking after 1973 which becomes more 'collaborative', 'anarchistic' and 'feminine' as well as more attuned to the mystical elements of his early writings.[20] The early period, which comprises *The Transcendence of the Ego*, *Sketch for a Theory of the Emotions*, *The Imagination* and *Being and Nothingness*, as well as *Nausea*, is the phase of Sartre's writing that has become popularized as denoting his true existentialism, containing many of the major philosophical themes – the imagination, bad faith, the look – for which he is well known. After the publication of *What Is Literature?* in 1949, Sartre's work turns towards Marxism as a form of dialectical and philosophical critique. Some scholars see a break between the early work and the later work (Warnock 1989), and by extension between the major philosophical works *Being and Nothingness* and the *Critique* that correspond to them, insofar as Sartre is seen to shift from individualist to collectivist categories and abandon his early theory of absolute freedom. The third phase of Sartre's thinking, in which he turns away from Marxism and his conception of the 'universal intellectual' is often overlooked, deemed not to be 'proper Sartre', but constitutes an important development in his philosophy, clarifying and expanding some of the themes of his early work on the imagination, as well as containing a rich repository of suggestions, such as that of '*le matriciel*' ('mother-matrix'), that foreshadow a posthumanist paradigm of thinking.

Although Sartre is well known for 'thinking against himself' and 'distancing myself from what I was the day before' (1984: 19), his philosophical trajectory is best read as a thesis of 'enrichment within continuity' (Perna 2007: 47) within an evolving scheme of 'diachronic development' (Caws 1984: 2–3). This accords with Sartre's own thoughts just before his death that 'despite everything I have always remained on a continuous line' (1980: 92). To understand him fully, he avers, 'I think that a study of my philosophical thought should follow its evolution' (1981: 9), despite the fact that many of his interpreters fail to do this. There is a 'change', as he himself identifies after *Being and Nothingness* (1974: 31), but this is more a change of *emphasis* than it is of direction or purpose. According to Sartre, his method became consciously dialectical only after *Being and Nothingness* but, as several scholars have convincingly argued,[21] and as I hope to demonstrate in the following chapters, he was a dialectician from his early years and the principles of his relational interpersonal ontology elucidated most fully in his later work were set in place from the outset in his very earliest thinking.

2

Heidegger, Derrida and the metaphysical charge

What the father kept silent, that comes in the son to be spoken and often I found the son to be the father's unveiled secret.

(Nietzsche, *Zarathustra* 2.7)

Both Nietzsche and Sartre recognized the fact that thoughts can operate 'out of season' when there is a diachronic time lag between life and epoch that operates prospectively and retrospectively so that the philosopher can be both behind and ahead of their contemporaries: 'the author cannot be the contemporary of his contemporaries unless he is, on the whole, behind them and ahead of them' (IF 3:424). This chapter looks at the denouement of the Nietzsche–Sartre story and the divisive influence of the French poststructuralists who split them into enemy camps of the 'New Nietzsche' and the 'old Sartre', construing their phenomenological and genealogical methods as antithetical approaches. This 'anxiety of influence' (Redeker 2002) or 'parricidal attack' (Howells 1999) on Sartre undertaken by Derrida, Foucault, Lacan and Lyotard had the effect of radically obscuring their multifarious philosophical connections and parallel thinking. My analysis begins, however, with Heidegger who saw some strong similarities in Nietzsche and Sartre but only by lumping them together as 'grand metaphysicians'.

The 'grand metaphysicians': Heidegger's verdict

Heidegger's thought stands as a gateway to the humanism–anti-humanism–posthumanism debate that dominates twentieth-century and contemporary philosophy, geared, as it is, towards the emergence of 'another beginning' in his attempt to go beyond Husserl and Nietzsche. His voluminous writings on Nietzsche (over 1,200 pages published in four volumes from lectures given at the University of Freiburg between 1936 and 1945) reveal a double relation. On the one hand, he positions Nietzsche as a significant moment in Western philosophy who made important contributions to traditional questions and brought the idea of 'being' into critical focus, and yet, on the other, he turns against Nietzsche, accusing him of the very errors (nihilism and metaphysical thinking) that Nietzsche himself had levelled against the Platonic and Cartesian tradition. In Heidegger's (1987: 1:204–5) estimation, Nietzsche is a Cartesian who 'performs the grandest and most profound gathering –

that is, the accomplishment – of all the essential fundamental positions since Plato in the light of Platonism', and his thought represents the 'consummation' and not the 'farewell' of metaphysical humanism. In his debunking of Plato's world of insensible forms, Nietzsche simply inverts and subordinates Platonic terms in favour of their opposite – being (becoming), stability, identity and number (fluidity and singularity), order or law (chance, contingency), objective truth as correspondence (perspective), transcendence (immanence), reason (instinct, drives), spirit or soul (body). This is evident in his theory of art, for instance. When Nietzsche states 'art is worth more than truth', he means that 'the sensuous stands in a higher place than the supersensuous' (1987: 1:74) in direct opposition to Plato.

For Heidegger (1977: 48), Nietzsche's metaphysics of subjectivity repeats the Cartesian subject as 'a ground lying at the foundation' by interpreting Being as will to power. This implies willing subjects who are 'centres of force' that strive to preserve and enhance themselves as they dominate the earth which is seen as a resource for development, something to be measured and directed. The theoretical consciousness attains its full power in the Cartesian *ego cogito*, grasping the world as a picture or model standing apart and against the perceiving subject. This reaches its culmination in Nietzsche's *Übermensch* which is conceived as will to power conscious of itself, with the distinction between it and the human as being one of cognition or awareness. With this consciousness of self all that is not self becomes an object over which dominion and control are to be exercised, a metaphysical configuration that posits the earth as other as an object of instrumental manipulation. Zarathustra is 'the being who appears within metaphysics at its stage of completion', and Nietzsche's exaltation of being is an obliteration of being in the metaphysical manner: 'this supposed overcoming is above all the consummation of nihilism. For now, metaphysics not only does not think Being itself, but this non-thinking of Being clothes itself in the illusion that it does think Being in the most exalted manner' (1977: 104). Nietzsche's metaphysics thus fits into the traditional formula of *essentia* (essence or possibility – will to power) and *existentia* (actuality – eternal return). It tries to think Being but succeeds only in naming it as a particular being.

For Heidegger (1977: 75), 'metaphysical humanism' is a way of looking at the world that makes the human subject the ground of its objectivity, starting with Plato's claim that the Good is the highest truth, thus identifying the world's essence in line with human moral values. This leads to nihilism since the world is said to exist only as far as it reflects human designs and values and also because if the world is nothing in itself, humans lose their sense of 'ontological security'. Nietzsche's 'value-thinking' falls into this metaphysical trap: 'values are the conditions of itself posited by the will to power.' This leads to the degradation of Being as it is posited as a 'mere' value, even if the highest value, giving rise ultimately to nihilism as values, can be chosen or unchosen by a subject who constitutes the ground for value: 'precisely through the characterization of something as "a value" what is so valued is robbed of its worth . . . what is valued is admitted only as an object for man's estimation' (1993: 251). The natural world is presented to the subject as an instrumental field for its own preservation and enhancement that denies the intrinsic value of that world which becomes a 'constant reserve' or resource for the 'enframing' of technology:

The uprising of man into subjectivity transforms that which is into an object . . . The doing away of that which is in itself, i.e. the killing of God, is accomplished in the making secure of the constant reserve by means of which man makes secure for himself material, bodily, psychic, and spiritual resources, and this for the sake of his own security, which wills dominion over whatever is – as the potentially objective – in order to correspond to the Being of whatever is, to the will to power. (1977: 107)

Heidegger undertakes the hermeneutical task of understanding the text not just as well but even better than its author. He limits his interpretation of Nietzsche to one single principle: 'Every thinker thinks only a *single* thought' (1987: 1:475). The will to power that emerges once we think the apparently irreconcilable thought of the will to power together with the eternal recurrence of the same in such a way that 'in terms of metaphysics, in its modern phase and in the history of its end, both thoughts think the selfsame' (1987: 3:161). Fused together, they become a '*sole* thought' (1987: 3:10) that fulfils 'the essence of modernity' and 'the metaphysics that is approaching consummation' (1987: 3:163). For Heidegger, however, this central thought isn't really present in Nietzsche's works or in an afterthought but could be realized only through a proper hermeneutical understanding.[1]

Although he claimed to go beyond him, Heidegger's attitude to Nietzsche was generally one of respect and fascination, evidenced by how long he spent writing about him. This was not the case with Sartre, however, whom Heidegger had little time for. Reportedly, nearly all the pages of Heidegger's copy of *Being and Nothingness* were left uncut, and even in his *Letter on Humanism*, there are only three actual citations from Sartre, all from *Existentialism Is a Humanism*.[2] That said, in philosophical terms, he saw Nietzsche and Sartre as following a similar path. Heidegger's critical reading of Nietzsche fed into a wider rejection of existentialism and what he saw as its central tenets (value-thinking, subjectivity, the will and the metaphysics of essence/existence). Heidegger criticizes Sartre's existentialism alongside Nietzsche's philosophy on these same points. The 'Humanism Debate' was precipitated by Jean Beaufret in 1946 when, with the intention of re-establishing a French-German dialogue after the war, he invited Heidegger to comment on Sartre's citing of him as a fellow existentialist. In *Letter on Humanism*, Heidegger wrote approvingly of Marx for realizing the historical nature of Being but accused Sartre of blatantly failing to come to this realization. Sartre's 'existence precedes essence' simply reverses Platonism and therefore, Heidegger (1993: 243) argued, is more of a metaphysics than a fundamental ontology.

Sartre's attitude towards Heidegger is harder to gauge than Heidegger's one of perfunctory dismissal towards the French philosopher. When Sartre's essay 'Legend of Truth' was published along with a French translation of Heidegger's 'What Is Metaphysics?' in the review *Bifur*, Beauvoir (1983: 92) reports that they failed to see the interest in it and hardly understood a word of it. After reading the same text again along with *Being and Time*, Sartre acknowledged an influence on his own thinking in his *War Diaries*, declaring that Heidegger 'supervened to teach me authenticity and historicity just at the very moment when war was about to make these notions indispensable to me' (WD 182). Scholars are divided on the extent of Heidegger's influence on Sartre's

Being and Nothingness,³ but in this text Sartre is both complimentary and critical of Heidegger's theory of the Other (praising his presupposition of the Other through his notion of 'thrownness' but charging him with failing to provide a phenomenological proof of the Other). He also accuses Heidegger of a sleight of hand (BN 683) in configuring death as always being one of my possibilities, which Sartre interprets as a form of life-denying Nietzschean resentment. For Sartre, death 'is an essential structure of the fundamental relation that we have called "being-for-the-Other"', a fact of my facticity that escapes me, and not my innermost possibility (BN 704).

Just as Heidegger's identification of Nietzsche as the 'consummate metaphysician' can be viewed as inapposite, so too his portrayal of Sartre. Although some follow Heidegger in classifying him as 'the best-known metaphysician in Europe' (Murdoch 1999: 1) or 'among the metaphysicians in whom the metaphysical tradition culminates' (Trottignon 1966: 27), others argue that Sartre 'is in no way a metaphysician' for he rejects any principle 'with a metaphysical foundation' (Perrin 2020: 264). Sartre didn't consider himself to be 'interested in metaphysics' (1990: 144). In his early writings, he rarely mentions metaphysics and when he does so, it is in derogatory terms, seeing it to contain 'abstract thoughts and empty intentions' (1995a: 147). In *The Transcendence of the Ego*, he 'shuns metaphysics at one fell swoop', especially 'the metaphysical hypothesis . . . according to which my Ego would not construct itself of elements having existed in reality' (TE 59). Alongside his critique of metaphysical idealism, he also emphasizes 'the absurdity that is metaphysical materialism' (TE 28). He talks of 'wiping one's hands of all metaphysical postulates' and abandoning 'the metaphysical theory of the image' (I 109) that makes the image a copy of the material thing as posited in 'the great metaphysical systems' of Aristotle, Descartes, Spinoza, Leibniz and Hume (I 7). Although Sartre's interest in ontology was accompanied by a growing disdain for metaphysics, his antipathy was relaxed in part in *Being and Nothingness*. In July 1940, he wrote, 'I have begun a treatise on metaphysics: *Being and Nothingness* and I will get back to it tomorrow' (WD 285). In this work he attempts 'a metaphysical theory of being in general' (BN 480). Metaphysical speculation, Sartre avers, is ineluctable and connected to the question of ontology – the 'why' and the 'how': 'the relation of metaphysics to ontology is like that of history to sociology' (BN 801). This raises the metaphysical quandary, '[w]hy is it that *there is* being?' (BN 801), but this is a question Sartre generally avoids as idle metaphysical speculation, preferring to ask 'how' but not 'why'.⁴

In several respects, Sartre's relation to metaphysics is similar to Nietzsche's, in general working to overcome it, but in part, repeating it. Nietzsche maintains a 'double relation' to modernity and any metaphysical grand narrative, undermining it while knowing that he cannot fully reject it. He suggests this himself when he concludes in *The Gay Science* that he should be counted among the 'metaphysicians' he attacks: 'Even we seekers after knowledge today, we godless anti-metaphysicians still take our fire, too, from the flame lit by a faith that is thousands of years old, that Christian which was also the faith of Plato, that God is truth, and that truth is divine' (GS 344). As Derrida argues, there is thus in a sense something inescapable about the integration of the dialectic. Every attempt to state a truth is to invoke reason which Foucault found out in his attempt to state the truth of madness where he subjected madness to the power of reason: 'Hegel, who is always right as soon as one opens one's mouth in order to articulate meaning' (1978: 263). In deconstructing metaphysical humanism, 'one risks ceaselessly confirming, consolidating, relieving at an always more certain depth that which one allegedly deconstructs' (1982: 135). In understanding the 'metaphysics' of Nietzsche and Sartre, one should not conflate the general (a philosophical inquiry that uncovers the basic nature of reality) and the pejorative sense (metaphysics as 'being' and 'dualism') of the metaphysical speculation that they distinguish.[5] It would have helped in this respect, as Mitchell (2020: 110) remarks, if Heidegger had clarified exactly *how* Sartre reinforces metaphysics and what it would mean to use the terms 'existence' and 'essence' non-metaphysically. The irony of Heidegger's interpretation of Nietzsche is that he relies heavily on Nietzsche's account of nihilism in metaphysical thinking but is guilty of the same charge of failing to overcome the nihilism in his own philosophy that he falsely accuses Nietzsche and Sartre of in his own 'metahistory of philosophy'.[6] Nietzsche is not just a precursor to Heidegger in this way but beyond him in several respects. Heidegger's own approach, for instance, pays very little attention to concrete political practices, approaching nihilism idealistically through the inner contradictions of metaphysics rather than the concrete political practices out of which it emerges as Nietzsche and Sartre do in their genealogical/historical investigation. For Derrida (1978: 281), although 'Nietzsche ... worked within the inherited concepts of metaphysics', he continually stretched their very limits, 're-animalizing' philosophy in a way that supervenes Heidegger's own philosophy:

> [E]very particular borrowing brings along with it the whole of metaphysics. This is what allows these destroyers to destroy each other reciprocally – for example, Heidegger regarding Nietzsche, with as much lucidity and rigor as bad faith and misconstruction, as the last metaphysician, the last 'Platonist'. One could do the same for Heidegger himself. (1978: 281–2)

Saints and sinners in Nietzsche's France

What charity and delicate precision those Frenchmen possess!
(Nietzsche, The Wanderer and his Shadow 214)

France was always of special importance to Nietzsche. He described it as 'a halfway successful synthesis of the north and south' (BGE 194) and declared its 'cultural superiority over Europe' (BGE 193). He felt more affinity with the French culture and language than with his own Teutonic tongue and regretted having to write in German rather than in a more fluid, playful and musical language like French (BGE 246). In philosophical terms, he preferred the companionship of Voltaire, La Rochefoucauld and Montaigne (whose books 'contain more real ideas than all the books of German philosophers put together' (WS 214)) to that of Leibniz, Kant and Hegel (though he was, of course, heavily inspired by Schopenhauer in his early writings).

It is perhaps fitting then that, having been dragged through the mud of Nazism in Germany in the early part of the twentieth century, the Nietzschean corpus was rejuvenated in Paris following the Second World War. Philosophically speaking, for the French poststructuralists, this meant confronting Heidegger's interpretation of Nietzsche and showing what Nietzsche's thought truly heralded. For Foucault, there are two main aspects of his thought that come to the fore. Firstly, 'Nietzsche the philologist' (1973: 305) who connects philosophy with a reflection upon language and secondly, the Nietzsche who awakens us from our 'anthropological sleep' and attempts 'the dissolution of man':

> Nietzsche rediscovered the point at which man and God belong to one another, at which the death of the second is synonymous with the disappearance of the first, and at which the promise of the superman signifies first and foremost the imminence of the death of man. (1973: 342)

The doctrine of the *Übermensch* signals Nietzsche's overcoming of nihilism and the passage beyond humanity. The 'Last Man' in *Zarathustra* is literally the last of man and the *Übermensch* breaks from metaphysical humanism. Rather than the death of God, 'Nietzsche's thought heralds the death of his murderer . . . the absolute dispersion of man' (1973: 385), signifying 'the threshold beyond which contemporary philosophy can begin thinking again' (1965: 353). In his essay of 1971 'Nietzsche, Genealogy, History', Foucault outlines Nietzsche's view of history as *genealogical history* based on the contingency of events, the episodes of history, the games of chance outside any preconceived finality (1977: 76) and utilizing the concepts of 'emergence', 'origin', 'descent' and 'birth' in delineating the origins of morality, asceticism, punishment and sexuality (1977: 77–8). Nietzschean genealogical history demonstrates there is no secret atemporal essence lying behind things but reveals 'the accidents, the minute deviations – or conversely, the complete reversals – the errors, the false appraisals, and the faulty calculations which gave birth to those things that continue to exist and have value for us' (1977: 81). This is contrasted with teleological or metaphysical history that views events from the perspective of the endpoint within a scheme of anticipated meaning. All in all, '[i]t was Nietzsche', Foucault states, 'who burned for us, even before we were born, the intermingled promises of the dialectic and anthropology' (1973: 263).

In *Nietzsche et la métaphore*, Kofman reiterates Deleuze's (1983: 220) comment that 'Heidegger gives an interpretation of Nietzschean philosophy closer to his own thought than to Nietzsche's'. For Kofman (1987: 54), the influence of Heraclitus in Nietzsche shows that it is not easy to reduce Nietzsche to a metaphysician: 'It is precisely in order to carry out this operation and to shake off the ghost which haunts him that I suspect Heidegger did not always use an honest, straightforward, and rigorous philological approach in his reading of Nietzsche.' Kofman's criticisms also echo those made by Eugen Fink, Heidegger's pupil at Freiburg, who argued that, by reducing all of Nietzsche's thought to metaphysical thinking and the 'single thought' of eternal recurrence, Heidegger neglects the element of *play* that grounds Nietzsche's philosophy, passing over the fact that 'Heraclitus remains the originary root of Nietzsche's philosophy' (1960: 13). For Fink (1960: 41), in Heraclitean play 'Nietzsche finds his deepest intuition of the reality of the world as grandiose cosmic metaphor'. Rather than the culmination of metaphysics, Nietzsche's thinking operates at the boundary of metaphysics, sometimes imprisoned within, and sometimes liberating itself from, metaphysics. Positing becoming and appearance as alternatives to Being and Truth keeps Nietzsche within the metaphysical paradigm, in Fink's (1960: 188) view, but when his thinking highlights on the cosmic play of forces 'beyond all valuation, precisely because all values emerge *within* this play', his philosophy is no longer metaphysical: 'where Nietzsche grasps being and becoming as *Spiel*, he no longer stands in the confinement of metaphysics.'

As we will see in Chapter 4 when we scrutinize the area of ontology, Nietzsche finds in Heraclitus a kindred spirit in whose company he feels 'altogether warmer and better than anywhere else' (EH 3BT3). Heraclitus' tragic wisdom supports a Dionysian philosophy which affirms 'passing-away and annihilating... the yea-saying to contrariety and struggle, becoming, with a radical repudiation of the very concept "Being"' (EH 3BT3). In particular, Nietzsche adopts Heraclitus' 'aesthetic fundamental-perception as to the play of the world' (PTAG 7), allowing him to escape the 'metaphysical matrix' of oppositional thinking by refusing 'every conception of affirmation which would find its foundation in Being, and its determination in the being of man' (Deleuze 1983: 220). For Nietzsche, play is the highest form of human activity directed towards the overcoming of nihilism through the creative transvaluation of values. The eternal return is the existential and playful challenge to raise 'the stakes of the game' to the limit that is 'eternity' (KGW 5.2. 11). Indeed, thought itself is, for Nietzsche, a form of play: 'The *playful pondering of materials* is our continuous fundamental activity.... This spontaneous play of phantasizing force is our fundamental intellectual life' (KGW 5.1.10).

In Derrida's (1998: 19) view, Heidegger is mistaken to say that Nietzsche's thought remains trapped within metaphysics by inverting Platonism since Nietzsche goes further and displaces the ingrained oppositions of that tradition. In his own work, Derrida expands the Nietzschean critique of binary thinking, the metaphysical '*faith in antithetical values*' (BGE 2). This means refusing to privilege hierarchical relations between conceptual oppositions: 'Nietzsche, far from remaining *simply* (with Hegel and as Heidegger wished) *within* metaphysics, contributed a great deal to the liberation of the signifier from its dependence or derivation with respect to the logos and the related concept of truth or the primary signified.' As developed by Derrida, Nietzschean deconstruction involves a biphasic movement, a 'double writing' that dismantles these oppositions. In overturning a metaphysical hierarchy, one must avoid reappropriating the hierarchical structure and remain within the closed field of binary oppositions. In the first phase, one overturns the privileged relation between the two values, then, in phase two, displaces the opposition altogether by showing it to result from a prior value imposition that itself requires critique. In denying the possibility of an unmediated, non-interpretative apprehension of reality, Nietzsche displaces the opposition of truth/falsity altogether. The key question is not whether a perspective is true or false but whether it enhances life or not. Similarly, Nietzsche goes beyond the binarism of good/evil in moral thinking through his transvaluation of values, a new mode of ethical thinking of playful experimentation and 'new interpretive possibilities' that Derrida calls 'active interpretation' (1998: 157–64).[7] Derrida celebrates Nietzsche's turn towards infinite interpretation, the plurality of style and the affirmation of the world as play. He views Heidegger's reading of Nietzsche as an extreme kind of unifying, truth-oriented and schematizing hermeneutics that, because of Heidegger's own attachments to metaphysics, misconstrues the multiple subtleties and play of styles within his texts: 'there is no such thing as the truth of Nietzsche, or of Nietzsche's text', they are only 'multiple, variegated, contradictory even' (1979: 103).[8]

Divisive Derrida

The same restraints that held Nietzsche's thought on the boundaries of metaphysical humanism, as well as the 'lines of escape' that went beyond it, were also evident in equal part in Sartre's existentialism but this was not acknowledged in anything like the same measure by the poststructuralists (with the exception of Deleuze and Guattari). Foucault's (2001: 54) cutting remark that Sartre and Merleau-Ponty were nineteenth-century philosophers trying to think the twentieth started a rally of words[9] and, by the late 1960s, swords were drawn between Sartre and the poststructuralists.[10] In the Heidegger–Sartre debate, the French poststructuralists followed the German philosopher in conjoining existentialism and humanism, and this view prevailed in French academic circles in the 1960s. Derrida in particular was critical of Sartre in his 1968 talk 'The Ends of Man', picking up on the fact that Sartre used Henry Corbin's translation of *Dasein*, from *Being and Time*, as 'human-reality'. Describing this as a 'monstrous translation' (1982: 115), he seized upon Sartre's anthropocentric bias that he identified as a theoretical commitment to an isolatable domain of the human: 'To the extent that it describes the structures of human-reality, phenomenological ontology is a philosophical anthropology' (1982: 115–16). In *Glas*, Derrida mocked Sartre as the 'onto-phenomenologist of freedom' (1986: 28), always in search of an original project to explain the entirety of an individual's life, while in 'The Ends of Man' he labelled as 'daring' and 'risky' Sartre's critique of Bataille for displaying a shaky grasp of German philosophical terms and an inadequate understanding of Hegel, Husserl and Heidegger (1982: 111–19). Later, he accused Sartre of also misunderstanding (or just ignoring) the important intellectual developments of his time, such as psychoanalysis, structuralism and the literature of Bataille and Blanchot. In an interview in *Le Nouvel Observateur* in 1983, while showing affection and praising Sartre for guiding him towards authors such as Bataille, Blanchot and Ponge, he describes his influence in excoriating terms as 'nefarious and catastrophic' and judges his renown as reflecting badly on French society:

> What must a society like ours be if a man who, in his way, rejected or got wrong so many of the theoretical or literary events of his time – let us mention for the sake of speed psychoanalysis, Marxism, structuralism, Joyce, Artaud, Bataille, Blanchot – who multiplied and broadcast unbelievable nonsense on Heidegger, sometimes

on Husserl, if such a man could come to dominate the cultural scene to a point of becoming a great popular figure? *(1999: 131)*

Following the lead of Howells, several scholars have noted the 'simplifying parricidal generational conflicts' in Derrida's reading of Sartre that largely takes the form of a 'philosophical psychodrama' (Davis and Davis 2019: 4) and ignores the many 'hereditary' Sartrean influences in his own thinking.[11] Derrida belonged to a generation which often seemed scornful of its existentialist forbears, of whom Sartre was the most prominent representative. His early references to Sartre tend therefore to be 'critical, dismissive, or just plain wrong' (2019: 3). As Howells (1992: 349) observes, Derrida's *La Voix et le phénomène* 'repeated in part, and probably unwittingly, Sartre's own deconstruction of the Husserlian subject'. Twenty years later, Derrida still seems unwilling to acknowledge that Sartre 'is not merely a forerunner but a real originator of much of what Deconstruction has to say on the subject'. This manifests a 'Bloomian anxiety of influence' in which Derrida attributes to Sartre positions diametrically opposed to those he in fact holds. Having falsified Sartre's views, Derrida himself 'appears to be repeating the broad lines of an analysis he is unwilling to recognize as constituting a precursor text' (Davis and Davis 2019: 28). His reticence to recognize Sartre's importance can be viewed as a form of parricide, asserting his autonomy by denying the father his due, killing him and claiming as his own what in fact was his father's. In Derrida's own words, 'the disciple must break the glass, or better the mirror, the reflection, his infinite speculation on the master. And start to speak' (1978: 32). It is only when Sartre is actually dead that Derrida can properly overcome his parricidal anxiety. By 1996, we finally see a change in attitude in Derrida when he acknowledges the positive influence of Sartre and gives a generous-spirited tribute to his existentialist forebear.

In the name of the father

Having deposed the subject with murderous haste in the 1960s, the French philosophers later suspended the radical finality of the 'death of man' and the 'ends of man' that they had celebrated twenty years earlier, retracting their animosity to Sartre and recognizing their myopia in consigning him to an uncomplicated humanism and a reductive Cartesian reading. In a version of 'loser wins' (*qui perd gagne*), one might ask whether the retrieval of 'existential pathos' (Derrida) and 'care for the self' (Foucault) in their later work signify a return to Sartrean concerns and a victory for the vanquished existentialist. Despite his previous criticisms of Sartre in the 1960s and 1970s, in the lead article for the commemorative fiftieth-anniversary issue of *Les Temps Modernes*, Derrida expresses 'boundless gratitude' and acknowledges the 'immense debt' he and others owe to Sartre. He confesses that in previous years he 'wouldn't have dared' admit his affection for Sartre and *Les Temps Modernes* but that he is now moved to 'do justice' to them and recognize the value of Sartre's philosophical oeuvre (1996: 44, 40). He also confesses to an amnesia for forgetting that Sartre had put into question the rhetoric of 'fraternity' (1996: 12) and now claims to be the heir of 'Sartre's opposition to himself and his antinomies'. It is Sartre's self-contradiction that most touches him, Derrida confesses, and his 'disaccord' or disagreement with self that he most admires (1996: 23, 32). Furthermore, he acknowledges 'Sartre's refusal of antinomies' that prefigured his own deconstruction of oppositional thinking (1996: 14). In other interviews, Derrida (2001: 40) states that, although he distanced himself from a certain existential interpretation of Husserl, his 'intention was certainly not to draw away from the concern for existence itself, for concrete personal commitment, or from the existential pathos that, in a sense, I have never lost'. His later writings, as Reynolds (2006: 167) notes, amount to a 'quasi-existentialism' based on a Sartrean notion of undecidability, responsibility and decision-making which Derrida describes as an 'existential pathos' (2001: 40) that maintains a perpetual openness to the future and to what might come.

Derrida's tribute to Sartre and *Les Temps Modernes* in 1996 came as somewhat a surprise. By reconciling himself to Sartre's ghost, was he finally reconciling himself to his youth when Sartre was one of his main influences? As Baugh (1999: 66) asks, by hunting Sartre, was Derrida actually 'pursuing his double'? Derrida, who has written so much of the ghost that returns to haunt (the revenant), appears haunted by the philosopher who wrote of a human-reality haunted by the totality it aims for and cannot attain. Is he playing the philosopher who, in his own words, '*himself* pursues relentlessly someone who almost resembles him to the point where we could mistake one for the other, a brother, a double, thus a diabolical image' (1994: 134)? Rather than being radically at odds with Sartre's philosophy, Derrida's philosophy of *différance* brings out the radical nature of the conclusions that can be drawn from it – 'despite Derrida's explicit repudiation of Sartre, the similarities with Sartre are striking' (Baugh 1999: 69). This, as we will see, applies not only to Sartre's theory of subjectivity and freedom but also extends to his philosophical theorizing in the areas of ontology, ethics and politics.

Compared to his poststructuralist colleagues, Deleuze had always been more reverent towards his existentialist predecessor and complimented his philosophy of 'immanence and becoming' in *Being and Nothingness* where others had seen only the influence of Descartes and Husserl: '[phenomenology and existentialism] were already history by the time we got to them: too much method, imitation, commentary and interpretation, except for the way Sartre did it' (1987: 12). Distinguishing Sartre's philosophical method from that of other phenomenologists, Deleuze praised Sartre for being 'the first to have considered the Other as a real structure' (2004: 373).[12] In an article devoted to Sartre entitled 'Il a été mon maître' published in a special 1964 issue of the periodical *Arts*, Deleuze (1964: 8–9) expresses his admiration for 'the private thinker [who] introduced new themes, a new style, a new polemic and a new way of raising problems as well as a hatred for all modes of "representation"'. He reiterates this in a series of interviews with Claire Parnet published in 1977, where he speaks enthusiastically of his respect for Sartre, explaining that 'Sartre allows us to await some vague future moment, a return, when thought will form again and make its totalities anew, like a power that is at once collective and private'. 'This is why', he adds, 'Sartre remains my teacher' (1987: 79) since he opened up new avenues for those like himself who came after:

> Fortunately there was Sartre. Sartre was our Outside, he was really the breath of fresh air from the backyard. . . . And Sartre has never stopped being that, not a model, a method or an example, but a little fresh air – a gust of air even when he had just been to the Café Flore – an intellectual who singularly changed the situation of the intellectual. (1987: 12)

Guattari also acknowledged a huge debt to Sartre, taking inspiration from his existential/ontological insights in *Being and Nothingness* as well as from his dialectical innovations in the *Critique*. Modelling his own distinction between *subject group* and *subjugated group* on Sartre's contrast between the *serial group* and the *fusing group*, Sartre showed the way, in Guattari's view, for diagnosing the 'degraded forms of subjectivity' (2000) that were endemic in Capitalist and Communist societies, and also sketched the direction for an affirmative countermovement or 'ethics of authenticity' to go beyond them. He also commended Sartre's prescience and his relevance for philosophy of today, thinking of him 'as a verb that should be conjugated in the present tense'.[13]

Even Foucault's mood had cooled when the general feeling towards Sartre changed from enmity to eulogy after the late 1960s. He paid homage to the 'immense work' of Sartre's and applauded him especially for his critique of 'the idea of the self as something which is given to us' (1983: 64) and for his idea of non-self coincidence or what Sartre called the ability 'to live without an ego' (NE 414):

> I think the immense work and political action of Sartre defines an era. . . . I would never accept a comparison – even for the sake of a contrast – of the minor work of historical and methodological spade work that I do with a body of work like his. (*La Quinzaine Littéraire*, 1968: 20)

In an interview in the 1970s, Foucault suggests that he and Sartre are philosophical brothers and sons of Nietzsche when he expresses enthusiasm for the fact that Sartre's first paper written as a student was on Nietzsche:

> Did you know that Sartre's first text – written when he was a young student – was Nietzschean? 'The History of Truth', a little paper first published in a Lycée review around 1925. He began with the same problem and it is very odd that his approach should have shifted from the history of truth to phenomenology while for the next generation – ours – the reverse was true. (in Raulet 1983: 204)

As was the case with Derrida, Foucault turned towards Sartrean vistas in his later phase, relaxing his previous 'anxiety of influence' towards him. Reinvigorating his own form of 'camouflaged existentialism' (Flynn 2004: 49), he performed a remarkable inversion by returning to themes he had previously denounced in Sartre guided this time by Sartre's own innovations.

Phenomenology and perspectivism

My eyes, however strong or weak they may be, can only see a certain distance, and it is within the space encompassed by this distance that I live and move, the line of this

> horizon constitutes my immediate fate, in great things and small, from which I cannot escape. Around every being there is described a similar concentric circle, which has a mid-point and is peculiar to him.
>
> (Nietzsche, *Daybreak* 117)

Foucault viewed the embrace of Nietzsche by poststructuralists in France in the 1960s as a movement away from Husserlian and Sartrean phenomenology: 'everything began from a dissatisfaction with the phenomenological theory of the subject and involved different escapades, subterfuges, breakthroughs . . . in the direction of linguistics, psychoanalysis or Nietzsche' (Raulet 1983: 199). It was a matter 'of calling this theme of the subject into question once again, that great fundamental postulate which French philosophy, from Descartes until our own time, had never abandoned' (1991: 56). Against Foucault's view expressed here of a disjunctive relation between Nietzschean perspectivism and phenomenology, many scholars view them to be mutually compatible and characterize Nietzsche as a proto or quasi phenomenologist,[14] finding an affinity between the phenomenologists' attack on the subject/object dichotomy and the radical reflection on language that Nietzsche articulated in the 1880s. Even Foucault's early works on madness show the connection between his preoccupation with the experience of madness and the phenomenologists' preoccupation with getting back to 'the thing itself'. Foucault, it should be remembered, was influenced by the existential psychoanalysis of Ludwig Binswanger (he wrote the introduction for the French translation of the essay 'Dream and Existence' and was in turn an influence on R. D. Laing who also took Sartre as an inspiration). Although, in *The Archaeology of Knowledge*, Foucault attacks *History of Madness* for having accorded 'far too great a place, and a very enigmatic one too, to what I call an "experience"' (1972: 16), the 'adventure of the gaze' looms large throughout his work from beginning to end.

Sartre's dense, colourful and affective phenomenology (as Deleuze recognized) was not a relapse into Husserlian idealism but a concerted effort to 'get back to things themselves' in a realist 'dialectical' account where things always evade and overflow our perception of them in a surplus dance of qualities:

> In the world of perception, no 'thing' can appear without maintaining an infinity of relations to other things. Better, it is this infinity of relations – as well as the infinity of relations that its elements support – it is this infinity of relations that constitutes the very essence of a thing. Hence a kind of overflowing in the world of 'things': there is, at every moment, always infinitely more than we can see; to exhaust the richness of my current perception would take an infinite time. (I 9)

When Sartre states the study of human-reality must begin with the cogito, we must be careful not to equate this with the Cartesian cogito,[15] for what he means to get across is the indispensability of lived experience and the importance of embodied consciousness and perspective. In his phenomenology of immanence and becoming, there is no detached or objective or spectatorial truth that doesn't involve the viewpoint of the agent: 'The point of view of pure knowledge is contradictory: the only point of view is that of *committed* knowledge' (BN 415). Building on Nietzsche's critique of 'the backworlds illusion' (BN 2) promulgated by Plato, Descartes and Kant, he takes the 'monism of the phenomenon' (BN 1) as the guiding methodological and substantive principle of his phenomenology. In his later 'progressive-regressive' method in the *Critique*, his task is to draw philosophical significance from concrete descriptions of experience whereby lived experience is shown to bear and to be borne by social and historical structures and personal-intentional singularities. '*What do we see?*' (CDR 2:23) is the essential starting pointing to his philosophical investigation. Even in his 1965 manuscript 'Morale et histoire', his method is still strongly descriptive: 'Before reducing ethical structures – or affirming their irreducibility – we must describe them and fix them with their specific characteristics ... Our first task is phenomenological.'[16]

Sharing Sartre's emphasis on embodied experience, Nietzsche's philosophical method can also be described as 'simply descriptive, quasi-phenomenological' (Haar 1988: 25). Although some scholars perceive a clash between Nietzsche's externalist 'scientific' method and the phenomenological first-person approach,[17] it is wrong to say that Nietzsche abandons the personal viewpoint and adopts the impersonal as a methodology. As Richardson (2009: 315, 318) notes, Nietzsche's interest in psychology looks for reasons not just descriptions: 'to do psychology ... one requires first-personal acquaintance with those wills oneself.' Furthermore, 'the new psychology' that Nietzsche calls for 'involves a kind of "subjectivity" at odds with the "objectivity" called for by science so far'. Nietzsche's proclivity to emphasize the first-person perspective is evident in the central importance he ascribes to *affect*. For Nietzsche, affects are conscious symptoms of the valuations of drives related to the success or otherwise of achieving their aims. This 'evolution-driven phenomenology' (Richardson 2020: 237) is a reflection of the organism. Our experience of objects as valuable is the product of projecting qualities and such affects onto the objects of those experiences. 'Whatever has *value* in the present world', Nietzsche states, 'has it not in itself, according to its nature – nature is always given value-less, but has been given, granted value, and *we* were the granters and givers' (GS 301).

In Safranski's (2003: 208) view, Nietzschean perspectivism is fully a phenomenological inquiry. Like Sartre in *Being and Nothingness*, Nietzsche had no intention of reviving artificial solipsistic doubts about the reality of the external world. Instead, he regarded the inner world as an internalized outer world that is only revealed to us as a phenomenon. Consciousness itself, however, is always in an intentional arc with the world, neither inside nor outside, but somewhere in-between, always alongside of what it is conscious of. Nietzsche hoped to heighten our awareness and attention, guided by the insight 'that all of our so-called consciousness is a more or less fanciful commentary on an unknown, perhaps unknowable, but felt, text'. Our intentions and drives are thus a form of directedness towards the world. An object is never registered in neutral terms but is grasped with an emotional valency in terms of our moods: 'Nietzsche was a master of shading the particular tinge, color, and mood of experience, and since he used his own suffering as a springboard to construct his philosophy, we find in his writings exquisite depictions of experiencing the world while racked with pain. Phenomenologically speaking, these are model analyses of an intentional design of the world' (2003: 209).[18] As Safranski (2003: 218–19) comments, Nietzsche's 'phenomenological attentiveness' to the world of consciousness requires an attitude that clashes with the complexities and demands of everyday life and in which we are sufficiently composed 'to let the world work its magic'.

From this, it is clear that Nietzschean perspectivism invites a comparison with Sartre, for whom Nietzsche paved the way with his analyses of consciousness, prefiguring the intentional structure of consciousness and the concept of 'outer-directedness' that Sartre and other phenomenologists developed further. His emphasis on instinct and preconscious drives also suggest a form of pre-reflective consciousness which formed the nucleus of Sartre's philosophy in *Being and Nothingness*: 'All of life would be possible without, as it were, seeing itself in a mirror, as in actuality even now the major part of our life unfolds without this kind of mirroring' (GS 354). Like in Sartre's phenomenological approach, Nietzsche recognizes that 'we see from the most particular *out*' rather than 'from the general to the most particular case' (LN 159). He insists that knowledge is always shaped by the perspective of its knower against 'high-altitude thinking',[19] the remote, neutral and objective standpoint of analytical reason in which 'we are asked to think an eye which cannot be thought at all, an eye turned in no direction at all, an eye where the active and interpretative powers are to be suppressed, absent, but through which seeing still becomes a seeing-something' (GM 3.12). Contemplation without interest, Nietzsche exclaims, is a 'nonsensical absurdity' (GM 3.12).

Nietzsche defines his perspectivism as the ability to multiply our perspectival affects: 'the *more* affects we allow to speak about one thing, the *more* eyes, different eyes, we can use to observe one thing, the more complete will our "concept" of this thing, our "objectivity", be' (GM 3.12). The free spirit must 'be able to gaze with many eyes and consciences from the heights into every distance, from the depths up to every height, from the corner onto every expanse' (BGE 211). This he contrasts with 'Socrates' one great Cyclopian eye' that can only see the world through the optics of rationality and so is unable to appreciate 'the lovely madness of artistic enthusiasm' (BT 14). Affirming the multiplicity of perspectives reformulates our notion of objectivity in opposition to the Kantian 'disinterested spectator'. Nietzsche posits Argos, the hundred-eyed monster, as a paradigm of perspectivism, a master of interpretation who 'sets every thing in the best light and observes it carefully from all sides' (HH 636). He presents the 'new philosopher' as a 'manifold plurality' who

> needs to have been a critic and a sceptic and a dogmatic and an historian, and in addition a poet and collector and traveller and puzzle-solver and moralist and seer and 'free spirit' and nearly all things, so that he can traverse the range of human values and value-feelings and *be able* to look with many kinds of eyes and consciences from the corners into every wide expanse. (BGE 211)

It is clear that Nietzsche's perspectivism – 'the ability *to control* one's Pro and Con and to dispose of them, so that one knows how to employ a *variety* of perspectives and affective interpretations in the service of knowledge' (GM 3.12) – dovetails with Sartre's phenomenology of lived experience, both placing affective moods, drives and states at the core of embodied consciousness. The notion of 'aesthetic perspectivism' has been suggested by Higgins (2000: 52) to capture Nietzsche's epistemology since the term 'aesthetic' gets at the root and range of the perspectival variables that are relevant to a true picture of the situations in which we experience the world. Many of Nietzsche's images are drawn from the sphere of art and aesthetics, illuminating features of life and lived experience that 'dethrones traditional epistemology from its queenly place in philosophy in favor of aesthetics, the study of perception and value within the perceptual sphere'. As Higgins argues, relating perspectivism to aesthetics brings perspectivism back to its original ground of sensation and perception, which are key elements, as we will see, in Nietzsche's and Sartre's rapturous aesthetic and ethical vision.

In the next chapter, I look at how these similarities in method between Sartrean phenomenology and Nietzschean perspectivism crystallized into their parallel thinking on the *decentred, non-egoic, affective self*, an emergent aesthetic view of subjectivity that would in turn greatly influence poststructuralist and posthumanist thinking.

3

The decentred self

> *What separates me most deeply from the metaphysicians is: I don't concede that the 'I' is what thinks. Instead, I take the I itself to be a construction of thinking ... in other words to be only a* regulative fiction *with the help of which a kind of constancy and thus 'knowability' is inserted into,* invented into, *a world of becoming. Up to now belief in grammar, in the linguistic subject, object, in verbs has subjugated the metaphysicians: I teach the renunciation of this belief.*
>
> (Nietzsche, LN 20-1)

There is no lack of confusion when it comes to Nietzsche's and Sartre's view of self and freedom. In Nietzsche's case, this usually means classifying him as eliminativist of both self and freedom, denying them altogether as illusory. For Sartre, this means attributing to him either (or both) absolute freedom (*Being and Nothingness*) or full-blooded determinism (the *Critique*). Such characterizations are a form of metaphysical parody, tying them to binary divisions and rigid oppositions that in actual fact their thinking works vehemently against. As we will see, they are both compatibilists and offer deconstructive and reconstructive poles of explanation that run in tandem.[1] Absolute freedom or hard determinism is anathema to their 'mediated' view of consciousness and world. As Solomon (2003: 181) observes, although Nietzsche's views on freedom are 'complex and confusing', a 'paradox of fatalism and self-creation', we should not understand fatalism straightforwardly as determinism. This is not a paradox but the essence of his perspectivism – they are two perspectives on ourselves – like a Kantian antinomy in which what appears to have two contradictory appearances turns out to be the expressions of two different standpoints that we often take up one or the other sequentially (2003: 184–5).

In the quest to create 'new subjectivities', Nietzsche puts an end 'to the superstitions which have so far flourished with almost tropical luxuriance around the idea of the soul', as well as the doctrine of the will that accompanies it (BGE 12). He rejects the 'atomistic' idea of a substantial soul but warns against rejecting 'new versions and refinements of the soul hypothesis', suggesting concepts like the 'mortal soul', the 'soul as multiplicity of subjects' and the 'soul as a society constructed out of drives and effects' (BGE 12). Equally, Nietzsche argues, 'our body is ... a society constructed out of many souls', and it is from this 'society' we get the 'performance' and 'successes' of willing (BGE 19). Conscious agency is only the directing (not driving) force of action.

To think otherwise is to mistake 'the helmsman for the stream' or the 'match' for the 'powder keg' (GS 360). Although he firmly debunks the idea of willing as a *causa sui*, an incompatibilist stance 'with a temerity greater than Münchhausen's, to pull oneself into existence out of the swamp of nothingness by one's own hair' (BGE 21), he does not dissolve the agential self altogether. As Riccardi (2018: 187) avers, 'Nietzsche's take on the conscious self is not eliminativist but rather profoundly revisionary'. His ideal of accomplished selfhood consists in 'the harmonious... relation between one's bodily self and one's (revisionarily understood) conscious self'. This is linked to a normative project of sketching and eliciting a harmonious psychological make-up that enables one to overcome the kind of self-division caused by the internalization of ascetic morality and the imposition of a certain form of social discipline. This is when the animal that makes promises can become a 'free spirit' or 'sovereign individual', an instance of 'rare freedom' and even a 'master of free will' (GM 2.2).

Against misreadings of Sartre that view him as a metaphysical thinker of 'absolute freedom' or 'hard determinism', it is clear that his dialectical view of freedom and necessity is consistently compatibilist that, like Nietzsche, he apprehends through a sublimating or supplementary logic of perspectival difference. Eshleman (2011: 42–4) makes this point well, identifying two views of freedom and subjectivity in Sartre's *Being and Nothingness*. According to the first, 'well-recognized but implausible' view, freedom is continuous creation ex nihilo, free of constraint from being-in-itself. The second, 'unrecognized but plausible view', developed later in *Being and Nothingness* starting from the role that others play in conditioning my becoming a person (through consciousness of shame), and, elaborating Sartre's concomitant notions of self, limit, and project, argues that 'freedom and power are intertwined'. In Sartre's 'considered view', freedom can only be 'an aberrant synthesis of the in-itself and nothingness', an admixture of social and material determinants and our free internalization of them (BN 688–9) within an intrinsically ambiguous process where we 'make something out of what is made of [us]' (1974a: 35). Similarly, the charge of 'crude materialism' in the *Critique* is equally inaccurate.[2] In this work, Sartre develops further his dialectic of freedom and situation that he began in *The Transcendence of the Ego* and worked through in *Being and Nothingness*. Freedom and necessity are, he consistently argues, dialectically coextensive and mutually implicative within a process of 'trans-substantiation' (CDR 178): 'man is mediated by things to the extent that things are mediated by man' (CDR 82). A true dialectical understanding of the subject, Sartre insists, must involve 'the perpetually renewed contradiction between man-as-producer and man-as-product' (CDR 158).

Before we look in closer detail at their dialectical view of freedom through the model of the 'three ecologies of self' (Guattari 2000), it is worthwhile to consider in brief the Cartesian model of self that they critiqued through their twin notion of the self as 'embodied consciousness'.

The bewitched ego

We find ourselves in the midst of a rude fetishism when we call to mind the basic presuppositions of the metaphysics of language – which is to say, of reason. It is

> this which sees everywhere deed and doer; this which believes in will as a cause in general; this which believes in the 'ego', the ego as being, in the ego as substance, and which projects its belief in the ego-substance on to all things.
> (Nietzsche, *Twilight of the Idols* 3.5)

Nietzsche acknowledges that philosophers are at last beginning to distance themselves from the metaphysical view of the Kantian and Cartesian self: 'Now, with admirable tenacity and cunning, people are wondering whether they can get out of this net – wondering whether the reverse might be true: that "think" is the condition and "I" is the conditioned, in which case "I" would be a synthesis that only gets *produced* through thought itself' (BGE 54). For Nietzsche, the idealists have got things the wrong way round: 'insofar as we are in the habit of overlooking and deceiving ourselves about this duality by means of the synthetic concept of the "I", a whole chain of erroneous conclusions, and, consequently, false evaluations have become attached to the will, – to such a degree that the one who wills believes, in good faith, that willing *suffices* for action' (BGE 19). Instead of being the cause of willing, the subject is the effect of it – willing is believed to be 'an activity and effect of a being who is thought of as a cause' (BGE 17). In rejecting standard views of agency, Nietzsche objects to the attempt to isolate discrete causes of actions: 'Cause and effect: there is probably never such a duality; in truth a continuum faces us, from which we isolate a few pieces, just as we always perceive a moment only as isolated points, i.e. do not really see, but infer' (GS 112). It is an 'error of false causality' in which '[w]e believe that we are the cause of our own will'. The inner world is full of 'phantoms and illusions' and, Nietzsche states, the will is one of them: 'The will no longer moves anything, hence does not explain anything – it merely accompanies events; it can even be absent' (TI 6.3).

Nietzsche conceives the 'I' as a synthetic construction, but by posting it behind actions, as a doer behind the deed, it 'has become a fairy tale, a fiction, a play on words: it has stopped thinking, feeling, and willing altogether' (TI 6.3). This bewitchment amounts to a 'rude fetishism' (TI 3.5) and Descartes is the philosopher most seduced by this linguistic illusion:

> 'There is thinking: therefore there is something that thinks': this is the upshot of all Descartes' argumentation. But this means posting as 'true a priori' our belief in the concept of substance: – that when there is thought there has to be something 'that thinks' is simply a formulation of our grammatical custom that adds a doer to every deed. (WP 484)

Even subjective experience is an effect rather than a cause of the will to power that interprets physiologically without a subject: 'The will to power interprets . . . it defines limits, determines degrees, variations of power' (WP 643) but '*[t]he mistake lies in the fictitious insertion of a subject*' (WP 632). For Nietzsche, it is false to consider consciousness to be indicative of the unity of the organism. Feelings are spontaneously felt without being articulated and most of our actions are undertaken without reflection or second-order awareness. It is the act of thinking that gives rise to the awareness of an 'I' and only the confusion of grammar that leads us astray to assign a subject as agent. The will is not a fixed unity but rather a swarm of diverse affections, voices, drives and energies. These are evaluative affectively loaded dispositions that are proactive, actively seek discharge and have a strong compelling force. They are in constant tension but form alliances of rank within a hierarchically structured order that is the driving force behind our acts, feelings and consciousness. This, Nietzsche argues, demonstrates the fictive and superficiality of the unified rationalist ego:

> It must be shown to what extent everything conscious remains on *the surface*: how an action and the image of an action *differ*, how *little* one knows of what *precedes* an action . . . *how essential* fiction and imagination are in which we dwell consciously: how all our words refer to fictions (our affects, also) and how the bond between man and man depends on the transmission and elaboration of these fictions. (WP 676)

In a bid to understand the self as an agential capacity capable of forming 'new subjectivities', Nietzsche prioritizes the role of instinct and subconscious physiological drives over conscious thought, Cartesian transparency and reflection: 'whatever *becomes* conscious becomes by the same token shallow, thin, relatively stupid, general, sign, herd-signal: all becoming-conscious involves a great and thorough corruption, falsification, reduction to superficialities, and generalization' (GS 354).

Although Sartre confessed his own childhood idealism in *Words* and that he had been tempted by the idealist teachings of his professors at the Sorbonne, he soon moved away from Husserl's philosophy because of its 'idealist turn'. In *The Transcendence of the Ego*, he critiques the idealism of Descartes, Kant and Husserl, arguing that they transform the real world of objects into the sanctuary of inner life, dissolving it into nothing but 'contents of consciousness'. Equating knowledge with consumption, 'they ate it with their eyes' (TE 87–9). In attacking idealism, Sartre develops Nietzsche's insights on the superficiality of the ego, portraying the belief in the ego or substantial self as involving a form of philosophical bewitchment where one reverses the order of things by deriving consciousness from ego instead of ego from consciousness:

> The ego is an object apprehended but also *constituted* by reflective consciousness. It is the virtual foyer of unity, and consciousness constitutes it as going in *the reverse direction* from that followed by real production. . . . As a consequence, consciousness projects its own spontaneity into the object Ego so as to confer on it the creative power that is absolutely necessary to it. However, this spontaneity, *represented* and *hypostasized* in an object, becomes a bastard and degraded spontaneity, which magically preserves its creative potentiality while becoming passive. Hence the profound irrationality of the notion of Ego. (TE 34–5)

According to Sartre, the transcendental ego of the idealists is neither necessary nor desirable (TE 7). The ego is simply the object pole of reflective consciousness and it is only through a magical reversal that we think it to be the origin or owner of it. Pre-reflective consciousness has its own synthetic unity without a transcendental

'I': it 'constitutes a synthetic, individual totality . . . and the I can, clearly, be only an *expression* (and not a condition)' (TE 7):

> When I run after a tram, when I look at the time, when I become absorbed in the contemplation of a portrait there is no *I*. There is a consciousness of the *tram-needing-to-be-caught*, etc., and a non-positional consciousness of consciousness. In fact, I am plunged into the world of objects. (TE 13)

For Sartre, positing the 'I' or 'me' behind consciousness is obstructive to a true understanding of consciousness: 'this superfluous *I* is actually a hindrance. If it existed, it would violently separate consciousness from itself; it would divide it, slicing through each consciousness like an opaque blade. The transcendental I is the death of consciousness' (TE 7). Since consciousness is pure activity, a transcending towards something it is not, to posit the I is to introduce 'a centre of opacity' (TE 8).

The I comes to be purely through reflection: 'The I only ever appears on the occasion of a reflective act . . . when reflected consciousness becomes the object of the reflecting consciousness' (TE 16). It is therefore not originary but a transcendent existent that always accompanies acts of reflection. Sartre describes how 'it is in exclusively magical terms that we have to describe the relations between the *me* and consciousness' (TE 26). Magic arises from 'impure reflection' (TE 23) that reverses the real phenomenological order of things, making primary things derivative and secondary reflected-upon things primary. My actions are seen to flow from me, whereas in fact my 'me' is the reflected synthesis of my actions. Unlike pure reflection that 'stays with the given . . . [and] disarms unreflected consciousness by giving it back its instantaneous character' (TE 24), impure reflection effects a magical reversal whereby it carries out 'an infinitization of the field' (TE 23), creating a transcendent object that serves as an imagined origin and cause 'in the past and the future' (TE 23). Thus, for Sartre, reversal and hypostasis signify the bewitching, magical way of relating to our own ego in which a more elemental, pre-reflective consciousness imbues its own creation with a pseudo power that allows consciousness to escape and even suppress aspects of itself. This is a form of pseudo-activity where all our states, emotions and actions through a relation of 'creation' are 'attached directly (or indirectly, through quality) to the Ego as to its origin' (TE 32). Consciousness has no originary ego or contents within but is 'a sliding beyond itself' and 'absolute flight':

> Consciousness is purified; it is clear as a strong wind. There is nothing in it but a movement of fleeing itself, a sliding beyond itself. If, impossible though it may be, you could enter 'into' a consciousness, you would be seized by a whirlwind and thrown back outside, in the thick of the dust . . . for consciousness has no 'inside'. Precisely this being-beyond-itself, this absolute flight, this refusal to be a substance, is what makes it to be a consciousness. (1970: 4)

Against the Cartesian notion of interiority, Sartre emphasizes the 'public' nature of the ego and the fact that there are objective psycho-physiological aspects to ourselves of which we are most often consciously unaware. The fact that the nature of reflective consciousness makes itself an object for such consciousness means that, for Sartre, the

'I is *an other*' (TE 46). We are always obliged to view ourselves from another-person perspective, even when we use 'I'. The ego is a public phenomenon, conditioned and shaped through societal and interpersonal forces. In overemphasizing one's interiority, Sartre warns, the I is magically hypostasized which leads to bewitching and 'impure' relations with oneself and others. When we encounter the Other, the direction of magic is reversed in which the world itself 'reveals itself to consciousness as magical just where we expect it to be deterministic' (STE 46). For Sartre, 'there is an existential structure of the world which is magical' (STE 46) because of the Other's inherent freedom, their unpredictability inscribed in their language, bodily movements and actions that do not obey strict causal laws: 'the category of "magic" governs . . . interpsychic relations between men in society' (STE 56). It is in this way we can become affectively captivated or disgusted by others.

For Sartre, even when psychological bewitchment seems to come 'wholly' from within (e.g. anger) or without (e.g. fright), consciousness and world are always locked in a fused dynamic. Because a study of the phenomenon requires a transphenomenal being and because consciousness cannot be 'constitutive of its object's being' (BN 21), there is a demand for a universal *'plenitude of being'* (BN 22) as a possibility for both phenomena and consciousness alike. As we have seen, for Sartre the 'I' is a synthetic construct of consciousness in a derivative reflexive mode of becoming, that which offers itself only 'through successive, fleeting profiles' (BN 22). Consciousness confronts its past and future as facing a self which it is 'in the mode of not being' (BN 111), a being that has 'an infinity of possibilities' (BN 192). The *pour-soi* always 'becomes itself by surpassing' (BN 179) towards an ever-higher value since emotion is 'coexistent' (BN 182) with the *pour-soi* and its desires. Value is hence nothing less than the being of the self (BN 179) and the 'circuit of ipseity' (BN 771–2) that we call the 'I' does not stem from any transcendental ego but is simply the projective unity of 'the myriad concrete desires which constitute the fabric of our conscious life' (BN 735–6). In the lived dynamic and concrete synthesis of 'man in the world' (BN 34), consciousness experiences a 'trinity of ontological affectivity' – nausea (world), anguish (consciousness), shame (other) – that relates to the three ecologies or dimensions of lived experience. For Sartre, affectivity is 'an existential mode of . . . human reality' (STE 12). All perception is accompanied by an 'affective reaction' (IM 28) to the extent 'each affective quality is so deeply incorporated in the object that it is impossible to distinguish between what is felt and what is perceived' (IM 139). In this way, affectivity ontologically grounds emotion and carries with it an evaluative charge that can lead to forms of captivation with ourselves, the world and with others. Anguish is felt as 'freedom's reflective self-apprehension' (BN 79), nausea as our immediate and basic affective recognition of the 'original contingency' (BN 178) of the world, stripped of all meaning and reason, while shame refers to my loss of transcendence in the presence of the other when I am no longer the centre of the world.

Many interpretations of Sartre, as O' Shiel (2019: 101) notes, are 'rationalistic', 'overly cerebral and reflective' and overlook the central importance of affectivity and magic in his phenomenology. The relation of consciousness to things and to others is one of dialectical interdependence where emotions and affectivity are constitutive components of this relation. Discussing the concept of possession, Sartre describes this as 'a magical bond' (BN 765) between consciousness and things where there is an 'impossible synthesis' (BN 751) of 'the me and the not-me' (BN 750). Consciousness and world implicate one another in a dynamic dyadic (BN 766) within which there is a 'syncretic movement . . . [of] the me becoming not-me and the not-me becoming me' (BN 764). Our experience of the 'viscous' (*visqueux*) particularly illustrates this: 'the viscous reverses the terms: suddenly the for-itself is *compromised*' (BN 788) by qualities that seem to 'become animated by a kind of life' and 'turn against me' (BN 789). This is a 'symbol of an anti-value' (BN 791) where materiality presents such a challenge in which our values are so affected that we feel strong visceral emotions like disgust. Like Nietzsche, Sartre abandons the idea of a unified rational subject or ego, immersing the self externally in the social and material world and multiplying it internally through the pre-reflective interplay of diverse affects, emotions and states. By dissolving the fictitious 'hindrance' of the ego, they both offer us a form of psychological therapy[3] or 'purifying reflection' that enables an escape route from the captivity and magical hold of the emotions only through rare moments where the subject apprehends her feelings as involving some form of self-deception.

The three ecologies of the self

Nietzsche's and Sartre's shared project to theorize 'new versions and refinements of the soul hypothesis' (BGE 12) presents a model of the self as an emergent 'unity within a multiplicity' locked in an interplay of elements with the social and material world. This is best understood, I suggest, through the trivalent model proposed by Guattari in *Les Trois Ecologies* of (i) *a material environment in the process of being reinvented*, (ii) *a constantly mutating socius* and (iii) *a nascent subjectivity*. Like Guattari (who was influenced heavily by them both), their affirmative reconstructive project emphasizes the need to create transversal lines and connections through them within 'a common ethico-aesthetic' viewpoint. Their descriptions of becoming are open-ended and allow for a notion of the subject that is precarious, shaped by the external world, the social sphere and the individual's internal forces and critical reflection. Describing each of these forces as an 'ecology' incorporates the idea of each as a living system that has a dynamism of its own but which intersects transitively with the other two. The 'new subjectivity' that they advance is a living, evolving triptych of material, social and psychological forces, a 'psycho-social-somatic unity' that is able to install itself simultaneously 'in the realms of the environment, in the major social and institutional assemblages, and symmetrically in the landscapes and fantasies of the most intimate spheres of the individual' (2000: 69). Both philosophers show the formidable weight of material and social forces while providing the lightness required to elide or direct them through 'purifying reflection', the formation of the 'intellectual conscience' and Dionysian 'flights of escape'.

(i) The body and environment

Body am I through and through and nothing besides.

(Nietzsche, *Zarathustra* 1.4)

In broad terms, Heidegger had a valid point – both Nietzsche and Sartre invert Platonism to the extent that they privilege the body over any transcendent conception of mind. In his rejection of 'soul atomism' – 'the belief which regards the soul as something indestructible, eternal, indivisible, as a monad, as an *atomon*' (BGE 112) – Nietzsche extols the 'great wisdom' of the body and debunks the rationality of the soul. As in Sartre's ideas of 'trans-substantiation' (CDR 182) and 'connective tissue' (BN 755), Nietzsche posits an intimate connection of transitive exchange between self and world, using the guiding metaphors of *incorporation* and *assimilation* to explain this. He conceives the body as a vehicle of assimilation that digests all kinds of material that are processed and modified into emotions and psychological states. Our character is susceptible and modifiable through the effects of inheritance, diet, exercise and environment: 'These small things – nutrition, location, climate, recreation, the whole casuistry of selfishness – are inconceivably more important than everything one has taken to be important so far. Precisely here one must begin to *relearn*' (EH 2.10). He connects environmental and dietary factors directly to certain psychological states. Too much rice in India leads to a lack of vigour and the nihilism of Buddhism, while the malaise of the German spirit is a result of poor air and 'winter sickness' from spending too much time indoors in front of burning stoves (GS 134). Conceiving the self as a 'psycho-somatic continuum', Nietzsche telescopes the strong effects of physiology – 'life style, nutrition, or digestion, perhaps a deficit or excess of inorganic salts in their blood and brain; in brief, in their *physis*' – on judgements, feelings, moods and tastes (GS 39). He recommends dietary change and physical labour for psychological disturbances or 'distress of the soul' (D 269). His own physical ailments and sufferings made him sensitive to the 'great reason' of his body and to decipher which foods and environments were conducive to well-being. He was, as he records in his writings, preoccupied practically and philosophically with finding ways to improve health and recover from illness (HH P4).

Reversing the transcendental conception of self of Plato and Descartes as sealed off from the world, Nietzsche plunges the self into matter: 'The inorganic determines us through and through: water, air, earth, the composition of the soil, electricity and so on. We are plants under such conditions.' The denial and ignorance of the body is accompanied by a misplaced arrogance on the part of humanity: 'How strange and superior we are towards the dead, the inorganic, and meanwhile we are three quarters a column of water, and have inorganic salts in us that probably have more influence on our fortunes than the whole of living society.'[4] In *Zarathustra*, Nietzsche distinguishes two notions of self proposed by Zarathustra in his famous speech 'On the Despisers of the Body'. The *Selbst* 'lives in your body . . . is your body'; it's 'a great reason, a multiplicity with one sense, a war and a peace, one herd and one shepherd'. The *Ich*, by contrast, corresponds to the conscious self and, though worshipped by the metaphysicians, amounts to little: 'Your small reason, what you call "spirit" is also a tool of your body, my brother, a small work and plaything of your great reason.' Ultimately, the *Ich* is ruled by the *Selbst*: 'The body is inspired, let us keep the "soul" out of it' (EH 9.4).

Alongside environment, Nietzsche also includes genetic inheritance as a constituent feature of *Selbst*, a fact that has divided scholars over the extent of his Lamarckism.

Discussing the concept of learning in D 540, Nietzsche states, 'Michelangelo saw in Raphael study, in himself nature: there *learning*, here *talent* . . . For what is talent but a name for an *older* piece of learning, experience, practice, appropriation, incorporation, whether at the stage of our fathers or an even earlier stage!' In BGE 200 he expresses a direct correlation between ancestral background and inner drives, skills or emotional dispositions: 'Human beings have in their bodies the heritage of multiple origins, that is . . . drives and value standards that fight each other and rarely permit each other any rest.' The results of 'racial mixing' give rise to two different types – those who seek rest and calm and those rarer types who have 'inherited and cultivated' self-control such as Caesar, Alcibiades and 'perhaps Leonardo da Vinci' (BGE 200). This is reinforced in D 30 where Nietzsche connects race to inner drives that form part of human nature, such as the drive to cruelty that has become sublimated but not extinguished for 'we moderns'. In BGE 264 he argues for the generational transfer of traits through 'corrupted blood': 'If one knows something about the parents, an inference about the child is permissible . . . that sort of thing must as surely be transferred to the child as corrupted blood; and with the aid of the best education one will at best *deceive* with regard to such a heredity.'

While Nietzsche attaches importance to inherited racial and psychological dispositions, he also connects 'the cultivation of race' to a self-perpetuating system of acculturation. Clark (2013: 287) argues in this respect that when Nietzsche states that 'a type with few but very strong traits . . . is fixed beyond the changing generations' and has 'staying power' (BGE 262), he does not refer to biologically inherited traits but uses the notion of breeding (cultivation) as an analogy to show how selective cultural practices, such as marriage, education, customs and penal laws, have produced human types with a strong 'staying power'. In the trivalent model of the three ecologies that I propose as a framework for understanding the Nietzschean self, all three factors – body/environment, socius and psychological – form a network of transversal interplay or a 'nature-culture continuum', articulated through Nietzsche's idea of a 'transfigured physis'.[5] Although the body is the 'great reason' of the self, Nietzsche does not conceive this in mechanical terms and distinguishes between the body as an object for medicine (*Körper*) and the living body as phenomenologically felt (*Leib*). Central to this is the notion of 'affect' (*Affekt*) that always plays a role in perception, selecting and avoiding things (BGE 192) or evaluating what is valuable for the overall growth and health of the organism (BGE 23). The *Selbst*, one's 'for and against' (BGE 284), is, for Nietzsche, an active force whose physiological state, felt through sensory perception and mood, involves interpretation and the projection of value and, as we will see below, links closely to Sartre's notion of embodied consciousness and pre-reflectivity.

Nietzsche's 'reason of the body', as Gerhardt (2006: 73, 85) suggests, has both 'a polemical and a systematically foundational sense'. It is polemically opposed to the dualist Christian-Platonic conception of being and becomes an earthly immanent replacement for God and also has ontological primacy in defining what a human is and how its 'great reason' functions as a creative physiological intelligence which is pursued through action in the world. The body is axiological in Nietzsche's account of art and in his Dionysian affirmation of life. For Nietzsche, art is a name for a dimension of *physis*: 'Art itself wells up in man as a force of nature and disposes of him, whether he wills it or not' (WP 798). Even 'creative thought' is the work of the body and its ancient wisdom: 'when they are asked to question how they performed their master stroke and from what sphere the creative thought came to them . . . hardly do they dare to say, "It came out of me, it was my hand that threw the dice"' (WP 659). Central to Nietzsche's artistic experience is *rausch* (rapture), an 'intoxication of the senses' and a heightened physiological state that increases the affective powers of the experiencing subject, felt at its most intense in the Dionysian force of music which hails the body directly. The body also figures centrally in Nietzsche's reconstructive project of 'giving style to oneself' (GS 290) in which he sketches out the contours of a 'positive asceticism', a form of self-discipline based on 'a powerful "no" and an exuberant "yes"' lodged between Stoicism and Epicureanism.[6]

Sartre's view of the body, both philosophically and personally, was complex. Beauvoir (1984: 117) records that he revealed to her, 'I found it hard to have a body.' He first became acutely aware of his own body as seen by others when, at the age of seven, he was taken to have his long flowing locks shorn and experienced a severe 'narcissistic wound' as a result. He had been a beautiful baby adored by his mother but, in the flash of the scissors, 'I turned as ugly as a frog' (1983: 12). Alienated by his own body and his diminutive stature, he would imagine himself to be Pardaillan, a tall and athletic comic book hero, feeling 'like a powerful warrior' as an imaginary 'kind of compensation for my shortness' (1981: 313).[7] Up until his final months, Sartre's 'imaginary body' had for all his life turned his interest away from his real body as a defence against vulnerability. His Stoicism was a form of sadism inflicted on his body that often turned into masochism: 'What is the point of good health? I prefer to have written *Critique de la raison dialectique* – I say it without pride' (1976: 153). It was not until the severities of chronic ill health forced him to take notice in the 1970s that he grew more in touch with his body and with a more inclusive acceptance of his feminine side.[8]

Throughout his writings, Sartre was cognizant of the physical connections and neurological/pharmacological dimensions of consciousness. Vulgarized descriptions of the *pour-soi* of *Being and Nothingness* as a 'disembodied consciousness' or some kind of 'Cartesian ghost' are absurdly misrepresentative and have led many to overlook his theory of the body. In his early phenomenological works, Sartre describes consciousness and body as intimately intermingled, such as they form a psychosomatic continuum or unity.[9] He shows how the body is intimately involved in belief. Emotion is conjoined with physiological changes in the tensing of muscles, sobbing, clenching of fist and gesticulations: 'during emotion, it is the body which, directed by consciousness, changes its relationship with the world so that the world should change its qualities' (STE 41). To believe in the magical behaviour of emotions we must be physically upset since our bodies are the 'instruments of incantation' through which they are lived out. In his description of anger, for example, the body is presented as a composite synthetic totality of life and action:

> Doubtless there is a cryptology of the psyche; certain phenomena are 'hidden'. But this does not mean at all that the meanings refer to something 'beyond the body' [. . .] these frowns, this blushing, this stammer, this slight trembling of the hands,

these sly looks which seem to be at the same time timid and threatening do *not* express anger; they *are* the anger. (BN 462)

For Sartre, there is unequivocally no disembodied 'pure knowledge'. Consciousness, he insists, 'exist[s] its body' (BN 441) and is body 'in its entirety' (BN 412) since the body is its 'sensory centre of reference' (BN 437). Presenting consciousness and body as a living unity, he argues against the idea that 'the psyche is *united* to a body' since 'the body is its substance and its constant condition of possibility' (BN 452). Invoking the difference between *Leib* and *Körper*, as Nietzsche did, he insists that '[t]he body is "*lived*, and not *known*"' (BN 435). 'We do not employ this instrument', he adds, 'for we *are* it' (BN 434). When there is a world, we are necessarily saying that there is a body (BN 413).

This is not to say, however, that there aren't any difficulties with his theory of the body in *Being and Nothingness* that has been described as 'puzzling' and 'multiply ambiguous' as well as 'groundbreaking' and 'pioneering'.[10] According to Morris (2020: 233–7), Sartre's conception of the body is 'complex and multi-faceted' with some lacunae and blind spots but is, in its phenomenological descriptions, 'remarkable and insightful' and in places (e.g. his description of shyness and the caress) unparalleled. For Morris, Sartre says too little about bodily needs (thirst, hunger, fatigue) and what he says is 'somewhat confusing'. By placing the body on the facticity side of facticity/ transcendence, he is unable to appreciate the body as having *teloi* and desires as in acute pain when the body 'emerges as an *alien presence* that exerts upon us a *telic demand*'. This is also the case with modes of bodily 'dys-appearance', such as acute pain, which are affectively felt by the body as negative thematizations of the body demanded by the body itself which affects an 'internal disruption' and 'spatiotemporal constriction' (as Sartre recognizes in our being-for-others). This connects with criticisms made by Howells who, while recognizing that Sartre is resolutely 'anti-dualist' and views the body as an 'essential condition for consciousness to exist', asserts that he is still 'arguably unable to accept all the implications of embodiment' (2011: 30, 26). For Howells (2011: 46), Sartre falls short in this respect of Merleau-Ponty in showing fully how the body is an 'intrinsic element in the activities of consciousness' whose examples of phantom limb pain and of brain damage (compared to Sartre's anodyne examples of stomach ache and eye strain) are 'indicative of the seriousness with which he takes the body'. If, for Sartre, we can choose how to relate to the sick body, for Merleau-Ponty 'it is only through illness that we exist at all'. There is also an inconsistency in Sartre's account of bodily states and drives evidenced in the disparate accounts he gives of hunger and sexual desire. Sexual desire, he states, reveals the indissolubility of consciousness and body wherein both are reciprocally transformed. Desire reveals the incarnation of consciousness (BN 516): 'in desiring, consciousness chooses to exist its facticity at another level. It no longer flees its facticity, but it attempts to submit to its own contingency, in so far as it apprehends another body . . . as desirable' (BN 512–13). This, as Morris (2020: 237) and Howells (2011: 173) note, is very different to his treatment of hunger, thirst, pain and illness that '*does not compromise* the very nature of the for-itself' (BN 511).

Despite these lacunae, Sartre's theory of the body in *Being and Nothingness* contains many insights that later philosophers, not least Merleau-Ponty himself, incorporated into their own view of embodied consciousness. For instance, Sartre anticipates the notion of 'habit' or 'motor skill' that Merleau-Ponty utilizes in his own work. Sartre recognizes that there are socially induced ways of moving the body, 'techniques of the body' or 'collective techniques' that 'determine my membership of communities' (BN 666). He uses the example of skiing to illustrate how the *pour-soi* appropriates such techniques (BN 667) and internalizes them (BN 680) before re-externalizing them in the form of kinaesthetic bodily movements. Although this was left undeveloped (on a physiological if not on a social level) by Sartre, it anticipates Merleau-Ponty's idea in *Phenomenology of Perception* that the body has its own 'intentional arc' and modes of 'proprioception' in which it incorporates the gestures and movements of others (1962: 94). Furthermore, Sartre also introduced the concept of 'the flesh' (*la chair*) integral to Merleau-Ponty's later philosophy. Although many scholars accuse Sartre of a totally negative view of the flesh as 'nauseous', Morris (2020: 231) notices, for instance, the seamless mix of phenomenology and ontology in *Being and Nothingness* where Sartre's description of flesh in the sexual caress overflows his other more negative descriptions of the flesh. His 'often beautiful descriptions' of the caress[11] show there are various non-instrumental ways of encountering one's own body and that of others, including the *aesthetic*, the *nurturing* and the *sensuous*.

Rather than try to solve the mind–body duality and explain it away in metaphysical terms of exclusion and separation, Howells (2011: 165–6) highlights how Sartre brings to light the many conceptual ambiguities and paradoxes bound up with it, thus resisting a point of certainty or analytic closure. He shows, as did Beauvoir, how identity and alterity are mutually productive, how transience is constitutive of experience and how freedom is always already conditioned by necessity. Presenting the situation as an ambiguous phenomenon in which it is impossible to distinguish the contribution of freedom from that of the brute existent (BN 662), Sartre demonstrates how we must assume our ambiguity (as facticity *and* transcendence) and not flee from it, thus coming to recognize that one's ambiguity is the necessary precondition of the moral life.

Despite some of her reservations about Sartre's philosophical treatment of the body in *Being and Nothingness*, Howells (2011: 33) is careful to observe that his concept of embodiment develops and expands over the course of his lifetime, his later work ever more attuned to embodied experiences of desire, suffering and pain and dispositional states of the subconscious.[12] In the *Critique*, he set about reinterpreting his philosophical categories by connecting them even firmer to the material world in order to overcome some of the unresolved ambiguities in *Being and Nothingness*. 'Consciousness' is reinscribed as 'praxis', while the idea of 'lack' is replaced by the notion of 'need' which, Sartre emphasizes, is 'the first totalising relation between the material being, man, and the material ensemble of which he is a part' (CDR 80). The category of need overcomes the difficulties that stemmed from the hegemony of the individual project in *Being and Nothingness* since it denotes a material relation with the world that is given independently of the rationalizing project. Faced with hunger, for instance, the subject totalizes the material field before him as an opening onto a complex reality and his praxis involves unifying and reorganizing the transcendence of existing circumstances towards the practical field (CDR 310). It is only by working on and transforming matter that he can go beyond existing circumstances and overcome need. Caught in a 'dialectic of circularity' (CDR 80), however, praxis preserves what it totalizes and becomes itself an embodiment of the inert quality of the material world. In order to transform the material field the individual must introduce into himself features of that field and make of his body a tool. Thus, in the course of praxis, he undergoes a profound interior alteration taking on or, in Nietzschean terms, *incorporating* the qualities of an object. The living act of his praxis is in turn absorbed into matter and transformed into an inert material fact. Sartre describes praxis in this way as 'a passage from objective to objective through internalisation' (SM 97). At the heart of praxis lies the totalizing project which, 'as the subjective surpassing of objectivity towards objectivity, and stretched between the objective conditions of the environment and the objective structures of the field of possibles, represents in itself the moving unity of subjectivity and objectivity, those cardinal determinants of activity' (SM 97).

Materiality is viewed by Sartre as the primary bond between the organism and its environment, but one that can be understood only in conjunction with human praxis. Materiality and praxis are dialectical coordinates, each contiguous to, and dependent on, the other. It is the presence of inorganic matter that makes praxis possible and, in satisfying organic need, praxis finds itself subject to the laws of inorganic matter even as it negates and totalizes it (CDR 82). For Sartre, this circularity of praxis and matter always reveals a double element at work: 'objectification (or man working upon matter) and objectivity (or totalized matter working upon man)' (CDR 284). Hence, a true dialectical understanding of the subject, Sartre states, involves 'the perpetually resolved and perpetually renewed contradiction between man-as-producer and man-as-product' (CDR 158).

(ii) The mutating socius

The way in which we are educated nowadays, we first acquire a second nature: *and we have it when the world calls us ripe, mature, and useful. Some are snake-like enough to shed this skin one day when underneath this cover their first nature has ripened. With most people, the germ has dried up.*

(Nietzsche, *Daybreak* 455)

Throughout his writings, Nietzsche emphasizes the 'heaviness'[13] of our social conditioning and the way in which social and historical forces produce, penetrate, assemble and also delimit the individual. His early work presents the individual as a cipher and singularization of the collective (a 'Universal Singular') bound by an objective spirit which ushers in a horizon of myths that 'completes and unifies a whole cultural movement' (BT 23). The past has layered structures within us, deposited through language, constituted meaning and memory: 'the human carries around the memory of all previous generations' (PTAG 35) unaware that she is voicing '[t]he spiritual activity of millennia laid down in language' (PTAG 31). In his 'middle phase', Nietzsche weighs the formidable forces of social acculturation in the formation of our 'second skin', a socially shaped self that enables one to function in the world moulded by familial influence, education, interpersonal relationships and one's social positioning terms of gender, age, class, ethnicity, ability and occupation (D 455). Although he puts more emphasis on biological and Lamarckian factors in certain passages (BGE 264, BGE 200, D 30, D 540), he often views genetic inheritance as modifiable through socialization. In D 34 he views familial influence more on the level of *modelling* and *behavioural transmission* than genetic inheritance. Moral feelings and dispositions are passed onto children through observation of their parents and siblings (GS 95).[14] Beyond the family, the force of circumstance and the necessity to survive in the social world can lead to the desuetude and loss of one's primary talents and traits: 'Circumstances do not only conceal and reveal . . . they magnify and diminish' (D 326). Learned traits and social roles become habituated traits that come to appear as naturally given. Moreover, people overidentify with their social role and social mores such that 'they become victims of their own good performance': 'they themselves have forgotten how much accidents, moods, and caprice disposed of them when the question of their "vocation" was decided . . . the role has actually *become* character; and art, nature' (GS 356).

Nietzsche links self-consciousness with sociality (D 26), arising paradoxically through the process of socializing or herding individuals in order to make them conscious of herd requirements (GS 354). He demonstrates the force of social interpretation and the power of appearances, the way in which presentation determines the character, the reputation or name of a thing. This is often arbitrary and inaccurate 'foreign to their nature and even to their skin – all this grows from generation unto generation, merely because people believe in it, until it gradually grows to be part of the thing and turns into its very body' (GS 58). The individual is created and directed socially: 'every man comes to know himself almost solely in regard to his powers of defiance and attack' (D 212). The other functions as a mirror and through the other we can learn 'the art of staging and watching ourselves' (GS 78). Nietzsche does not dismiss the possibility of individuals withdrawing from social roles, 'to stand alone and give an account of themselves' (BGE 210), but considers it a rare occurrence. In words that portend Sartre's idea of bad faith and seriality, he concludes that in this conformist social world governed by herd mentality and social mores, '[e]veryone is farthest from himself' (GS 335).

Central to the 'reality of the Other' as constituent of the self is the phenomenon of language since consciousness, according to Nietzsche, develops only under 'the pressure of the need for communication' (GS 354). Positing the subject as a mere effect of linguistic and grammatical codes, he argues that '[p]eople used to believe in "the soul" as they believed in grammar and the grammatical subject' (BGE 54). But the subject derives from the outside born out of intersubjective practices and forged out of collective demands rather than emanating from inside as in the cogito. He thus theorizes a historical, emergent view of the self that has developed as a societal product or herd requirement.[15] The constituent power of the imagination that lies at the heart of the conscious self is, first and foremost, an *intersubjective* thing, a social and historical act of singularity expressed within and through language:

> The development of language and the development of consciousness go hand in hand. . . . Add to this that language serves not only as a bridge between human

beings, but also as a mien, a pressure, a gesture. . . . The human being inventing signs is at the same time the human being who becomes ever more conscious of himself. It was only as a social animal that man acquired consciousness – which he is still in the process of doing, more and more. (GS 354)

Extending his metaphor of diet and incorporation to a social level, Nietzsche shows how the will to power absorbs forces from the outside to make its own powers and values (D 171) influenced and directed by the force of the objective spirit of the culture where it develops to the extent that it can strongly determine (national) character (BT 23, Z 4.12, BGE 47, TI 6.1).

From his earliest writings, Sartre viewed his self as outwardly dispersed in the Other and not inwardly generated by any ego or soul:

in vain we seek the caresses and fondlings of our intimate selves . . . like a child who kisses his own shoulder – for everything is finally outside; everything, even ourselves. Outside, in the world, among others. It is not in some hiding-place that we will discover ourselves; it is on the road, in the town, in the midst of the crowd, a thing among things, a human among humans. (1970: 5)

He writes in his *Notebooks from Youth* in 1924 (when just 19), 'I have looked for my sense of self: I have seen it manifest itself in my relationship to my friends, to nature, to the women I have loved. I have found in myself a collective soul, a group soul, a soul of the earth, a soul of books. But my sense of self, as such, outside of human beings and of things, my real self, unconditioned, I have not found it' (EJ 471–2). In his *War Diaries*, he describes the existential dislocations he would later theorize in *Being and Nothingness* through the experience of 'the look': 'I had the impression', he records, 'at every instant, that my friends were reading my innermost self; that they could see my thoughts forming . . . I could feel their gaze to my very entrails' (WD 271). As mentioned, it was the *syncategorematic* or social nature of the Sartrean self in which we find 'the structure of the Other' (2004: 383) that attracted Deleuze to his early phenomenology. Sartre argues in *Being and Nothingness* that Kant and Husserl misunderstood the determining presence of the Other. In their idealist ontology, the constituting negation is 'an external negation', separating me from the Other 'by a real or ideal space' in which the Other is only an 'indifferent exteriority' who cannot affect me in my being (BN 423). Sartre insists that interpersonal relations are, by contrast, an 'internal negation' which posits the original distinction between the Other and myself as being such that it determines me by means of the Other and determines the Other by means of me (BN 453). When fixed by the gaze of the Other, this decentres my world and causes me to experience 'a new type of intraworldly haemorrhage' (BN 400) in which all the constituents of my world flow towards the Other. Forms of self-experience thus depend internally on the constitutive importance of the Other in which the mediation of the Other throws me 'out of myself' and reveals to me new dimensions of who I am (BN 337).

In the *Critique*, Sartre extends his analysis of the Other from a dyadic level to a collective and institutional level in which he considers larger historical and social forces. At the heart of his conceptual apparatus is the 'practico-inert' which, as Jameson (1991: xxiii) describes, is a 'new concept and a new and durable philosophical term ... a more precise way of designating objects which are not mere things and agencies which are not exactly people either'. For Sartre, the dialectical circularity of praxis and matter gives rise to contingent social arrangements and relations that, once fixed, serve to limit and circumscribe the very freedom from which they originate. These relations form the practico-inert and represent the accretions and the sedimentations of past action in the form of a network of meanings and demands to be interiorized by totalizing individuals and groups, referring to the role of human action in the constitution of an inert social reality that in turn comes to dominate further action. Sartre describes this process in the following way:

> in dissolving the inherited practico-inert, the sovereign and, through him, the society, interiorize the social structures it conditioned; and the transcendence of this interiorization, that is, its practical re-exteriorization, has as its outcome, in a slightly different context, the constitution of another practico-inert that reconditions men, into personal structures and finally praxis itself. (CDR 2:288)

Like Nietzsche's 'memory of all previous generations' (PTAG 31), the practico-inert is the sedimentation of past praxes, 'simply the activity of others in so far as it is sustained and diverted by inorganic inertia' (CDR 556). It forms an 'objective spirit' which acts as 'the medium for the circulation of significations' (CDR 776) and exerts its force as a shifting and dynamic 'quasi-totality' that conditions modes of subjectivity and intersubjectivity (CDR 324). In this way, Sartre asserts that 'a man totalizes his epoch to the precise degree that he is totalized by it' (IF 3:426). Social life is composed of three different 'modalities of action' that combine free praxis with practico-inertia – individual ('constituting') praxis, common ('constituted') praxis and praxis-process (unites praxis with otherwise 'necessary' social relations). Sartre demonstrates how impersonal practices populate the social field as 'full of acts without an author' (SM 163–4) but, at the same time, are dependent upon human praxis for their genesis and perpetuation.

As Sartre's work progresses, the subject becomes increasingly enmeshed in social and historical forces:

> The historical whole determines our powers at any given moment, it prescribes their limits in our field of action and our real future; it conditions our attitude toward the possible and the impossible, the real and the imaginary, what is and what should be, space and time ... it is history which shows some exits and makes others cool their heels before closed doors. (1968: 80)

Self-determination is conceived as a process of reworking and integrating an already sculpted material. Agency is found in this sense only *within* the limits of our given psychological, biological and historical influences and not *in spite* of them. Indeed, what is perhaps most striking about these texts are Sartre's numerous concessions to Freudianism, a theory he had criticized heavily in *Being and Nothingness*. This conversion is also evident in *Search for a Method* where Sartre speaks of psychoanalysis as the 'one privileged mediation' in understanding how a child lives his family relations inside a given society (SM 61). The examination of the individual within the family which psychoanalysis undertakes alone enables us, according to Sartre, 'to study the process by which a child, groping in the dark, is going to attempt to play, without understanding it, the social roles which adults impose on him' (SM 60). In *The Family Idiot*, Sartre deepens this Freudian perspective and sets out to show how, in the case of Flaubert, 'the structures of [his] family are internalized in attitudes and re-externalized in practices by which the child makes himself be what others have made of him' (FI 3). Tracing this back to the very earliest stages of childhood, he describes the way in which the infant Gustave is structured by the loving attention or by the indifference of his mother: 'To begin with, the baby internalizes the maternal rhythms and tasks as the lived qualities of his own body. . . . His own mother, engulfed in the depths of his body, becomes the pathetic structure of his affectivity' (FI 57–8). The lack of love shown by Gustave's mother, who was only a 'mother out of duty', formed a deep frustration that 'penetrates him and becomes within him an impoverishment of his life – an organic misery and a kind of ingratitude at the core of experience' (FI 129–30). Inevitably, Flaubert is pathologically impelled towards art by damage inflicted by his bourgeois upbringing (where the imaginary was prioritized above the real and words above things): '[t]he prehistoric past comes back to the child like Destiny' (FI 55). Sartre shows how the child's 'first project' develops positively or negatively in relation to the mother's affection, either creating a sense of self-worth and value or preventing it. The mother's tenderness in words and touch leaves the child with 'a kind of religious optimism based on the abstract and calm certainty of his own value' (FI 129–30). A person's ability to confront the world around them with hope and optimism has its foundation in early experience for 'in order to love life, to wait each minute for the next with confidence, with hope, one has to have been able to internalize the Other's love as a fundamental affirmation of the self' (FI 392). The values, passions, goals, prides and prejudices that guide adult experience are grounded in experiences initially lived 'in the depth and opaqueness of childhood' (SM 62). Even individual preferences, talents and interests are the result of societal and familial forces that inhibit or develop potentiality: 'the dunce and the prodigy are both monsters, two victims of the family institution and institutionalized education' (IF 3:24). The subject is therefore formed predominantly by the opaque forces of history and family destiny as

> a function of the society in which he lives, of the mode of production, of the technical knowledge available at the time, of the structure of the family, of antecedent circumstances, of the historic *future* which reveals itself as his destiny, but also of the singularity of his own previous history and of his biological characteristics, inherited or acquired. (IF 3:442)

In his psychoanalytic study of Flaubert, Sartre replaced his earlier idea of the 'original project' to understand the total meaning of as person's life with the dialectical process of 'personalization', a long and evolving process of assimilating, integrating and transcending one's past, especially childhood (FI 2:6). In the unfolding of a person's life, key elements from childhood return in new forms and manifestations. Key stages are like 'spirals' which the person revolves around, the deposited meanings of earlier experiences always developing, evolving and forming richer aggregates. For Sartre, dialectical development has a horizontal or a longitudinal dimension of spirals that unfold over time in an individual's life as well as a vertical dimension that intersects with the cultural and historical epoch in which she lives. The self is thus a composite of the individual factors that conditioned the spirals of an individual's life (the experiences of childhood) with the social forces that unfold around them (and how they are internalized by the individual). As 'singular universals', individuals totalize a particular cultural and historical moment by expressing its values, detotalize it by challenging certain aspects of it and retotalize it by producing changes that further impact future time and meaning.[16] Where the first two volumes of *The Family Idiot* establish Flaubert's subjective neurosis on the basis of his family origins, his 'personalization' through friendships, reading, writing and significant childhood experiences, in the third Sartre, shows the 'objective neurosis' of his times, revealing how the two coincide in parallel:

> Thus the diachronic finitude of an individual is particularized by the finitude of the social projects which envelop him and give him – by enlarging or shrinking the field of his possibilities, hence of his choices – his destiny as a finite man and his particular alienations. (IF 3:440)

The 'Objective Spirit' of one's time circulates as a network of institutional discourses, ideologies, received truths, cultural significations and mystifications that present or articulate 'the totality of imperatives imposed upon a person in a particular society' (IF 3:48). The articulated knowledge does not determine what one thinks, but it necessitates that one responds within its given terms like a structural grammar where to refuse those terms only becomes another concretization of (and accession to) the imperative of those same terms.[17] As Sartre describes this: 'The individual interiorizes his social determinations: he interiorizes the relations of production, the family of his childhood, the historical past, the contemporary institutions, and then re-exteriorizes these in acts and options which necessarily refer us back to them' (SM 45).

Through his concepts of 'Objective Spirit' and 'practico-inert', Sartre follows Nietzsche in acknowledging the seminal role of language in constituting subjectivity. His early work defines language as 'being-for-other from the outset' (BN 493) that extends to 'all expressive phenomena' (BN 494), including gestures, body language, mannerisms and dress, but it is in his work after 1945 that he stresses our essential situatedness in language which he now describes as the 'objectification of a class, the reflection of conflicts, latent or declared, and the particular manifestation of alienation' (SM 113). In *Saint Genet*, language is said to become Genet's 'most inward reality and the most rigorous expression of his exile' (SG 276), while, in *What Is Literature?*, writing and words are seen as the essential medium for the expression of freedom in communication with others. By the time of Sartre's later period, self and language have become deeply and irrevocably intertwined:

significations come from man and from his project, but they are inscribed everywhere in things and in the order of things. Everything at every instant is signifying and significations reveal to us men and relations among men across the structures of our society. But these significations appear to us only insofar as we ourselves are signifying. (SM 156)

Sartre's autobiography can be seen in this light as a deliberate attempt on his part to theorize this dialectical interdependence of the subject and language by showing how identity is formed through its expression in words. In Lyotard's (1986: xii) view, Sartre is one of the first to grasp the 'ontological thickness' of words in this text and to appreciate their power over the subject who is 'spoken' by them. Sartre realized that 'words could not be dissipated in the transparency of a signifying intention'. His later texts in particular (that still predate the main wave of poststructuralist texts in the 1960s and 1970s) can be seen in this way to directly anticipate the decentred subject popularized by poststructuralists. For instance, he accepts Lacan's interpretation of the Unconscious as the 'discourse of the Other':

As far as I'm concerned, Lacan has clarified the unconscious as a discourse which separates through language or, if you prefer, as a counterfinality of speech: Verbal structures are organized as a structure of the practico-inert through the act of speaking. These structures express or constitute intentions that determine me without being mine. (1977: 10:97)

In *Search for a Method*, Sartre reiterates the linguistic encoding of the self, showing the ways in which language and culture (as constituent features of the practico-inert) 'are not inside the individual like stamps registered by his nervous system. It is the individual who is inside culture and inside language (SM 113). 'Man is for himself and for others', he asserts, 'a *signifying* being ... a creator of *signs*' (SM 152). He develops this deconstructive impetus further still in the *Critique* writing openly of 'acts without an author' (CDR 152) and 'constructions without a constructor' (CDR 754).

Although Sartre agrees with Lacan and presages poststructuralist accounts in recognizing that 'structure produces behaviour', he warns that we should not pass over 'the reverse side of the dialectic in silence' (1977: 9:86): 'Man can only "be spoken" to the extent that he speaks' (FI 2). Commenting on the rising tide of anti-humanism in an interview in 1966, he observes that the subject as 'a sort of substantial I, or central category, always more or less given ... has been dead for a long time'. What is missing in the anti-humanist discourse, however, is how 'the subject ... constitutes itself from a basis anterior to itself by a continual process of interiorization and re-exteriorization' (1966: 91). Although the self is penetrated and intersected by social and historical forces, it does not lose its existential signature and trace for it maintains its capacity to go beyond immediate circumstances and, whatever its limitations are, to 'make something out of what is made of [it]' (1974a: 35):

Totally conditioned by his class, his salary, the nature of his work, conditioned in his very feelings and thoughts, it is he [the proletarian] who freely gives to the proletariat a future of relentless humiliation or one of conquest and victory, according as he chooses to be resigned or revolutionary. And it's for this choice that he is responsible. (1977: 2:27–8)

(iii) A nascent subjectivity – Nietzschean style and Sartrean authenticity

Our opinion of ourself, however, which we have arrived at by this erroneous path, the so-called ego is thenceforth a fellow worker in the construction of our character and our destiny.

(Nietzsche, *Daybreak* 115)

Against eliminativist accounts that Nietzsche simply denied the self, it is clear that he was obsessed with (his) self from a young age. Between the ages of thirteen and twenty-four, he produced at least six autobiographies, books he wrote in order to discover who he was in a bid to plot his existence as 'the sequent development of an autonomous self' (Blue 2016: 3). In his final phase, he returned to this autobiographical task of discovery and projection in *Ecce Homo*. In notes written in 1867, he assesses the pros and cons of self-portraiture and self-observation: 'it deceives . . . [it] inhibits energy: it separates and breaks apart'; 'Self-observation as a developmental illness'; 'Instinct is best', 'our acts must occur unconsciously', 'know yourself through actions, not by watching'. The only advantage he lists for self-observation is as 'a weapon against outside influences' (KGW 1.4.489). For Nietzsche, one always invents, imagines or performs a self in a process of 'mnemotechnics' (BGE 68) even as one attempts to remember it accurately.

It is wrong to think that Nietzsche excludes creative agency and the formation of a 'revised self' from his picture of the individual, for without these, his critique of moral values and his project of 'self-overcoming' makes little sense. However much our natures are given, we are responsible for cultivating our character, though this, he recognizes, can be perilously difficult: 'Giving style to one's character – a great and rare art' (GS 290). Rejecting idealist notions of free will as a human conceit, Nietzsche envisages us as less the heroic captains of our fate but more like oarsmen, capable of heroic self-movement but also swept along in a sometimes cruel but glorious sea.[18] Although Nietzsche avoids talk of conscious agency regarding intentional action and describes acts in terms of a 'quantum of energy' that discharges itself (GS 360) within processes, such as 'instinct', 'drive' or other biological 'agencies', he argued against the mechanization of such processes. He speaks pretentiously in *Ecce Homo* of his life as a 'destiny', but this includes responsibility for realizing our potential and underscores not only his fatalism but also his existential resolve.[19]

Nietzsche's Schopenhauerian injunction to 'become those we are – human beings who are new, unique, incomparable, who give themselves laws, who create themselves' (GS 335) involves liberating oneself from circumstances that have limited one's view of the world, 'the musty agreeable nooks into which preference and prejudice, youth, origin, the accidents of people and books or even exhaustion from wandering seem to have banished us' (BGE 44). Nietzsche finds the metaphysical concept of character as unchanging or constant as implausible because of the constant becoming of our underlying drives (D 560): 'you are always another person' (GS 307). Transformation is thus a key element of self-overcoming – Zarathustra is transformed into a child (Z P2), in the chorus in *The Birth of Tragedy* one sees 'oneself transformed before one's eyes' (BT 8) and change is the key element in a process of becoming oneself (GS 335). Nietzsche is in tune with the existentialist notion of the self as something one *achieves* or *becomes*. The self arises from an activity, and since this activity can be lesser or better performed, it can be more or less adequately formed. As the self is a *relation* (like the *pour-soi*) and not a substance, it arises through self-relation or reflexivity. This reflexivity develops into more complex structures that are built out of drives both by biological and historical processes. In 'giving style to oneself' (GS 290), Nietzsche proposes a next step to this reflexivity of creating 'one's own, ownmost ideal' (GS 335).

Nietzsche's position on the self, as Richardson (2020: 401) observes, is often 'unsettled or ambiguous' as there is a deep ambiguity as to where exactly to locate the self in the reflexivity he celebrates. This ambiguity plays out in a series of three oppositions that Nietzsche 'the therapist' attempts to resolve and sublimate as a complex balance and interplay of opposing factors.

Self-affirmation versus self-denial

There is a constant tension in Nietzsche between expressions of self-affirmation and self-denial. Although he preached evangelically against asceticism, he was himself prone to its Stoic, self-abnegating logic.[20] For Nietzsche, contempt of self is necessary for self-overcoming since it draws out what is noble in one's self:

> This secret self-ravishment, this artist's cruelty, this delight in imposing a form upon oneself as a hard, recalcitrant suffering . . . [is] the womb of all ideal and imaginative phenomena and perhaps beauty itself. – After all, what would be 'beautiful' if the contradiction had not first become conscious of itself, if the ugly had not first said to itself: I am ugly? (GM 2.18)

Disgust can produce positive effects as when Zarathustra admits that there is 'much filth in the world' but 'nausea itself creates wings and water-divining powers' (Z 3.12.14). Contempt is a vertical emotion that elevates providing distance and height and giving the free spirit a 'bird-like freedom, bird-like exuberance, and a third thing in which curiosity is united with a tender contempt' (HH P4).

This is, of course, offset by the affirmation of self that Nietzsche locates in his positive avatars, the free spirit, Dionysus and the *Übermensch*, but his search for a 'curiosity united with a tender contempt' reveals a sublimating logic at play. This is how Manschot (2021: 88) interprets Nietzsche in attributing to him a project of 'positive asceticism', a perspective situated between Epicureanism and Stoicism that incorporates a form of self-discipline based on 'a powerful "no" and an exuberant "yes"'. Against pure Epicureanism which can be too idyllic, Arcadian or 'typically decadent' (A 30), Nietzschean Epicureanism is 'a reflective, refined way of living hedonistically – not a flat, blind, impulsive hedonism that aimlessly follows impulses but a serene ability to be gladdened by life because nature invites you to be so' (2021: 92). This runs in conjunction with a Nietzschean Stoicism that adopts certain ascetic practices as an art of hardening oneself as a protection from external temptations, incorporating a more rationalistic approach to morality in terms of living in tune with the cosmos.

Multiplicity versus unity

Although Nietzsche was praised by the poststructuralists for multiplying the subject and for shattering the unity of the transcendental ego, his philosophy plots a complex dialectic between multiplicity and unity. In the *Nachlass*, for instance, he argues in several places for the idea of 'the subject as multiplicity': 'The assumption of *one subject* is perhaps not necessary: perhaps it is just as allowable to assume a multiplicity of subjects, whose interplay and struggle lie at the basis of our thinking and of our consciousness generally' (WP 490). He refers to the 'perspectival *illusion*' of unity, even the 'guide of the body', which we think of as a unified organism with a single purpose, 'shows a tremendous *multiplicity*' (WP 518). Elsewhere, by contrast, he conceives of the body as a self-relating unity (a drive unit). It 'does not say I but does I' (Z 1.4), a unified centre of agency beneath consciousness without words:

> If *I* have anything of a unity within me, it certainly doesn't lie in the conscious I and in feeling, willing, thinking, but somewhere else: in the preserving, appropriating, expelling, watchful prudence of my whole organism, of which my conscious I is only a tool. (LN 2)

Although, for Nietzsche, '[a]ll unity is unity *only as organization and interplay*' (WP 561) and '[t]he "I" (which is *not* one with the unitary management of our being!) is indeed only a conceptual synthesis' (WP 371), he highlights the necessity of imposing a 'single taste' (GS 290) if only to provide a simplified version of oneself in public as an instrument of communication (D 182, GS 356). He presents a positive characterization of the philosopher as comprehensive and multi-perspectival, a 'wholeness in multiplicity' (BGE 212), not as a fragmented dissolution of identity.

Nietzsche's principal lesson from his fragmentation of the self is not to give up on unity but to work to make, so far as we can, a single thing out of our multiplicity, albeit the right kind of unity.[21] The philosopher of the future will incorporate all aspects of his drives into a productive unity, a witness 'to one will, one health' (GM P2). Viewing fragmentation as a problem for the individual (Z 2.20) or for a culture (UM 1.1, Z 2.14), he praises Goethe's belief that 'everything is redeemed in the whole' (TI 9.49) for it is true that 'a person *is* in the context of the whole' (TI 6.8). Goethe was Nietzsche's paradigmatic example of greatness since he organized the multiplicity of his drives into a whole or form of 'completeness': 'What he willed, was *totality*; he fought the separation of reason, sensibility, feeling, will . . . he disciplined himself to wholeness, he *created* himself' (TI 9.49) Art is not simply the immersion in a world of illusion since when the artist 'forgets himself' in rapture, it is on the basis of an emergent subjectivity in the process of articulation immersed in worldly practice: 'Every artist knows how far any feeling of letting himself go his most natural state is – the free ordering, placing, disposing, giving form in the moment of "inspiration" – and how strictly and subtly he obeys a thousand laws precisely then' (BGE 188).

Nietzsche thus does not seek complete disintegration – 'I sought a new center' (WP 417) – but a new individuality based on a reflexive understanding of social and historical practices as well as an ability to recognize and sublimate one's drives. As Richardson (2020: 317–22) notes, freedom is an adaptive skill (*dunamis*) which has evolved through biological and social processes and which has three principal stages or phases that map on to Nietzsche's schema of animal–human–superhuman where each involves a certain capacity or skill and a conception of itself as free. Animal freedom can be found in all organisms and amounts to drive unity, whereas human freedom involves a 'second-order standpoint' or self-conception as a 'sovereign individual'. This, in Nietzsche's words, is 'a true consciousness of power and freedom' of the individual as 'the possessor of a long, unbreakable will', without which he is but the slave 'of momentary affect and desire' (GM 2.2). The freedom of the *Übermensch*, 'freedom by genealogy', deploys the *wissenschaften* of psychology and history as indispensable tools for a revaluation of our values, a form of demystification for which 'we need a knowledge of the conditions and circumstances out of which [our values] have grown, under which they have developed and shifted' (GM 6). Exposing controlling forces makes a new freedom possible. With this knowledge at her disposal, the superhuman represents, in Richardson's (2020: 416) words, 'a new kind of self, crystallized more fully out, as a full-fledged thing, in the ontological space between its parts – its drives – and wholes of which it's a part – the group, the society, the species'.

Centrifugal (instinct) versus centripetal (reason)

In understanding Nietzschean freedom, we should not over-rationalize it and foreground Apollo at the expense of Nietzsche's chosen Dionysus, forgetting the central importance of affect and rapture in his aesthetic alongside the more reflexive pursuit of the 'intellectual conscience' and 'genealogical history'. Nietzsche wants to advance, not obviate, freedom by naturalizing (severing it from the metaphysical subject) and historicizing it, conceptualizing freedom genealogically as a particular historical phenomenon or development. Our animal freedom has evolved in conjunction with a conception of how we view ourselves as free subjects, but it is clear that Nietzsche values this freedom and laments the loss of its vital Dionysian energies under Christianity's 'internalization of man' and its suppressing of instinct. There is a double movement in Nietzschean freedom of *in* and *out*, doing and reflecting, of de-egoization (multiplicity) and of reflective unity (the intellectual conscience), but Nietzsche makes clear his preference for instinct over reason. In his attempted sublimation of the two, sensuous activity enjoys the lion's share of his attention, with conscious thought conceived as secondary and derivative: 'So long as life is ascending, happiness equals instinct' (TI 2.11). In *Ecce Homo*, he warns against the conscious adoption of 'great imperatives' as an obstacle to self-overcoming: 'That one becomes, what one is, presupposes that one is furthest from suspecting what one is . . . One must keep the whole surface of consciousness – consciousness *is* a surface – clean of all great imperatives' (EH 2.9). Although Nietzsche's middle phase exudes a more reflexive spirit, he is otherwise fairly dismissive of rational reflection of the conscious *Ich* in relation to the 'greater wisdom' of the bodily *Selbst* and pre-reflective subconscious desires: '*Before* the judgment occurs, *the process of assimilation must already have been done*: thus here too there lies an intellectual activity that doesn't enter consciousness' (WP 532). Nietzsche recognizes another level of thinking than the conscious, an unconscious and wordless thinking which accounts for much of what the self is: 'The entire full deep belief in subject and predicate or in cause and effect is stuck into every judgment' (WP 550) and 'sunk "into the unconscious"' (LN 104). We should, he advises, '*Not wish to see too soon*': 'As long as one lives through an experience, one must surrender to the experience and shut one's eyes instead of becoming an observer immediately. For that would disturb the good digestion of the experience: instead of wisdom one would acquire indigestion' (WS 297). In Humean terms, our ideas are much weaker than our impressions: 'Thoughts are the shadows of our sensations – always darker, emptier, simpler than these' (GS 179). The body remains Nietzsche's prime focus in the project of self-overcoming and rapture is the key element in this. For Nietzsche, rapture is a form of self-exceeding, an affirmative projectivity in which one 'goes out of himself'. Nietzsche's paean to the Dionysian is a call for the intensification of the affects: 'In the Dionysian state . . . the entire affect-system is aroused and heightened', there is an 'inability not to react', one 'enters into every skin, into every affect' (TI 9.10). The ecstatic produces the highest possible intensification of experience in which, in Heidegger's (1987: 1:14) words, 'the entire emotional system is alerted and intensified so that it discharges all its powers of representation, imitation, transfiguration, transmutation, every kind of mimicry and playacting conjointly'. Art is especially important in the production of affects, our 'greatest natural powers' (WP 386), and reminds us of our animal vigour: 'it is . . . a rousing of the animal function through pictures and wishes of intensified life' (WP 802).

Although Heidegger charges Nietzsche with an 'inverted Platonism' in his glorification of affect and sensuality, it is more accurate to view this in terms of a projected sublimation on Nietzsche's part. His goal of 'giving style to oneself' is the sublimation of the drives – 'mastery over the passions, *not* their weakening or extirpation' (WP 933), giving the free play over one's desires 'which knows how to take these magnificent monsters into service' (WP 933). Nobility embodies a naturalness (in a non-Stoic sense) of being attuned to one's drives rather than controlled by reason (TI 2.5). The free spirit experiences passions as a wild nature and the normal state as 'tranquilly beautiful' (D 502), aiming for the 'spiritualization' of passion rather than its extirpation (TI 5.1). Passions can be 'stupid', 'destructive' or 'ugly', Nietzsche warns, like the passions Wagner influenced (WC 6), or they can be ennobling and sublime, such as when passion is spiritualized into love (D 27). In line with his deconstructionist logic, he blends conscious and subconscious together in a shifting and dynamic dialectic. This consists both in a 'losing of oneself' in rapture and a 'gathering of oneself' within the more reflective intellectual conscience. This works on a centrifugal more than centripetal level, though Nietzsche seeks a healthy sublimation of the two in dissolving metaphysical oppositions – '"*being conscious*" is not in any decisive sense the *opposite* of what is instinctive' (BGE 3) – even if language 'will not get over its awkwardness and will continue to talk of opposites where there are only degrees and many subtleties of graduation' (BGE 24). The Dionysian and the Apollonian intersect for Nietzsche and, though he valorizes the 'greater wisdom of the body', he does not efface conscious thought altogether. Genealogical history and the intellectual conscience can, in the form of a therapeutic praxis, enable us some awareness of the complexities of our unconscious motivations where emotions deceive us as to their genuine motivation.[22] It is, for Nietzsche, a false dichotomy, after all, to separate reason and passion: 'the misunderstanding of passion and reason, as if the latter were an independent entity and not rather a system of relations between various passions and desires; and as if every passion did not possess its quantum of reason' (WP 387). He makes it clear that we cannot survive by looking directly at the Dionysian but must create the Apollonian veil of the aesthetic. This is the inner contradiction of 'the terrible joy' of Dionysian experience. The self must be lost in Nature but remain intact to have the experience as a form of comprehension. In gaining itself, the self must somehow lose itself, becoming submerged but not entirely lost in the Dionysian.[23]

In short, Nietzsche's affirmative reconstruction of the 'soul hypothesis' (BGE 12) displays a sublimated Dionysian logic (inversion leading to displacement) that elides firm differences between reason and passion, conscious and subconscious. This relates transversally to the other two ecologies of self. Nietzschean freedom works on two levels in terms of the body and the social.[24] To overcome the problem of fragmentation, Nietzsche finds value in unification, creating a 'new center' (WP 417) that orders the multiple drives and 'spiritualizes' them into a healthy configuration or alliance. But although unification is valuable insofar as it makes a 'one' that is greater by virtue of the many that it unites, it also needs to preserve the difference in that many. Each part should be not just 'one more of the same' but also contribute something its own.[25] As we will see in the next chapter, Nietzsche's idea of 'wholeness in multiplicity' (BGE 212) feeds into his wider ontological thinking, which I characterize (following Deleuze and Guattari) as a 'monistic pluralism'. His '*self out of enveloping other*' addresses the problem of assimilation, that is, the challenge in making a self is to crystallize it out of the social matrix in which it is originally set. Like Sartre's observations on seriality, Nietzsche recognizes that when we merge into the group, we most often lose our individuality: 'Nothing is rarer than a personal action. A class, a rank, a *Volks-Rasse*, an environment, an accident – all express themselves sooner in as work or deed than a person' (WP 886). Cultures and customs make people sick or healthy just like the environment or food can, and when social mores are restrictive, we become 'entwined in an austere shirt of duty' (BGE 226) and unable to express the creative impulses of our will to power.

Sartre's defence of existential authenticity follows many of the same paths of ambiguity and sublimation as Nietzsche's did, conceiving freedom not as an ontological predicate or metaphysical property but as a becoming or activity, something the subject *does* more than has:

> freedom represents something that doesn't exist but that gradually creates itself, something that has always been present in me and that will leave me only when I die. And I think that all other men are like me, but that the degree of awareness and the clarity with which this freedom appears to them varies according to the

circumstances, according to their origins, their development, and their knowledge. (in Beauvoir 1984: 361)

At the heart of Sartrean freedom lies the *imagination* which appears as the correlative of the freedom of human consciousness, and it is this which helps Sartre to link his interest in art to his overriding preoccupation with human liberty and social commitment. However, this carries a certain ambiguity: on the one hand, imagination enables the self to overcome its engulfment in reality and to escape the travails of the practico-inert, being thus vital to any project of change; yet it can also alienate the very liberty it makes possible, leading the individual to deny the real and to value fantasy above reality.[26] Imagination is the dynamic force in the process of becoming, allowing us to see things differently from habituated and encoded significations and to move beyond static conceptions of 'being' or character, but a force that can also lead us away from the world and the reality of our situation.

As early as the 1920s, Sartre eschewed a dry conceptualism with the appeal to 'feelings' and 'affect', following very much a Nietzschean course. His phenomenology is a form of empiricism that accepts and seeks intuitive knowledge.[27] Although there are strong continuities between Sartre's early and later thinking, there are shifts of emphasis, however, and this is evident in the idea of self-transparency which was seen as essential to existential freedom in his early works but fades into the background as his work progresses.[28] In the *Critique*, Sartre modifies the self-transparency of the *pour-soi* of the early phenomenology into a pre-reflective comprehension of 'the translucidity of praxis to itself' (CDR 74), a 'totalizing grasp of any praxis in so far as it is intentionally produced by its author or authors' (CDR 776). Although his emphasis is now much more practical than theoretical and so less prone to charges of Cartesian mystification, he still allows a transparency that is accessible to conscious reflection. This he uses to access the lived experience of individuals in his existential biographies of Baudelaire, Mallarmé and Genet, involving a form of comprehension that is holistic, relating whole to whole which 'it is possible to comprehend ... not to explain it. At most one can make it felt' (1981b: 1685). Although praxis 'is self-explanatory and transparent to itself, it is not necessarily expressible in words' (CDR 93).

Looking back in an interview in the 1970s, Sartre felt that *Being and Nothingness* 'dabbled' in 'apparently non-rational processes' but didn't analyse them deeply enough:

My early work was a rationalist philosophy of consciousness. It was all very well for me to dabble in apparently non-rational processes in the individual, the fact remains that *L'Etre et le néant* is a monument of rationality. But in the end it becomes an irrationalism, because it cannot account rationally for those processes which are 'below' consciousness and which are also rational, but lived as irrational. (1974a: 41)

In his early phenomenology, Sartre suggests that authenticity and freedom of the self can be found in what he terms 'purifying reflection'. Whereas impure reflection is contaminated by the desire to make myself an object, purifying reflection is a form of reflexivity that can reveal to us our freedom and image of ourselves as if we were seeing ourselves in a mirror. This is the 'simple presence' of the consciousness reflecting to the consciousness reflected on a kind of 'reflective "reflection-reflecting"' (BN 219). The nothingness that consciousness is cannot be known to pre-reflective consciousness nor grasped as an object by impure reflection but 'is accessible only to purifying reflection' (BN 279), allowing us to grasp all the reflective distortions and mystifications, often formed in childhood, that keep us mired in patterns of bad faith.

In terms of our emotional life, purifying reflection involves uncovering 'ulterior motives' of various emotions and moral sentiments and their strategic deployment in negotiating the world around us.[29] Emotion, in Sartre's view, is about transforming the world. Psychologists studying emotion 'try to confront their subject as the physicist confronts his' (STE 1), working from the essential principle 'that their enquiries should begin first of all from facts' (STE 2). This commits the error of treating consciousness as a physical thing, falling prey to the bewitchment of the ego and thus losing the experiential quality, magical nature and phenomenological dynamic of emotion. Sartre is aware of the need to explain emotional behaviour as involving both a genuine belief in the projected quality and an awareness of its falsity and allows an escape route from the captivity and magical hold of the emotions only through rare moments of 'pure reflection' where the subject apprehends her feelings as involving some form of self-deception. The aim of this purifying reflection, as of Nietzsche's intellectual conscience, is to discern whether our captivating emotions are 'life-enhancing' or 'life-stultifying'.

An offer from John Huston in 1958 to write a screenplay about Freud led Sartre to a deeper appreciation of the unconscious and a reconsideration of Freud's writings. In his notion of 'lived experience' (*le vécu*) developed after the 1960s, he acknowledged that there are elements of psychological life that remain hidden from rational awareness: 'There is, indeed, an unconscious lodged in the heart of consciousness' (1988: 83). They can be understood metaphorically but not 'named or known' (1974a: 42). The introduction of 'lived experience', as Sartre describes, was a refinement of pre-reflective consciousness in *The Transcendence of the Ego* and *Being and Nothingness* used to enrich the subconscious and situational aspects of consciousness that were not fully elaborated in his early work:

> What I call *le vécu* is precisely the whole of the dialectical process of psychic life, a process that remains opaque to itself for it is a constant totalization, and a totalization *that cannot be conscious of what it is*. (1977: 10:108)

As 'the equivalent of unconscious-conscious', *le vécu* no longer shares the self-transparency of consciousness, Sartre maintains, but involves forgetting, opacity, unselfconsciousness and a lack of self-knowledge. Even his previous sanctuary of infallible self-awareness, the pre-reflective cogito, is now opened up to external influence: 'presence to self for each of us possesses a rudimentary structure of praxis.... At the very level of nonthetic consciousness, intuition is conditioned by individual history' (FI 148).

Sartre's notion of 'lived experience', in Flynn's (2014: 221, 394, 294) view, denotes 'a certain functional equivalent of the unconscious' and reveals the 'ambiguous mixture of equally deep attraction and repulsion' with the idea of the unconscious within his thinking. His growing acknowledgement of a quasi-unconscious dimension to our lived experience enables him 'to appeal to "Freudian" concepts without resorting to the opaque realm of the unconscious'. Striving for a dialectical account of lived experience as an amalgam of 'conscious-unconscious', he presents self-awareness as 'life aware of itself', without implying any thetic knowledge or consciousness. In the case of Flaubert, this involves a comprehension of 'how Flaubert did not know himself and how at the same time he understood himself admirably' (1977a: 127–8). In the transition from consciousness to praxis to lived experience, we witness a certain 'clouding' of the translucency that marked Sartrean consciousness from the outset, as Flynn (2014: 410) notes, but not a *full reversal* of his early opposition to the unconscious. As Sartre described his purpose:

> I want to give the idea of a whole whose surface is completely conscious, while the rest is opaque to this consciousness and, without being part of the unconscious, is hidden from you. . . . For Flaubert, the lived is when he speaks of illuminations that he has and which suddenly leave him in the dark so that he cannot find his way. He is in the dark before and after, but there is a moment in which he has seen or understood something about himself. (1977a: 128–9)

When asked in 1971 if purifying reflection and therefore authenticity were impossible, Sartre responded, '[y]ou know that I never described this kind of reflection, I said that it could exist, but I only showed examples of accessory reflection. And later I discovered that nonaccessory reflection was no different from the accessory and immediate way of looking at things but was the critical work one can do on oneself during one's entire life, through praxis' (1977a: 121–2). Sartre describes this critical undertaking in regard to oneself guided by 'praxis' as a kind of 'katharsis' (BN 219) in which we 'turn back upon ourselves' and catch consciousness on the wing without objectifying the ego (BN 222). Like Nietzschean freedom, Sartrean freedom is lived in the main pre-reflectively gravitating more towards the affective Dionysian than the structuring Apollo but aiming ultimately towards a sublimation of the two.[30] Preontological comprehension is a valuable source of primitive, infallible awareness for Sartre (like Nietzschean instinct) that appropriates features of the Freudian unconscious, unveiling an immediate non-cognitive access to the world. Practices of de-egoization, Sartre attests, must rid consciousness of any ontological mirage of self, creating an 'original temporality' (BN 222) in a unity of experience with the body that, like Nietzschean drives that interpret and engage in reflexivity, has its own form of wisdom that belongs to the structures of 'non-thetic self-consciousness'. Purifying or 'kathartic' praxis is to be found most of all in the activity of *play* which Nietzsche and Sartre place at the centre of their philosophy.

A playful wisdom: *Homo Ludens*

It is strange to take everything so seriously.

(Nietzsche, KGW 4.1.6)

Nietzsche characterizes gay science as a 'saturnalia' of the mind (GS P1). It is a light-hearted or playful pursuit of truth (GS 382) opposed to the scholarly goal of certainty (GS 366). Just as the Roman festival of Saturnalia exhibited the contingency of social mores by temporarily permitting their contravention, Nietzsche opposes the carnivalesque spirit of *The Gay Science* to the view of 'moralities and religions' that attempts to ground our practices in timeless, authoritative norms that are independent of culture and history. For Nietzsche, the world or 'beautiful chaos of existence' (GS 277) that was previously taken to be an organized collection of purposes appears as beautiful precisely because its lacks any intrinsic values or purposes that may constrain human life. Since many aspects of existence are contingent or transformable, affirming them means modifying them so that they please us aesthetically: 'For one thing is needful: that a human being should attain satisfaction with himself – be it through this or that poetry or art' (GS 290). 'Giving style' to oneself is a two-way process of deconstructing and reconstructing. First one has to gain knowledge of everything that is 'lawful and necessary' in nature as well as everything particular and distinctive in oneself. Hitherto, Nietzsche claims, 'all valuations and ideals have been built on *ignorance* of physics or in *contradiction* to it' (GS 335). To construct well requires us to have knowledge of the materials deployed and it is with such knowledge that we can take the second step of giving style by shaping it in accordance with an aesthetic ideal. The end product is less important than the activity or process itself of imagining, sculpting and transforming: 'In the end, when the work is complete, it becomes clear how it was the force of a single taste that ruled and shaped everything great and small – whether the taste was good or bad means less than one may think; it's enough that it was one taste!' (GS 290).

From his earliest to his final writings, Nietzsche placed *play* at the centre of his affirmative thinking. Play is associated directly with creation, a cosmological game in which the events of the universe occur, like with a child who builds and scatters her playthings (BT 24). He consistently associates the child with innocence and creativity (UM 2.1, BGE 57) and urges us to emulate this – in the 'genuine man, a child is hidden: it wants to play' (Z 1.18). The laughter of the child is an antidote to Christian seriousness, where to 'live and laugh gaily' (GS 324) is the mark of one who has learned to live without 'metaphysical consolations' (BT A7).[31] In the passage 'On the Three Metamorphoses', Zarathustra exclaims that the child's play makes possible a transvaluation of values and a passage to a higher level of moral thinking. Where the camel could only follow rules given to it (passive nihilism) and the lion was only capable of saying no (reactive nihilism), the child playfully creates its own values (active nihilism): 'The child is innocence and forgetting, a new beginning, a game, a self-propelled wheel, a first movement, a sacred Yes. For the play of creation, my brothers, a sacred Yes is needed: the spirit now wills *its own will*, and he who had been lost to the world now conquers *his own world*' (Z 1.8). Zarathustra himself, as teacher, is a 'prelude to better players' and it is the *Übermensch* who, as the superior player, masters the play of forces to give meaning to herself and to the earth (Z 3.12.20).

Although the idea of play plays a lesser role in Nietzsche's later work and he offers no explicit typology of it, he draws upon three interrelated concepts of play. First, *Schauspiel* involves theatrical play and performance where we are all actors with an assortment of masks and where the most highly valued responses are joyful laughter and dance (HH 34). This takes the place of 'metaphysical comforts' in compensating for the horrors of existence and becoming. Second, Nietzsche conceives play as *Weltspiel*, the play of the world, and a play of forces in which nothing stands fast (WP 1067). The individual is himself a 'play of forces' and his task as self-legislator is to create the rules for this play: 'It is a measure of the degree of strength of will to what extent one can do without meaning in things, to what extent one can endure to live in a meaningless world because *one organizes a small portion of it oneself*' (WP 585A). Finally, *Kinderspiel* denotes the play of the child, the most important sense of play that animates the other two. This is 'serious play' but a kind of seriousness qualitatively different than that of the metaphysical comforters who preach salvation. The seriousness of the child is a form that recognizes the contingency of the world while fully affirming its own play: '"Play", the useless – as the ideal of him who is overfull of strength, as "childlike", the "childlikeness" of God, *pais paizon*' (WP 797).

In parallel with Nietzsche, the principal aim of Sartre's existentialism is to abandon 'the spirit of seriousness'. The spirit of seriousness, he contends, 'regards values as transcendent givens that are independent of human subjectivity, and it transfers the character of being "desirable" from the ontological structure of things to their simple material constitution' (BN 809). The theme of role playing and dramaturgy forms an important element in Sartre's life, from his childhood days acting out the hero Pardaillan, to his phenomenological analysis of impersonation, to his descriptions of inauthentic role playing in his examples of bad faith in *Being and Nothingness*. In his play *Kean*, he addresses what Diderot referred to as 'the paradox of the actor' – who is the person behind the role? To answer this, he distinguishes the actor from the player. The player returns home after the performance 'whereas the actor plays himself every second of his life . . . He is no longer able to recognize himself, no longer knows who he is. And finally is no one' (1976: 243). He revisits this question through his analysis of bad faith in *Being and Nothingness*. In bad faith, one separates and opposes the two poles of our ontological and existential condition, facticity and transcendence, whereas '[t]hese two aspects of human reality are, in truth – and ought to be – capable of being validly coordinated' (BN 99). Authenticity, by contrast, must be understood in terms that do not collapse or conflate the two poles of facticity and transcendence but take into consideration the interplay and 'valid coordination' between them as a matter of degree. It embodies celebrating the perpetual and continuous play that is at the heart of transcendence and facticity and all decision-making.[32]

In his *War Diaries*, Sartre repeats Schiller's remark that 'man is fully a man only when he plays', asking '[h]ow can we fail to see that play, by its very nature, excludes the very idea of seriousness?' Anticipating his analysis of bad faith, he contrasts play with the seriousness and analytical reason of the engineer: '"game" . . . is the happy metamorphosis of the contingent into the gratuitous . . . why the assumption of oneself is itself a game' (WD 313–14). Play represents, symbolizes and manifests the 'first principle' of human freedom:

> It's not possible to grasp oneself as consciousness without thinking that life is a game. For what is a game, after all, but an activity of which man is the first origin:

> whose principles man himself ordains and which can have consequences only according to the principles ordained. But as soon as man grasps himself as free, and wishes to use his freedom, all his activity is a game: he's its first principle; he escapes the world by his nature; he himself ordains the value and rules of his acts, and agrees to pay up only according to the rules he has himself ordained and defined. Whence the diminished reality of the world and the disappearance of seriousness. (WD 326)

Towards the end of *Being and Nothingness*, Sartre suggests there is a way out of bad faith[33] and the contradictory desire to become God through play, an activity in which we are the 'first origin' and in which we set our own rules (BN 753). In the activity of play

> the function of the action is to manifest and presentify *to itself* the absolute freedom that is the person's very being. This particular type of project, which has freedom for its foundation and its aim, deserves special study. Indeed, it differs radically from all the others in aiming at a radically different type of being. We ought to explain in detail its relations with the project to-be-God that we have taken to be the deep structure of human-reality. But we cannot pursue this study here; in fact it belongs to an *ethics*. (BN 754)

Sartre associates play with a kind of purifying praxis that works against seriousness: 'play, in opposing itself to the spirit of seriousness, seems to be the least possessive attitude' (BN 752). The activity of play leads to psychological instants that 'provide the clearest and most moving image of our freedom' (BN 622), moments of 'a twofold nihilation' (BN 572) where past and present, self and world change together in new directions.

Sartre develops the idea of authenticity further in *Notebooks for an Ethics* where he describes it as 'a conversion from the project to-be-for-itself-in-itself . . . to a project of unveiling and creation' (NE 482). The goal of his freedom ethic is that 'the only meaningful project is that of doing (not that of being) . . . authenticity consists in refusing any quest for being' (NE 475). He reaffirms this just before his death in *Hope Now*: 'I think there is a modality other than the primary modality. . . . It's the ethical modality. And the ethical modality implies . . . that we stop wanting to have being as a goal, we no longer want to be God. . . . We're looking for something else' (HN 59). Hence, Sartrean authenticity is not a serious project but a playful one: 'Sincerity is excluded therefore because it bears on what I am. Authenticity has to do with what I will. Sincerity presents itself as contemplation and an announcement of what I am . . . [A]uthentic reflection is a willing of what I will' (NE 479).

The quintessential expression of play is produced through art: 'the artist is, on the one hand, the man who chooses really to create imaginary objects, but he is also and above all (if we place ourselves in the ontological point of view) the man who chooses to create imaginarily the real world; he is the one for whom perception is already unreal creation' (NE 554).[34] Sartre suggests that it is only through art and play that we are able to overcome the separation of subject (*pour-soi*) and object (*en-soi*), the aesthetic object (e.g. the novel) representing an end product and grand fusion that is 'fully myself and fully beyond myself' (WL 53). Unlike the psychological freedom which torments what it lacks (i.e. being), the freedom of art uplifts: '[t]he recognition of freedom by itself is joy' (WL 52). Art embodies an authentic response to the spirit of seriousness as a form of 'serious play' (akin to Nietzsche's *Kinderspiel*) in which the self is taken up into a transcendent world of immanence and rapture from which a return to normality, mundanity and seriousness can be crushing:

> Aesthetic contemplation is an induced dream and the passage to the real is an authentic awakening. We often speak of the disappointment that accompanies the return to reality. . . . In fact the discomfort is simply that of the sleeper on awakening: a fascinated consciousness, stuck in the imaginary is suddenly freed by the abrupt ending of the play, of the symphony, and suddenly regains contact with existence. Nothing more is needed to provoke the nauseous disgust that characterizes the realizing consciousness. (IM 193)

Although Derrida attributes his concept of 'play' to the influence of Nietzsche, it is also evident, as Sawyer (2015: 34, 38) points out, how Derrida's concept of 'play' operates within Sartre's analysis of the spirit of seriousness and its relationship to bad faith. There is a philosophical bridge between the concepts of play in Derrida and the *pour-soi* in Sartre – play deconstructs structures, and the *pour-soi* deconstructs facticity and the *en-soi*. Derrida's Nietzschean affirmation of play is an existential one, and not merely linguistic. It is akin to the Sartrean affirmation of human freedom. Furthermore, like Sartre, Derrida highlights the way that freedom and anxiety, play and structure, facticity and transcendence are all interrelated and interact with each other. Derrida's analysis of structure finds its parallel in Sartre's view that humanity desires to be God, a desire in which we are both free from external constraints and completely at one with our identity. As Sartre highlights repeatedly in his writings, the unavoidable ambiguity endemic to decision-making is what enables ethical possibilities in the first place, pre-empting Derrida's idea that decision and responsibility are not simply calculations and rule following but are shot through with undecidability. This simultaneously opens up the alterity of the ethical relation with the Other who is not just the Other who looks at me but one which is unforeseeable, beyond my grasp, and hence the result of play.

The posthuman self: A Nietzschean/Sartrean hybrid

In deconstructing the self, the French poststructuralists acknowledged their debt to Nietzsche who was the first philosopher to 'dissolve man' (Foucault 1973: 342). The problematic Nietzsche has left us, in Foucault's (1977: 42) view, is to plot '[t]he breakdown of philosophical subjectivity and its dispersion in a language that dispossesses it while multiplying it within a space created by its absence'. In his 'ethical' phase, Foucault (1983: 64) also credits Sartre as an influence on his own reconstructive 'technologies of self', sharing his (and Nietzsche's) idea that self-overcoming and the practices of freedom that support it should be conceived in aesthetic terms. Foucault's later work can be viewed as a form of 'camouflaged existentialism' (Flynn 2004) in which, as Sutton Morris (1997: 544) points out, 'Foucault not only shares with the early Sartre the view that there is no fixed original essence of an individual, but also shares the view that instead of seeking to discover a nonexistent, original, true self, one might engage in actively forming the self as a work of art'.

Like Nietzsche and Sartre, Foucault conceives of striving 'to give your existence the most beautiful form possible' (1984: 353) and 'creat[ing] ourselves as a work of art' (1984: 321) on the model of the sublimation of Dionysian or centrifugal acts of de-egoization that take us 'outside the self' conjoined with Apollonian reflective practices of self-fashioning that act as 'a weapon against outside influences' (KGW 1.4.489).[35] Whereas, for example, Foucault positions thought in his early 'archaeological phase' as constrained by linguistic conditions to the extent that we cannot even render an account of the limits a particular thought is constrained in, he suggests later that the practices of philosophy in reflection are themselves ways to free our thoughts: 'Thought is a freedom in relation to what one does, the motion by which one detaches oneself from it, establishes it as an object, and reflects on it as a problem' (1984: 388). In a later interview, he reinstates philosophy as a form of Sartrean 'purifying reflection', arguing that the role of the philosopher is 'to make oneself permanently capable of detaching oneself from oneself [while] altering one's thought and that of others' (1988: 263–4). Centrifugally, Foucault also follows the path of Nietzschean instinct and Sartrean pre-reflectivity in which a Nietzschean ideal of becoming-multiple is attained through what he calls 'transgressive practice' (1984: 48). This involves particular practices (e.g. sexual, aesthetic) that deliver us to the limit of our (normalized) identities without attempting to live securely beyond it. According to Foucault (1991: 31), we should look for 'limit experiences' within experimental practices which tear the subject apart from itself in an attempt to 'reach the point of life which lies as close as possible to the impossibility of living'. He points to the Dionysian realm as a potential repository for somatic freedom in which we can escape the psychological training of the body and effect 'the destruction of the subject as pseudo-sovereign' (1977: 222).

In his later 'ethical' period, Foucault gives particular primacy to aesthetic forms of self-cultivation as a means of 'refusing the type of individuality that has been imposed on us for several centuries' (1984: 308). Since there is no essential subject, no self grounded in biological or ontological necessity, 'there is only one practical consequence: we have to create ourselves as a work of art' (1984: 321). It is through art that the imagination is nurtured in a realm of possibility, difference, sense experience and renewal. It is only when we begin to give ourselves style through self-reflective forms of aesthetic and experimental practice that we are able to withstand the impact of historical, objectifying forces. If we see ourselves as a 'work of art', continually being made and unmade, we become constant activists for whom it is necessary to prevent enabling limits from congealing into constraining limitations and to generate new limits and new forms of subjectivity which constitute selves. Transgressive and aesthetic practice is vital for the creation of new forms of subjectivity, Foucault (1977: 190–1) argues, because it shakes us out of our usual categories, enabling us to think in different ways by unifying and differentiating experience in unusual ways. This makes possible a form of self-understanding through self-expression that takes us beyond the 'given' of our historical, social and linguistic conditioning.

There are also striking similarities, as several scholars have noted,[36] between Sartre's idea of a non-identical, relational subject and Derrida's theory of *différance*. Like the Derridean sign, Sartrean consciousness differs from itself through a temporal movement of 'deferral' whereby the present can be what it is only through the mediation of the future. This gives the clue to Sartre's famous description of consciousness as 'being what it is not and not being what it is' (BN 27). Since all consciousness is intentional (consciousness *of* something), it is nothing other than this activity of directing awareness towards an object. This awareness comes about by consciousness transcending the immediate appearance of the object and projecting towards the 'horizon' of other possible appearances of the object, the sum of which define it and which constitute the future consciousnesses of that object. The present of consciousness (awareness of an object) is thus defined on the basis of a future and irreal totality of consciousness which is *not yet*:

> The nature of consciousness implies ... that it project itself in front of itself in the future; one can understand what it is only through what it will be, it is determined in its actual being by its own possibilities. (1977: 1:96)

And yet, Sartre maintains, consciousness is unable to fix itself to this future totality which defines it since consciousness cannot be anything other than consciousness *of* its object. The totality that consciousness seeks is something *irréalisable*: it will never find it since such a totality would involve the impossible synthesis of *pour-soi* and *en-soi*, openness and completion, transcendence and determinacy. Consequently, consciousness both *is* and *is not* the totality of future consciousnesses through which it defines itself and suffers the absence of that totality as a 'lack' of its own being (BN 207). This lack must necessarily remain unsatisfied since this totality could only become closed and completed if consciousness ceased to be intentional and transcendent. Sartre argues as such that human-reality is perpetually haunted by a totality which it is without being able to be it, precisely because it cannot attain the in-itself (closure, identity) without losing itself as for-itself. The Sartrean subject is constituted by a temporal deferral which means that it 'has its being outside, in front of and behind itself' (BN 184), always caught between a future which is not yet and a 'never present past' or 'original contingency' (BN 202) that coincides with its facticity and thrownness. The temporality of consciousness means, for Sartre, that the subject is non-identical and non-contemporaneous with its present, a relation to self-grounded in self-difference and self-otherness that is inadequate to itself.

Viewed in this light, Sartrean consciousness can be seen to fit closely Derrida's description in *Of Grammatology* of 'a self presence that has never been given but only dreamed of and always split, incapable of appearing to itself except as its own disappearance' (1976: 112). In the same way that Sartrean consciousness is separated from itself by a temporal deferral, in Derrida's analysis of signification 'an interval must separate the present from what it is not in order for the present to be itself' and hence 'this interval that constitutes [the present] as present must ... divide the present in and of itself' (1982: 13). Derrida draws the conclusion from Saussure's linguistics that, as a 'duality-in-unity' of a material signifier and a conceptual signified, the linguistic sign 'is never present in itself' since it is 'essentially inscribed in a chain or system within which it refers to . . . other concepts by the systematic play of differences' (1982: 140). Each term is caught up in 'infinite implication, the indefinite referral of signifier to signifier' in which each signified concept 'always signifies again' (1978: 25). In this way, a concept never is what it is since it is constituted by its difference with other concepts so that what it lacks is constitutive of what it is – it is what it is not (BN 27).

Thus, rather than being an obvious or natural target for Derrida's critique of a 'metaphysics of presence', Sartre's early theory of consciousness can be seen to prefigure it in several respects. Although denounced by Derrida in *Glas* as 'the onto-phenomenologist of freedom' (1986: 28) who is oblivious to the interminability and undecidability of signification, Sartre fulfils in *Being and Nothingness* and elsewhere the Derridean project of deconstructing the self-identical and self-present metaphysical subject. His ethical theory of authenticity, like Derrida's theory of *différance*, valorizes an acceptance of 'distance from self', openness, incompletion and contingency, pointing towards an ideal of a subject which chooses not to *reappropriate* itself, but to flee itself, not to coincide with itself, but to be always at a distance from itself. In common with poststructuralist deconstructions of the subject, Sartre takes the 'I' to be no more than a synthetic construct of consciousness which is impermanent and fluid: 'the intuition of the Ego is a perpetually deceptive mirage' (TE 69). He argues against the idea of an authentic or 'deep' self which is pregiven or original, insisting instead that the *pour-soi* is fundamentally a *relation* (BN 181) or a 'perpetual deferring'. In his later work, such as *Words* and *The Family Idiot*, this is re-emphasized once more where his own and Flaubert's self is theorized throughout as an imaginary construct rather than an original source.

Deleuze's and Guattari's posthumanist self as 'folded interiority' can also be viewed as a Nietzschean–Sartrean composite. In their quest to escape the 'rigid segmentary lines' that construct fixed and normalized identities, they advocate 'lines of flight' as full deterritorializing movements away from molar identity where 'cracks' grow into 'ruptures' and the subject is 'shattered' in a process of *becoming-multiple*. Lines of flight constitute full expressions of subjectivity and take place on the plane of creativity, desire, possibility, experiment, death and destruction (1987: 26–38). The Nietzschean affirmation of becoming-multiple is reflected in their normative ideal of the Schizophrenic (in *Anti-Oedipus*) and of the Nomad (in *A Thousand Plateaus*). The 'Schizo-Subject' embodies their conception of the subject as multiple, decentred and fragmented since she does not see her behaviour as belonging to a conscious, encompassing 'I', often referring to herself in the third person and refusing to speak the word 'I'. Their ideal of the Nomad is similarly one who is never static, enduring or fixed but who must 'keep moving, even in place, never stop moving' (1987: 159). In *What Is Philosophy?*, they reiterate this idea of multiplicity and becoming, calling for the creation of forms of de-subjectification that involve the exploration of different forms of consciousness beyond the confines of molar normality. They celebrate the death of the majoritarian individual subject by invoking experimental modes of consciousness which are excluded from normalizing reason, such as those esoteric and

Dionysian practices which involve rapture, excess and intoxication (1994: 44). These are full-fledged lines of flight that combine 'travel, hallucination, madness, the Indians, perceptive and mental experimentation, the shifting of frontiers, the rhizome' (1987: 520).[37]

In *Les Trois Ecologies*, Guattari (2000: 59) calls for the 'praxic opening-out' of the three ecologies of body, socius and psychology in the form of radical 'eco-art' that subsumes all existing ways of domesticating existential territories and is concerned with intimate modes of being and the expansion of alternative experiences 'centred around a respect for singularity, and through the continuous production of an autonomizing subjectivity that can articulate itself appropriately in relation to the rest of society'. 'Mental ecosophy', as Guattari terms it, will lead us to reinvent the relation of the subject 'to the body, to phantasm, to the passage of time, to the "mysteries" of life and death'. Interiority will establish itself at the crossroads of multiple components, each relatively autonomous in relation to the other, and, 'if need be, in open conflict', configuring a self that is 'intersectional' and 'polyvocal', operating on a plane incorporating the real 'territorialized existential territories' and the real that is virtual 'deterritorialized incorporeal universes' (2000: 35, 36). From this, there will emerge a collective and individual subjectivity that 'completely exceeds the limits of individualization, stagnation, identificatory closure' and that inhabits 'new aesthetic worlds' as well as 'a new "pre-personal" understanding of time, of the body, of sexuality' (2000: 68).

Anticipating Guattari's three existential territories, Nietzsche and Sartre theorize a dynamic trivalent model of the self in which *body*, *socius* and *psyche* confront us as 'not given, as an in-itself, closed in on itself, but instead as a for-itself that is precarious, finite, finalized, singular, singularized, capable of bifurcating into stratified and deathly repetitions or of opening up processually from a praxis that enables it to be "habitable" by a human project' (2000: 53). Furthermore, their quest for 'new versions of the soul hypothesis' promotes the depersonalization of subjectivity such that the subject identifies with the multiplicity while at the same time inventing and experimenting with re-singularizing subjectifications. In the next two chapters, we will see in ontological and ethical terms how Nietzsche and Sartre theorize their revised deconstructed self in concrete relation to the Other and the natural world.

4

Smooth ontology

a play of energies and waves of energy at the same time one and many, increasing here and at the same time decreasing there; a sea of energies flowing and rushing together, eternally moving, eternally flooding back ... with an ebb and a flood of its forms; out of the simplest form striving towards the most complex, out of the stillest, most rigid, coldest form towards the hottest, most turbulent.

(Nietzsche, *The Will to Power* 1067)

In this chapter, I look at the ontologies of Nietzsche and Sartre and examine them in the light of the distinction made by Deleuze and Guattari (1987) between 'smooth' and 'striated' space. In Nietzsche's case, this involves reconstructing his ontological scheme as outlined primarily in his *Nachlass* and, in Sartre's, through a close examination of his two main philosophical treatises, *Being and Nothingness* and the *Critique*. I argue that Nietzsche and Sartre present a *dialectical* and *relational* ontology of forces, best described as a 'pluralistic monism', that surpasses the disjunctive approaches of methodological individualism (atomism) and holism in the search of a ternary or supplementary mode of comprehension.

Smooth and striated

In *A Thousand Plateaus*, Deleuze and Guattari distinguish between (postmodern) smooth space and (modern) striated space: 'in striated space, one closes off a surface and "allocates" it according to determinate intervals, assigned breaks; in the smooth, one distributes oneself in an open space' (1987: 481). Following the 'grand compromise' of Spinoza, they argue that the immanence of nature demonstrates both the unity of things (univocity of being) and their endless differentiation (multiplicity of beings):

> A single and same voice for the whole thousand-voiced multiple, a single and same Ocean for all the drops, a single clamour of Being for all beings. (1994: 36)

This they encapsulate in their 'magic formula' of 'PLURALISM = MONISM' (1987: 20). Deleuze, in particular, criticizes the 'logic of identity' that lies at the heart of Hegelian rationalism in which what is deemed other to reason (desire, emotion, the body, the mad, the feminine) is subsumed under a reconciliation of differences within a totality that leads to totalitarian thinking. Against this, Deleuze finds in Nietzsche a 'logic of difference' that affirms difference in itself rather than subordinating differences to a logic of identity. Nietzsche's will to power represents a monistic 'differential of forces' from the perspective of a 'pluralist or polyvalent monism' in which *becoming-Übermensch* denotes an active process of assembling rather than the hypostatization of an endpoint to be assembled.[1] Despite the clear antipathy he shows in *Nietzsche and Philosophy* to the Hegelian 'logic of identity', Deleuze does not seek simply to refute all versions of dialectical thinking but refers to the long history of the *distortion* of the dialectic (1994: 268).[2] Deleuze and Guattari, as Schrift (1995: 257) notes, follow Nietzsche in their willingness to utilize binary concepts *strategically*, seeking to multiply rather than dissolve dualistic concepts in a non-oppositional way. Deleuze replaces the old dualisms of his early work (active/reactive, master/slave) with a whole new series of dualisms (rhizome/tree, nomadic/sedentary, molar/molecular) but these are not used in a straightforward way. Instead, they are woven into complex webs of interconnections. The rhizome, for instance, is heterogeneous, a multiplicity or plateau on whose surface intensities are in a state of constant variation. In their tactic of multiplying difference, each dualism is always broken down into a complex series of overlapping terms that are made to do new work. Rhizomatic thought, proposed by Deleuze and Guattari (1987: 220), is a kind of thought that proceeds by connections, bringing things together in proximity through deterritorialized flows that boost one another, accelerate their shared escape and augment their quanta. Dualistic thought, by contrast, involves 'the conjugation of these same flows, indicates their relative stoppage, like a point of accumulation that plugs or seals the lines of flight, performs a general reterritorialization, and brings the flows under the dominance of a single flow capable of overcoding them'. As we will see, the tactic of exploding dualisms rhizomatically through their strategic deployment in order to 'make them work' in proper dialectical fashion is one that forms the core of Nietzsche's and Sartre's philosophy.

The will to power: Nietzsche's relational ontology

every centre of force adopts a perspective toward the entire remainder
(Nietzsche, *The Will to Power* 567)

Nietzsche traces his ontological conception of the will to power back to Heraclitean philosophy. In his analysis of becoming, he frequently alludes to Heraclitus' example of the changing river (Z 2.12), opposing the dynamic process of becoming to the static metaphysical idea of being that presents things and values as unchanging. Following Heraclitus, he posits cosmic history as a collection of processes that interact to produce temporary forms that then dissolve only to reconfigure and form new ones (UM 2.9). Within the dynamic of becoming, all unities are multiplicities that are in a state of constant change and development in relation to themselves and to others. The cosmos is, for Heraclitus, a constant process of becoming, governed by a law of cyclical creation and destruction, a law that constitutes the cosmos as a process of eternal and interconnected creation and destruction that *just is*. Nietzsche connects this cosmology with children's play (*Kinderspiel*), a theme he further links to the artistic drive to creation. The significance of both the child and the artist, for Nietzsche, is that they engage in processes of creation and destruction that are removed from *moralism* and from *teleology*. In his lecture on Heraclitus in *The Pre-Platonic Philosophers*, he writes:

> only in the play of the child (or that of the artist) does there exist a Becoming and Passing Away without any moralistic calculations. [Heraclitus] conceives of *the play of children* as that of spontaneous human beings: here is innocence and yet coming into being and destruction. We find here a purely aesthetic view of the world. We must exclude even more any moralistic tendencies to think teleologically here. (PP 70)

The tragic wisdom of Heraclitus, in Nietzsche's view, resides in his embrace of *non-oppositional thought*. While dualistic thought arose with Socrates and Plato, the thought which reigned in the tragic age of the Greeks, that of the pre-Platonic philosophers, was one which thought in terms of *co-compositional forces*. Tragic thought involves a kind of duality and opposition, but one which recognizes in the opposite of a thing the condition for that thing, and thus sees opposite tendencies as necessary. Tragic wisdom presents the world as *justified* in its dualistic and contrary forces, which involve both creation and destruction, and that it is justified precisely as an aesthetic phenomenon. Nietzsche credits Heraclitus with repudiating both the appearance-reality distinction that emerged with Anaximander and the notion of being. The nature of reality is nothing other than its effects (PTAG 5). He claims that science will dispense of the thing in itself which is empty of significance and 'worthy of Homeric laughter' (HH 16). Things are fabricated beings, 'unities which do not exist' and instead of thinking a thing is a material substratum, the 'whole procedure of science has pursued the task of resolving everything thing-like (material) in motions' (HH 19). *Metaphysical* philosophy strictly divides opposites, demanding separability of them, and claiming that phenomena emerge from things in themselves, 'assuming for the more highly valued thing a miraculous source in the very kernel and being of the "thing in itself"' (HH 1). Unlike metaphysical philosophy, Nietzsche's historical philosophy follows Heraclitean principles in denying 'the duality of totally diverse worlds' (PTAG 5) and discovering 'that there are no opposites' (HH 1) but only differences of degree: 'There are no opposites: only from those of logic do we derive the concept of the opposite – and from them falsely transfer it to things' (WP 552). For Nietzsche, absolute reality and being-in-itself are contradictions: 'In a world of becoming, "reality" is always only a simplification for practical ends, or a deception through the coarseness of organs, or a variation in the tempo of becoming' (WP 580). Even the laws of logic, identity and contradiction are not 'forms of knowledge at all! They are regulative articles of belief' (WP 530).

Another way that Nietzsche denies opposite values is by insisting that values are never instantiated purely or completely.[3] This involves seeing the 'reverse side' of good and bad things (WP 1015) since opposite values are mixed together in things bivalently. No person is purely good or bad, and this also applies to experiences and actions that often contain a mixture of motives and a psychic economy of competing drives that motivate them. Opposite values are *comparative* and *scalar* rather than intrinsic to things and bifurcated. Good contains bad and it is incoherence to think one could exist without the other since creating includes destroying (Z 2.12) and affirming means negating: 'negating and destroying are conditions of Yes-saying' (EH 4.4). Nietzsche argues that the law of non-contradiction might have limited application in the field of logic but does not apply to value or to truth in general where opposites evolve out of prior evaluations, such as evil out of the noble concept of good and truth out of error. There is a key sense in which he doesn't deny 'opposites' but indeed affirms and promotes them as real and as valuable if considered non-metaphysically. As with Deleuze and Guattari, certain opposites play a strategic role in Nietzsche's analysis. Apollonian and Dionysian are described as opposites (BT 1–2) but he conceives the relationship of them as co-compositional since both of these artistic drives are required to unfold their energies in reciprocal proportion. They are 'necessarily interdependent' and 'Apollo could not live without Dionysus' (BT 4). He describes himself and Dionysus as opposite to Christ and Christianity (EH 4.9), and he praises new philosophers as the stimuli for 'opposite values' (BGE 203). Denouncing the 'hemiplegia' of the 'good human' who separates off one side of a dualism and insists on it alone, teaching 'that it is a higher thing to be efficient on only one side' (WP 351), he proclaims that the greatest are those like Zarathustra who combine opposites (EH 3Z6).

In terms of Nietzsche's wider ontology, Richardson (2020: 356) notes how Nietzsche's simultaneous decrying and celebration of oppositional thinking opens up a 'great tension' or 'apparent contradiction' in his thinking. On the one hand, he is 'a vigorous opponent of dualism'[4] but he is 'repeatedly pulled back from this monism to dualist views at seeming odds with it'. Pulled in both directions, it is part of his philosophical method to give free play to these countervailing impulses and not subject them to a finished theory or consummation, keeping them in dialectical tension and avoiding metaphysical closure. Nietzsche's sine qua non for creative power is 'the vehement struggle' of 'deep feelings with their opposites' into a sublimation of a harmonious whole (KSW 9.6.207). Although one must be 'rich in oppositions' (TI 5.3), this is conceived in a strategic way as an 'inverse ideal' (BGE 56) to metaphysics in generating a productive 'scalar logic' of difference, 'containment' and 'gradation' (Richardson 2020: 372).

Relationality

For Nietzsche, events are not constituted by items but by the interaction *of* things. To view things discretely in isolation from their relations to other things is a philosophical error. As we saw with the self in Chapter 3, for example, individual consciousness is the product of linguistic forces and not their origin (GS 354). This relationality is developed further in Nietzsche's broader ontology in which he defines a thing as 'the sum of its effects, united by a concept, an image' (WP 551). If one removes other things, an object has no properties therefore 'there is no things without other things' and no 'things-in-themselves' (WP 557). Since independently existing things are inventions 'owing to the requirements of logic' (WP 558), if everything we projected onto the world in order to make it intelligible were eliminated, 'no things remain but only dynamic quanta, in a relation of tension to all other dynamic quanta: their essence lies in their relation to all other quanta, in their "effect" upon the same' (WP 635). The world is therefore 'essentially a world of relationships' (WP 568).

In his unpublished lectures from the early 1870s, Nietzsche draws upon the work of von Helmholtz to argue that the natural sciences of his day confirm the Heraclitean precept that everything is in flux: 'nowhere does an absolute persistence exist, because we always come in the final analysis to forces' (PP 60). In the 1880s, he endorses a relational ontology of force by appealing to the authority of the mathematician and physicist Roger Boscovich. In a letter to Köselitz (1882), Nietzsche writes, '[s]ince him, there is no longer any matter – except as a popular simplification. He has thought the atomistic theory through to its end. Gravity is most certainly not a "property of matter", simply because there is no matter. Gravity is, just like *vis inertiae*, certainly an appearance of force (simply because there is nothing else other than force!)' (KSB 6.213).

Nietzsche's relational ontology of forces based on the precept that the world is will to power 'and nothing else besides' (WP 1067) positions him, according to Meyer (2018: 370, 375–6), as 'a forerunner to Ontic Structural Realism' because he inflates the ontological priority of structure and relations and takes these structures to be real and discernible by science. Responding to criticisms that Nietzsche's relationism and his elimination of individual 'things in themselves' is incoherent for it violates the claim that relations require *relata* and leads to a circularity of regress in defining what a thing is, Meyer argues that Nietzsche agrees that a relational ontology is conceptually incoherent. He acknowledges that Heraclitus' unity of opposites doctrine violates Aristotle's principle of the law of non-contradiction (PTAG 5), a reason why Parmenides rejects Heraclitus' relational ontology (PTAG 10). However, 'Parmenides' prejudice' assumes that there is a neat conformity between how we think the world to be and how it actually is, positing an isomorphism between thinking and being, and falling prey to the vanities of anthropomorphism by forcing us to believe the little 'it' of logicians (BGE 17). For Meyer (2018: 378), although some might try to avoid this Nietzschean scepticism by rethinking our comprehension of relations and *relata*, they are fighting against what Nietzsche calls a 'logical anthropomorphism' (KSW 7.19) that cognitively predisposes us to think that relations need independently existing relata endowed with some intrinsic properties.

While Meyer is right to highlight the importance of relationality in Nietzsche's ontology and his scepticism concerning our 'logical anthropomorphism', Nietzsche is best understood as keeping open the tension between *relata* and relations and resisting metaphysical closure. The subject is a relational entity 'designated by the effect it produces and that which it resists' (WP 634). Will to power is productive, not something the subject 'has', but the productive force of interpretation of which the delimited subject is an effect. As Schrift (1996: 341) argues, Nietzsche sought to keep the will to power multiple so that it might appear in multiple forms, 'at once producer and product, a monism and a pluralism'. In his attempt to think difference differently, Nietzsche's recasting was not reductive, nor should it be seen as privileging exclusively one analytic framework. Instead, 'the monistic framework of will to power supports Nietzsche's pluralist response to the privileging of oppositional thinking' (1996: 345). In Nietzsche's philosophy of 'originary multiplicity', things are derivative from a complex and rich multiplicity of forces:

> All unity is only as *organization and interplay* unity: not
> otherwise than how a human community is a unity: so,
> *opposite* of atomistic anarchy; therewith a *complex of rule*, which
> *signifies* One, but *is* not one. (KSW 12.2.104)

For 'the human being as multiplicity', physiology 'gives only an imitation of an astounding intercourse among this multiplicity and subordination and integration of parts into a whole. But it would be false to conclude from a state the necessity of an absolute monarch (the unity of the subject)' (KSW 11.27.276). In this way, Nietzsche's concept of unity is equidistant from an originary unity on one side and from atomistic chaos on the other. Self-organization is an emergent play among constituents, all seeking out the resistance of antagonists in order to overpower (subordinate and integrate, or functionalize) them.[5] Nietzsche's idea of the subject as *emergent* represents a striving to think post-metaphysically. By conceiving of multiplicities and unities in conjunction as evolving and ephemeral but not as mutually exclusive, his position aligns closely with Sartre and with philosophical posthumanism.[6] In a tactic of sublimation, the atom/subject is inverted by a logic of relationality and then displaced in a new configuration where it is recast as emergent, generated by certain confluences of the creative will to power into a unity or 'detotalized totality'. For Nietzsche, life is a combination of forces that seeks assimilation, incorporation and expansion, 'the feeling of increased power' (BGE 230). The will to power is in this sense an assemblage both individually (in terms of inner drives) and collectively (in terms of its relation to other things), a variable and relational multiplicity that is kept together 'by an "organization" understood in the sense of a verb and not a noun since it is in continual movement, always reorganizing' (Aydin 2007: 30). Following Plank (1998: 395, 14), we may conceive this as a process of 'aleatory and recurrent cyclical patterns of the Will to Power as non-teleologically locally maximized centers of the configurations of energy discharges', a series of recombinative particles/energy centres/entities that are immanent in the system, not transcendent to it. In Nietzsche's ontology of 'dissipative systems' (1998: 433) there is no need for hidden variables or metaphysical postulations since reality is simply a process of combination, recombination, alignment and dissonance between energy centres.

Sartre's dialectic with holes: A ternary logic

Despite the fact that Sartre was an adherent of the Cartesian method of systematic doubt, we should definitely not stray too far down the Cartesian path in interpreting him, for, as Mary Warnock warned with good reason more than thirty years ago, '[t]here is no more determining factor in [his] thought than the rejection of Cartesian dualism' (1989: 15).⁷ In Sartre's own view (1981a), his method became consciously and fully dialectical only after *Being and Nothingness* but Sartre was a dialectician from his early years, evident in both his ontology and his social philosophy.⁸ His philosophical trajectory is most fruitfully read in this light as a thesis of 'enrichment within continuity'. This accords with Sartre's thoughts expressed in an interview just before his death that 'I myself think that my contradictions mattered little, that despite everything I have always remained on a continuous line' (1980: 92).

Despite Sartre's own preference for the *Critique*, *Being and Nothingness* is still the most discussed and celebrated of his two grand philosophical treatises but also the most divisive among Sartrean scholars. Many see it as a thoroughly Cartesian tract wrapped in dualistic thinking (McCann 2011; Solomon 1988; Grene 1993), but this view is now increasingly in decline as a 'vulgarization' superseded by a more nuanced perspective that follows Warnock's anti-dualist reading in opening up new pathways of understanding his philosophy. As Gardner felicitously describes the situation:

> All great structures of thought in the history of philosophy achieve a kind of pictorial, visionary force, and consequently allow themselves to be reduced for purposes of rapid reference to a cluster of images and bold slogans. *B[eing] & N[othingness]* is no exception, and in the course of its reception and the conversion of existentialism into a diffuse cultural movement Sartre's early philosophy has been subjected to exceptional simplification, not to say vulgarization. (2009a: 36)

Part of the difficulty in understanding *Being and Nothingness* is the text itself, which has been variously described down the years as 'a thankless task', 'endlessly repetitive', 'full of ugly neologisms', 'in places quite unintelligible' (Olafson 1958: 276), as well as 'a rambling work', 'demonstrably in need of editing' and 'often inconsistent' (Richmond 2013: 101). It is perhaps due to these factors that it has been so variously interpreted since, as Richmond (2013: 101) states, 'a question remains as to whether some cogent position . . . can be extracted from what Sartre says.' Nonetheless, the time is propitious for a radical revaluation of Sartre's ontology and, as Heldt (2020: vii) suggests, to give his 'early ontological idiom . . . a good shake'. This means, for example, foregrounding neglected terms such as 'multiplicity', 'virtuality', 'actuality', 'Gestaltic', 'egological', 'complicity', 'totalization' and '(non-)thetic'. These are conceptions that have traditionally been dwarfed in the literature by the usual classical terminology associated with *Being and Nothingness* (e.g. *pour-soi/en-soi*, facticity/transcendence) often bent by interpreters into a Cartesian shape. Sarah Richmond's recent new translation of this seminal text into English in 2018 can be viewed in part as a response to this reinterpretation process, clearing up some of the locutionary, terminological and conceptual misunderstandings that might have arisen from Hazel Barnes' 1956 translation. It is symbolic of a fresh attempt among many Sartre scholars to view this work with different eyes, to rethink some of its central categories and distinctions, to amend hasty and simplified conclusions and to reposition it in the trajectory and development of Sartre's thinking.⁹

It is ironic and 'a curious twist of fate', as Ally (2017: 82–4) remarks, that Sartre was squarely accused of dualism as he was 'unequivocal on the matter of his monism', a philosophy in which 'world and body and consciousness are ontologically *one*'.[10] Near the beginning of *Being and Nothingness*, Sartre insists that we must 'explain how these two regions of being can be placed under the same heading . . . it is clear that we will not be able genuinely to apprehend the meaning of either of them until we have established their real relations with the notion of being in general, and the relations that link them' (BN 25). The internal coherence of Sartre's monism is revealed through the logical structure of *Being and Nothingness* that runs from the abstract to the concrete, starting with consciousness as a procedural method and moving on to the body, world and others. To avoid significant misunderstandings, it is thus essential to treat *Being and Nothingness* as a whole with the 'simple imperative of interpretative holism' due to its 'precisely calibrated internal logic' (Ally 2017: 66). As Eshleman (2020a: 144–5) explains, the text is comprised of a horizontal axis that moves from the analysis of highly abstract simples to increasingly concrete, complex wholes based around his cardinal ontological distinction between being-for-itself and being-in-itself. Following Husserl's part/whole method as laid out in *Logical Investigations*, Sartre decomposes concrete wholes into increasingly abstract parts until he reaches the simplest points possible. Thus, his distinction between *pour-soi* as free and temporal and *en-soi* as '*massive*', 'full positivity', 'escapes temporality', 'has no secret' and 'alterity is unknown to it' (BN 28) reaches a conclusion that is only 'provisional' (BN 25). The second part, by contrast, follows Heidegger and gives priority to wholes. In the case of human-reality, this is lived as an internally related, synthetic totality whose sum comprises more than its parts and not just a compilation of externally related, independent pieces. It is the introduction of discussion of others in part 3 that leads Sartre to abandon the abstract unconditional theory of freedom since freedom is now lost and finds its limit in the free objectifying power of Others.[11]

Sartre makes it clear that body and consciousness are two aspects of the ambiguity of lived experience that cannot be separated until after the event: 'We know that there is not, on the one hand, a for-itself and, on the other, a world, as two closed wholes, whose means of communication it is necessary afterwards to seek. Rather, the for-itself is by itself a relation to the world' (BN 413). As 'a duality that *is* a unity' (BN 125), or as Gardner (2009a: 97) calls it, a 'duality-in-unity', body and consciousness represent two abstract poles and Sartre's method can be seen as a 'rheostatic gyration' between these poles, 'a relentlessly recursive logic' that goes forward and backward.[12] *Being and Nothingness* is replete with phenomenological descriptions that highlight 'the difficulties encountered by the Cartesian theory of substance' (BN 766), and Sartre is clear from the outset that he is eschewing dualistic thinking, insisting that there is no way of separating appearances from the thing itself: 'That is why we can, in the end, also reject the dualism of appearance and essence. Appearance does not hide essence, but reveals it; it is the essence' (BN 3). Sartre's method proceeds analytically from abstract and simple concepts to a concrete and complex whole. As his analysis develops, he significantly revises abstract claims made early in the text and abandons all claims to the unlimited (and unconditioned) nature of freedom in the second half. We misunderstand his phenomenological ontology if we ignore this progression of analysis in which he weaves the ontic facts of our current existence into the more generalized ontological structures of existence.[13] In the conclusion to *Being and Nothingness*, Sartre is unequivocal: 'we have just shown that the in-itself and the for-itself are not juxtaposed. Quite to the contrary, the for-itself without the in-itself is something like an abstraction: it can no more exist than a colour without a shape, or a sound without a pitch and a timbre' (BN 803).

This method continues and intensifies as his work progresses. In his later philosophy, his focus shifts from a largely dyadic perspective to a collective analysis that takes account of wider groups, multiplicities and historical structures. He defines comprehension as 'nothing other than my real life; it is the totalizing movement which gathers together my neighbor, myself, and the environment in the synthetic unity of an objectification in process' (SM 155) and sets out philosophically, or 'mereologically', to understand the part in the whole and the whole in the part. To achieve comprehension, Sartre explains, 'two dialectical procedures are possible', one centripetal and the other centrifugal: 'On the one hand, a procedure of decompressive expansion which starts off from the object to arrive at *everything*, following the order of significations. . . . On the other hand, a procedure of totalizing compression which, by contrast, grasps the centripetal movement of all the significations attracted and condensed in the event or in the object' (CDR 2:49). Sartre employs both of these procedures and ends up with a 'mediated' account that maintains 'the relative irreducibility of social fields' (SM 82), which are real but still remain dependent or 'parasitic' on free organic praxis (SM 77). Hence, in Sartre's social ontology we find a relentless tug of war or boxing match between Kierkegaard the 'Singular Universal' and Hegel the 'Universal Singular' (BN 330).[14] Although Kierkegaard marks progress towards realism since he insists above all on the primacy of the specifically real over thought (SM 12), for Sartre, 'Hegel's brilliant intuition is to make me depend on the Other *in my being*' (BN 328).

In a footnote in *What Is Literature?*, Sartre signals his interest in the development of dialectical history, an area that his earlier phenomenology had left untouched: 'Some day I am going to try to describe that strange reality History, which is neither objective, nor ever quite subjective, in which the dialectic is contested, penetrated, and corroded by a kind of antidialectic, but which is still a dialectic' (WL 333–4). He continues this dialectical search in *Notebooks for an Ethics* where he proposes an 'existential dialectic' or a 'dialectic with holes in it' (NE 449), a historical process where individual agency and moral responsibility can produce 'an irrational leap into another dimension of being, a new dialectic and a new leap' (NE 458).[15] As Badiou (2009: 43) describes it, the *Critique* was Sartre's attempt to provide a dialectical comprehension of history composed 'as a symphony in two movements', a regressive movement (a theory of practical ensembles) and a progressive movement (a rational reconstruction of history as a 'totalization without a totalizer'). Out of this symphony crystallizes Sartre's version of the dialectic which, according to Badiou (2009: 167–8), 'is not the synthetic neutralization of two pre-existing but contradictory terms, but the discovery of the articulation that deploys the dimension along which they suddenly emerge as "sides"'. It designates 'the active unity of an operation as a preliminary to any determination of a duality'. The dialectic is hence 'never a dualized sequence of concepts . . . [but] is the polarization of a space that is articulated'. In the Sartrean dialectic, we find an 'index of complementarity' between opposing pairs, as Ally (2020: 373) contends, that requires a ternary or sublimating logic of comprehension in which '[c]ontradictions abound, and paradox lurks in the nearby ternary shadows'. Following the threefold stages of 'contradictions, surpassing and totalization' (SM 34), Sartre's dialectical method offers a way out of metaphysical dualism and protection against analytical closure by transforming opposing pairs into a displaced or sublimated third in the same way Nietzsche sought to. Within his surpassing of opposites, for example, *real-imaginary* becomes *possible*, *pour-soi/en-soi* becomes *for others*, *praxis-practico inertia* becomes *praxis-process*, *totality-totalization* becomes *totalization of envelopment* and *need-scarcity* is sublimated into *abundance*. As Ally (2020: 365) explains, in Sartre's thought ternary logic continually infuses binary logic: 'We might call this the *immanent imminence of the ternary*, both immanent and imminent. The third is *always coming* and *always nearby* and *always already there*. When we think with Sartre, if we look for a Third, we will find one.'

For Sartre, 'reciprocal ternary relations are the basis of *all* relations between men whatever form they take' (CDR 111). Ternary reciprocities ground and mediate all abstract dualities and form a bond of sociality: 'a ternary relation, as the mediation of man amongst men, is the basis on which reciprocity becomes aware of itself as a reciprocal connection' (CDR 109). In explaining totality and multiplicity by this ternary logic, Sartre demonstrates a sensitivity to parts and wholes that is missing from atomistic or holistic accounts. A totality is never fixed or static but is always in motion and always in process. Totalization hence relates to becoming as an activity of an intentional, integrative and open-ended development. It 'delineates a practical field [and] attempts the most rigorous synthesis of the most differentiated multiplicity' (SM 46). As individuals or collectivities, we are never completed totalities but 'detotalized totalities' that are both constituted and dissolved by the transcendence towards future possibilities (NE 543). Hegel's dialectic assumes the viewpoint of the whole or Absolute with no respect to particular determinations or individual instances, but 'no totalitarian and unifying synthesis of 'Others' is possible' (NE 339). The group is dispersed by contingency into a plurality of beings who nonetheless mutually determine each other, a 'detotalized totality' (NE 17). Thus, Sartre's ontology reveals an intrinsic *relationality* or interconnectedness – '[e]verything is always revealed as united to everything' (CDR 360) – in a kind of feedback system of mutually constitutive parts that also accounts for singularity and individuality:

> Humans are singular beings who belong to historical ensembles. They cannot be compared to atoms or body cells. United? Separated? They are both. There is no separation that is not at the same time a mode of presence, nor a bond so intimate that it does not incorporate a secret absence. (1977: 6:197)

Emergent interactionism

Although the 'old Sartre' is classically seen as 'the ultimate individualist' who subscribes to a social ontology of methodological individualism,[16] this is now commonly seen as a misrepresentation of his complex dialectical position. As far back as the 1930s, Sartre preached against social atomism, attributing it to the bourgeois analytical point of view that, as he would later argue in the *Critique*, is incapable of grasping collective realities or synthetic wholes such as social class, as opposed to synthetic or dialectical reason, which is totalizing and 'thinks in terms of solidarity' (CDR 375, 468). This difference 'expresses itself as a conflict of rationalities' (CDR 802). Analytical reason, which constitutes bonds between individuals only 'in the milieu of exteriority', forms the basis of capitalist hegemony, he contends, by reinforcing the 'absolute separation between people which is so crucial to the continuing domination of the individualistic bourgeoisie' (CDR 285, 297).

Unlike methodological individualism, Sartre's social theory of 'emergent interactionism' (Farrell Fox 2020) or 'Dialectical Nominalism' (Flynn 2010) recognizes the synthetic enrichment of social phenomena and their irreducibility to their parts. Viewing subjectivity and intersubjectivity as *emergent* explains how a higher order is founded on a lower one and in a sense contains it but at the same time takes it over and integrates it into new structures which cannot be explained by those that are taken over. This is not just a simple mixing of elements but more a chemical reaction that yields a new substance with different qualities from its constituents. For Sartre, consciousness emerges on the intersubjective level as an ongoing totalization between subjectivities that becomes a 'totality' but is always open to detotalization (CDR 404). Community is not a simple collection of discrete individuals but is informed by a unity of existence that penetrates and transcends their private worlds. A *totality* is thus defined

> as a being which, while radically distinct from the sum of its parts, *is present in its entirety*, in one form or another, *in each of these parts*, and which relates to itself either through its relation to one or more of its parts or through its relation to the relations between all or some of them. (SM 45)

When two or more for-itselfs enter into relationship, as Flynn (1992: 216) observes, 'there is a reciprocity that is an *existential modification of each*' that forms an inter-individual reality which transforms individual praxis. This accords broadly with a Spinozean ontologico-ethical position, articulating an ethico-political subjectivity that is elaborated neither in terms of a monadic individual nor of a collective entity but of an essentially self-creating, internally related multiplicity of singularities that interrelate according to intrinsic, spontaneous movements. When they move towards common ends, the singularities give rise to ontological dislocations – that is, the formation of more complex singularities in 'constellations of reciprocities' (CDR 367). All of reality is a congregation of individual singularities freely configuring and reconfiguring themselves according to different, spontaneous modalities.[17] Sartre's 'pluralistic monism' is thus kaleidoscopic composed of singularities in constant becoming that coalesce and merge together in the production and creation of a composite whole. Free praxis becomes constituent power in this process and it is within this continuous movement of becoming that the multitude or group discovers itself as subject. This gives us a rationality that goes beyond the dualisms of modernity, outlining a new form of thinking that represents itself in a logic of the singularities in process, in fusion and in continual surpassing.

Throughout his writings, Sartre makes clear his intention to steer a path between the metaphysics of idealists who 'reduce matter to mind' and the materialist who 'reduces mind to matter' (1995a: 204). As Flynn (2014: 250) notes, Sartre holds an 'emergentist' form of materialism where mind develops from matter but is irreducible to matter in its distinctive features, the chief of which is intentionality which Sartre consistently takes to be the defining characteristic of the mental. In the *Critique*, he defines his ontological position as a 'monism of materiality' (CDR 29) and as a 'realistic materialism' (CDR 181). A person is 'wholly matter' (CDR 180), an organism symbiotically related to its environment through need, and engaged in a reciprocal dialectical process of 'trans-substantiation' (CDR 178). It is this material process of exchange that establishes our interconnectedness: '[when something] has taken on the character of materiality it enters into relation with the entire Universe' (CDR 163). This is continuous with *Being and Nothingness* where Sartre refers to the distinction between *en-soi* and *pour-soi* as an 'abstraction' and seeks a 'concrete ontology' instantiated in the world. As Eshleman (2011: 33) points out, his philosophy never talks about different kinds or types of being but always different *modes* of being:

> In Sartre's considered view, the universe contains only one *kind* of being that can be divided into different modal categories. When understood in this way, Sartre subscribes to a version of substance monism (materialism) conjoined with a modal pluralism (in a way perhaps distantly influenced by Spinoza).

This Spinozian heritage aligns Sartre's ontology with Deleuze's and Guattari's magic formula of 'PLURALISM = MONISM' (1987: 20) and their general ontology of the 'intermezzo' (1987: 277).[18] Although linking Sartre's dialectical ontology with 'anti-dialectical' Deleuzian thinking may seem like a false move, as we have seen, Deleuze does not condemn all dialectical thinking and the strategic use of dualisms,[19] merely those uses that lead to 'dialectical *exclusion*' (1992: 67) or to 'the *distortion* of the dialectic' (1994: 268). Sartre's dialectic is not a Hegelian one based on exclusion or identity but is rather an open-ended 'decapitated dialectic' (Flynn 2010: 28), a 'dialectic with holes in it' (NE 449). For Sartre, dialectical enrichment lies in the transition from the abstract to the concrete, that is, from elementary concepts to notions of greater and greater richness. This movement of the dialectic is the reverse of the dialectic of (Cartesian) science and the analytic spirit. The latter is blind to totalization, ignores the existence of socioeconomic classes and is individualist in its metaphysics and ethics. Sartre's dialectical reason is opposed to the stance of the de-situated experimenter that perpetuates analytical reason as the model of intelligibility in the 'milieu of exteriority' (CDR 285). The Sartrean dialectic, by contrast, as 'the living logic of action', is invisible to a contemplative reason. It appears in the course of praxis as a necessary moment of it and is created anew in each action: 'man must be controlled by the dialectic insofar as he *creates* it, and *create* it insofar as he is controlled by it' (CDR 35).

Nietzsche's gay science

An absolutely burning thirst took hold of me: from then on I actually pursued nothing more than physiology, medicine, and the natural sciences.
(Nietzsche, *Ecce Homo* 3HH3)

Nietzsche's writings manifest a great deal of ambiguity concerning the status of science. In the early works, it is cast as primarily negative, engendering a cold rationalism that leads to the Socratic degradation of life, an epitome of seriousness that destroyed the 'tragic wisdom' of the Greeks and their instinctive ability 'to play around life with lies' (EH 3BT1). The spirit of science is the belief, which first came to light in the person of Socrates, 'that the depths of nature can be fathomed and that knowledge can heal all ills' (BT 82). But '[w]hat is science for *at all*', asks Nietzsche, 'if it has no time for culture?' (UM 1.8). Disenchantment with Wagner in late 1870s, however, precipitated a reconsideration in which Nietzsche looked to science as a weapon against the prejudicial illusions of romanticism, religion and morality, praising the scientific spirit of neutrality and autonomy (D 36, GS 293). In the middle works, he esteems science and draws heavily on the natural sciences in explaining moral sentiments and human psychology:

Long live physics! . . . We, however, want to *become who we are* – human beings who are new, unique, incomparable, who give themselves laws, who create themselves! To that end we must become the best students and discoverers of everything lawful and necessary in the world: we must become *physicists* in order to be creators in this sense – while hitherto all valuations and ideals have been built on *ignorance* of physics or in *contradiction* to it. So, long live physics! And even more long live what *compels* us to it – our honesty! (GS 335)

In his final period, his view shifts again to a more nuanced position. *Zarathustra* marks the transition to a more mythic and poetic mode of philosophy, the third phase of his thinking towards science which is one of overall scepticism based on a critique of its metaphysical foundations. Whereas in *The Gay Science* he had viewed science as an opportunity, valuing the scientific spirit for its honesty and critical potential (GS 7), in *Beyond Good and Evil* he now sees it more as a danger for engendering a form of religious nihilism (BGE 204). Despite its pretensions of objectivity, science is not immune from morality and its belief in truth makes it the spiritual descendant of the ascetic ideal and not its opponent (GM 3.23–4). In seeking detachment and objectivity, the scientist falls victim to 'the dangerous old conceptual fiction' of a 'pure, will-less, painless, timeless knowing subject' (GM 3.26) who sees a faithful 'mirror' of events: 'The objective man is an instrument, a precious, easily injured and clouded instrument for measuring and, as an arrangement of mirrors, an artistic triumph that deserves care and honour; but he is no goal, no conclusion and sunrise . . . still less a beginning' (BGE 207). For Nietzsche, modern science involves a flight from the actual, for it relies on ideal fictions, such as number, atom, substance, pure observation and law (Z P3) and has filled the vacuum of nihilism with a timid, sterile conformity to law (BGE 30). He talks of the 'fictions of logic' and the 'purely invented world of the unconditional and the self-identical' (BGE 5) created by conceptual thought. There is a gulf between our rational understanding and our primal experience, between 'pale, cold, gray concept nets' and 'the motley whirl of the senses' (BGE 14). People have wrongly taken concepts for the world as it really is and consequently we have created a symbol world of cause, sequence, relativity, number which 'we project and mix . . . into things as if it existed "in itself"' (BGE 21). He questions the adequacy of reason and concepts to reality and identifies Socrates and Plato as 'symptoms of decay', 'conceptual mummies' who sacrificed instinct to 'the daylight of reason' (TI 2.10).

Although critical of modern science in its Socratic-Platonic form, Nietzsche's thought becomes increasingly naturalistic, however, as it evolves into his later philosophy. Friedrich Albert Lange's *The history of materialism and critique of its meaning for the present* (which he read in 1862 while at Pforta) was a major influence on Nietzsche's turn to naturalism, but he had also long held an interest in the scientific thinking of the Presocratic Greek philosophers.[20] Alongside Heraclitus, it was Democritus who led Nietzsche towards the natural sciences, breaking away from anthropomorphism by extracting all moral projections and any form of teleology or meaning from the indifferent and random universe. Contrary to the Platonic worldview, Democritus' 'disenchantment of being' grasped the world in its contingency as entirely without reason or *telos*.[21] In the 1870s and 1880s, Nietzsche drew upon the naturalism of Darwinism and Lamarckism in forming an evolutionary perspective. In line with Darwin, he believed that humans evolved from other forms of animal life and adopted a non-teleological view of nature as a blind play of forces or accidental process. However, he criticized Darwin's idea of an organism's passive adaptation to the environment and Darwin's 'will to life', preferring instead the concept of will to power as an internal creative force (which Lamarck allowed for in his theory). Nietzsche's criticism of Darwin's theory of 'passive adaptation' to external forces fed into his wider criticism of modern (Newtonian) science that he charged with being too mechanistic and failing to incorporate intentional directedness into its framework of understanding: '"Mechanistic interpretation": desires nothing but quantities; but force is to be found in quality. Mechanistic theory can therefore only describe processes, not explain them' (WP 660). Despite these criticisms, Nietzsche prides himself on his realism, his 'courage before reality' (TI 10.2), and embarks upon a 're-aiming of science' to give us power over our own values. His attacks against science are directed only against 'science so far' and he projects a 'new science' that acquires a 'new charm' after the removal of morality (WP 594). In his *1888 Notebooks*, he opens up a dichotomy between 'old' and 'new' science. Where the old science is mechanistic and only explains things from the outside, ignoring their inner will in which their qualities reside (WP 625), the new science will rid itself of metaphysical fictions and constitute reality as a play of forces with intentionality and directedness: 'The victorious concept "force" . . . still needs a completion: an inner will must be ascribed to it, which I designate as "will to power"' (WP 619).

For some scholars, Nietzsche's 'new science' finds its home in the principles of quantum physics. Megill (1985: 38), for instance, draws a comparison between the duality of Apollo and Dionysus and that of particle and wave in quantum physics. Where Apollo (particle) seeks to grant form to individual being by drawing boundaries around them, Dionysus (wave) can break these 'little circles' when Apollonian tendencies 'congeal the form to Egyptian rigidity and coldness' (BT 9). This reflects in the visual bias of Apollo, 'the shining one' and 'the deity of light' and the non-imagistic bias of Dionysus, the musical one (BT 1). In Plank's (1998: 65, 508) view, there are striking similarities in Nietzsche's ontology of 'dissipative systems' and quantum mechanics. Nietzsche's relational will to power and rejection of idealist metaphysics finds a consonance in the holism of quantum mechanics and its rejection of classical accounts of reality. Nietzsche 'had a primitive quantum theory of force' as early as the 1880s, describing the will to power as a quantum state in which observer and observed form an inseparable system (BGE 36) and anticipating Bohm's panpsychism of 'somasignificant' or 'signasomatic' events where there are different levels of mind but where all particles have some state of mind and awareness.

In general, Nietzsche is strongly inconsistent in regard to the Socratic spirit, viewing the will to truth as *both* poison and medicine. On the one hand he stresses repeatedly how it can be bad for us to uncover the truth about values – how it is leading to the loss of values, nihilism, the great problem of the modern age. But, on the other hand, and seemingly contrary to that advice, he is also constantly thrusting upon us stark and pressing insights about our values, thus forcing these truths to our attention. This can be viewed in the light of the 'tragic wisdom' he extols in *The Birth of Tragedy* and the gay science he advocates later. The figurehead of Nietzsche's tragic wisdom is the 'musical Socrates' (BT 15) who represents a synthesis of Dionysian and Apollonian drives. We cannot just eliminate the Socratic drive for knowledge and science, in Nietzsche's sublimated view, but must complement it with the qualities of the artist in whom Heraclitean tragic cosmology is manifest (PTAG 62). In *Human, All Too Human*, Nietzsche talks of 'two chambers of the brain, as it were, one to experience science and the other nonscience' (HH 251) and searches for a harmonious interplay of the two, an aesthetic morality based on the physics of the body and its sensorial apparatus (GS 33). He envisages a time when science is not abandoned but is cross-fertilized with art into a *gay science* in which 'artistic energies and the practical wisdom of life will join the scientific thinking to form a higher organic system' (GS 113).

Sartre's dialectical science

While it is slightly hyperbolic to charge Sartre with being 'incapable of science' (Plank 1998: 493), it is fair to say that he is not known for his refined scientific sensibilities and love of lab coats. According to Beauvoir (1983: 39), 'he flatly refused to believe in science', going so far as to maintain 'that microbes and other *animalculae* invisible to the naked eye simply didn't exist at all'. Taking psychology as his example, he complains that psychologists who seek to establish a science in attending solely to the facts prefer 'the accident to the essential, the contingent to the necessary, disorder to order'. They do not notice 'that it is just as impossible to attain the essence by heaping up the accidents as it is to arrive at unity by the indefinite addition of figures to the right of 0.99' (STE 4). The task of existential psychoanalysis, Sartre insists, is hermeneutical (BN 810). He calls us to 'abandon the primacy of knowledge' (BN 9) that leads philosophers to consider existential relationships as epistemological ones (e.g. the existence of other minds). Conceptual knowledge is secondary to intuition: 'Deduction and discourse, which are incorrectly labelled as "knowledge", are only instruments leading to intuition' (BN 246). Generally, Sartre held science at a distance, openly acknowledging its considerable explanatory power but criticizing its 'concept of absolute objectivity' (BN 414) and its analytic/positivistic character (CDR 32). Beguiled by 'objective relations' and sunken in 'the world of objects' (BN 419), science aims at establishing relations of 'pure externality' (BN 414). The scientist posits herself as 'a de-situated investigator' (CDR 2:2), but the point of view of pure knowledge is contradictory for the known is never separated from the knower: 'the only point of view is that of *committed* knowledge' (BN 415). Modern science, as Sartre perceived it, was simply an instantiation of analytical reason, a positivist reason that views the world dispassionately as a set of objects for neutral observation presupposing an all-seeing, knowing subject who stands outside of the domain she investigates. Such a position masks the ideological construction of reality and the fact that 'we are up to our eyebrows' (1977a: 77) in history, always *in* a situation rather than above or beyond it.

Against the analytic gaze of the modern scientist, Sartre counterposes *dialectical reason* that recognizes itself as *situated* and begins with an embodied and situated perspective, 'the *life*, the objective being of the investigator, in the world of Others' (CDR 51). Dialectical reason starts at the most abstract point possible with an investigation of praxis as a purely individual undertaking: 'Critical investigation will set out from . . . the individual fulfilling himself in his abstract *praxis*, so as to rediscover, through deeper and deeper conditionings, the totality of his practical bonds with others and, thereby, the structures of the various practical multiplicities' (CDR 52). Dialectical enrichment lies in 'the transition from the abstract to the concrete, that is, from elementary concepts to notions of greater and greater richness' (1995: 209) spreading out to ever-widening spirals of analysis of connections in exteriority with social and historical forces, thus demonstrating that 'there is no such thing as an isolated individual' (CDR 677).

As Ally (2017: 158) observes, despite his misgivings about modern science, 'the prospect of a better science seems always to have lurked in the back of Sartre's porous mind'. In *Being and Nothingness*, he obliquely shares Husserl's classification of philosophy as a rigorous science and in the *Critique*, he drives towards a deeper form of scientific understanding based on an open-ended integrativity (CDR 31–2). A few pages later, he invokes the prospect of 'the existence of dialectical connections in inanimate Nature' but quickly qualifies it: 'in the present state of knowledge . . . we are [not] in a position to affirm or deny it' (CDR 33). This equivocation stands in contrast to his unequivocal and forthright criticisms of Engels' *Dialectic of Nature* elsewhere in the text (e.g. CDR 33). He concludes that 'at present, the absolute principle that "Nature is dialectical" is not open to verification at all' (CDR 28) but entertains the idea that a future science might fulfil the conditions of dialectical intelligibility: 'We shall accept the idea that man is a material being among material beings and, as such does not have a privileged statute; we shall even refuse to reject *a priori* the possibility that a concrete dialectics of Nature will one day be discovered' (CDR 34). He suggests that if science were to progress from its positivistic methodology, then a dialectics of nature becomes feasible:

> It may be said that the metaphysical hypothesis of a dialectic of Nature becomes more interesting when it is used to explain the passage from inorganic matter to organic bodies, and the evolution of life on earth. This is true. But it should be noted that this *formal* interpretation of life and evolution will never be more than a pious dream as long as scientists have no way of using 'totality' and 'totalization' as a guiding hypothesis. . . . For the present, biology, in its actual research, remains positivistic and analytical. It is possible that a deeper knowledge of its object, through its contradictions, will force biology to consider the organism in its totality, that is to say, dialectically, and to consider all biological facts in their relation of interiority. This is *possible*, but not *certain*. (CDR 34n16)

Through its dialectical innovations, in Ally's (2017: 162–3) view, Sartre's philosophy 'obliquely anticipated' new forms of scientific explanation. His dialectical lexicon of *praxis*, *praxis-process* and *practico-inertia* is rich in philosophical significance and could be used to confound the linear analytical positivism of conventional (Newtonian) science. In principle, a natural science could include all life and non-living matter within its dialectical intelligibility into 'the real movement of a unity in the process of being made' (SM 69). Sartre's dialectical ontology thus connects productively with several strands of the 'new sciences of life and complexity'. Kauffman's molecular biology, for instance, follows Sartre's emergent interactionism in demonstrating the emergent order in complex systems and the origins of autonomy where complexity refers to a system of interacting units that displays global properties not present at the lower level, for example, ant colonies, schools of fish. Patterns emerge through interactions internal to the system involving information exchange, an autonomous and spontaneous activity leading to self-organization.[22] Sartre's dialectical mereology also anticipates the anti-Cartesian science advocated in *The Dialectical Biologist* by Levins and Lewontin. Criticizing analytical reason that fails to take account of numerous mediations and assemblages, they advance a dialectical worldview of parts and wholes remarkably close to Sartre's in the *Critique*:

> 'Part' and 'whole' have a special relationship to each other, in that one cannot exist without the other, any more than 'up' can exist without 'down'. What constitutes the parts is defined by the whole that is being considered. Moreover, parts acquire properties by virtue of being parts of a particular whole, properties they do not have in isolation or as parts of another whole. It is not that the whole is more than the sum of its parts, but that the parts acquire new properties. But as the parts acquire properties by being together, they impart to the whole new properties, which are reflected in changes in the parts, and so on. Parts and wholes evolve in consequence of their relationship, and the relationship itself evolves. These are the properties of things we call dialectical: that one cannot exist without the other, that one acquires its properties from its relation to the other,

that the properties of both evolve as a consequence of their interpenetration. (1985: 3)

In Sartre's ontology, the world is a dynamic, open-ended, integrative web of irreducible active connections and totalizations, a 'totalization without a totalizer'. The dialectic is 'not the study, not even the "functional" and "dynamic" study, of a unity already made' but *'the real movement of a unity in the process of being made'* (SM 69), just like Nietzsche's will to power: 'If totalization is really an ongoing process, it operates everywhere. This means both that there is a dialectical meaning of the practical ensemble – whether it is planetary, or has to become even interplanetary – and that each individual event totalizes in itself this ensemble in the infinite richness of its individuality' (CDR 2:17). In the opening page of *Principles of Biological Autonomy*, Varela quotes Sartre's footnote cited above (CDR 34n16) in its entirety. His principle of 'living systems as cognitive systems', in Ally's (2017: 167) view, 'is arguably an effort to fulfil some, if not all, of Sartre's demands, or more generally to render theoretical biology explicitly dialectical'. Central to Varela's and Maturana's dialectical system is the concept of *autopoiesis* that explains the intentional directedness of individual organisms and collective systems in symbiosis with the rest of nature. Sartre's dialectical comprehension captures 'autopoiesis in a nutshell' (2017: 444), where he describes 'the wealth of the organism' (CDR 404) and its reciprocal transformative connections to the rest of nature: 'For the organism, unity is the perpetual restoration of unity . . . [Its] functions, moreover, ceaselessly turn back upon themselves in a circularity that is only the first temporalization of permanence, since their tasks are always similar and always conditioned by the same "feedback"' (CDR 2:344–5).[23] Just as in Sartre's emergent interactionism, in Earth System Science (inspired by the 'Santiago School' of Varela and Maturana, as well as Lovelock's 'Gaia hypothesis'), the earth has an identity as a whole, an adaptable and plastic unity acquired through time in a dynamic partnership of circularity between life and its terrestrial environment. As a self-organizing unity, it is a relational and mediational process collectively generated by the various components (geosphere, hydrosphere, atmosphere and biosphere) and the networks of interconnections and feedback relations between them.

Alongside chemistry and biology, Sartre's idea of a 'new science' (based on the principles of dialectical totalization and emergent interactionism) can be cross-fertilized with many of the principles of quantum physics, such as *interrelatedness, indeterminacy, ambiguity, emergence, organization, reversibility, unity, plurality* and *situatedness*. Unlike Nietzsche's will to power, Sartre's relational ontology has yet to be firmly linked with quantum physics,[24] but they are very much continuous. First of all, both critique the standpoint theory of neutral observation and replace it with the importance of 'observer-participancy'. Indeed, Sartre appeals explicitly to a 'truth of microphysics [that] the experimenter is part of the experimental system' (SM 32), 'a practical organism producing Knowledge as a moment of its praxis' (SM 179).

Second, viewing subjectivity and intersubjectivity as *emergent* explains how a higher order is founded on a lower one and contains it but at the same time takes it over and integrates it into new structures which cannot be explained by those that are taken over. This is used in quantum physics, for instance, to show how higher consciousness or capabilities come into existence through the concatenation and organization of lower-level parts. A whole is not identical with the sum of its parts but is something new, and all its properties differ from those displayed by the parts of which it is composed. Association is in this way a productive phenomenon in itself, consisting in bringing to external relation established facts and formed properties.[25]

In quantum physics, as in Sartre's middle path 'between atomism and organicism' (1981a: 357–8), neither individuality nor relationship is lost, for neither has exclusive ontological primacy. A whole created through a quantum relation is a new thing in itself greater than the sum of its parts and, although there is no end to the process of quantum integration of particles into new wholes, each particle maintains facets of its identity (as fermions never merge completely).[26] Furthermore, in its dynamic transformation from one state to another, Sartre's emergent interactionism exhibits what quantum physics calls 'reversibility'. In the recursive movement from seriality to fusion, groups undergo a modal change, a 'constant transformation of energy' (CDR 549) from less energy and vibration to a greater amount of intensity and cohesion (just as electrons can move in any direction in the transition from a higher energy state to a lower one). In terms of Sartre's social ethic, a parallel can also be drawn between his dichotomy of fusion and seriality and Von Foerster's theory of quantum interaction (used originally to describe the behaviour of cybernetic systems that achieve internal, homeostatic control through the free exchange of information between the parts): 'The more [rigidly] connected are the elements of a system, the less influence they will have on the system as a whole. [...] The more [rigid] the connections, the more each element of the system will exhibit a greater degree of "alienation" from the whole.'[27] Quantum systems are delicately poised between order and chaos and so embrace *ambiguity*. Too static and they run down, too chaotic and they break apart like dissipative systems or Sartrean totalities.

As thoroughly relational, quantum and Sartrean consciousness elicit a social ontology that inverts the atomistic logic of Cartesian individualism and Newtonian physics. In the Newtonian universe, individuals are like indivisible billiard balls attracting, repelling and colliding in externality. By contrast, because wave functions can overlap and become entangled, quantum systems can 'get inside' each other and 'form a creative, internal relationship' through which they further evolve (Zohar 1991: 59). Sartre, as we have seen, argues along similar lines in *Being and Nothingness*, insisting that interpersonal relations are an 'internal negation'. When fixed by the gaze of the Other, this decentres my world and causes me to experience 'a new type of intraworldly haemorrhage' in which all the constituents of my world flow towards the Other (BN 400). In an interview with Michel Sicard shortly before his death, Sartre focuses on the issue of interconnectedness and entanglement[28] and takes a 'quantum view' by positing the existence of an internal *ontological* bond between human beings:

> Ontologically, consciousnesses are not isolated, there are planes where they enter into one another – planes common to two or to *n* consciousnesses ... [Humans'] perceptions or their thought are in relation one with others, not only by exposure to the other, but because there are penetrations between consciousnesses. (1979a: 15)

Consciousness and free will are seen as inseparable in quantum physics, reflecting the self-organizing capacity of living organisms to take unstructured, inert or chaotic matter from the surrounding environment and draw it into a dynamic, creative dialogue. Quantum indeterminacy arises from the 'creative thinking' of matter. Just as an electron sends out 'virtual feelers of possibility' in determining its motion, so does consciousness in deciding its course of action through imagining things differently or by running through different choices. Quantum indeterminism is based in this way on *creative thinking* when a person states or depicts 'what in fact does not exist', reflecting the inherent creativity in all self-organizing systems (Zohar 1991: 62, 172). This is akin to the creative power of the imagination in Sartre's terms and to the *pour-soi* whose spontaneous upsurge and decisionism is a 'pure event in the heart of being'. Just as in Sartre's idea of 'a duality that *is* a unity' (BN 125), the quantum worldview transcends the dichotomy between mind and body, inner and outer, showing that the building blocks of mind (bosons) and matter (fermions) arise out of a common substrate and share a mutually creative dialogue.

Assimilation and hodological space

Drawing on the work of Gestalt psychologist Kurt Lewin, Sartre describes 'the real space of the world' as 'hodological space' (BN 415). For Lewin, hodological space denotes the dynamic relation between agent and environment. Through goal-directed purposive activity, the individual delineates a world in which objects function as 'valences' that can be either positive and attractive or negative and unappealing. As we move towards or away from the valenced objects, we trace a path or 'vectors' that are a function of the strength or direction of the agent. These valences fluctuate and shift during the normal process of experience as the agent's goals change, and so vectors are constantly modified relative to changing valences. In this way, the subject generates a constantly fluctuating 'field of force' in the course of interacting with the environment.[29] As Sartre explains, 'around the other, an entire space is grouped, and this space is made with my *space*; it is a regrouping, at which I am present, and which escapes me, of all the objects that populate my universe' (BN 350). Space is thus not striated with strict divisions and boundaries but an open smooth space in which forces converge and coalesce, causing ontological dislocations in individuals through a state of transfer: 'Originally, space is a qualitative and magnetic field, because it is traversed, because one pursues there, because one flees there, and one is always on the plane . . . of the unveiling of the new' (NE 361). Unlike Euclidean space that has fixed coordinates, hodological space is generated relative to each subject and is constantly fluid. Space is not merely an anatomical entity possessing clearly delineable boundaries but is coextensive with one's range of possibilities and field of force: 'my body is . . . everywhere . . . [it] is always extended through the tool that it utilizes . . . my body is at the end of the stick on which I leaning . . . it is at the end of the telescope which shows me the stars; it is . . . in the entire house, because it is my adaptation to these tools' (BN 436).

In his rich phenomenological descriptions, Sartre describes a reality in which *en-soi* and *pour-soi* share a depth or 'fusion of ends': 'the for-itself's absorption by the in-itself, [is] like ink by blotting paper' (BN 790). In describing the action of sliding in the snow, for instance, Sartre refers to the continuity of the *pour-soi/en-soi* as 'a synthesis of depth' (BN 757). Action reveals to us a 'relation between being and being which, even though the physicist apprehends it externally, is neither pure externality nor immanence, but which refers us to the Gestaltist notion of *figure*' (BN 808). There is 'a tactile fascination' in the viscous where the 'suction of the viscous that I can feel on my hands is the beginning of a *continuity* between the viscous substance and myself' (BN 789).³⁰ For Sartre, my relation to objects is not just an instrumental and detached one like that of the analytical scientist, since possession is a 'magical relation': 'I *am* these objects that I possess, but outside and in confrontation with myself' (BN 767). He describes how emotions 'feed' or are 'nurtured' on objects as objects take on affective textures or moods; evocative qualities appear at the heart of objects in such a way that the affected subject and the affective objective are bound in an indissoluble synthesis. Perception has an affective coloration that reveals a union of the psychic and physiological and the point at which their boundaries run into each other:

> When feeling is directed on at [*sic*] a real thing, currently perceived, the thing sends back to it, like a screen, the light that it receives from it. And so, by a game of back and forth, the feeling is constantly enriched, at the same time that the object imbibes affective qualities [. . .] each affective quality is so deeply incorporated in the object that it is impossible to distinguish between what is felt and what is perceived. (IM 139)

This 'connective tissue' (BN 755) between objects and subjects in Sartre's ontology shares a close bond with posthumanist eco-aesthetics. Böhme (1995: 119), for instance, elaborates a form of biosemiotics where things in the environment are in communication with each other, a form of 'being-in-communication' in which beings 'tincture' the environment in which they are perceived. The universe is thus conceived as dialogically composed of a series of inter-animating relationships that emphasize multiplicities rather than individual subjects. *Relata* do not pre-exist relations but emerge through specific intra-actions in a world that unfolds indeterminately as a complicated tissue of events in which connections of different kinds overlap or combine and thereby form the texture of the whole.

Sartrean hodological space develops Nietzschean insights of assimilation and incorporation and configures reality as 'a play of energies and waves of energy at the same time one and many' (WP 1067), demonstrating '*the relational character* of all occurrence' (KSW 11.26.157). As we will see in further detail in the next chapter, this aligns Nietzschean and Sartrean ontology very closely with several philosophical strands in contemporary posthumanist thinking, such as *philosophical posthumanism*, *vibrant materialism*, *object-oriented ontology* and *eco-phenomenology* that follow Nietzsche and Sartre in emphasizing the view of the radical interconnection of the human, non-human and Other-than-human. Central to posthumanist thinking is the concept of 'autopoiesis' which, as we have seen, was prefigured in Nietzsche's and Sartre's 'new science' to explain the ability of a system/organism to creatively maintain and reproduce itself.[31] Philosophical posthumanism also follows Nietzsche (explicitly) and Sartre (implicitly) in rejecting standpoint theory in favour of a situated and pluralistic perspectivism where '[i]t is our needs that interpret the world' (WP 267). Additionally, posthumanism incorporates a Nietzschean–Sartrean model of the self as a 'relational, embodied, affective and accountable entity', engendering a 'mind-body continuum' sedimented within a 'nature-culture continuum' (Ferrando 2020: 154, 139). This recognizes 'the ontological inseparability of intra-acting agencies' and 'a posthumanist performative account of material bodies (both human and nonhuman)' (2020: 155, 136).

As Barad (2003: 801) complains, some of the constructive radicalizations of late postmodernity somehow lost track of the material: 'Language matters. Discourse matters, Culture matters. There is an important sense in which the only thing that does not seem to matter anymore is matter.' In this sense, Nietzschean and Sartrean ontology can be considered an improvement on Derrida's all-consuming textuality and phonocentrism. For Sartre, it is matter that connects us to all other beings (CDR 163), but matter is not something passive, fixed and inert to be shaped by some external force. Rather, it is a process of 'materialization' which is dynamic, shifting, entangled, diffractional and performative, always, as Deleuze and Guattari (1987: 451) describe it, 'matter in movement, in flux, in variation, matter as a conveyor of singularities and traits of expression'.[32] Indeed, Sartre's analysis of *practico-inertia* and counter-finality in the *Critique* gives us a vivid illustration of how, in Bennett's (2017: 447) words, 'non-human things and forces actively shape the bodies they encounter, including the humans'. In the form of the practico-inert, worked matter emerges as a shifting and transformative quasi-totality that surrounds and conditions us (CDR 324). In his example of the effects of deforestation in China, Sartre demonstrates how the farmer experiences a form of 'practical destiny' constituted by the 'magical field of counterfinality' (CDR 224). The material field, synthesized by 'the serial infinity of human acts' (CDR 219), becomes 'a strange and living being' (CDR 169). Continuing the theme of 'magical possession' (BN 767), in the *Critique* matter is conceived as a 'magical field' (CDR 224) full of 'vampire objects' (CDR 169) that soak up the lifeblood of praxis: 'All of us spend our lives engraving our maleficent image into things, and this image fascinates and bewilders us if we try to understand ourselves through it, even though we are nothing other than the totalizing movement which results in this particular objectification' (CDR 227, trans. modified). Illustrating the phenomenon of 'trans-substantiation' (CDR 178), in his example of female factory workers he shows how machine and the worker form a relationship of perfect symbiosis, each hosting the other. Through the free movement of her project, the worker becomes a machine of the machine bringing to the machine her experience and creativity, even the fantasies, which its mechanisms demand. The machine then dialectically shapes the experience she invests within it to the point that even her sexual reveries are subjected to the rhythms of the machine: 'The machine demands and creates in the worker an inverted semi-automatism which complements it' (CDR 233). From the dialectical mediation of the practico-inert comes the emergence of the 'homme-machine' (CDR 191), a hybrid form of being definitively non-human but not inhuman either, rather a composite or assemblage of 'the totalizing movement which gathers together my neighbor, myself, and the environment in the synthetic unity of an objectification in process' (SM 155). In this way, Sartre depicts socio-material reality as one of shifting, mutually transgressive contexts that challenges any straightforward differentiation between humanity and the worked-upon material that surrounds it in the practical field. In the *Critique*, freedom no longer refers to a 'choice' among possibles but to the necessity of totalization and praxis in response to external exigencies and demands within a network of intra-actions or transversal exchange of forces between different agencies. Within this relational assemblage, he posits only a small space for creativity within the singularity that marks my making of being what has been made of me (CDR 330), akin to an existential signature or trace.

In summary, Nietzschean and Sartrean relational ontology expands upon a 'Spinozian-Deleuzian genealogy', conforming to posthumanist thinking by recognizing itself as 'a monistic pluralist (or a pluralistic monist) form of becoming' (Ferrando 2020: 167) that avoids dualism as a metaphysical postulate but uses dualisms strategically within a ternary or sublimating dialectical logic. Nietzsche's and Sartre's innovative mereology shows that neither monism nor pluralism by themselves could be feasible to sustain a proper ontology. In thinking posthumanistically, we should thus follow Nietzsche and Sartre and deconstruct the either/or of the one/many binarism and avoid searching for priority or origin: 'The one is necessarily and constantly differentiating and so it (they) is (are), at the same time, many' (2020: 167). In Nietzsche's 'terra-sophy' and Sartre's 'hodological space', we find a *rich affective dialectic* and a magical, 'sympoietic' view of nature akin to 'the enchanting realm of physics' described by quantum physicists in which there is a reciprocal movement between consciousness and its noematic correlate where each affective quality is so deeply incorporated in the object 'that it is impossible to distinguish between what is felt and what is perceived' (IM 139). In Chapter 6, I delve deeper into this affective dialectic as I look at their posthumanist innovations in relation to their theorization of nature, animals, technology, ecology and the future.

5

A creative ethics and agonistic politics

> [S]upposing the recommendation appealed to mankind, it could in pursuit of it also impose *upon itself a moral law, likewise at its own discretion. But up to now the moral law has supposed to stand above our own likes and dislikes: one did not actually want to* impose *this law upon oneself, one wanted to* take *it from somewhere or* discover *it somewhere or* have it commanded to one *from somewhere.*
> (Nietzsche, *Daybreak* 108)

In this chapter, I look at Nietzsche's and Sartre's ethical theories as they progress from the early to their later work and examine how their 'creative ethics'[1] connects to their political writings. While, ethically speaking, they share much common ground in their respect for individual autonomy and in their endeavour to construct an affirmative ethics in the wake of the death of God, in a political sense, the elitist, aristocratic Nietzsche and the democratic, egalitarian Sartre prima facie seem diametrically at odds. This is so particularly in regard to Nietzsche's final period of 'Grand Politics' in which he proposes a radically aristocratic political vision predicated on a 'pathos of distance' (GM 2.18) and relations of exploitation between the 'higher type' and the 'herd' (WP 936). Despite Nietzsche's lurch towards aristocratism in his final period, however, scholars find a very different political philosopher in his middle writings and locate many resources for a radical form of democratic practice.[2] In the final part, I take a reconstructive approach to Nietzschean political thinking in the light of his middle writings and suggest common ground between Nietzsche and Sartre in the form of a politics of 'positive agonism' or 'pluralist anarchism' that grounds freedom in an open, emergent dialectic of self and Other, taking its momentum from his relational ontology of forces, from his perspectival notion of truth and from his genealogical deconstruction of power.

Sartre's unfinished Nietzschean ethics

One of the most mysterious texts by Sartre and one that it seems nobody has really read (it is not yet found and is probably lost) is a long study on Nietzsche that he began in the period of *Notebooks for an Ethics* (1947–8) and which, according to Sartre, was a part of his ethical research (EJ 194). Apart, that is, from Beauvoir who did read it (as she read all of Sartre's works before he published them) and refers to it in *Adieux* as 'a work on ethics', 'the book in which you wrote an important, long, and very fine study of Nietzsche' (1984: 180).³ Whatever Sartre wrote about Nietzsche in his ethical study would likely have been concerned with the question of *nihilism* and the creation of new values following the death of God as he indicates in the following passage:

> Monsieur Bataille is a survivor of the death of God. And, when one thinks about it, it would seem that our entire age is surviving that death, which he experienced, suffered, and survived. God is dead. We should not understand by that that He does not exist, nor even that he no longer exists. He is dead: he used to speak to us and he has fallen silent, we now touch only his corpse. (2010: 234)

The death of God, announced for the first time in Nietzsche's work by the madman (GS 125), marked a situation in which '*the highest values devalue themselves*' (WP 9), a 'pathological transitional stage' (WP 13) and 'the recognition of the long *waste* of strength' (WP 12A) invested in the ascetic Christian worldview. In Derrida's (1981: 70) view, nihilism functions for Nietzsche as a kind of 'pharmakon' which 'acts as both remedy and poison . . . can be – alternatively or simultaneously – beneficent or maleficent'. The term plays ambiguously between poles and exposes the limit of metaphysical thinking, for its movement cannot proceed as an opposed binarism. It is a conjunctive 'both . . . and . . .' rather than disjunctive 'either . . . or . . .'. Nihilism is thus poison (in its Christian-Platonic form), the expression of a decadent and sickly will to power, but also a remedy: 'nihilism, as the denial of a truthful world, of being, might be *a divine way of thinking*' (WP 15). For Nietzsche, despair in the absence of a goal constitutes 'passive nihilism' – 'a decline and recession of the power of the spirit' – in contrast to the active nihilism he affirms that represents 'a sign of increased power of the spirit' (WP 22). The passive nihilism of the 'last man' who 'makes everything small', invents happiness and 'blinks' is contrasted to the 'self-overcoming creature' who gives 'birth to a star' (Z P5). Nietzsche's 'active nihilism' is based on the premise that there are goals, but no single goal: 'Can we remove the idea of a goal from the process and then affirm the process in spite of this?' (WP 55). 'The formula of my happiness', he writes, is 'a Yes, a No, a straight arrow, a goal' (TI 1.44).

In Daigle's (2009: 56, 67) view, the crux of the connection between Nietzsche and Sartre is their diagnosis of nihilism (the loss of meaning that accompanies the death of God) and the reconstructive ethical programme ('an immanent humanistic ethics') they propose as a solution to it. We can view them in this light as 'two optimists' (2009: 61) replacing God by giving life a new meaning in a world with no intrinsic meaning through an aesthetic justification. Their ethics are humanistic insofar as they both focus on the individual and her flourishing. This is a humanism 'more demanding' than the humanism they criticize in that it requires no constraints to be put upon the individual in terms of moral or religious objectivity (2009: 63). In *Notebooks for an Ethics*, Sartre argues that the death of God means not only the death of transcendence but also 'the opening of the infinite' (NE 34), that is, the infinity of human possibilities: 'In this way, man finds himself the heir of the mission of the dead God: to draw Being from its perpetual collapse into the absolute indistinctness of night. An infinite mission' (NE 494). For Daigle (2009: 66–70), the figure of the *Übermensch* must be understood in terms of a moral ideal. It is meant as an emulative figure that illustrates human potential in the form of 'a constant striving' or activity of becoming just like Sartre's theory of consciousness and freedom: 'the Overman is essentially a Sartrean authentic person and vice versa'. Although Sartre is very close to Nietzsche in his dealings with the question of the meaning of life, there is a political separation in their respective ethics. Nietzsche's influence wanes on Sartre as his preoccupations become more political since Nietzsche's humanistic ethics 'remains individualistic'. In Nietzsche, there is no appeal to the Other', unlike Sartre, who presents an 'opening to the Other'. For Daigle (2009: 63), Nietzsche's 'virtue ethics' needs to become a 'virtue politics' in which flourishing is seen as important for all the group. This, as we will see, presents a problem in aligning Nietzsche and Sartre politically (if we take Nietzsche's aristocratism of his later works as his final word) but does not debar a rapprochement with a more dialectical reading of his view of the relation between self (individual) and Other (herd) evident in his relational ontology of agonistic forces and his more democratic writings of the middle period which do show 'an opening to the Other'.

Nietzsche's revaluation of values

The loss of a centre of gravity, resistance to natural instincts, in a word 'selflessness' – this is what has been called 'morality' so far . . . In Daybreak *I took up the fight against the morality of 'unselfing'.*

(Nietzsche, *Ecce Homo* 3D2)

Although there are differences between the three periods of Nietzsche's ethical thinking, there are many strands of continuity that form a consistent core. First, Nietzsche takes ethical values to be cultural constructions and adopts a historical/genealogical approach in which a critique of moral values depends on 'a knowledge of the conditions and circumstances out of which they have grown, under which they have developed and shifted' (GM 6). What appears virtuous in one time or place can be perceived as vice elsewhere: 'only something which has no history can be defined' (GM 2.13).[4] Second, Nietzsche's rethinking of morality aims to go beyond the binary thinking of Good and Evil to articulate a ternary level of ethical conception based on the sublimation rather than the disjunction of the opposed terms.[5] He condemns totalitarian thinking linked to universalizing morality (BGE 202) in opposition to Roman tolerance (BGE 46), for instance, but criticizes relativism (no moral idea is binding) as 'equally childish' (GS 345) since it jumps to a nihilistic conclusion and assumes the possibility of having values from the outside or having no values at all. Third, Nietzschean ethics holds a deep concern for the self-determination and autonomy of the individual but a form of individuality conceived in relational/dialectical terms with the collective.

Nietzsche's general view on ethics is encapsulated in his narrative 'Of the three Metamorphoses' in *Zarathustra*. The three figures of the camel, the lion and the child represent three evolving stages in the development of morality. The camel personifies traditional and customary morality and obediently carries the burden and weight of their duties and dictates. The lion represents a no-saying stage in human history where individuals question and destroy the existing tablets of morality in the name of freedom. The overcoming of these two disparate positions is represented by the figure of the child who negates the spirit of gravity and seriousness through play and affirmative projects of self-cultivation. Nietzsche's ethical views undergo both subtle transformations and dramatic shifts as we move between his three transitions. In his early writings, his moral sense is collective, aimed at bringing into existence a vibrant and noble moral culture based on, but not atavistically returning to, the Greek culture of tragedy. His moral paragon of the middle writings is the 'free spirit', a more individualist conception, but one of a liberal kind whose 'Epicurean garden' is a 'lovely, peaceful, self-enclosed garden . . . with high walls to protect against the dangers and dust of the roadway, but with a hospitable gate as well' (D 174). In the later writings, his individualism turns into one of an illiberal kind and forms the bedrock of his radical aristocratism. This is the bloody Nietzsche, or 'fire-and-brimstone moralist' (Solomon 2003: 62) whose rejection of bourgeois morality values the excellence of a noble few over the well-being of the multitudinous masses. Standing as the 'opponent of the disgraceful modern softening of feeling' (GM 6), this is very much a stoical Nietzsche who emphasizes suffering and struggle: 'do you know that only this discipline has created all enhancements of human so far?' (BGE 225). Alongside creation, there must also be the 'agony of the child-bearer' (TI 10.4): 'Creating . . . requires suffering and much transformation' (Z 2.2). What is common throughout Nietzsche's ethical outlook is his rejection of justificatory foundationalist theories. Philosophers, he comments, 'make one laugh' with their quest for a rational foundation for morality (BGE 186). Throughout his writings, Nietzsche vehemently rejects universalism and endorses plurality. He praises the Hindu Laws of Manu for dividing individuals into different castes and maintaining that different ethical claims pertain to different castes (A 56–7). In the absence of any ethical universality in modern societies, it is foolish to impose the demands of a single morality on people: 'what is fair for one cannot by any means for that reason alone also be fair for others . . . the demand of one morality for all is detrimental to the higher men' (BGE 228).

The principal target of Nietzsche's 'revaluation of values' is customary morality which he views as inimical to the emergence of the 'free spirit'. For Nietzsche, '[w]e are entwined in an austere shirt of duty' (BGE 226) and so the free spirit must be hostile towards what 'is familiar, traditional, hallowed' (GS 297). Customary morality defends conformity to the 'sanctity' and 'inscrutability' of tradition (D 19), an 'inexplicable, indeterminate power' behind our thinking that lies 'beyond the personal' (D 9). It requires a regime of habit and obedience that turns humanity into a self-undermining 'perpetual sacrifice' (D 18) and is motivated by a mood of fear of transgression that may result in revenge, resentment or punishment. A fearful person is never alone but intuits an enemy to be 'always standing behind his chair' (D 249). The deleterious effects of customary morality, driven by revenge and resentment, sicken the remaining ones who, to remain as free spirits, should seek solitude (D 323). Nietzsche urges them to be courageous and take responsibility for their health on both an individual psychophysical and a cultural level:

The number of these little revenge addicts, not to mention that of their little revenge-acts, is immense; the whole air is constantly buzzing from the arrows and darts launched by their malice such that the sun and the sky of life are darkened by it – not just for them but even more so for us, the others, the remaining ones: which is worse than the all too frequent barbs which pierce our hide and heart. (D 323)

Nietzsche recommends that we should take a gardener's approach to our multifarious competing drives and cultivate new moral values and virtues that we already find ourselves beginning to express (D 566). He lists the 'good four' ethical virtues that require us to be '[h]onest towards ourselves and whatever *else* is our friend; *courageous* towards the enemy; *magnanimous* towards the defeated; *polite*: always' (D 556) but also invites us to wonder about the creation of new values 'of purple-glowing galaxies and whole Milky Ways of the beautiful' where we can become 'astronomers of the ideal' (D 551).[6] He presents the image of creatures in flight, '*aeronauts of the spirit*', who fly higher and further away with all of our 'great mentors and precursors' who cannot fly any further. There still remains a 'vast and prodigious trajectory' to explore, and despite the fatigue of some including ourselves, we can take comfort in the knowledge that '[o]ther birds will fly further!' (D 573). To become a free spirit one must constantly engage in an art of self-overcoming that requires transformation and renewal as contained in the message of the phoenix:

> '*Poet and bird*'. – The bird Phoenix showed the poet a flaming scroll turning to ashes. 'Do not be terrified!' it said, 'it is your work! It does not possess the spirit of the times and still less the spirit of those who are against the times: consequently it has to be burned. But this is a good sign. There are many types of dawn'. (D 568)

For all living organisms, change is necessary for their health. Snakes that do not shed their skin perish, as do free spirits who never change their opinions (D 573). In the pursuit of health and flourishing held out in the possibility of a new ethic, we should experiment by engaging in '*tiny deviant actions*' (D 149), diverse ways of 'novel experiments' in our 'ways of life' and 'modes of society' to reinforce imaginative resistances to customary morality. The 'numerous novel experiments . . . made in ways of life and modes of society' (D 164) will create free spirits who engage imaginatively and creatively with ethical problems in the affirmation of a new ethic. To be free, one must experiment with conflicting beliefs, be prepared to suffer and renounce valued things and show 'a *tenacious* will to health' (HH P4). He exhorts his readers to experiment with different kinds of life-affirming practices (D 453) and test out new types of morality (D 164). To avoid indoctrination by collective and conformist systems of values, we must become drawn to what is strange and unknown and try out multiple perspectives (GS P3).

Broadly speaking, Nietzsche proposes what can be described as 'an ethical *eudaimonism* based on "experimentally" generated knowledge' (Ure 2015: 166). A strong 'Epicurean mood' pervades the middle writings, including a sense of moderation, tolerance and yearning for companionship. Unfortunately, this has led to a certain neglect of the middle writings as they fit uncomfortably with 'the bloody Nietzsche' of the late period who performs cold rationality and who, through prolonged suffering, grows 'a hard Stoic hedgehog skin' (GS 306). His later writings replace the 'free spirit' with the figure of Zarathustra and the *Übermensch* and take on a more prophetic tone in the anticipation of a new human being. The target of his ethical critique is 'the last man' who has reacted to the death of God and the commercialization of society through life-denying practices based on uniform values, sedated emotions, easy options and wretched contentment, a form of escapism and weak nihilism (Z P5). But who or what is the *Übermensch*, the antidote to the last man? In describing the 'new philosopher' in *Beyond Good and Evil*, Nietzsche gives us a clue:

> a human being who constantly experiences, sees, hears, suspects, hopes, and dreams extraordinary things ... struck by his own thoughts as from outside ... as by lightning bolts ... himself a storm pregnant with new lightnings; a fatal human being around whom there are constant rumblings and growlings ... uncanny doings. (BGE 292)

For Nietzsche, bad conscience, slave morality and 'the internalization of man' (GM 2.16) have made possible a strange leap in human evolution transforming humanity from a limited animal of instinct into an animal with tremendous possibilities for development. Thus, bad conscience is an illness inasmuch as pregnancy can be regarded as an illness:

> From now on, man is *included* among the most unexpected and exciting lucky throws in the dice game of Heraclitus' 'great child', be he called Zeus or chance; he gives rise to an interest, a tension, a hope, almost a certainty, as if something were announcing and preparing itself, as if man were not a goal but only a way, an episode, a bridge, a great promise. (GM 2.16)

He speculates about the appearance on earth of 'the earliest race of contemplative human beings' from which the philosopher and a more complicated kind of human will eventually emerge (GM 3.10) whose awareness of historical and psychological conditioning, love of freedom and will to know the world marks a decisive shift in humankind: 'Tremendous self-examination: becoming conscious of oneself, not as individuals but as mankind. Let us reflect, let us think back; let us follow the highways and byways!' (WP 585). Affirmation is conditional upon a 'no-saying' insofar as the dominant values one has internalized have to be overturned if an affirmative form of life is possible (EH 4.4). Nietzsche describes the overtaking of life by scientific history as a form of self-mummification (TI 3.1) and looks forward to a future 'that gives back to the earth its goal and to the human its hope' (GM 2.24).

In Conway's (1989: 212) view, we should not construe the *Übermensch* as a 'world-historical figure' with undue haste since Nietzsche is being ironic when he speaks of the 'man of the future' and the 'great redeemer from nothingness and God' (GM 2.24). The *Übermensch* ideal is only posited in the first two parts of *Zarathustra* and, in the second half, he renounces the ideal of perfection and a future redemption but sets out to replace pedagogy with self-creation through exemplification, replacing the universalist prescription for humanity with the idea of a 'local rebellion' against nihilism and pursuing the path of a 'quiet' *Übermensch*. Against this view, though, many attribute a more universalist perspective to Nietzsche's later ethics. For Siemens (2018: 319–20), '[w]hile his perfectionism refers to individual "impulses, deeds and works", it is important not to isolate it (as a concern for a few select individuals) from a generic orientation towards "humanity" and its growth, enhancement or intensification'. Nietzsche's perfectionism is a concern to extend the range of human capabilities and possibilities that enlarge the species or concept 'human'. His later ethics are an appeal, not to annul the concept of humanity 'but to rethink it by reapportioning and transvaluating the conscious and unconscious, purposive and affective determinants of human agency' in which humanity and nature are 'inseparably entwined'. In Ure's (2015: 169, 171) view, Nietzsche's ethical thinking changes in its later stages from 'ethical perfection to bio-political transformation'. In *Daybreak*, Nietzsche attacks the 'weakening and abolition of the *individual*' and her sacrifice to the whole or some larger group (D 132), asserting the right to self-determination (D 107), but argues for a radical commitment to the Enlightenment ideal of truth at any cost (D 429, D 45). In his later writings, he replaces the service to knowledge with the idea of species-enhancement, engaging a neo-Stoic therapy to eliminate any compassion or pity that might obstruct his political program of producing higher types. He radically transforms his political therapy to maximize flourishing, no longer offering it to all but only to those select few with the biological potential to facilitate the species' potential. In *Beyond Good and Evil*, Nietzsche uses the example of the Sipo Matador ('Murdering Creeper'), the parasitic Javanese vines that 'so often enclasp an oak tree with their tendrils until eventually, high above it but supported by it, they can unfold their crowns in the open light and display their happiness' (BGE 258), to justify exploitation and sacrifice of the masses for the essential characteristic of a good and healthy aristocracy. As we will see, for many scholars, the aristocratic declarations of his later texts betray the revolutionary promise of his critical project and, particularly, the more democratic or pluralistic ethos of his middle period, by falling back into the masculinist hope for Christian redemption and reinstating Platonic conceptions of political classes and the state.

Sartre's three ethics: Authenticity, reciprocity and the gift

Sartre never produced a full-fledged ethical theory, only provisional sketches for what a theory might contain. Although it is often thought that his ethics not only falls into two distinct periods but entails two discrete theories, the line of demarcation separating the first ethics from the second is sometimes difficult to discern, since, as Sartre indicates, 'the *Critique* is *Being and Nothingness*, and it is not possible to understand one without the other' (in Beauvoir 1984: 422). To complicate matters, some scholars demarcate a third ethics (an ethics of 'the WE') that Sartre formulated after the *Critique* in the late 1960s and 1970s. Although these demarcations are useful in mapping the changes of emphasis and perspective in his thinking as it developed, my general approach is to view Sartre's oeuvre as a process of 'diachronic enrichment'. There is no doubt that his understanding of intersubjectivity and collectivity deepens as his work progresses, but the seeds of his later ethical thinking are present, if sometimes subdued or not fully adumbrated, in his early phenomenology.[7] Simple characterizations of Sartre's early social ontology as that of an unshakeable negativism where 'hell is other people' tell only a fraction of the story, neglecting significant aspects of his thinking. Unlike Christian hell which is everlasting, one always has the possibility of freely choosing to leave the hell of *Huis Clos* as the door always remains unlocked.[8] Although he later described *Being and Nothingness* as his 'eidetic of bad faith' (1964a: 196), he lodges a promissory escape from bad faith in a footnote that 'would require corrupted being to reclaim itself. We will call this authenticity: its description does not belong here' (BN 117n27). Moreover, there are moments in gestate where Sartre suggests forms of intersubjectivity he would develop to a higher sophistication, outlining a 'We-Subject' where a plurality of subjectivities recognize one another as transcending-subjectivities: 'In the "we" subject, nobody is an object. The *we* encompasses a plurality of subjectivities, each of whom recognizes the others as subjectivities' (BN 544). He returns to this later in the text, describing 'the experience of the We-subject' as a kind of 'collective rhythm' (BN 559). This provides a valuable sketch of authentic relations based on recognition and reciprocity[9] later developed in *Notebooks for an Ethics* and the *Critique*.

Towards the end of the 1940s, Sartre embarked on a theory of 'committed ethics', declaring that the writer aims towards 'action by disclosure': 'What aspect of the world do you want to disclose? What change do you want to bring into the world by this disclosure?' (WL 37). The work of art, he argues, is both a gift and an exigence, 'an act of confidence in the freedom of men' (WL 67) and 'a task proposed to human freedom' (WL 65). Proposing a 'literature of production' to counter the bourgeois 'literature of consumption' (WL 119), Sartre cements the link between art and ethics: 'at the heart of the aesthetic imperative we discern a moral imperative' (WL 67). He likens moral choice to constructing a work of art but cautions, '[w]e are not espousing an aesthetic morality' (EH 45), a warning he would later repeat in *The Family Idiot* when criticizing the bourgeois idea of *l'art pour l'art*. In this period, Sartre confronts 'the present paradox of ethics' (WL 221) of acting morally in an immoral world: 'Ethics is *for us* inevitable and at the same time impossible' (SG 185). As it is impossible to treat people as ends in the present society, the task of the artist is to exhibit this paradox of means and ends (illustrated vividly in his play *The Devil and The Good Lord*).[10] His *Notebooks for an Ethics* is Sartre's attempt to work through this problem and formulate a 'morality of deliverance and salvation' (BN 543n34) to which in *Being and Nothingness* he promised he would 'devote a future work' (BN 811). This he arrives at through the notion of *authenticity* that lies in the unveiling of being through non-being, through *doing* rather than being. It consists 'in renouncing the category of appropriation' in order 'to introduce into the internal relation of the Person the relation of *solidarity*, which will subsequently be modified into solidarity with others'. At the same time 'it realizes a type of unity peculiar to the existent, which is an *ethical* unity brought about by calling things into question and a contractual agreement with oneself' (NE 479).

As Sartre later commented (1974b: 171), it was the perceived 'bourgeois individualism' of *Notebooks for an Ethics* that led him to abandon it. The second 'dialectical ethics' that he formulates in the 1950s and 1960s heralds a more collective orientation that goes beyond the dyad of self and Other and extends to wider groups and ensembles. The defining features of his dialectical ethics in the *Critique* are, as Flynn (2014: 311–12) notes, moral indignation, spontaneity, camaraderie, a heightened sense of disalienation, the distrust of party politics, confidence in 'direct action', a visceral dislike of authority and the ever-presence of violence in the form of 'fraternity-terror'. Like Nietzsche, Sartre identifies 'norms' with customary morality, a function of the practico-inert that restricts spontaneity and creative moral praxis, producing inauthenticity and patterns of bad faith. The inert structure of social life can be found in the *serial* group. Seriality involves a certain ordering of people that 'becomes a negative principle of unity and of determining everyone's fate as other by every Other as Other' (CDR 261). The series constitutes a negative unity of inertia, a reified totalization maintained by 'hexis' (habit) in which, rather than transforming a situation, individuals instead merely endure it. In this serial group, they are bound together from without by an object they do not control: 'The series represents the use of alterity as a bond among men under the passive action of an object' (CDR 266). Serial existence is a common feature of social life that can be found wherever individuals are brought together 'horizontally' in alterity under the directing force of the practico-inert, through which their relations become structured. My individual characteristics are inessential in the series since, as just 'one other' to the others, I am instantly replaceable by anyone else who might come along: 'In the series everyone becomes himself (as Other than self) in so far as he is Other than the Others, and in so far as the Others are Other than him' (CDR 262).

After describing the alienating experience of the series, Sartre counterbalances its negative gravity with a positive analysis of the fusing group (*groupe-en-fusion*).[11] Where inertia forms the basis of the serial group, *praxis* is the constituent feature of the fusing group: 'Praxis is the only real unity of the fused groups: it is praxis which creates the group, and which maintains it and introduces its first internal changes into it' (CDR 418). In place of the alienating or objectifying third, Sartre introduces the 'mediating third' that describes free organic praxis as constituting the fusing group in a network of reciprocity. In the fusing group, no individual sacrifices his freedom to the social whole since individual will coincides with the general will and each finds a confirmation of his own act in the actions of others. As a result, all signs of alterity between individuals dissolve: 'everyone continued to see himself in the Other, but saw himself there as himself . . . everyone sees his own future in the Other' (CDR 354). The fusing group represents a state of genuine organic community since it encompasses 'the individual discovery of common action as the sole means of reaching the common objective' (CDR 387). Since no praxis in the group serves to violate or to obstruct any other, but only to enrich it, 'the essential character of the group-in-fusion is the abrupt resurrection of liberty' (CDR 401).

While the fusing group becomes the prototype for authentic social relations, its existence is ephemeral and precarious. From the moment of its inception, the free praxis of the group 'carries a destiny of seriality' (CDR 679). Since the group emerges as a defensive reaction against fear and imminent threat, once this is removed, the group falls into dissipation since the practical basis of its unity no longer exists. In order to stop this process of fragmentation, the group must impose stability by other means. This happens through the introduction of 'fraternity-terror' that incorporates organization, function and the division of labour in addition to a pledge taken by the group for reciprocal protection against the relapse into seriality, alterity and indifference (CDR 422). In the 1970s, after the events of 1968, Sartre sketches out a third 'dialogical ethics' in the course of a series of interviews. Continuing the direction of the fusing group, he speaks in 1976 of the establishment of a non-hierarchical society in which 'a new form of freedom is established, which is the freedom of reciprocal relations of persons in the form of a we' (1980: 233). In other respects, however, he changes course and returns to concepts formulated in his earliest thinking: 'And I am trying to close the circle, to link my first thoughts with my latest, by giving up some of my ideas from BN and CDR' (1980: 234). Key to this was the development of a form of *fraternity* no longer based on violence and terror but on reciprocal connection, 'integral humanity' and the 'interpenetration of consciousnesses', continuing the process of de-egoization and an 'ethics of the gift' that Sartre had initiated in *Notebooks for an Ethics* but then put on hold in the *Critique*. A new era of 'integral humanity' will replace the 'subhumans' of the present deformed by the systematic processes and constitutive structures of capitalist society. Returning to the liberating power of the imagination to 'surpass the real' (I 186), his final period of interviews represents Sartre's attempt to construct a new collective ethics in order to bring this change about: 'Morality cannot be imposed from above. In fact, morality is not possible in a world of individuals . . . man's fulfilment is collective' (in Gerassi 2009: 120–1).

Nietzsche's grand politics

The great health – *Being new, nameless, hard to understand, we premature births of an as yet unproven future need for a new goal also a new means – namely, a new health, stronger, more seasoned, tougher, more audacious, and gayer than any previous health.*

(Nietzsche, *The Gay Science* 382)

There is perhaps no other philosopher one can think of whose philosophy has been appropriated by such a diverse range of ideologies as Nietzsche's, a spectrum that seems to encompass just about every conceivable political alternative. This is despite the fact (or maybe because of it) that nowhere in his writings does Nietzsche present a systematic account of his political thinking but merely different sketches that emerge in different periods.[12]

Raised in a conservative and religious household, when he came of age politically in the 1860s, Nietzsche's views were strongly royalist, extolling a deep respect for the grand heroes of history and the great nation. Once the war was underway with Austria in 1866, he supported the Prussian military machine, serving two stints in the army (as a soldier and medical orderly). In the 1870s, his 'Bismarckianism' expressed itself as an aloof disdain towards party politics, demanding a cultural rebirth inspired by Greek culture, the music of Wagner and the pessimism of Schopenhauer. Developing Schopenhauer's aristocratism and calling for tragic greatness in culture as the aspiration of the political state, Nietzsche argued that some political theories (e.g. Rousseau and Socialism) are unduly sentimental and fail to recognize that each culture must accept the necessity of slavery (BT 18) in order for great art to prosper.[13] He celebrated Schopenhauer initially as the philosopher of a regenerated Germany who became a cultural figurehead for his generation as Hegel had been for his in the 1830s. Although he later rejected his mentor, Nietzsche was attracted to his anti-orthodoxy, his aestheticism and his rousing call to follow our consciences, resist absorption into the masses and '[b]e your self! All you are now doing, thinking, desiring, is not you yourself!' (UM 3.127). Unlike 'we moderns' who glorify 'the dignity of man' and 'the dignity of labour', the Greeks understood that a life devoted to toil made it impossible to become an artist. The 'need for art' rests upon 'a terrible basis': 'In order that there may be a broad, deep, and fruitful soil for the development of art, the enormous majority must, in the service of a minority, be slavishly subjected to life's struggle, to a greater degree than their own wants necessitate' (G.S 6). In his essay 'The Greek State', Nietzsche laments the 'drone-like individuals' of the modern masses where culture and state are reduced to the furtherance of the wishes of egoistic individuals, propelling the 'deviation of the state tendency into a money-tendency' (G.S 7, 15). Modern humans are no longer political animals in the Greek sense, for we are unwilling to organize ourselves as 'material for society'. He advocates war in order to reinstate the collective purpose and body of the state: 'although it comes along like the night, war is nevertheless Apollo, the true divinity for consecrating and purifying the state' (G.S 15).

In the early 1880s, Nietzsche's political views underwent a decisive transformation. He became an earnest critic of modern German politics, viewing the Bismarckian state as a philistine enforcer of racist, nationalist and statist policies. This mirrors his split with Wagner who turned from libertarian revolutionary to the favourite of the king of Bavaria and a reconciled supporter of the Reich. His break with Wagner is equally a break with the political idealism and cultural romanticism of his youth. In this middle period, a 'milder Nietzsche' emerges, one who believes that 'democratic politics can promote and further culture, not that it necessarily has to destroy it, or that it is synonymous with decadence and degeneration' (Ansell-Pearson 1994: 95). What is needed to cure social ills, Nietzsche now suggests, 'is not a forcible redistribution of property but a gradual transformation of mind: the sense of justice must grow greater in everyone and the instinct for violence weaker' (HH 452). In *Human, All Too Human*, Nietzsche regards democracy differently than he had done in 'The Greek State'. It does not necessarily mean the death of culture but can offer the best protection of culture if it is kept separate from politics. He declares that 'the democratization of Europe is irresistible' (WS 275) and argues for a future 'democracy as something yet to come' (WS 293), which will overcome polarities of wealth and power and render obsolete the dangerous ideologies of nationalism and socialism. He even suggests an enlightened labour policy that will guarantee workers' protection against injustice and exploitation and secure the contentment of body and soul (WS 286). A strong pan-Europeanism and hope for a new European humanity is proposed as an alternative to nationalism:

> the separation of nations through the production of *national* hostilities . . . is in its essence a forcibly imposed state of siege and self-defence inflicted on the many by the few and requires cunning, force and falsehood to maintain a front of respectability. It is not the interests of the many (the peoples), as is no doubt claimed, but above all the interests of certain princely dynasties and of certain classes of business and society, that impel to this nationalism; once one has recognized this fact, one should not be afraid to proclaim oneself simply *a good European* and actively work for the amalgamation of nations. (HH 475)

In considering the question of how we prevent and guard against tyrannical concentrations of power, Nietzsche suggests democracy as a site of pluralism that incorporates resistance to, and emancipation from, tyrannical forces. From around 1880 onwards, however, he increasingly links democracy with tyranny in the form of popular sovereignty, the promotion of uniformity and the elimination of qualitative diversity. In the texts of his middle period, he recognizes the archaic nature of hierarchical social structures and traditional feelings of subordination but throws this out of the window and reverses direction in his mature aristocratic politics. He replaces the idea of social and moral change taking place through a process of liberal recommendation with a process of aristocratic legislation. In his mature political thinking, Nietzsche accepts a 'Machiavellianism' (WP 304) which, in the thought of his middle period, he associates with the despotism of socialism and clearly rejects because of its reliance on force, obedience and deception.[14] In the mid- and late 1880s, his middle insights fade away and he reverts back to the collective viewpoint of his early work, viewing people as pawns in the service of greatness, but viewed this time in more evolutionary/physiological terms than in cultural ones. In *Beyond Good and Evil*, Nietzsche asserts that every enhancement of the human type is the work of a society based on an order of rank and differences of value between humans. Society 'needs slavery in some sense' as 'scaffolding' (BGE 258) for some individuals to achieve 'the highest value' and 'deepest significance'. High culture requires a pyramid structure for the elevation of its highest specimens:

> The essential characteristic of a good and healthy aristocracy is that it experiences itself *not* as a function (whether of the monarchy or of the commonwealth) but as their meaning and highest justification – that it therefore accepts with good conscience the sacrifice of untold human beings who, *for its sake*, must be reduced and lowered to incomplete human beings, to slaves, to instruments. (BGE 258)

> The order of castes, *order of rank*, only formulates the supreme law of life itself; the separation of the three types is necessary for the preservation of society, for making possible higher and higher types. (A 57)

In the *Nachlass*, Nietzsche considered a political application of 'the eternal return of the same' that will lead to the 'foundation of an oligarchy over peoples and their interests: education to a universally human politics'. This will introduce a 'new Enlightenment' and a new order of rank (KSW 11.212–3). In *The Gay Science*, he talks of the 'children of the future' who are neither liberals working for progress nor 'socialists' who dream of equal rights and the abolition of slavery but 'conquerors' who love danger and war and who realize that every enhancement of the human requires a new kind of enslavement (GS 377).[15] Nietzsche justifies aristocratic rule by drawing on the notion of will to power that seeks to enhance its power, grow and become predominant: 'Exploitation does not pertain to a corrupt or imperfect or primitive society: it pertains to the *essence* of the living thing as a fundamental organic function; it is a consequence of the intrinsic will to power, which is precisely the will of life' (BGE 259). The exploitation of one group or individual by another, Nietzsche asserts, is 'the *primordial fact* of all history' (BGE 259).

Nietzsche's affinity with Fascism relates to his 'Machiavellianism', his advocacy of elitism, struggle, suffering and cruelty to achieve political ends, as well as his criticisms of compassion and pity. It was the popularity of his writings in Germany during the First World War that allowed the Nazis to exploit him as an ideological ally during the interwar period. Nietzsche gave the Nazis intellectual credence and substance, helped along by his literary executrix, Elisabeth, who presented him as a philosopher of German imperialism and militarism, even inviting Hitler to visit the Nietzsche Archive and, on one occasion, presenting him with her brother's walking stick. Academic philosophers, such as Baeumler and Rosenberg, were enlisted with the task of propagating Nietzsche's philosophy. In Baeumler's 1931 *Nietzsche as Philosopher and Politician*, Nietzsche is the philosopher of the Nordic race and his attacks on the German people were directed towards those non-Germanic elements of the German people, such as Christians and Jews. Other works reinforced this militaristic message of Nietzsche as the true philosopher of National Socialism, such as Härtle's *Nietzsche and National Socialism* and Oehler's *Nietzsche and the Future of Germany*. While eschewing these Nazi vulgarizations of Nietzsche, modern scholars often focus upon his elitism and his promotion of 'pathos of distance' (based on contempt and disgust) as a virtue, showing, in Alfano's (2018: 122) words, 'the bleak prospects for a Nietzschean democratic ethos'.

On the Left, the dissemination of his work after his mental collapse in 1889 was quickly taken up by socialists, anarchists and feminists who were inspired by his quest for individual self-realization and creative personality, highlighting his atheism and anti-nationalism that alienated him from German conservatism. Progressives see in Nietzsche the 'unmasking trope', his ironic stance to the modern world and his genealogical deconstruction of power, providing the material for the development of a new progressive politics, a 'radicalized liberalism' (Connolly 1988) or 'liberalism with teeth' (Hunt 1993). Connolly (1988: 136) privileges a 'Nietzschean perspective' for understanding modernity that 'insists upon thinking dangerously during a time of danger'. Those things, such as madness, irrationality, chaos, disorder, perversity that are deemed beyond the control of political and instrumental technologies are delimited as 'forms of otherness' in need of normalization. For Connolly (1988: 140), Nietzsche's genealogical thought 'eschews all transcendental and teleological justifications of the present and confronts history in all its contingency'. It does not contain within it a single theory of politics but 'a diverse set of ethical and political possibilities'. We need a 'post-Nietzschean' political theory made up of Nietzsche's counter-ontology of otherness that would 'turn the genealogist of resentment on his head by exploring democratic politics as a medium through which to expose resentment and to encourage the struggle against it' (1988: 175). Although Nietzsche's final phase of political thinking is 'deeply metaphysical' with 'regressive dimensions' that contravenes his earlier pluralistic logic (Ansell-Pearson 1994: 161), some view his advocacy of a pan-European plurality (BGE 241) and his 'ecological turn' as progressive aspects of his later 'grand politics'. As the central meaning of a future politics, he posits the question, '[h]ow shall the earth as a whole be governed? To what end shall "man" as a whole – and no longer as a people or a race – be raised and trained?' (WP 957). Furthermore, his 'politics of domination' is offset by another dimension in his thinking where he envisages the possibility of a peaceful coexistence among different human types in which the former pursue practices of artistic self-creation and others preoccupy themselves with quotidian pursuits and material interests. For Nietzsche, the *Übermensch* will exist free of political power and prestigious economic wealth. The goal is 'not to conceive of the latter as masters of the former', but rather 'two types . . . are to exist side by side' (KSW 10.244). In a dialectical relation of mutual enhancement, '[t]he same conditions that hasten the evolution of the herd animal also hasten the evolution of the leader animal' (WP 956).

Positive agonism

The will to power can manifest itself only against obstacles; it therefore goes in search of what resists it.

(Nietzsche, *The Will to Power* 656)

Influenced by Heraclitus' notion of strife as the basic motor behind change and becoming, as well as by his idea the cosmos as a battle of opposed forces, the concept of *agonism* lies at the explanatory heart of Nietzsche's social ontology. Just as trees in a jungle fight each other for power (WP 704), the will to power 'seeks that which resists it' (WP 656). In Ancient Greece, the *agon* represented freedom of mind in antiquity in the form of 'a measured discharge for the forces of nature' (Siemens 2018: 319), not their annihilation or negation. The Greek state was the watchdog of productive agonism, harnessing the *agon* to guarantee that the instinct for struggle is not discharged in a deleterious way that may threaten the polis. In the Greek *agon* (contest), Nietzsche identifies the socially binding force of myth that curbs the excesses of unidentified egoism by 'placing it in the service of the whole': 'For the ancients the goal of agonal education was the welfare of the whole, the state society' (KSW 1.7). For Nietzsche, agonism is productive when among relative equals it recognizes differences rather than collapses them. This he applies to Apollo and Dionysus (BT 1), cultural advancement

(HH 158, 170), scientific advancement (HH 634), friendship (D 192), gender (BGE 238), self-overcoming (Z 2.7, 2.12) and the need to order competing drives (HH 141).

As Siemens (2018: 329, 326) notes, Nietzsche's concept of the *agon* reminds us that 'the individualistic pathos of his texts notwithstanding, he is a profoundly social thinker who addresses fundamental ethical questions in relational terms'. The medial or relational sense of the agon presents a '*social ontology of tension*' in which '[e]very gift must unfold through contestation' (KSW 1.789). In the *agon*, the relations of tension define the *relata* – each capacity, force and subject needs agonistic relations with another in order to become what it is. The resistance offered by others compels me to assert myself and, since the resistance I encounter is unpredictable, continuous and contingent in origin, who I am and what I can do turns out to be highly dynamic and contingent. The community is constitutive of individual agency at the affective level of drives in sharp contrast to the capitalist society of possessive individuals who compete through egoistic drives. The meeting of forces gives rise to a process of assimilation, incorporation and expansion that aims towards 'the feeling of increased power' (BGE 230). A dominant organization attempts to incorporate a suppressed organization but must bring itself closer and accommodate it in order to do so. The process of incorporation is not a simple submission but is instead a shared becoming where each organization bends to form something new. This is to be understood not in dualistic terms of submission and dominance but instead as an agonistic model of transformation where striving between different and multiple forces allows intermingling and change to occur in each drive irrespective of which one is the incorporator.[16]

In Hatab's (1995: 68) view, Nietzsche opens up the possibility of reinscribing democratic practices in non-metaphysical terms that allows us to dispense with the notion of equality and replace it with the concept of agonistic respect or indebtedness in which the other is an indispensable part of my self-development, the annulment of whom would be like annihilating part of myself. Within relations of agonistic indebtedness, the other does not constitute a disabling threat to my identity but provides an alternative and enriching perspective through which I am able to grasp my own limits. Respect for others is based accordingly on a notion of indebtedness to those who prevent limits from congealing by sustaining contest between different ideas and identities. Through 'a cultivation of care for difference' (Connolly 1991: 64), we are able to respect others by seeing them as embodying and living out some of the possibilities and richness of life that we had to forego in order to be who we are. For Siemens (2015: 93), however, liberal notions of indebtedness tend to take only the positive aspects of Nietzschean antagonism and disregard Nietzschean hatred, assimilation, nourishment and 'pathos of distance'. In Nietzsche's 'spiritualization of *enmity*' (TI 5.3), one has to hate one's enemies and share in their power by rejoicing in their strength (Z 1.10). Hatred provokes a reciprocal dynamic of affirmation, stimulation and self-empowerment, a nuanced phenomenology of agonism where hatred is bound up with love just as friend and enemy are entwined. It is important not to confuse the concept of equality presupposed by the *agon* with the kind of equality Nietzsche criticizes so vehemently in the context of modern democracy (TI 9.37). For one, it concerns equal forces or capacities, not equal rights or equality as an ideal. Second, it does not exclude qualitative diversity in favour of uniformity. Siemens (2015: 95) concludes in this respect that Nietzsche's ontology of power culminates not in tyranny but in affirmative ideals that exclude domination, subjection and incorporation in favour of an approximate equality/equilibrium of powers that is compatible with a democratic politics of identity. This is why Nietzschean agonism opposes tyranny (which collapses power into a single individual) and state socialism (which tries to efface agonism and difference).

As we saw in Chapter 4, Sartre shares with Nietzsche a relational ontology of forces in which '[e]verything is always revealed as united to everything' (CDR 360). Sartre's ontology of forces constitutes a similar theory of *positive agonism* in his social ethics. In Sartre's phenomenological account of hodological space (BN 415), the valences of my field of force are directly affected by the presence of the other as an undermining or confirming presence who generates their own alien spatiality and valences: 'We are dealing with a relation . . . within which a spatiality that is not *my* spatiality unfolds because, rather than being a grouping of objects *towards* me, we have an orientation *that flees me*' (BN 349). The Other 'unfolds its own distances around it' (BN 350), which can disintegrate my spatiality and precipitate an 'intraworldly haemorrhage' in my consciousness. As an embodied consciousness, what I am at any instant is my pre-reflective interaction with the other as a field of force which is a function not of my interiority but of the other's presence. The Other directly shapes my embodied consciousness, whether her presence results in my field of force imploding, becoming decentralized or being challenged and supported. For Mirvish (1996: 67), Sartre's elucidation of 'conflict as a positive phenomenon' accords perfectly with details worked out later about the nature of authenticity in *Notebooks for an Ethics*, 'a positive analysis of interpersonal relations' that can 'be found early in Sartre's *oeuvre* and shown to rest on his ontology'. An example Sartre gives of positive conflict resulting from authentic relations is that of helping a man onto a bus by extending my hand out to him as he chases after the bus:

> Help . . . is opposition overcome, that is, makes use of the conflict between freedoms. You never help to help by letting yourself be helped, but – on the corporeal plane – by grasping this help. . . . If someone has to help me, I have to pull on the person pulling me, that is, I go in the opposite direction – the form of a struggle overcome. (NE 288)

Here, I relate to the Other as 'an alien freedom which is *in difficulty*' (NE 279). In hodological terms, I generate a field of force that has a dominant, positive valence on the other's goal that intersects and overlaps to generate new possibilities of force. As well as acting negatively when one oppresses another, intersections of force can also generate positive conflict. Sartre illustrates this in terms of a 'loved other', invoking a distinction between Annie the woman I love and her image which is a substitute in her absence. Unlike the real Annie, the image of her contains no real surprises: 'In every person we love, and for the very reason of its inexhaustible wealth, there is something that surpasses us, an independence, an imperviousness which exacts ever renewed efforts of approximation' whereas 'tenderness does not rebound on the unreal object; it has not just fed on the inexhaustible depths of the real: it remains cut off from the object, suspended' (IM 208, 204). With the real Annie there is a sudden tension and restructuring of my field of force as it intersects with her own. Empirically, this may well cause conflict as our choices and predilections differ, but this conflict can be positive: 'Help . . . is opposition overcome, that is, makes use of the conflict between freedoms' (NE 288).

As Mirvish (1996: 78) notes, Sartre begins to develop the 'creative and challenging' aspect of conflict in his account of authentic sexual desire in *Being and Nothingness*, although he only develops this fully in *Notebooks for an Ethics*. As a 'sublimation of passion', love involves treasuring and 'finding precious' the independence and spontaneity of the Other and their irreducible alterity. For Sartre, authenticity encompasses a 'certain kind of interpenetration of freedoms' (NE 290) where 'each freedom is wholly in the other one' (NE 288). Relations of this kind occur in authentic love and friendship, incorporating a 'unity of diversity' or a 'sameness' that both respects the other free individual and overcomes radical separation and otherness (NE 81). This involves the processes of assimilation and incorporation and a shared becoming but not coincidence or complete dissolution of individual singularity. Commenting on Sartre's rejection of the idea of coincidence as he describes the love between Eve and Pierre in *The Chips are Down*, Bell sums this up well: 'Human relationships that strive in a positive, authentic way for perfect coincidence, perfect confidence. Such coincidence . . . cannot be achieved. Ambiguity and a tension of opposites are ineradicably part of the human condition; yet the effort to harmonize and unify the inharmonious and disparate may well be vital to . . . authentic striving' (1989: 164–5). For Sartre, reciprocity lies in no generic essence but emerges through praxis and the transformation of the material field whether through mutual antagonism or reciprocal solidarity: 'It cannot be based on a universal abstract bond, like Christian "charity"; nor on an *a priori* willingness to treat the human person . . . as an absolute end; nor on a purely contemplative intuition revealing "Humanity" to everyone as the essence of his fellows' (CDR 109–10).

Self and Other: A dialectical exchange

Great star! What would your happiness be, if you had not those for whom you shine!
. . . Behold! I am weary of my wisdom, like a bee that has gathered too much honey;
I need hands outstretched to take it.

(Nietzsche, *Zarathustra* P1)

There is a certain paradox about Nietzsche and Sartre in that they are simultaneously heralded as *both* individualist and relational thinkers. As Ansell-Pearson (1994: 87) remarks, 'the widely held view of Nietzsche as an extreme individualist solely preoccupied with the nature of an asocial, isolated individual, is profoundly misleading'. Nietzsche's political thought is characterized from beginning to end by a desire to transcend the atomistic basis of modern societies and its narrow, 'bourgeois', individualism. The privatization of society, for Nietzsche, 'means the *end* of society'.

He understands his politics as being neither individualistic nor collectivistic since the former 'does not recognize order of rank' and the latter fails to generate a notion of individual greatness (WP 859). Along with Sartre, his ethics and politics can be viewed as an attempt to square this circle through a dialectical analysis of the various ways and means by which individuality and intersubjectivity mutually implicate and reinforce (or diminish) each other, forming richer or weaker expressions of subjectivity.

In Daigle's (2009: 70) view, what separates Nietzsche and Sartre is the German philosopher's inability to progress from an 'ethics of virtue' to a 'politics of virtue' due to his 'closure to the Other' and his distaste for the herd. There is in this sense a disjunction between Nietzsche's social ontology and his aristocratic politics. While recognizing the ontological entwinement of self and Other, his politics seem to separate them, imagining the *Übermensch* as distinct from and superior to the herd. For all this talk of 'wholeness', Nietzsche is not seriously concerned to envisage a whole *society*. He envisages the whole *individual*, but he shows insufficient interest in the social patterns that would facilitate and sustain his wholeness. His concern for the creative individual and the social needs of his creative individuality is gained at the expense of society's other members. Richardson (2020: 468, 443) refers to this as Nietzsche's 'predatory stance' towards the herd which surfaces in certain passages in his writings and raises the worry of whether Nietzsche cares at all about the herd given his insistence on 'rank-order': 'My danger is *disgust* with people' (EH 4.6). He often insists that he speaks only for a select few: 'let Zarathustra not talk to the people, but to companions! Zarathustra shall not become shepherd and dog to a herd!' (Z 1.9).[17] The fear is that Nietzsche is completely indifferent to the herd or, worse still, views it entirely as a slavish instrument for the elite (BGE 188, 239, GS 377) to the point of immolation, imagining a large cleft between the highest and lowest types (WP 886, 953).

As Richardson (2020: 224) notes, however, the common trend in Nietzsche's thinking is towards a more nuanced understanding of self and Other in which the operation of the common stands 'in a certain dialectical relation to the individual'. This relation changes from his early work where the Apollonian is seen as a principle of individuation inferior to the generality of the Dionysian (where we lose our identity as 'belonging to a higher community' (BT 1)) to his later judgement that seems quite the reverse when the common falls into disfavour and becomes 'the herd': '*Basic error*: to place the goal in the herd and not in the single individuals! The herd is means, not more!' (WP 766). Despite his positive attitude towards solitude and individuality as 'lone wolf' and 'outsider', however, Nietzsche does not want to cast off his social identity and argues for the indispensability of individual and herd: 'one should *not* evaluate the solitary type by the herdish, *nor* the herdish by the solitary . . . both are necessary; equally their antagonism is necessary' (WP 886). For Richardson (2020: 444, 447), rather than the inverse relation that Nietzsche's 'predatory' passages suggest, he thinks that progress depends on 'herds and individuals ascending together by a dialectic'. This denotes an 'intimate relation' between individual and herd comprised of mutual involvements in which even the most exceptional individual is still really a mixture of herd and individual traits. The herd establishes the ground out of which the individual can flourish or flounder since intersubjective practices or common culture are the essential springboard for individual singularity and excellence. The higher the herd, the more able the individual is to ascend even higher as their advances are in turn incorporated or absorbed into shared practices. There is 'a dialectical interplay between herd and individuals' (2020: 448) in which individuals, through their disenchantment and movement beyond the ethic of custom, generate new values and abilities that are in turn absorbed by the herd as new norms. Exceptional individuals are 'the seed-bearers of the future, the authors of spiritual colonizing and new-founding of states and communities' (GS 23). The herd in itself, in Nietzsche's view, exerts a gravitational pull towards the ordinary and mediocre – 'the tendency of the herd is towards stasis and preservation, there is nothing creative in it' (WP 285). It simply longs for comfort, lack of danger, alleviation of suffering and the state of 'green meadow happiness' (BGE 44).

This Nietzschean dialectic is sometimes conceived on a species level – 'My task, preparing for humanity's moment of highest self-reflection, a great noon when it will look back and look out, when it will escape from the mastery by chance and priests and for the first time pose the questions of why? and what for? *as a whole*' (EH 3D2) – but also in terms of the single transformative individual – 'this antichrist and antinihilist; this conqueror of god and of the nothing – *he must one day come*' (GM 2.24). For Nietzsche, as Richardson (2020: 232–8) observes, the individual's 'contempt' for the common is aimed at 'instituting a new common' by changing and improving the common, within and against it, rather than opting out of it. Revisionary work is carried out in solitude since an active stance towards the common requires periodic estrangement from it. The purifying turn towards oneself is contained within an overall will to improve the community or group. After leaving his hermitage, Zarathustra looks for a new community in order to make his 'individualized meanings' into a new common and a new language. Equally, free spirits are the work of high culture. They cannot be reduced to individual egocentric endeavours but are concerned with 'humanity' and are interventions within a culture. Their stance against the group is just another way of serving it. By means of her 'individualizing turn' the individual is a device of the common to improve itself. All individual spirituality belongs to a collective spirit: 'artists . . . as well as orators, preachers, writers . . . come at the end of a long chain' (GS 354). Stendhal and Bizet have achieved 'greatness' by embodying the 'inventive nobility' (BGE 253) of free spirituality, but this greatness is essentially a contribution to the 'France of the Spirit' (BGE 254), to the 'European soul' (BGE 245) and 'European consciousness' (BGE 259), not an individual concern. Humans have, in Nietzsche's view, a deep allegiance to their species, the closest in kind of all living things: 'nothing in us is older, stronger, more relentless and insuperable than this instinct' (GS 1). Each of us is an exemplar or representative of humankind, sharing a common link. The individual 'is an error: he is nothing for himself, no atom, no "link in the chain", no mere inheritance from the past, – he is the whole single line human up through himself' (TI 9.33). The human is not just an individual 'but the living organic totality in one particular line' (WP 678): 'the kind is everything, the one is always nothing' (GS 1).

In highlighting Nietzsche's individualism, it is easy to overlook the importance of wholeness in his philosophy and treat his thinking undialectically (metaphysically). The duties of the 'sovereign individual', he tells us, 'are not the duties of a solitary; on the contrary, they set one in the midst of a mighty community held together, not by external forms and regulations, but by a fundamental idea. It is the idea of culture, insofar as it sets for each one of us but one task: *to promote the production of the philosopher, the artist and the saint within us and without us and thereby to work at the perfecting of nature*' (UM 3.5). 'Humanity' is a constitutive feature of the practical standpoint itself that we come to inhabit in our role as agents, lending a certain coherence and imperishability to our individual lives by making them part of a collective project that is perpetually in the making and by means of which we become necessarily connected to each other:[18] 'our thoughts, our values, our yes's and no's and if's and whether's grow out of us with the necessity with which a tree bears its fruit – all these things are related and interconnected as the testimony to One Will, One Health. One Soil, One Sun' (GM P2). For Nietzsche, great experimenters realize a perfectionist demand that has a general orientation beyond the individual towards humankind.[19]

Nietzsche 'individualizes individuality' by aspiring to show us how to be an individual in a new way, a fuller and better way that can be incorporated into ongoing practice within groups.[20] He recognizes that in groups with shared social practices and norms we become a superorganism, 'masters of the earth' in which each member feels himself amplified by belonging to this greater power and 'communal power-feeling' numbs the individual's discontent with himself (GM 3.19). Reading Nietzsche dialectically within a framework of positive agonism gives a grounding for a more dynamic conception of self and Other that brings him closer to Sartre and to a more democratic political orientation. Even his advocacy of '*strong* selfishness' as 'the deepest necessity for flourishing' (EH 4.7) is not simply self-absorption but rather a form of storing up for the purpose of enhancing expressive capacities and sharing them with others. In the '*right ideal* selfishness' we 'care and watch for the *benefit of all*' (D 552), setting a model for all to come as a pioneer for the whole type. There are, he argues, many kinds of selfishness that are 'despicable' (UM 2.7), such as the 'phantom' ego (D 105), the idea that one's self should become a universal law (GS 335) and the 'tidal waves of selfishness' found in previous ages (BGE 212). Noble selfishness, by contrast, is entwined with magnanimity (GS 49), love and friendship (GS 14) and an extended sense of self for the growth of humanity (D 547), like the love and selfishness of a mother caring for her child (EH 2.9, D 552). Whether selfishness is 'strong' or 'weak' depends on if it represents the 'ascending or the descending line of life' (TI 9.33).

So, what examples of positive intersubjectivity (akin to *fusion* in Sartre's) can we find in Nietzsche's writings? First, his early thinking in *The Birth of Tragedy* provides us with a prototype of the collectivist self based on the participatory model of tragic art and Dionysian rapture. The intoxication of the participants is *transformative*; they are seized by moods and insights so powerful that they are liberated from the dominion of concepts and all the divisions between one human being and another, giving way to the overwhelming feeling of unity and 'the destruction of the *principium individuationis*' (BT 2). Dionysian 'affirmative effects' enable us to grasp the constitutive links between individual and whole where the redemption of existence is dependent upon the individual being able to attain the perspective of the will, itself expressed by the wisdom of the chorus. Nietzsche returns to this idea in his later writings in his 'Dionysian affirmation of the world as it is' (WP 536), which gives the sense of the wider whole of which one is a part. This is an affirmation of life from the viewpoint of an individual, but 'an individual drawn out of himself', 'an ecstatic affirmation of the total character of life' (WP 539). Greatness does not issue from the individual but from the power of the whole manifesting itself through the individuals: '[O]ne belongs to the whole, one is the whole . . . *nothing exists apart from the whole!*' (TI 6.8).

Second, some scholars point to Nietzsche's theorization of *friendship* in his middle and later writings as a positive model of social relations (in microcosm) that can be developed as a 'practical ethics of reciprocity' against 'the revenge of institutions and rationalism' (Stauth and Turner 1988: 14). In Verkerk's (2020: 2) view, his 'ethics of friendship' provides a positive model of sociality that complicates a simple characterization of him as an individualist thinker and delineates other modes of interaction beyond that of agonism alone. He encourages free spirits who seek 'one's own way' to separate themselves from society and to 'live in seclusion' but also encourages them to have friends and help others (GS 338). Within the three types of friendship Nietzsche outlines (joyful friendship, agonistic friendship and bestowing friendship), he promotes the virtues of shared experiences and mutual becomings. Joyful friendship is a healing balm from pity and suffering '*to share not suffering but joy*' (GS 338). Friends can provide a kind of meta-perspective on oneself that challenges beliefs and ingrained habits (GS 355), enabling a vital means for self-overcoming, a 'secret path' to expose parts of oneself of which one is unaware: 'The actual fortress is inaccessible, even invisible to him, unless his friends and enemies play the traitor and conduct him in by a secret path' (HH 491). As a mirror of recognition, friendship can provide a form of illuminating external critique that helps us to shed a skin and renew ourselves (GS 307).[21] Demonstrating the compatibility of egoism and friendship, agonistic friendship involves a form of 'spiritualized enmity' that provides the opportunity for self-examination and growth through cooperative competition: 'In one's friend one should have one's best enemy. You should be closest to him in your heart when you strive against him' (Z 1.14). Enmity is transformed into a tool for mutual growth and self-overcoming where friends engender qualities that we hope to accrue through mutual endeavour and striving. Nietzsche places the highest worth of all on the bestowing friendship: 'the highest virtue is a bestowing virtue' (Z 1.22.1). The bestowing friend offers potential and wisdom to others to use for their own growth, believing that 'to *give* is more blessed than to *have*' (WS 320). Her own capabilities, attributes and wisdom are offered in the form of a gift to others who in turn reciprocate their own bestowing:[22] 'I teach you the friend and his overfull heart . . . in whom the world stands complete, a vessel of goodness – the creating friend, who always has a complete world to bestow' (Z 1.17). When Zarathustra declares, '[n]ot the neighbour do I teach you but the friend' (Z 1.14), he is making a distinction between positive and negative forms of sociality.

The 'herd', like many of Nietzsche's terms, carries different force and connotation in different places but is more generally equated with a will to obey moral norms or an 'ethics of custom' (BGE 199) and, akin to the Sartrean serial group, is viewed as promoting an annihilation rather than enhancement of individuality. As we have seen, his view of intersubjectivity 'contains both enabling and disabling aspects' (Ansell-Pearson 1994: 157). His 'politics of domination' is offset by another dimension in his thinking where he envisages the possibility of a peaceful coexistence among different human types. Here, in this more dialectical scenario, the *Übermensch* is not viewed as a master of the herd but rather the 'two types . . . are to exist side by side' (KSW 10.244). In Safranski's (2003: 297) view, Nietzsche doesn't really develop this dimension of his thinking sufficiently and was ultimately 'incapable of reconciling the ideas of self-enhancement and solidarity, or at least allowing them to coexist'. Although he recognizes the alienation of solitude (Z 4.13), he remains a paragon of independence, keeping a 'pathos of distance' with his fellow human being. It is indicative that in the final book, Zarathustra leaves the cave when visited by the 'higher men', disgusted by the human smell, preferring the company of his animals untouched by rules, mores and regulations. In the absence of any community, as Solomon (2003: 127) contends, Nietzsche turned his own personal suffering into a heroic campaign and ended up defending a crude notion of self-assertion, 'generalized to all nature as "the will to power"', reducing the notion of his later aristocratic ethics 'to a combination of aggressive banality and energetic self-indulgence' and turning his back on the insights and openings of his middle works.

In his dialectical view of individual and herd, his Dionysian affirmation of life and his ethics of friendship, Nietzsche began to explore the intersubjective conditions of self-cultivation, but this is something that Sartre's philosophy develops significantly, particularly his theory of groups which is one of the main sociological innovations of his philosophical legacy.[23] Connecting selves rather than constituting the self is something Sartre thinks through more than Nietzsche. Prior to the 1940s, it is thought that Sartre valorized the Nietzschean ideal of the lone intellectual who stands aloof from society, embracing individualism and non-conformity while maintaining a relatively indifferent attitude towards political matters. Although his apoliticism in the 1930s may be overstated – Beauvoir notes their many political discussions and the fact that Sartre considered joining the Communist Party before 1939[24] – he nonetheless describes his political consciousness at this time as 'petit bourgeois, individualistic and democratic' (Gerassi 2009: 120) and as a 'morality of *complaisance*' (1983a: 385). Despite its many insights on the syncategorematic nature of the self in which, as Deleuze commented, 'Sartre . . . is the first to have considered the Other as a real structure' (2004: 373), *Being and Nothingness* had left intersubjectivity relatively unexplored in his own view: 'What is particularly bad in *L'Etre et le néant* is the specifically social chapters, on the "we", compared to the chapters on the "you" and "others"' (1981a: 13).

It was Sartre's experience as a prisoner of war that taught him solidarity, brought about, as much as anything, by being in the 'absolute proximity' (1964a: 348) of others: 'I have seen crowds of all kinds, but the only other time I have witnessed that nakedness, that sense of everyone's direct relationship to everyone else, that waking dream, that dim consciousness of the danger of being a man, was in 1940 in Stalag XII D' (W 121).[25] Presenting space as an affective terrain of competing, overlapping and assimilating forces with others, he describes entering a café after his release from the Stalag:

> I was lost, the few drinkers that were there seemed more distant than stars; each of them claimed a wide space on the banquette, a whole marble table to themselves,

and to touch them I would have to cross the 'polished floor' which separated me from them. If they seemed inaccessible to me, these twinkling human stars, quite at ease in their atmospheres of rarefied gas, it was because I no longer had the right to put a hand on their shoulder or thigh, nor to call them 'little one'; I had found bourgeois society again, and I had to relearn a life of 'respectful distance'; my sudden agoraphobia betrayed a vague sense of regret for the unanimous life from which I had just been forever rescued.(1964b: 348–9)

For Sartre, political ideologies are inscribed or embodied in the phenomenological experiences of different spaces. This is shown in his contrast of the ceremonial and hierarchical theatre with the maternal informal space of the cinema, a *'chambre obscure'* or dark room removed from paternal vigilance and surveillance. Where the theatre is composed of rituals and rites that separate bodies and social groups from each other in order to prevent violent conflict kept at bay through distance and ceremony, the cinema is popular and democratic like a form of detoxication or a point of entry into a new space and a hitherto undiscovered form of sociality. This new space, as ffrench (2013: 39) describes, is 'a space of desire, pregnant with the possibility of affective contact', an 'urban dark' in which the body's freedom is generated enabling a form of togetherness based not on violence but on proximity and 'adherence' where nothing now regulates the distance of one from another. Sartre's thinking fixes upon the emergent and shifting dialectic between self and Other that can be 'either positive or negative' (CDR 113) depending on its unfolding within the practico-inert. In his dialectical analysis, he demonstrates how the fate of the individual is bound up with the structure and dynamic of the group. His main target of critique is the institution which he interprets as the group's most inert and degraded form. For Sartre, the *passive seriality* of the institution differs from the *social inertia* of the series in that it is the result of a collective operation, 'a systematic self-domestication of man by man' (CDR 606) in favour of a common regulative practice. Also, the *vertical* otherness of the institution differs from the *horizontal* otherness of the serial group in that, in the latter, each is united to the others from without via a collective object, whereas, in the former, each is united to the others primarily through a bond of interiority, the command-obedience relation. This relation is founded upon a network of *authority*, the acceptance of which involves the 'interiorization of the impossibility of resisting it' (CDR 630). The sanctions of this authority can range from minor rebuke to physical torture and death, but in each case, the authoritarian structure will inevitably produce 'internal anxieties' for those who wish to resist it. If an individual does rebel through radical conscience or through the demand for creative praxis, his acts are treated as the acts of 'the alien, the suspect, the trouble-maker' (CDR 656). The vertical otherness of the institution is thus structured in a way that guarantees 'the mineralization of man at every level, except the highest' (CDR 658).

Despite the constraints and alienations of social ensembles, Sartre does not lapse into Nietzschean solitude and lose sight of the intersubjective conditions for individual freedom and creative praxis: 'I think that an individual in the group, even if he is a little bit terrorized, is nonetheless better than an individual alone and considering separation. I don't think that an individual alone can accomplish anything' (1974b:

171). Charting the passage from alienation to fusion (and back again), Sartre shows how connections in exteriority can transform into 'interior connections' within the fusing group when the 'mediating third' constitutes a potential regulatory third without becoming a transcendent other to the group and all are seen as co-sovereigns and as organizers of a common project. It represents the archetype of a genuinely free, egalitarian and reciprocal community which has managed to overcome alienation and serial existence and effect 'a transition from the Other to the same' (CDR 612). Within the reciprocal exchanges of the group, the other no longer signifies the one who objectifies and steals my world but one who enables, confirms, reflects and enlarges my possibilities as a partner in common action. Presaging 'the beginning of the existence of men who live for each other' (HN 110), Sartre's later thinking of the 'WE' pays testament to the 'ontological interdependence of consciousnesses' and the 'singularity of the individual', illuminating, in political terms, the complex and ambiguous dialectic of self and Other. His goal was to find a political creed that went beyond Marxism, deploying its heuristic apparatus while avoiding its recodification of authority and the institution (as in Stalinist Communism). This would recapture a beatific feeling he first felt as a child at the Lycée in 1915 when he experienced fusion while playing with a small group of friends, running and shouting in the Place du Panthéon: 'Without aim, end, or hierarchy, our society wavered between complete fusion and juxtaposition' (W 139). The Other is, for Sartre, a source of enrichment and collective becoming and not just the alienating and objectifying Other who condemns our freedom to dissolution under the tropes of bad faith: 'Through the Other I am enriched in a new dimension of Being: through the Other I come to exist in the dimension of Being, through the Other I become an object' (NE 499).

Anarchism, freedom and plurality

a hitherto shy and unavowed species of 'beautiful soul', the species anarchistica
(Nietzsche, *On the Genealogy of Morals* 3.26)

Curiously, although his writings pervade a strongly anarchistic ethos,[26] many of Nietzsche's direct comments on anarchism were overtly critical. He charges anarchism with purporting to be different to other ideologies like democracy, equality or socialism but is really of the same kind as it is founded on *ressentiment* and reaction (GS 370, GM 2.11), expressing a desire for pity and the herd (BGE 202). Anarchists can be individuals of great power but this can express itself in self-denial and simple destruction (D 184, GS 370). The anarchism Nietzsche had primarily in mind when denunciating it was nineteenth-century Russian anarchism. Anarchists like Kropotkin were deluded, he thought, in believing that there could be a quick and painless transition to a world of mutual cooperation. Revolutionary anarchists (such as Bakunin who was Wagner's ally in 1848) were nihilists whose violence and terrorism were fuelled by a raging *ressentiment*. Their activities would only encourage the state to intensify its own violence and declare states of exception. Despite his mainly negative comments, however, it is arguable that Nietzsche's political view finds its home most readily in some form of anarchistic viewpoint or variant of 'the *species anarchistica*' (GM 3.26). His critique of the state, his defence of plurality and individual freedom, as well as his recognition of the importance of intersubjective practices for the cultivation of that freedom, would seem to support a broadly anarchist position.

Nietzsche's writings are laced with a dark image of the modern state moving towards a form of 'nomad thought' (Deleuze 1977) that is broadly anarchist, calling for a new form of democracy yet to come (WS 293). Rejecting contractarian narratives, he makes no bones about the fact that the state was formed through blood and conquest and not consensus:

> blond beasts, a conqueror and master race which, organized for war and with the ability to organize, unhesitatingly lays its terrible claws upon a populace perhaps tremendously superior in numbers but still formless and nomad. . . . He who can command, he who is by nature 'master', he who is violent in act and bearing – what has he to do with contracts! (GM 2.17)

The oldest state thus appeared as 'a fearful tyranny, as an oppressive and remorseless machine, and went on working until this raw material of people and semi-animals was at last not only thoroughly kneaded and pliant but also *formed*' (GM 2.17). Its existence is predicated on a form of 'organized immorality': '*internally*: as police, penal law, classes, commerce, family; *externally*: as will to power, to war, to conquest, to revenge' (WP 717). Nietzsche's middle writings mark the beginning of him posing the question of the state's legitimacy, its nationalist ideological fervour and noise, its aversion to nomadism and its reactive security hysteria. He recognizes how the state uses exaggerated emergencies to beguile the public with 'investigations, undertakings, reorganizations' (HH 448, D 179). In the face of democratic forces, rulers 'cling with their teeth to their dignity as warlords: for this they require wars, that is to say states of exception in which that slow constitutional pressure of the forces of democracy lets up' (WS 281). The state is incompatible with great culture as education becomes corrupted, turning citizens into state functionaries and wasting the talent of exceptional individuals (HH 481): 'Culture and the state – one should not deceive oneself about this – are antagonists. . . . All great ages of culture are ages of political decline: what is great culturally has always been unpolitical, even *antipolitical*' (TI 8.4). Most importantly, the state is bound up with political theology: 'The belief in a divine order in the realm of politics, in a sacred mystery in the existence of the state, is of religious origin: if religion disappears the state will unavoidably lose its ancient Isis veil and cease to excite reverence' (HH 472). He briefly entertains an alternative vision of a reformed state that employs religion as a mythical instrument (HH 472) and is founded on a meritocracy (HH 2.318), but without the buttress of a political theology, 'a later generation will see the state to shrink to insignificance in various parts of the earth' (HH 472). Over time, the state will dissolve and some other 'organizing power' will emerge just as the state superseded previous forms of association, such as the clan, family or polis.

Nietzsche brings his critique of the state to a crescendo in *Zarathustra*, viewing it as the enforcer of a slow euthanasia for its people: 'State I call it where all are poison drinkers, the good and the base; state, where all can lose themselves, the good and the base; state, where the slow suicide of all is called – "life"' (Z 1.11). While staying in his rented room in Sorrento, Nietzsche could see two islands from his window – the 'blessed isle' (the island of Ischia, bathed in the light of the sun) and next to it the 'Fire Hound Isle' (the volcano Vesuvius, full of smoke, lava, noxious emissions and explosive violence).[27] In *Zarathustra*, the state is symbolized by the 'Fire Hound Isle':

> At best I could regard you as the ventriloquist of the earth. . . . You've learned more than enough about bringing mud to the boil. . . . Like you yourself the state is a hypocrite hound; like you it likes to speak with smoke and bellowing – to make believe, like you, that it speaks from the belly of things. For it wants absolutely to be the most important animal on earth, this state; and people believe it, too. (Z 2.18)

The 'hypocrite hound' is the engine of an 'Infernal Racket' that signals the violent changes it forces through, although these are not a change of values but ones of expediency (Z 2.18). As 'the coldest of all cold monsters' (Z 1.11), the state enacts its violence through the 'scarlet judges' who cruelly enjoy sending the criminal to his death (Z 1.6). Despite the 'Fire Hound', however, in *Zarathustra* the undertone is of hope and comfort, of courage and confidence, despite the seriousness of the situation since Zarathustra has embarked on a journey towards 'the great health' that 'makes the will free again, which gives earth its purpose and man his hope again' (GM 24). Zarathustra is, in many ways, the anarchist par excellence. He seeks out friends to share joy and agonistic tension with but finds only disciples. At the end of the first part, he leaves his companions because they have become followers instead of believing in themselves: 'Now I bid you lose me and find yourselves; and only when you have denied me I will return to you' (Z 1.22.3). He seeks equals, creators, harvesters and celebrants: 'Companions the creator seeks and not corpses, not herds or believers either. Fellow creators the creator seeks, those who inscribe new values on new tablets' (Z P9). Against the scarlet judges of the state, Zarathustra endorses an anarchistic community of self-policing autonomous individuals: 'Can you give yourself your own evil and your own good and hang your own will over yourself as a law? Can you be your own judge and avenger of your law?' (Z 1.17).

As a community grows stronger and more self-confident, its penal law becomes more lenient: 'It is not impossible to imagine society *so conscious of its power* that it could allow itself the noblest luxury available to it, – that of letting its malefactors go *unpunished*' (GM 2.10). This would be a society in which the individual 'calls himself to account and publicly dictates his own punishment' (D 187).[28] Someday, 'we will no longer have the heart for the logical sin that lies concealed in anger and punishment, whether practiced individually or socially' (WS 183). For Nietzsche, lives should be lived from the inside, for an individual is 'entitled to determine what they understand by an endurable life' (HH 438). This is in opposition to the (socialist) state which 'outbids all the despotisms of the past' and aims at the 'annihilation of the individual' by reducing her to an 'organ of the community' (HH 473). True justice originates between parties of approximately equal power 'where there is no clearly recognizable superiority of force': 'Justice is thus requital and exchange under the presupposition of an approximately equal power position' (HH 92). Against the expedient warmongering of the state, he champions the values of peace and cooperation, describing the wisdom of neighbouring chieftains who came to the recognition 'how each could even assist and rescue the other in times of need instead of exploiting and augmenting this need of his neighbour as heretofore' (WS 190).

In Warren's (1991: 74) view, Nietzsche's political thinking suggests an alternative to statist politics, one 'reminiscent of the anarchism of Godwin'. Foreshadowing the objections of later anarchists, such as Emma Goldman, against Marxists, 'Nietzsche believed that revolutionaries harbor a "reactionary" desire to reassert the power of the state over the individual' (1991: 222).[29] The problem Nietzsche acknowledges, but leaves unresolved, is how to institute a society with a shared ethical life which allows for the recognition of otherness and the affirmation of difference. He recognizes collective culture as a horizon for self-constituting practices – 'collective self-esteem is the great preparatory school for personal sovereignty' (WP 773) – and fully acknowledges the deep interdependence of the individual and society even while he speaks on behalf of the individual. Although he does suggest these might coincide (in his more dialectical moments), he is so taken by the opposition between the individual *qua* existential agent and the 'herd' tendencies of society that he sees it as a permanent and tragic feature of the human condition. In particular, his later aristocratic politics undermine the pluralistic implications of his philosophy of truth, following instead the ancient aristocratic idea that 'the best should rule, and that the best should also want to rule'. Thus, his later thinking in many respects misunderstands the innovative implications of his philosophy and of his middle writings, which, in Warren's (1991: 223) words, 'suggest that all politically hierarchies . . . are inconsistent with the intersubjective space of individuation'. This is 'to think with Nietzsche against Nietzsche' (Ferry and Renaut 1997: vii), using the wider logic of his thinking to critique the irresponsibility, irrationalism and anti-democratic sentiment (as well as the unquestioning acceptance of tradition and authority) of his aristocratic phase. Nietzsche's will to power (as an organized capacity for action) is not inconsistent with social and political equality simply because the universal motive identified by the concept of the will to power is not domination but self-constitution. His future vision of strength is not Caesar but 'Caesar with Christ's Soul' (WP 983).

Despite his diatribes against socialism, Nietzsche displays a sensitivity to the worker and the oppressed, decrying how in modern society, 'man is in ruins and scattered over a battlefield'. Zarathustra laments the death of peoples unified 'by tablets of the good' and the birth of 'the new idol', the state that tells 'lies in all the tongues of good and evil' (Z 1.11). Nietzsche criticizes the diminution of man in commercial society, of 'turning humanity into *sand*!' (D 174) by grating off the rough edges of life in a collective drive towards timidity and uniformity. The capitalist work ethic is self-destructive, and work a mere 'mechanical activity', resulting in 'absolute regularity, punctilious and unthinking obedience, a mode of life fixed once and for all, fully occupied time, a certain permission, indeed training for "impersonality", for self-forgetfulness, for *incuria sui* [lack of care for the self]' (GM 3.18). This is a process of collective loss in which 'man is diminished' (WP 866). Modern workers are perhaps, even though this is 'slavery in a higher sense' (A 54), worse off in some ways than slaves (HH 457) since factory work robs the worker of his artisanal craft and obliterates individuality (D 173). Moreover, industriousness infects all aspects of life in modern capitalism from science and art (UM 1.8), religion (BGE 58) and relations between women and men (BGE 239).

Hatab (1995: 70) joins Warren's defence of a pluralistic democratic Nietzsche, pointing to his idea of agonism as an alternative to the idea of equality as a basis for democracy, emphasizing difference above sameness. Nietzsche's perspectivism lends itself to an ethic that subverts normalization and allows 'space for difference to be', undermining traditional and aristocratic justifications that invoke timeless truths and historical necessity: 'Aristocracies and authoritarian regimes have historically defended their right to dominance and unchecked power by way of confident knowledge claims about the nature and order of things.' In *Human, All Too Human*, Nietzsche defends the right of the masses to determine their own existence and government:

> if the purpose of all politic really is to make life endurable for as many as possible, then these as-many-as-possible are entitled to determine what they understand by an endurable life; if they trust to their intellect also to discover the right means of attaining this goal, what good is there in doubting it? (HH 438)

Nietzsche defines democracy as the form of political organization that 'wants to create and guarantee as much independence as possible: independence of opinion, of mode of life and of employment' and speaks of a *new form of democracy* 'as of something yet to come', characterized by the independence of opinion and new modes of life and employment: 'That which now calls itself democracy differs from older forms of government solely in that it drives with new horses: the streets are still the same old streets, and the wheels are likewise the same old wheels' (WS 293). He praises democracy as a provisional instrument for overcoming militarized nationalism (WS 275) and for breaking up rigid class hierarchies and liberating individual ambition (GS 348, 356). The 'new democracy' is one that will allow 'a plurality of norms', honour 'the right of individuals' and avoid the 'rigid consequence of the teaching of one normal-human' (GS 143). Even in *Beyond Good and Evil*, while arguing that moral notions of equality and democracy have created a mixture of cultural and biological types that causes new problems (BGE 208), he also thinks that this creates new possibilities and opportunities (BGE 223–4). Races are constantly evolving and it is possible for a people over time to define itself as a race (BGE 200).

In his conjecture of a society in which 'politics will have a different meaning' (WP 960), Nietzsche is primarily opposed to statist thinking based on the erasure of individuality in the name of a uniform and homogenous identity and on the fixing of sharp boundaries between inside and out in the form of national territorialism. In Shapiro's (2016: 138) view, beyond the boundaries of political power blocs and across lines drawn by nation states, Nietzsche's perspective calls for new forms of kinship and solidarity. This is signalled in his notion of '*Menge*' (BGE 256) that, as 'a multitude of diverse individuals' (GS 149), represents a more positive view of groups in Nietzsche's philosophy than that of the 'herd'. Often wrongfully translated as 'masses' (which conveys the sense of homogeneity), it denotes rather a 'multitude' or a hybrid nomadic and diverse grouping. Nietzsche is never derogatory about the *Menge* 'with its duties and virtues' (BGE 213), although he does set himself apart from it. The multitude is not read as a territorial or political unit but more as an audience who impose a form of selectivity in their desires, as opposed to the herd and masses. He associates this with Europe which has become a spawning ground for spiritual hybridity (BGE 251) and those who see 'the wretched ephemeral chatter of politics and national egoism *beneath* themselves' (A 1). As Shapiro (2016: 92) notes, the concept of *Menge* denotes people as 'multitudes' full of 'productive possibilities' and though Nietzsche's concept is much more theatrical (as a group of spectators) rather than revolutionary or active (as in the 'multitude' of Spinoza or Negri), it formulates the idea of an inclusive affective community. Like Deleuze, Shapiro (2015: 132) points to Nietzsche's 'spiritual nomadism' (HH 2.11, D 452) in which he heralds a 'new politics' of nomadic thought that decodifies the state without recodifying it (1977: 149). Bringing together Nietzsche's ecologism and anarchism, Deleuze and Guattari (1994: 102) identify this along political lines as Nietzsche's 'geophilosophy', an approach that avoids teleology and statism, emphasizing a plurality of forms of human habitation, including nomadic and other non-state groupings in which seas, deserts, caves and mountainous terrains all become forms of smooth space, fields of unconstrained movement of bodies and thought.

As his mother described him, Sartre was 'a nice little anarchist surrounded by his books' (1983b: 129). In a 1975 *New York Review of Books* interview, he acknowledges himself an anarchist his entire life: 'I have never accepted any power over me, and I have always thought that anarchy, which is to say a society without powers, must be brought about' (1975). Of course, he is well known as a Marxist (and heavily criticized as a 'fellow-traveller' with the French Communist Party (PCF) in the 1950s), but this was a label he rejected in his later years. Whereas in 1957 he had declared that Marxism was the unsurpassable 'philosophy of our time' (SM 31), describing it as 'simultaneously a totalization of knowledge, a method, a regulative Idea, an offensive weapon, and a community of language' (SM 6), in a 1975 interview with Michel Rybalka, he answered 'no' to the question of whether he was still a Marxist. In other interviews, he continued to distance himself from Marxism and associate his thinking with anarchism: 'I was always more of an anarchist than a Marxist. . . . [My] anarchism . . . was really an expression of freedom, the freedom I described earlier, the freedom of a writer' (Gerassi 2009: 44). 'I was an anarchist without knowing it when I wrote *Nausea*', he affirmed, and 'I have always thought that anarchy – which is to say, a society without powers – must be brought about' (1977a: 389).

As Betschart (2020: 29) notes, Sartre's alliances with the Communists (France 1952–6, Soviet 1954–6, Algerian rebels 1955–62, Castro's Cuba 1960–1 and the 'Maoist' New Left groups 1970–3) were not ideological partnerships but rather 'cases of tactical cooperation'. Sartre was faithful only to his own values, to his 'big four no's to militarism, colonialism, racism, and bourgeois morality'. He was, for instance, an early supporter of Russian dissidents against Stalinism (by 1963 *Les Temps Modernes* had already published three of Solzhenitsyn's novels). After 1968, Sartre and Beauvoir became 'the godparents' of the political movements of individual freedom based around gender, ethnicity and sexual orientation, articulating a politics which, in Aronson's (1995: 34) words, is 'feminist, pro-gay liberation, anti-racist and ecological'. Showing a concern for individual freedom, autonomy and subjectivity, like Nietzsche, Sartre feared the totalistic, state-centric varieties of socialism. Many scholars now acknowledge that Marxism was a heuristic tool in his thinking and a springboard towards a more refined political trajectory that he identified as anarchism.[30] Sartre's anarchism is suspicious of all social groups, appealing directly to the power of artistic self-development and individual authenticity in and against a social world of oppression and conformity. He conceives society not as an organic whole but as a complex collection of separate individuals and assemblages and is consistently anti-Hegelian in arguing against organicism, preferring to see society as a 'detotalized totality'. This, in Heter's (2020: 532) view, makes Sartre a 'syndicalist', both fearful and in awe of the transformative power of group being. This places him at a distance from individualists (such as Stirner) and collectivists (such as Hegel).[31] Like the social anarchists, he imagines a socialist alternative to the capitalist state, but he values collectivity as a process of freely configuring or pluralistic emergent assemblages that enable the kaleidoscopic expression of individualities as opposed to degraded serial forms of social existence that inhibit it.[32]

Sartre's view of the state as a totalized monolith very much runs in parallel with Nietzsche's, expressing a 'nomadic' wish, in Deleuze's terms, to decodify its apparatus. He discards the liberal idea that democratic states express a social contract among equals since citizens obey the law not by choice but as a result of mystification and violence. The state is not a neutral arbitrator that mediates the interests of smaller groups or communities but operates through ruses or 'traps', especially voting, where the ruling class creates the spectacle of a collective will. Society is not a genuine group but an atomized mass forming the 'container' and 'battlefield' for competing groups: 'Thus it would be wrong to see the State *either* as the concrete reality of society (as Hegel apparently wished or believed), *or* as a pure, epiphenomenal abstraction' (CDR 639). For Sartre, '[t]he state can never be regarded as the product or expression of the totality of social individuals' (CDR 636) since it is characterized by seriality and 'other-directedness' (CDR 646): 'the relation of the State to concrete society can never, even in the best of circumstances, transcend other-direction' (CDR 654). In the 1970s, he wrote two essays, 'Election: A Trap for Fools' and 'Justice and the State', in which he appeals to the ideal of non-oppression to reject both thick and thin justifications of the state: 'State Justice was created precisely in order to perpetuate exploitation' (1977a: 175).[33] Political representation is but 'a falsification of the popular will' (1977a: 176), a type of 'blackmail' that creates inert gatherings of people who 'cannot resist the State' (CDR 636). Sartre illustrates this through the phenomenology of the secret ballot and its other-directedness: 'No one can see you, you have only yourself to look to; you are going to be completely isolated when you make your decision' (1977a: 200). For Sartre, '[u]niversal suffrage is an institution and therefore a collective which atomizes or serializes individual men. It addresses the abstract entities within them – the citizens, who are defined by a set of political rights and duties, or in other words by the relation to the state and its institutions' (1977a: 202).

Although Sartre states in the conclusion to *Being and Nothingness*, '[o]ntology itself is unable to formulate moral prescriptions', it does allow us, he concedes, 'to glimpse what an ethics that took up its responsibilities by confronting a *human reality in situation* might be' (BN 809). In looking to a future beyond the state, Sartre's anarchist syndicalism, exemplified by his prototype of the fusing group, is an expression of his ontology of emergent interactionism, offered as a sublimation of multiplicity and unity, self and other. He describes his vision of 'a flourishing humanity' as an individual adventure in the dimension of the universal shot through with possibilities: 'But my destiny is me coming to myself as an image. What is more, humanity is an individual adventure that takes place in the dimension of the universal. The individual coming to himself in terms of the features of the universal, this is humanity's destiny' (NE 422). Key to this are the notions of intersubjectivity and reciprocity: 'we can conceive of an absolute conversion to intersubjectivity. This conversion is *ethical*. It presupposes a political and social conjuncture (suppression of classes and the State) as its necessary condition, but this suppression is not sufficient by itself' (NE 407). In building and forging a flourishing humanity, we pass from the particular to the universal, thereby transcending the old society and the old History. In a classless society where there is no oppression that 'breaks apart intersubjective solidarity' (NE 427), it 'can also be love, that is, the project undertaken confident that freedoms evaluated as such and willed as such will take up and transform my work and therefore my Ego, which will thus lose itself in the absolute dimension of freedom' (NE 418). Flourishing humanity will not be marked by division and hierarchy but by integration and love, a new phase of existence based on the model of the festival which we must work for:

> it is a break with the spirit of seriousness, expenditure, nihilation, passage to the *festival*. Indeed, the festival is liberation from the spirit of seriousness, the end of economies, the overthrowing of hierarchy, and the absorption of the Other by the Same, of the objective by intersubjectivity, of order by disorder. This will turn out to be the *apocalypse* as one of the extreme types of interhuman relations. (NE 374)

In interviews in the 1970s, he conceives democracy not merely as a type of government but as a *form of life* where (a post-*Critique* conception of) fraternity forms the bond of relationships between people in society: 'our goal is to arrive at a genuinely constituent body in which each person would be a human being and collectives would be equally human' (HN 67). In Sartre's final ethics, the future 'is a pure future beyond the system' that has 'to be created – not by building a system (not even a *socialist system*) but by destroying every system' (1974a: 251). This would be a witnessing of 'what Malraux, in *Days of Hope*, called the Apocalypse, that is to say, the dissolution of the series into a group-in-fusion. And this group, though still unstructured, that is to say, entirely *amorphous*, is characterized by being the direct opposite of alterity' (SG 357). Fired by the imagination and realized through praxis, 'humanity' is an evolving notion designating a power of political transformation and invention: 'The essential moment therefore is that of creation, that is, the moment of the imaginary, of invention. . . . And naturally the negative moment is essentially bound to the imaginary since man chooses to illuminate what is, in the light of what is not' (NE 464). Sartre's anarchistic political vision would in years to come prove important as a philosophical resource for poststructuralists, such as Foucault, Derrida and Deleuze/Guattari, who drew heavily on key Sartrean ideas, particularly his theory of commitment and seminal analysis of the fusing group.[34]

6

Posthuman progenitors

A new world view is settling itself into the minds of humanity. It goes about like a virus.
(Carl Fortlage, 1857 cited in Blue 2016: 237)

I know my fate. One day my name will be associated with the recollection of something tremendous – of a crisis such as there has never been on earth, of the most profound collision of conscience, of a decision evoked counter *to everything that had hitherto been believed, demanded, hallowed.*
(Nietzsche, Ecce Homo 4.1)

Posthumanism and transhumanism

Inspired by Derridean deconstruction, the Deleuzian critique of 'oppositional thinking' and Foucault's wake-up call to release us from our 'anthropological sleep' (1973: 370), posthumanists have embraced a new direction in philosophical thinking that addresses itself to the pressing ecological and ethical issues of the Anthropocene.[1] Although there are different variants of posthumanism (as the word has become somewhat of an umbrella term), I refer to Ferrando's 'philosophical posthumanism' (2020) as a statement of the philosophical thinking that derives most closely from French poststructuralism and, in turn, from the philosophical insights of Nietzsche and Sartre. This can be contrasted, for the sake of illustration, with transhumanism that, although it shares common features with posthumanism, can be seen in some important respects as antithetical to it in philosophical form. According to Ferrando (2020: 118), philosophical posthumanism is a 'non-hierarchical system of thought' in which alterity (human and non-human) is embraced as 'an open and constantly evolving frame, not as the undisciplinable chaos to be normalized, otherized, or divinized'. It adopts an onto-epistemological approach, as well as an ethical one, 'manifesting as a philosophy of mediation, which discharges any confrontational dualisms and hierarchical legacies . . . approached as a post-humanism, a post-anthropocentrism, and a post-dualism' (2020: 22). The type of dualism deconstructed by philosophical posthumanism is a strict, rigid and absolute metaphysical form of dualism, and not the liquid, shifting and intra-changing form of duality – 'an explicit duality expressing an implicit unity' (2020: 60). Although it cannot be assimilated to it completely, philosophical posthumanism continues the postmodernist quest for proliferating difference and acknowledging 'the voices of the subjectivities which have been historically reduced to the realm of the "Other"' (2020: 24). By contrast, transhumanism (as derived from Julian Huxley) can be characterized as 'anthropocentric' and based on human exceptionalism with its roots in the Enlightenment, valorizing progress, linearity, science, technology and rationality, a form of 'ultra-humanism' (2020: 35). Transhumanists endorse the coming of the posthuman condition brought about through a rapid technological and scientific acceleration, including computing, information and media technologies, genetic engineering, nanotechnologies, artificial intelligence, virtual realities, prosthetic enhancements, robotics and space colonization as common themes. Transhumanists hope for enhancements in all aspects of human beings, eliminating pain and suffering and enhancing pleasure and experiences.[2]

Scholars have placed Nietzsche on both sides of the posthumanism–transhumanism debate, and there is no doubt he displays some ambiguity in his writings regarding the status of the *Übermensch*, his superhuman prototype of the future, influenced to a large extent by the varying attitudes he adopts towards science during the three phases of his thinking. Sorgner (2009: 38), for example, claims Nietzsche as an ally and precursor of transhumanism since he proposes a dynamic view of nature and values in which the cosmos undergoes endless change as well as a revaluation of all values in which a scientific form of thinking replaces the religious and the imperative to enhance human values and capacities: 'The overhuman comes about via an evolutionary step which originates from the group of higher humans. Nietzsche does not exclude the possibility that technological means bring about the evolutionary step.' In Mellamphy's (2015: 143) view, the overhuman should be read 'physiologically' (as the choreographic motor of a transhuman chthonic machine which directs life's form – giving activities by way of a-signifying forces) rather than juridically (as a framework of morals or ideals to be followed). In support of this, Zarathustra hints at the biologistic contents of the *Übermensch*, while in the *Nachlass*, Nietzsche suggests a strongly physiological/ biological vision of the *Übermensch*: 'I write for a species of man that does not yet exist' (WP 958). The 'goal' of the higher human, he states, was the 'evolution of the entire body and not just of the brain' (KSW 10.506). In the spirit of experimentation and adventure trumpeted by transhumanists, Nietzsche exhorts us to take chances and to 'live dangerously!' (HH 283, BGE 224).[3]

However, in *Ecce Homo* Nietzsche is keen to strip the *Übermensch* of any Darwinian or idealist conceptions (EH 3.1) and elsewhere in his writings justifies his future philosophy in juridical terms of (aesthetic) values.[4] Furthermore, as Ansell-Pearson (1997: 3) argues, it is wrong to view the *Übermensch* as involving a systematic effacement of all supposed anachronistic traces of our past. Nietzsche looked back to the Renaissance and the past to find those 'exemplars' of humanity and – who embodied the desire and will to power of the prospective *Übermensch*, such as Goethe, who manifested greatness and wholeness (TI 9.49). Although there is a certain temporal ambiguity in the superhuman insofar as he sometimes futurizes it (not even his hero of the past Goethe can achieve it) as a new species or epoch (WP 958), elsewhere he uses the term to apply to past heroes (A 4) and the present as an existential imperative, asking 'not what will replace humanity in the sequence of beings' but 'what type of human one shall *breed*, shall *will*, as of higher value, more worthy of life, surer of a future' (A 3). In *Zarathustra*, Nietzsche emphasizes the continuity between past, present and future that overlap and interlink. The humanity of today are the parents of tomorrow, 'fragments of the future' (Z 2.20), since the power of their self-realization will one day 'ignite the light of the future' (Z 3.16.1). Humanity 'should be a bridge, and not a purpose' (Z P4).

Guided by Nietzsche's sublimating logic, it could be said that the *Übermensch* is a new type the human grows into which both is and isn't 'human'.[5] Whereas the '[h]uman is *nonanimal* and *superanimal*', the higher human 'is nonhuman and superhuman: they belong together' (WP 1027). Becoming *übermenschlich* involves a state of being called 'post-metaphysical' (Ansell-Pearson 1997: 1),[6] embodying a spiritualized physics that incorporates the truth and complexes of our natural drives and affects as well as sharable practices that affirm human capacities and promote new forms of individuality. For Ansell-Pearson (1997: 144), 'Nietzsche does not think this overcoming in terms of the abolition of the human but rather only in terms of the destruction of its anthropocentric determination as the superior point of evolution'. The transhuman condition 'is not about the transcendence of the human being but concerns its non-teleological becoming in an immanent process of "anthropological deregulation"' (1997: 163). The transhumanist overemphasis on technology often results in a technocentric transcendence of biology that ignores the situated aspect of the body, obscuring difference and plurality.[7] Pursuing radical life extension and immortality, transhumanist technologism takes on the character of a religion in the form of an other-worldly striving for transcendence and salvation. From a Nietzschean perspective, transhumanism has become transformed into a 'classic expression of an ancient ideal': 'it is no longer Christianity fulfilling the role of Platonism for the people, but rather a cyberspace cult' (1997: 2). By projecting a redemptive future and an ascetic ideal to overcome suffering, transhumanism takes the form of religious nihilism: 'All that which Nietzsche regarded as providing fertile soil for an immanent process of continual self-overcoming is here treated as a condition that is to be escaped from' (1997: 32–3). In contrast to philosophical posthumanism, transhumanism employs simple dichotomies that Nietzsche's thought problematizes (human/posthuman, organic/technological) and involves anthropomorphic projections onto nature: 'The positing of themselves as the meaning and measure of evolution is the anthropocentric conceit of humans that is exposed with the advent of nihilism' (1997: 161). Evolution is conceived by Nietzsche as non-teleological and appears to be a highly contingent and random process, but in some forms of transhumanism, has become a grand narrative taking the form of 'a facile quasi-Hegelianism in which the rise of the machine is construed in linear and perfectionist terms' (1997: 4).

Stiegler (2015) echoes Ansell-Pearson's concerns about annexing Nietzsche's thinking to a transhumanist grand narrative. He criticizes transhumanism for being complicit with, and serving as an ideological support for, capitalism and imperialism which are seen as the culmination of a historical process geared towards progress, a 'natural selection' of evolutionary processes. Contemporary information technologies – 'big data' and the algorithms that control it – bring nihilism to completion faster than Nietzsche prophesied because of the *levelling* effect. Such technologies function in conjunction with capitalism in a way that simultaneously targets individuals more comprehensively than ever before possible, shaping their thoughts and desires in conformity with statistical averages, producing a domesticated 'quantified' or 'data' self. In his critique of the 'last man' for which the *Übermensch* is his proposed antidote/solution, Nietzsche's principal target is the reactionary individualism of the calculating utilitarian shopkeeper parodied by Napoleon. For Nietzsche, people have become slaves in the worship of the 'god of machines and crucibles' (BT 18), constrained within the 'spider's web of reason' and enslaved to labour under a 'servitude of purpose' (Z 3.4). Like Marx, he recognized the hardship of those subjected to the mechanical grind and indignities of the labour market and condemned the hypocrisy of the 'pale religions' offered as a palliative to the slaves (BT 18). In Stiegler's (2015: 45–8) view, transhumanism is nothing but a wholesale embrace of this form of calculative rationality and thus a justificatory ideology for 'cognitive capitalism'. It seeks to reengineer the human being so that only averages are possible, and exceptions – those which escape algorithmic control – are eliminated. Since we are *constituted* by our technologies that condition our existence and our nature as human, technologies are paramount when considering what the human race is becoming. While the effect of technology is to reinvent and bring about changes in the function of human organisms that would otherwise risk enslavement to biological drives, Stiegler repeatedly refers to 'the ambivalent therapy – toxicity of the technological object', both cure and poison, wherein the very technologies that 'liberate', or 'disautomate', us can also induce regression to pathological modes of automation.

This Nietzschean critique of the levelling effects of cognitive capitalism can also be found in Sartre's philosophy. As his analysis of the 'homme–machine' (CDR 191) illustrates, neotechnic and prosthetic technologies form a continuum with the human 'body-machine' alongside a domain of virtuality and incorporeality that offers a 'potential space' involving interrelations, interfaces and autonomous becomings or, conversely, mystifications and impoverishments. Sartre's thinking points towards a view (consistent with posthumanism's 'Precautionary Principle')[8] of the dangers of our 'machinic becomings' (Guattari 2000: 38) for human projects of freedom. This signals a move away from a Faustian view of technology as a form of ultra-humanistic control to one of undecidability and non-calculability in relation to both our machinic enslavement and technics of becoming. As Sartre shows, our captivation by the practico-inert can often take the form of 'dark magic' as in psychopathology and addiction. As technology advances in a digital society, the captivating powers of the image have intensified through advertising and consumer capitalism in a semiotic system of simulacra and hyperreal objects.[9] Sartre touches upon this in his early work on the imagination, where he writes about the 'statics of the image' (IM 16) and its poverty compared to the real-life inexhaustibility of things, their peculiar '*flesh*' or 'intimate texture' (IM 16). Synaesthetic perception and the inexhaustibility of the real is always more powerful than the imaginary and the one-dimensionality of the reproduced image (IM 144–5).[10]

Perhaps we should not get too carried away with the *Übermensch* in interpreting Nietzsche's philosophy of the future since it is but one among several ideals or 'masks' that Nietzsche adopts. Although the *Übermensch* is used in *Zarathustra* and does not disappear (A 4, TI 9.37, EH 3.1), it is in general rarely employed by Nietzsche who also projects the ideal of Dionysus (BT, EH Z6), 'free spirits' (D, HH, GS), 'new philosophers' (BGE 2) or 'experimenters' (BGE 42) and Zarathustra (GS 342, TI 4, EH Z1). Another paragon he suggests for a new mode of thinking that goes beyond metaphysical humanism is the figure of the *musical Socrates* (BT 15). Nietzsche recalls in the *Phaedo* that Socrates, waiting for his execution, regrets he had never made music. He realizes his previous mistake that the theoretical attitude cannot redeem existence, and an aesthetic attitude is superior and necessary. This figure also symbolizes, for Nietzsche, one of the reasons he believes that tragic myth is ready for a rebirth in the form of the *self-critique* of the theoretical attitude in the contemporary era. Nietzsche does not propose an eradication of the theoretical tendency and a return to the double-intuitive tendencies of Apollo and Dionysus. Socrates and Dionysus are the modern tendencies which should be brought into a kind of harmonious relation in tension, a co-constitution which would combine science and art. Through the 'musical Socrates', Nietzsche suggests that art can be accompanied by a science that involves a self-critique of its own limits. It denotes the advent of the posthuman as an aesthetic space in which values, and knowledge as well, are reflected on and critiqued, as well as constructed through the activity of creative play.

In his writings, Nietzsche does not mention technology (and technological promise) very much, but his allusions to it tend to the phobic, complaining about typewriters, the empty repetitive soulless 'music' of a barrel organ or decrying the enslavement of the worker to machines under capitalism. It was *nature* that attracted Nietzsche where he found solace from the technological buzz and noise of the city and where he found creativity all around him as well as the symbiotic communion with the senses that he craved within his idyll of the 'Epicurean Garden'. The central question for his philosophy of the future, as several scholars have highlighted,[11] is an aesthetico-politico-ecological one – 'how shall the earth as a whole be governed?' (WP 947), a question that runs through *Zarathustra*, Nietzsche's symphonic paean to nature.

Nietzsche's nature

Remain faithful to the earth

(Nietzsche, *Zarathustra* 1.22.3)

Nietzsche had a deep love for nature and its transformative, generative powers. Aged eight, he felt happiness, companionship and a sense of fusion when out hiking in the countryside on school field trips singing patriotic songs and playing humorous games.[12] Later in life, he walked in the mountains near Nice for seven or eight hours at a time, joyful among the cypresses and cistuses and Nature's abundant gifts to the senses. He likened his solitary treks in the mountains to Zarathustra's ascent, a 'wandering exile' looking down from the summit like in Caspar David Friedrich's painting 'The Wanderer above the Mist'. Influenced strongly by Ralph Waldo Emerson whose essay 'History' in praise of 'spiritual nomadism' he copied into his notebooks during his adolescence, he was fascinated by the intimate connection between self and environment and how one's habitat can warp or mould desires and mood. Emerson also alerted him to the importance of instinct and the fact that the self operates beyond the reach of consciousness. Many of Nietzsche's early literary compositions celebrated nature, harking back to the pastoral setting of his childhood at Röcken. In 1861, he wrote an anthropological essay 'Hunters and Fishers' where he sought a naturalistic rather than religious explanation for the development of human civilization. He posits the self as 'a repository of tendencies' that environmental factors rouse or repress just as the vagaries of weather affect the growth of a plant: 'Only now do I recognize how many experiences have affected my development, and how heart and intellect have been formed under the influence of surrounding circumstances' (KGW 1.2.258). In 1863, he returns in his writings to the comparison of human beings with plants, finding comfort in the exigencies of genus and species, the way vegetation expresses and develops into the plant it was born to be (KGW 1.3.193–6).

Nature is woven into Nietzsche's writings. His concept of the free spirit was inspired by the coast of Sorrento which he observed from his rented room watching the fathomless sea and the rushing of the waves, 'the sea, with its rippling snake-skin and beast-of-prey beauty' (HH 49). For Nietzsche, our relation to the environment is one of incorporation and assimilation, a transfer of energies and forces between things. In determining who we are, 'nutrition, place, climate', he writes, 'are inconceivably more important than everything one has taken to be important so far . . . [i.e.] "God", "soul", "virtue", "sin", "beyond", "truth", "eternal life"' (EH 2.10). As Manschot (2021: 151) notes, Nietzsche is a 'philosopher of atmospherics' and a phenomenologist of nature by delineating space as an affective medium of interchange and transfer. From 1880 onwards, he became fascinated with the metabolic processes that take place between people and the environment. On 6 August 1881, he experienced his transformative moment of eternal return in front of a pyramid-shaped boulder on his way to the mountain lake at Silvaplana-Surlej, a region he described as 'the sweetest corner of the earth'. This was a moment that marked his decisive step to his 'naturalization' as he called it. His years of wandering were a process of healing of body and mind. Out of a sick and degenerate situation 'one returns newborn, having shed one's skin, more ticklish and malicious, with a more delicate taste for joy, with a tenderer tongue for all good things, with merrier senses, with a second dangerous innocence in joy, more childlike and yet a hundred times subtler than one has ever been before' (GS P4).

For Nietzsche, all things are dependent on the environment for their flourishing and the expansion of their creative will to power: 'Every living thing needs to be surrounded by an atmosphere, a mysterious circle of mist: if one robs it of this veil, if one condemns a religion, an art, a genius to orbit as a star without an atmosphere: then one should not wonder about its becoming withered, hard, and barren' (UM 2.7). His affective sensitivity to the environment provides an ecological logic that warns against pollutants, whether they be chemical or social, alerting us to the 'atmoterrorism' (Manschot 2021: 152) of polluted cities, concrete jungles, drone warfare, aerial bombardment, nuclear radiation, radio waves and microwave toxicity – 'I need *solitude* . . . the breath of a free, playful air' (EH 1.8). His pagan encomium to nature in *Zarathustra* is woven around Zarathustra's injunction to '[r]emain faithful to the earth' (Z 1.22.3) and is Nietzsche's attempt to develop a new philosophy in which the earth would be central rather than the instrumental designs of humankind. As Zarathustra marvels, nature not only provides food for nourishment but does so in an aesthetic way, with beautiful and beckoning colours, tastes and aromas. However, human despoliation of the earth has caused it to suffer through exploitation and pollution: 'The earth has a skin; and this skin has diseases. One of these diseases for example is called "human being"' (Z 2.18). It is the 'last man', in particular, who threatens environmental health: 'For the earth has now become small, and upon it hops the last man, who makes everything small' (Z P5). However much the earth is despoiled and polluted, Zarathustra declares that it still retains tremendous possibilities for growth and renewal as 'the heart of the earth is of gold' (Z 2.19). In his more optimistic moments, he imagines the earth as a vast health resort and gigantic tree of life (WS 188–9) but voices apprehension for the '*Menschen-Erde*' (human earth) that can manifest itself as a hell or a garden.[13]

A significant metaphor for encapsulating Nietzsche's ecology is that of the *garden*. Convalescing from his 'abysmal thought' of eternal return, Zarathustra is cheered by his animals' news that the world is awaiting him as a garden (Z 3.13) before he concludes the third part with 'The Seven Seals', his celebratory song of the earth (Z 3.16). In Nietzsche's aesthetic-political vision of earth's transformation, gardens are sites of becoming that offer aesthetic and multisensory stimulation, earthly experiments that are responsive to variations in their surrounding environment and which offer a diversity of possibilities. Gardens are not just empty spaces but distinctive places like Foucauldian heterotopias with pervasive affective qualities that can nurture or block creativity. They represent the perfect metaphor for human inventiveness and creativity, an experiment and conversation with nature in the form of a nature-culture hybrid.[14] Nietzsche extends the metaphor of gardening also to the care of one's self in which we sculpt and impose aesthetic order on natural forces: 'One can dispose of one's drives like a gardener and, though few know it, cultivate the shoots of anger, pity, curiosity, vanity as productively and profitably as a beautiful fruit tree on a trellis' (D 560). The interplay of passions and drives do not create beauty by themselves but need care and cultivation:

> Out of damp and gloomy days, out of solitude, out of loveless words directed at us, conclusions grow up in us like fungus: one morning they are there, we know not how, and they gaze upon us, morose and grey. Woe to the thinker who is not the gardener but only the soil of the plants that grow in him! (D 382)

In advice to the 'good Europeans', 'free spirits' and 'philosophers of the future', Nietzsche sounds an ecological plea: 'please don't forget the garden, the garden with the golden trellises!' (BGE 25). In Shapiro's (2016: 136) view, Nietzsche's idea of the earth as garden(s) is his attempt 'to sketch an aesthetic politics of the human-earth or a geoaesthetics and geopolitics of the Anthropocene'. He offers an 'earth-centred reversal' of biblical themes, from the innocence of the Garden to the terror of the Apocalypse and Antichrist in which his correlation of garden-happiness with sensuality reverses the biblical garden story where Eve and Adam feel shame in the discovery of their nakedness and sensuality. In a sublimating movement, he puts forward the garden as a perfect nature-culture continuum, subscribing not fully to Emersonian wilderness but favouring the flourishing of style 'within a *half wild* environment' (KSW 9.256).[15] For Manschot (2021: 75), Nietzsche's overhuman who 'speaks from the heart of the earth' (Z 2.18) and the free spirits whom he urges to take on the task of the management 'of the earth as a whole' (HH 24–5) herald 'a new direction in philosophical cosmology that makes the relationship between humans and the earth the central concern of our twenty-first century understanding of ourselves'. This he terms 'terrasophy', a philosophical viewpoint that takes the earth 'as not an object but a partner' and recognizes the will to power as a universal and abundant creative force in nature and in things, transforming our relationship to Gaia from one of a furious and vengeful goddess to the face of a caring mother (2021: 131). Deleuze and Guattari (1994: 102) identify this along political lines as Nietzsche's 'geophilosophy', an approach that avoids teleology and statism, emphasizing a plurality of forms of human habitation, including nomadic and other non-state groupings within fields of the unconstrained movement of bodies and thought.

Contra Heidegger, an ecological reading of Nietzsche's philosophy dispels the view that his will to power involves the domination and 'enframing' of the earth by humans. Instead, it recognizes Nietzsche's view of the will to power as a universal creative force in nature, traces his relational ontology of assimilating and incorporating forces and follows his numerous injunctions to remain true to the earth, establishing it as an Epicurean garden of 'free air' that offers solitude, creativity, play and satiates (what Plank (1998: 102) refers to as) his 'Sensism':

> The most spiritual men feel the stimulus and the charm of sensuous things in a way that other men – those with 'fleshy hearts' cannot possibly imagine. . . . The strength and power of the senses – this is the essential thing in a well-constituted and complete man: the splendid 'animal' must be given first. (WP 1045)

Animals

Of all modern philosophers, Nietzsche mentions the largest number of animals in his writings, a diverse array of no fewer than 120, some encountered on his walks in nature and others discovered in his reading.[16] Throughout his writings, animals were vital sources of nourishment for his philosophical thinking, and no more so than in *Zarathustra*. When Zarathustra is discontent and lost in the human world, animals enable him to find the right track towards happiness. After leaving the ugliest human being, he is cold and lonely but feels 'warm and lively' when he stumbles across a herd of cows huddled together on a knoll, finding a beggar in the midst of them who is there 'to learn from these cows' (Z 4.8). The cows teach him to 'chew the cud', to ingest food slowly and gather his thoughts gradually rather than be dazzled by a superabundance of impressions as in life in the city. During the course of conversation with his animals,

Zarathustra learns much from them, including the central truth of Heraclitean wisdom which they speak to him: 'Everything goes, everything comes back; the wheel of being rolls eternally. Everything dies, everything blossoms again, the year of being runs eternally' (Z 3.13). Significantly, after conversing with the 'higher men' in his cave, he chooses to slip outside to talk to his animals: 'Tell me, my animals: these higher men all together – do they perhaps not *smell* good. Oh clean fragrances around me! Only now do I know and feel how I love you, my animals' (Z 4.14.1). As the *Übermensch* appears only on the distant horizon, Zarathustra can only feel at home with his animals who provide him with philosophical solace. The eagle and the snake accompany him at all times. The eagle represents a view from above, seeing what's ahead, 'the tree called future' with its clear vision and sharp eyes, while the snake, 'the wisest animal under the sun', symbolizes the eternal return and the circularity of time, keeping its body close to the earth.

Alongside Darwin, Nietzsche was a stentorian voice of the nineteenth century in eliding the Christian or Enlightenment distinction between humans (as possessors of souls or rationality) and animals (as creatures of pre-programmed instinct and desire). The will to power is conceived as a natural motivation or creative force that applies to *all* organisms: 'every animal . . . instinctively strives for an optimum of favourable conditions under which it can expend all its strength and achieve its maximum feeling of power' (GM 3.7). 'To understand what life is', Nietzsche writes, 'the formula must apply to trees and plants as well as to animals' (WP 704) and 'for each of these there is a small corner from which it measures, is aware, sees and doesn't see' (LN 129). Indeed, he insists, '[t]*he organic process constantly presupposes interpretations*' (WP 643). All organisms have 'a biological intentionality or perspectivity', a minimal consciousness that forms 'the foundation of the affects' (BGE 258). He even extends this beyond animals and plants to include all organic and inorganic things: 'the will to power . . . guides the inorganic world as well. Or rather, that there *is* no inorganic world' (LN 15). In Nietzsche's view, it is erroneous to think that we are different to other animals. What we think of as the protocols of 'social morality' can be found everywhere in a simple form 'even down to the deepest depths of the animal world' (D 26). This includes the drive to truth as well as other values that we think to be quintessentially and uniquely human, such as morality: 'The beginnings of justice, as well as of prudence, moderation, valor – in short, of all we designate as the *Socratic virtues*, are *animal* in nature . . . it is not improper to describe the entire phenomenon of morality as animal' (D 26). Like humans, animals have self-consciousness motivated by sociality. The animal 'observes the effects it produces upon the representing of other animals, from this it learns to look back upon itself, to take itself "objectively", it has its degree of self-knowledge' (D 26). They can show 'sympathy' or 'empathy' and are capable of representing what another is experiencing (e.g. in the predator's interpretation of the prey), making animals capable of pity or cruelty (HH 2.62). This also gives them a sense of cause and effect, the ability to see 'intentions in *all* happening' (WP 550). Indeed, Nietzsche talks of 'the sagacity of plants' (WP 660) and attributes memory to all organisms due to the intelligence and intentionality of their drives: 'memory is older than consciousness. E.g., we have memory in the mimosa [tree], but no consciousness. Memory naturally without *picture*, in the plant'. This, he elaborates, is a kind of muscle memory or bodily intentionality found in its 'reflex-movements' (KSW 72-3.19). Finding the power of recognizing and concluding as common to all organisms, he even finds the origin of logic in the protoplasm which 'makes what it appropriates equal to itself and fits it into its own forms and files' (WP 510). As Solomon (2003: 37) remarks, Nietzsche would be very sympathetic to charges of speciesism when defining universal principles of humanity for, like Darwin, he sees humans and other organisms as continuous in exhibiting similar qualities. When speaking of becoming, this applies to all biological forms of the will to power, to become *what* one is rather than *who* one is. This connects to his perspectivism and his 'interpretative pluralism' in which he engages with a 'plurality of gazes' by viewing the human perspective from the outside, imagining what animals actually think about humans: '*Humanity*'. – We do not regard the animals as moral beings. But do you suppose the animals regard us as moral beings? – An animal that could speak said: 'Humanity is a prejudice of which we animals at least are free' (D 333).[17] Humanity, he surmises, must appear very strange indeed to the rest of the animal kingdom:

> I fear that the animals regard man as a creature of their own kind which has in a highly dangerous fashion lost its healthy animal reason – as the mad animal, as the laughing animal, as the weeping animal, as the unhappy animal. (GS 224)

And yet, Nietzsche, of course, does not avoid ambiguity or contradiction altogether on the matter for there are metaphysical residues in his thinking that surface in places displaying an anthropometric or humanist bias that Heidegger identified but exaggerated. Although in the *Nachlass* Nietzsche ascribes memory to all organisms, elsewhere he takes memory of the past as a capacity that distinguishes humans from animals: 'Human . . . braces himself against the great and ever greater pressure of what is past' (UM 2.1). This requires a separation of the self from immediate experience which allows him to consciously will: 'this mastery over himself also necessarily gives him mastery over circumstances, over nature, and over more short-willed and unreliable creatures' (UM 2.1). The animal lives unhistorically, its existence consumed by the present moment and the satisfaction of its immediate desires and needs. It cannot dissimulate for 'it conceals nothing and at every instant it appears as wholly as it is'. With humans, however, the knowledge of the past 'pushes him down and bends him sideways' and shows him the cruelty, suffering and imperfection of his life (UM 2.1.61). Nietzsche argues that the memory of the past emerged through the primitive relation between 'buyer and seller, creditor and debtor' that preceded societal organizations and norms. Over time, the community became the creditor to whom the individual owed a 'moral debt' internalized through common values and the human became 'the creature who measures values, who values and measures, as the "calculating animal in itself"' (GM 2.8). It is as the 'esteeming animal' that humans have become the 'undetermined animal' (BGE 62) since they are able to gain some latitude from the play of their biological drives in accordance with created and assumed values. In certain passages, Nietzsche seems to adopt an exclusivism in regard to humans that elsewhere he is quick to reject. This is evident in the following passage from *Daybreak* where he considers the viewpoint of a butterfly:

In the meantime I have come to look with new eyes on the secret and solitary fluttering of a butterfly high on the rocky seacoast where many fine plants are growing: it flies about unconcerned that it has but *one* day more to live and that the night will be too cold for its winged fragility. For it too a philosophy could no doubt be found: though it would no doubt not be mine. (D 553)

Here Nietzsche emphasizes discontinuity between humans and other creatures while acknowledging the butterfly worthy of a philosophy of its own. We may question, however, why he should assume the butterfly to be 'unconcerned that it has but *one* day more to live and that the night will be too cold for its winged fragility'. Surely such existential concerns pertaining to survival, life and death are common to butterflies as much as to beavers or viruses and are evident within their intentions, actions and interpretations. In perhaps Nietzsche's worst humanist faux pas, he agrees with Schopenhauer that humans suffer more than animals – 'the human is the most suffering creature' (WP 990) – and thinks that the difference is so great as to constitute a vast difference in kind. Suffering is a key (exclusive) feature of our psychic economy, Nietzsche claims, such that the sufferings of all animals undergoing vivisection don't compare to 'one painful night of a single hysterical educated female' (GM 2.7). Even in *Zarathustra*, among all of Zarathustra's close connections with his beloved animals, there is to be found a certain bias contained in the hierarchical symbolism of his ape-human-*Übermensch* compound: 'What is the ape to a human? A laughing stock or a painful embarrassment. And this is exactly what the human should be to the *Übermensch*: a laughing stock or a painful embarrassment' (Z P3).

Nietzsche identifies humanity as the bearer of a *multiplicity* of drives that have been created through historical existence: 'Human has, in contrast to the animal, bred large in himself an abundance of *opposite* drives and impulses; by this synthesis he is master of the earth' (WP 966). The human creation of 'bad conscience' within Christianity is a dramatic turn in animal development, 'an animal soul turning against itself', internalizing a morality based on guilt before God for one's biological drives, body and earthly existence: 'Oh this insane, pathetic beast – man! What ideas he has, what unnaturalness, what paroxysms of nonsense, what *bestiality of thought* erupts as soon as he is prevented just a little from being a *beast in deed!*' (GM 2.23). This has made humanity into 'the sick animal human' in painful denial of its animalistic and biological nature: 'human is sicker, less certain, more changing, more unsettled than any other animal. Of this there is no doubt – he is *the* sick animal' (GM 3.13). There is hence an ambiguous sense in which Nietzsche makes a distinct place for humanity while simultaneously animalizing it, revealing the human as *pharmakon* – both poison and cure. Characteristically, he tries to deflate our pride in these human values and suggests they are less reliable guides than our animal drives and affects. However, he also sees the possibility for change, conceiving the human as a (rickety) bridge that threatens to disintegrate in modernity[18] but which at the same time 'could *transform* itself from a moral to a wise humanity' (HH 107), forming a link of evolution in terms of the historical configuration of the will to power from the past into the future. Whatever differences Nietzsche suggests in his writings, it is clear that the general thrust of his thinking is towards effacing or diminishing these differences for which he always gives a *genealogical* rather than metaphysical explanation:

> For to translate man back into nature; to master the many vain and fanciful interpretations and secondary meanings which have been hitherto scribbled and daubed over that eternal basic text *homo natura*; to confront man henceforth with man in the way in which, hardened by the discipline of science, man today confronts the *rest* of nature, with dauntless Oedipus eyes and stopped-up Odysseus ears, deaf to the siren songs of old metaphysical bird-catchers who have all too long been piping to him 'you are more! you are higher! you are of a different origin!' (BGE 230)

Posthumanism has drawn heavily on Nietzsche's insights in eliding strict alterities or separations between humanity and the rest of nature (conceived autopoietically). Developing Nietzsche's notion of affectivity, Massumi (2015: 8–9) compares animal instinct to how a musician plays improvisational variations on a theme as 'a spontaneous excess of creative self-consistency', a force not of impulsion or compulsion but of *'affective propulsion'*. Following vitalist biologist Jacob von Uexküll, as well as Nietzsche, Deleuze and Guattari (1994: 185) propose 'a melodic, polyphonic and contrapuntal conception of nature', emphasizing the musical character of complex evolution. This replaces a teleological conception of nature with a melodic one in which the boundary between art and natural technique is an arbitrary one. They point to relations of 'counterpoint' in nature, such as that of the hermit crab and the shell of the dead mollusc, which join planes together as 'a double articulation' (1987: 51) and form blocs of sensation and longitudinal and latitudinal lines of becoming (1994: 185). To view the world in this way is to construct '[n]ature as music' (1987: 314) and to recognize that artifice is fully a part of nature.[19] Such a rhizomatic or involutionary perspective, they claim, carries not 'the slightest risk of anthropomorphism' (1987: 318). This, of course, is fully in accord with Nietzsche's observations in WP 808 where he also conceives nature as an *aesthetic* network of becoming:

> Art does more than merely imagine; it even transposes values. And it is not only that it transposes the *feeling of values*. . . . In animals, this condition produces new weapons, pigments, colours, and forms; above all, new movements, new rhythms, new love-calls and seductions. It is no different with man.

As Ansell-Pearson (1997: 117, 163) argues, Nietzsche's speculations on the becoming of the animal 'contain a radical and far-reaching overturning of anthropocentric naivety'. Moreover, his vision of the future for humanity is necessarily bound up with the non-human, prefiguring a posthuman subject as, in Deleuze's (2004: 107) words, a 'free, anonymous, and nomadic singularity which traverses men as well as plants and animals independently of the matter of their individuation and the forms of their personality'. What Nietzsche's relationism and 'atmospherics' tell us is that a lifeform is never separable from its rapport with the world. For Nietzsche, the organism is not to be reified as a monadic entity but rather as a 'complex of systems struggling for an increase in the feeling of power' (WP 703). Symbiosis in nature teaches us that the human is an integrated colony of amoeboid beings just as they are integrated colonies of bacteria. Biological cells in our bodies can evolve only through the acquisition of bacterial symbionts and in this way we can say, with some literal sense, that each individual is 'a tremendous *multiplicity*' (WP 518) with an infinity of living individuals inside.[20]

Sartre *in Naturabilis*

Sartre's personal aversion to nature is no secret, thanks in the main to Beauvoir, who describes how the efflorescence and rugged power of the natural world did not provision any great joy for him: 'More than the pure air of the mountain peaks or the open sea, he enjoys an atmosphere full of tobacco smoke and warmed by human breath.' She likens his attitude to nature to Roquentin's aversions to it:

> Roquentin's crisis reaches its paroxysm in a public park, and nowhere does the presence of things show itself with more indiscretion than in the heart of nature. Sartre detests the country, with its proliferation of plants and swarms of insects. At most, he tolerates the level sea, the smooth desert sands, or the mineral coldness of mountain peaks, but he is really happy only in cities, at the heart of a universe constructed and populated with fabricated objects. (2004: 230)

In the light of these comments, many scholars cursorily condemn Sartre for holding a jaundiced view of nature, often pointing to *Nausea* as a prime example of his literary distaste for all things composed of matter, vegetation and flesh. Kohak sums this up when he writes that, for Sartre, 'the nonhuman appears as also inhuman, absurd and nauseating'. According to Kohak (1984: 4, 76–7), 'his descriptions of the natural world ... stress its repugnant absurdity', leading him to adopt a 'mechanistic nature-construct' in which he posits a 'radical difference ... between the being *en-soi* of nature and the *pour-soi* of humans'. Kirsner (1985: 225) expands this view, claiming that '[i]n his personal and philosophical refusal of surrender, Sartre wants consciously directed activity to dominate the body and nature', thus repeating the view of the body and the world that has enshrined the project of Western civilization for many centuries. 'This is the logic of domination', Kirsner states, 'which views the world as there to be subdued and controlled and uses an instrumental, managerial form of rationality that regards oneself, others and the environment as objects to be quantified and manipulated.'

Although scholars are not altogether incorrect in pointing, along with Thody (1992: 31), to the fact that Sartre's literary writings 'come back again and again to the same images of sickness and discomfort, of the plethoric unpleasantness of nature', this tells only half the story for he also presents nature in a very dynamic way, as a vibrant network of overlapping energetic forces and living phantasmagoria. It is true, of course, many of his descriptions border on the unpleasant or grotesque. Stricken by a state of metaphysical nausea, for instance, Roquentin sees the natural world seeping through the flesh of others. Hands become white worms and crabs; woman's sex becomes ants, centipedes and ringworm. When he picks up a pebble, this causes a 'sweetish sickness' and 'nausea in the hands'. The sea from which the pebble emerges holds no relief from this nausea as the '*real* sea is cold and black, full of animals; it crawls under this thin green film which is designed to deceive people' (N 179). As Mussett (2020: 518) observes, Roquentin experiences 'a melding of the organic, inorganic and human' in which 'things behave like living organisms, seething, growing, threatening him by their mere presence'. He is sunken in phenomenology, experiencing a rich affective dialectic with the outside world that gets inside consciousness and the body 'penetrating me all over, through the eyes, through the nose, through the mouth' (N 181): 'everywhere blossomings, hatching out, my ears buzzed with existence, my very flesh throbbed and opened, abandoned itself to the universal burgeoning' (W 133). Objects and bodies are far from dead lifeless matter but are alive with their own intentionalities, qualities and dynamic uprisings, 'every now and then objects start existing in your hand' (N 176), '[t]hings have broken free from their names. They are there, grotesque, stubborn, gigantic' (N 180).[21] In his Dionysian experience of the chestnut tree, Roquentin is not an active agent but the passive recipient of sensation: 'The chestnut tree pressed itself against my eyes. . . . The soft sound of the water in the Masqueret Fountain flowed into my ears and made a nest there, filling them with sighs; my nostrils overflowed with a green, putrid smell' (N 183). Objects carry their own agency – 'A tree is scratching the earth under my feet with a black nail' (N 181) – and place Roquentin under their influence: 'I was inside; the black stump *did not pass*, it stayed there, in my eyes, just as a lump of food sticks in a windpipe' (N 188–9). Things themselves are the carriers of sensation – 'they will feel something gently brushing against their bodies' (N 226) – and the body itself has its own motility or 'motor intentionality' irrespective of consciousness: 'My body turns very gently towards the east, wobbles slightly and starts walking' (N 227); 'the arm trembles, the nail scratches, scratches, the mouth smiles under the staring eyes and the man endures without noticing it this little existence which is swelling his right side, which has borrowed his right arm and his right cheek to fulfil itself' (N 181):

> Objects ought not to *touch*, since they are not alive. You use them, you put them back in place, you live among them: they are useful, nothing more. But they touch me, it's unbearable. I am afraid of entering into contact with them, just as if they were living animals. . . . Now I see; I remember better what I felt the other day on the sea-shore when I was holding that pebble. It was a sort of sweet disgust. How unpleasant it was! And it came from the pebble, I'm sure of that, it passed from the pebble into my hands. (N 22)

In dissociating Sartre from Nietzsche, scholars often mention the passage where Roquentin alludes to the frailty of existence in contrast to what some refer to as the vitality of the will to power, but elsewhere in the text, he emphasizes its vibrancy and vigour:

> My eyes never met anything but repletion. There were swarms of existences at the end of the branches, existences which constantly renewed themselves and were

never born. The existing wind came and settled on the tree like a big fly; and the tree shivered . . . a thing-shiver flowed into the tree, took possession of it, shook it, and suddenly abandoned it. (N 190)

More importantly, Roquentin sees himself as continuous with nature (though he finds it repugnant) for '[his] body is co-extensive with the world, spread right through things' (BN 428), sharing a common existence of superfluity and contingency: '*Superfluous*: that was the only connexion I could establish between those trees, those gates, those pebbles. . . . And I – weak, languid, obscene, digesting, tossing about dismal thoughts – *I too was superfluous*' (N 184). His fate, he concludes towards the end of the novel, is to '[e]xist slowly, gently, like these trees, like a puddle of water, like the red seat in the tram' (N 223).

Of all those who have discerned a nascent ecological logic in Sartre's dialectical philosophy,[22] Ally's *Ecology and Existence* is by far the most systematic investigation in both a deconstructive sense (of interpreting his range of writings) and a reconstructive manner (of seeing through some of his blind spots and developing his fledgling ecology to the full). Ally shows how Sartre's philosophy is rife with ambiguity where nature is concerned but far from the purely negative view many scholars all too readily ascribe to him through a superficial and simplified reading. If we scan the range of his writings, we can find a multivalent formulation of nature (as threat, as 'Feminized Other', as escape and cradle of retreat, as rapture) and a burgeoning ecological perspective from which it is possible to articulate 'the broad contours of a new socioecological imaginary' (2017: 323).[23] On the negative side, Ally addresses the four theoretical charges brought against Sartre in addition to *ad hominem* (he personally disliked nature) and *ad usum* arguments (he neglected the ecological narrative throughout his work). These are 'reflexive anthropocentrism', 'heuristic exceptionalism', 'categorical exclusivism' and 'naïve instrumentalism' (2017: 26). These factors wax and wane throughout his writings (and sometimes even within the same passage!) but are not essential, in Ally's (2017: 360–1) view, to the structure of his wider ontological thinking. Although none of them is easily dismissed, we should be careful of 'throwing out the baby with the bathwater'. Instead, a reconstructive reading of his oeuvre shows that nothing of his fourfold flaw – failing, fallacy, error, lacuna – is foundational for his wider ontology. Furthermore, criticisms of Sartre often overlook the subtlety and nuance of his thinking and 'obscure the interpretive latitude that is the hallmark of his manner of thinking things through' (2017: 385). It is in the nature of Sartre's methodologico-substantive apparatus 'to leave itself open to further development' and of his philosophizing that is always open to 'the integration of new insights and pathways' (2017: 25).

As we saw in Chapter 4, Sartre's descriptions of the *en-soi* as brute Being, opacity, inertia, pure exteriority and raw passivity – '[i]t is what it is' (BN 28) – are considered by him in the wider denouement of *Being and Nothingness* as 'provisional' and 'abstract' and give way to a dialectical view of the relation between *pour-soi* and *en-soi* as one of 'connective tissue' (BN 755) as his investigation proceeds. On this point, Sartre is unequivocal: 'Man and world *are* relative beings, and relation *is* the principle of their being' (BN 415). Mediation is at the very heart of Sartre's ontology as the phenomenological and dialectical condition of experience and history. In

Search for a Method onwards, Sartre's treatment of nature also matures in a similar manner to his developments with freedom. In elucidating his notion of history, he introduces the concepts of material need and scarcity as key explanatory factors: 'Whatever men and events are, they certainly appear within the compass of scarcity; that is, in a society still incapable of emancipating itself from its needs – hence from nature' (SM 132).

Doubtlessly, Sartre's writings display a great deal of ambiguity insofar as he both uproots us *from* Nature and roots us *in* it. In *Materialism and Revolution*, for instance, he presents us as trapped in a hostile adversarial nature:

> It is not true, then, that man is outside Nature and the world, as the idealist has it, or that he is only up to his ankles in it, baulking like a bather having a dip while her head is in the clouds. He is completely in Nature's clutches, and at any moment Nature can crush him and annihilate him, body and soul. (1977)

When asked about ecology and class in interview in the 1970s, however, he argues in opposition to this:

> The development of the human species has placed it in conditions that are no longer natural; but it nevertheless retains relations to Nature. The real problem of the human species today, the problems of class, capital, and so on, are problems that have no relation to Nature. They are posed by the human species in its historical movement, and that leaves Nature outside of them. (1981a: 29)

This ambivalence increases further when we bear in mind what he had previously stated in the same interview: 'I raise the class question, the social question, starting from being, which is wider than class, since it is also a question that concerns animals and inanimate objects' (1981a: 14). As Ally (2017: 361) observes, however, although Sartre's ambivalence ripened and never completely went away, he made better sense of it over time as his dialectical view developed through the *Critiques*.

While it is true that the four charges levelled against Sartre do relate to certain assumptions that surface in his writings, they are often overstated or neglect other elements that work against such readings. The charge of instrumentalism, for instance, in many ways misreads his wider philosophical orientation. Although he writes, '[m]y surroundings are the implement-things that surround me' (BN 657) and '[e]very praxis, whatever else it may be, is first an instrumentalization of material reality' (CDR 161 – translation modified), it is grounded as a real dimension of the relational nature of lived experience and does not vitiate the core substance of his thought. What scholars often miss is that he also writes in *Being and Nothingness* of an open-ended, integrative orientation towards instrumentality, describing instrumentality as a 'categorial classification' (BN 60). His aim is phenomenological not metaphysical – to describe the structure of instrumentality not to posit it as our *only* means of relating to the world.[24] Indeed, he highlights the pitfalls of an 'instrumentalist humanism', insisting that relations of modification and subjection are just one aspect of our multifaceted relationality to the world (CDR 2:316).

Equally, it might be said that Sartre's exclusivism is one of *degree*, not one of kind, despite the fact that it returns as a 'bad habit' or as 'a cognitive spasm' in his thinking (Ally 2017: 363). It is often noted how Sartre configures praxis in exclusivist terms as a distinctly human activity.[25] In his lecture 'morale et histoire', he discusses a monkey in terms of its being an actor and rearranging its environment in a purposeful way in order to satisfy a need but doesn't call this praxis. He reiterates this viewpoint in the *Critique*:

> The whole complex of behavior patterns of certain insects and mammals may be called action or activity. It can even be noted that activity on earth begins with single-celled creatures themselves. At all events, the questions posed by such activity have nothing in common with those ... posed by the existence of practical multiplicities ... equal or superior to our own. (CDR 2:384)

For Sartre, the distinguishing human feature of praxis is 'constituent interiority', the 'motive force of everything' (CDR 322). This, he states, is 'phenomenologically temporalizing', 'dialectically totalizing' and uniquely human: 'We affirm the specificity of the human act, which cuts across the social milieu while still holding on to its determinations, and which transforms the world on the basis of given conditions. For man is characterized above all by his going beyond a situation, and by what he succeeds in making of what he has been made' (SM 91). His transitional essay of the 1940s 'Materialism and Revolution' explicitly rejects Engels' dialectic of nature and argues for the specificity of human acts: 'it is obvious that the notion of *natural history* is absurd ... only human history is possible' (1995: 192). Adopting an analytical viewpoint (that, ironically, he trenchantly criticizes in the *Critique*), he argues that biological change across time is 'of a mechanical and not dialectical order' (1995: 192–3). In *Search for a Method*, this exclusivism is still, albeit more subtly, at play in his thinking: 'What we call freedom is the irreducibility of the cultural order to the natural order' (SM 152). Considering only *Anthropos* as relevant for his social ontology, he poses the fundamental question, '[d]o we have today the means to constitute a structural and historical anthropology?' (SM xxxiv). As Ally (2017: 153, 224) observes, despite Sartre's increasingly dialectical sensibilities, his propositions 'carry the burden of a familiar supposition that humankind and nature are somehow radically distinct *from* each other – even if they are, and at the same time, fundamentally wrapped up *with* one another'. His reflex position is to ascribe value singularly to human beings, and his 'anthropogenesis of the ought' is evident throughout all of his scattered ethical writings: 'Sartre's anthropogenic axiology and humanist metaethics provide some of the best evidence of the deep continuity of his thought.'

In other passages and parts of his writings, however, Sartre's view is more nuanced, parenthetical and ambiguous, suggesting more of a continuum with the rest of nature rather than a separation from it.[26] In the *Critique*, he defines his 'monism of materiality' as 'the only monism which makes man neither a molecular dispersal nor a being apart, the only one which starts by defining him by his praxis in the general milieu of animal life, and which can transcend the following two true but contradictory propositions: all existence in the universe is material; everything in the world of man is human' (CDR

180-1). The *Rome Lectures* (1964) marks something new in Sartre's thinking where he takes up our animality not simply as an ontological structure but as a positive region of ethical investigation. The bond between our lived animality and our lived moral experience is, he argues, *felt need*, something common to all living organisms. When commenting directly on animals in 1943, he takes a resolutely anti-Cartesian view: 'I do think that animals exist as consciousness, and as such, nihilate. . . . I am not at all Cartesian on this point, I've always believed in the intelligence and passions of animals' (2014). He returned to this theme in interview in the 1970s:

Nature is not exclusively in-itself. A plant that is growing is no longer altogether in-itself. It is more complex. It is alive. (1981a: 40)

I think animals have consciousness. In fact I have always thought so. (1981a: 28)

Although it was left to others, such as Merleau-Ponty, Deleuze and Derrida, to fully confront the notion of animal psychism and human animality from a posthumanist perspective, Sartre's 'existential limno-phenomenology' suggests and illustrates it with some phenomenological richness.[27] In some passages, Sartre takes a Dionysian view of nature alluding to its manifold secrets and a forgotten sense of its abundance and beauty: 'man is everywhere crisscrossed by Nature. He himself is a natural being, to the extent that Nature is magic' (NE 352). In *Words*, he associates closeness to nature with a pre-reflective sapience or comprehension: 'truth flows from the mouths of babes and sucklings. Still close to Nature, they are cousins of the wind and the sea: their stammerings offer broad and vague teachings to him who can hear them' (W 28–9). He repeats this magical conception of nature in his essay 'Black Orpheus' as a creative power, a kind of Mother Goddess, 'an enormous perpetual birth' (1964a: 40). In the final phase of his thinking, he re-imagines this celebratory pagan conception, formulating the concept of the 'mother-matrix' that he hoped to develop into a philosophy of 'Mother Earth' (HN 90).[28]

In Ally's (2017: 154–5) view, Sartre's account of nature rides on a thin ambiguous line, a 'line without thickness' (CDR 2:329), of keeping the human and non-human heuristically apart while insisting that 'they are ontologically cut from the same metaphysical cloth'. This functions as a 'lived contradiction' in his schematic philosophy that his dialectical approach illuminates. By decoupling his errors from the best of his insights, however, it is possible 'to naturalize or . . . ecologize' (2017: 214) his ethics and ontology in the service of an 'existential ecology' that yields a 'hybrid existential-ecological axiom' of 'existence precedes essence because it's all related' (2017: 506). Sartre can be viewed in this light as a thinker who stands on the cusp of the 'Holocene-Anthropocene transit' between a waxing Earth and a waning world (2017: 353). His designation of the Earth as 'the Elsewhere of Elsewheres' as absolute Otherness (CDR 323–4) signifies just the tragic underside of late-Holocene thinking since, as he recognizes in *Saint Genet*, the environment is all around us: 'We rapidly cart away the dead, we stealthily recover waste, every day we mask, in the name of cleaning up, the destruction of the day before. We conceal the pillaging of the planet' (SG 24). Despite the fact that Sartre did not make more explicit his parenthetical self and was guilty of some elements of anthropocentrism, if we look past his professed intentions and expectations for his time, it is possible, as Ally contends (2017: 371–3), to see new meanings for ours. Reading *through* the late-Holocene denotations of the *Critique* we can read *above* them and *beyond* them.

If we explore Sartre's work deeply enough, it is thus possible to discover an '*ecology of intelligibility*', 'a vital community of logics' and 'an inferential ecosystem of sorts' peppered with 'emergent ecological sensibilities and earthly sensitivities' (2017: 364, 392) that can illuminate our present Anthropocene predicament. In just four pages out of over a thousand in the *Critique* in which he describes the 'destructive apparatus' of the Chinese peasant and the practice of deforestation (CDR 162), he demonstrates how worked-over matter takes on an alien presence, resisting us through passive action and confronting us as a counter-finality that can have disastrous consequences. Matter is conceived in these terms as an actant within a human/non-human assemblage and far from the 'passive unity' of the inert *en-soi* that scholars hastily take to be his overriding viewpoint. In the *Critiques*, he recognizes our Anthropocene collective fragility, both in terms of our self-induced suicide through ecological despoliation or atomic annihilation (CDR 2:306) in the face of planetary contingencies, such as 'some sidereal catastrophe' (CDR 2:310) or some 'cosmic cataclysm' (CDR 2:321) that might 'exterminate our species' (CDR 2:326).

Eco-phenomenologists

The work of Sartre's friend and erstwhile colleague, Maurice Merleau-Ponty, is scriptural for many eco-phenomenologists[29] and is often viewed as a philosophical bridge between existentialist phenomenology and poststructuralism. Sartre and Merleau-Ponty became good friends in their university days at the ENS, co-edited the journal *Les Temps Modernes* together, but parted ways over ideological issues in the 1950s not long before Merleau-Ponty's death in 1961. In his obituary 'Merleau-Ponty vivant', Sartre spoke warmly of his former friend and heralded the contemporary resonance of his philosophy: 'Merleau-Ponty is still too much alive for anyone to be able to describe him' (1961). Merleau-Ponty's writings on Sartre's philosophy were an admixture of the positive and negative. In his review of *The Flies* published in 1943, he commends Sartre's conception of freedom – 'flaw in the world's diamond, splinter in nature's skin' – as comparable to Nietzsche who showed 'the basis of terror and cruelty on which the Greeks made freedom appear' (1997: 63–4). In the second issue of *Les Temps Modernes* in November 1945, he defends *Being and Nothingness* against those who view it as a 'poison' against which is needed a 'quarantine' (1964a: 71), arguing it posits neither a materialism nor a 'residual idealism' (1964a: 77), since Sartre's central concern is 'man's relationship to his natural or social surroundings' and 'our corporeal and social ties' (1964a: 71, 72).

Despite this recognition, elsewhere Merleau-Ponty is highly critical of Sartre's 'flat ontology' of *pour-soi* and *en-soi*, charging him of conceiving of nature as being 'is what it is', a plenum of undifferentiated full positivity: 'Sartre speaks of a world that is . . . in itself, that is, flat, and for a nothingness that is absolute abyss. In the end, for him, depth does not exist, because it is bottomless' (1968: 237). Ontological space, Merleau-Ponty argues, is unified as space of disparate unity in which both sides of Being implicate each other, intermingle and share a depth of flesh between them. For Sartre, however, the two sides are faced off against each other in incommensurable opposition and lack a 'between space' (1968: 75). In 'the look', for instance, the Other is perceived negatively as a 'not-me' who apprehends an aspect of me that I myself cannot, but according to Merleau-Ponty (1968: 82), the phenomenological expressivity of the embodied other comes before the conflictual relations evinced by 'the look': 'we are not two nihilations installed in two universes of the in-itself, incomparable, but two entries to the same Being, each accessible to but one of us'. Failing to recognize this, Sartre lacks an interworld: '[i]n Sartre, there is a plurality of subjects but no intersubjectivity.... The world and history are no longer a system with several points of entry but a sheaf of irreconcilable perspectives which never coexist and which are held together only by the hopeless heroism of the I' (1973: 205).

As Beauvoir pointed out in the 1950s in her essay 'Merleau-Ponty et le pseudo-sartrisme' (1955) written in response to Merleau-Ponty's criticisms of Sartre, Merleau-Ponty presents a false image of Sartre as an idealist who disregards the body and lacks a theory of intersubjectivity. Not only does he vulgarize Sartre's ontology in *Being and Nothingness* as being one of exclusion and 'abstract removedness', it is wrong to say also that he fails to supply a concept of 'objective possibility' as the negative dimension, as a mediation of the negation of the negation (1973: 122).[30] Furthermore, Beauvoir accuses Merleau-Ponty of acting in bad faith because he knew Sartre was in the process of developing his social ontology in the *Critique*. In this vein, Caeymaex and Cormann (2020: 476) accuse Merleau-Ponty of criticizing Sartre for his own gain, 'thinking about himself through a Sartrean lens, exploiting for himself the tensions that create difficulties in Sartre's thinking'. Throughout his works, Merleau-Ponty did not stop testing out his own theories in the light of Sartre's, 'in an explicit dialogue, admiring and critical at once' (2020: 478). Hyppolite and Saint-Aubert concur with this. According to Hyppolite (1991: 719), 'the difference that separated these two men ... sometimes allowed them to switch positions with the other'. Up until his death in 1961, Merleau-Ponty 'exploited ... the fecundity of the tension that inhabited Sartre's philosophy from the beginning', a 'living and uninterrupted dialogue' (1991: 687). In Saint-Aubert's (2011: 60) view, Merleau-Ponty secretly ate away at Sartre's ontology and anthropology under the appearance of camaraderie, involving a strategy of turning Beauvoir against Sartre by playing on 'what still remains non-Sartrean in Beauvoir'. More than this, he borrows heavily from Sartre as he 'disguises, wears costumes, and willingly attributes to others what he himself has done on the pretence that he is interpreting others' work according to his own intuitions ... even Sartre, sometimes re-clothed in the least expected clothing'.

There are three clear areas – reflection, the body and intersubjectivity – in which Merleau-Ponty can be said to have stolen Sartre's clothes, even though he developed, refined and enlarged them to fit a larger frame. First of all, in *Phenomenology of Perception* he follows Sartre's idea of the pre-reflective cogito, which he defines as a 'glimpse of myself', a 'tacit awareness' and 'inarticulate grasp' that precedes knowledge and speech (1962: 404). Dismissing the 'view from above' (1968: 69) as Sartre had done in relation to lived experience, he posits the pre-reflective cogito as an immanent modification of lived experience. Establishing a 'living link' between the I and world, and exploring preferentially the zones of experience 'in which being and consciousness coincide' (1962: 492), Merleau-Ponty proposes a form of embodied philosophizing or 'true reflection' (1962: 452) that bears close similarity to Sartre's 'purifying reflection' and 'comprehension'. This is a form of reflection that recognizes its own contingency and dependence on the pre-reflective givenness of the world prior to Cartesian separation and mechanistic determination, 'a creative operation which itself participates in the facticity of that [unreflective] experience' from which philosophy springs (1962: 61–3). Philosophy provides us with an indissoluble bond between our openness to a world that remains resolutely other and our reflective return to ourselves, an intertwining of immanence and freedom. '[T]rue philosophy' thus involves 'leaving oneself' and 'retiring into oneself' (1968: 49, 199), a 'double movement of perspectivism' (centrifugal and centripetal) that, as we saw in Chapter 3, is intrinsic to Sartre's (and Nietzsche's) therapeutic psychology.

Just as Merleau-Ponty draws heavily on Sartrean ideas, the same can be said in reverse. Their thinking is best conceived in this sense as involving 'relations of reciprocal influence' (Churchill and Reynolds (2013: 222)). In many ways, Sartre's focus became more Merleau-Pontyian in his later phase of thinking that evolved after his friend's death. In his final years, for instance, he became more celebratory of nature and attuned to Merleau-Ponty's 'chiasmic thought' (1968: 141). According to Colombel, Sartre had been discussing the concept of 'le matriciel' (the mother as 'matrix') with him for three years. He also told Sicard that he was writing a work that was to transform completely what he had previously thought in philosophy based on the 'interpenetration of consciousnesses' (1979b: 15).[31] This echoes passages in *Hope Now* where Sartre refers to a tribal view of totemism for a model of human interconnection by recapturing the sense of the Mother Goddess as a totem: 'When I see man, I think: he has the same origin as myself, like me he comes from Mother Humanity, let's say, Mother Earth as Socrates says, Mother' (HN 90).

Although deeply intersubjective in its positing of the self as syncategorematic, Sartre still thought that the section on 'being-for-others' in *Being and Nothingness* was the weakest one: 'What is particularly bad in *L'Etre et le néant* is the specifically social chapters, on the "we", compared to the chapters on the "you" and "others"' (1981a: 13). No doubt influenced by Beauvoir's concept of the 'social Other' and by Merleau-Ponty, Sartre buttressed his concept of intersubjectivity in the *Critique* to move fully beyond a dyadic level of explanation. His concept of the practico-inert (and 'objective spirit') bears similarity to Merleau-Ponty's idea of an interworld of mediations woven by intercorporeality and language (1962: 354) This was developed by Merleau-Ponty into the 'flesh of the world', a dense multilayered field of relationships, 'intermundane spaces' and forces, a 'pell-mell ensemble of bodies and minds, promiscuity of visages, words, actions, with, between them all, that cohesion which cannot be denied them since they are all differences, extreme divergences of one same something' (1968: 84). Like Sartre, Merleau-Ponty (1968: 214) views subjectivity as emergent, arising from the inter-corporeal exchange between self and others. Perceptibility is diacritical and reversible, a doubling up of seen/being-seen, uttering/being-heard, a 'relation of reciprocity in which neither of the relata is intelligible apart from the other' (1968: 264). Emotions, for instance, are not felt within the subject but acquire meaning intersubjectively in a 'between space' or 'interworld'. In the case of anger, 'the location of my anger ... is in the space we both share' (2004: 84). Following Sartre, he theorizes emotions as bound up with corporeal articulations, an 'expressive space' in which our body is thought to be 'comparable to a work of art' (1962: 151). Merleau-Ponty's idea of bodily expressivity and the direct perception of others in conceiving the body as a synthetic totality of life and action draws upon Sartrean insights regarding the idea of the body as a 'nexus of living meanings' (BN 462). Mirroring Sartre's emphasis on the 'connective tissue' (BN 755) between *pour-soi/en-soi*, Merleau-Ponty theorizes subject and object as 'not two opposed domains to be somehow united, they are both aspects of the same flesh: the flesh seeing itself, turned upon itself, overlapping itself, folded upon itself, reversible' (1968: 111). There is, he argues, 'incipient significance' in the living body: 'our gaze, prompted by the experience of our own body, will discover in all other "objects" the miracle of expression' (1962: 197). Just as in Sartre's theory of sexual desire and 'the caress' (BN 508), he shows how eroticism reveals the force of desire and the blind bodily links that 'cross over' from one person to another (1968: 264). In the conveyance of emotional meaning, it is 'as if the other person's intention inhabited my body and mine his' (1962: 185). Experience is transitive – what happens in me can pass over into the other – arising from an early affective 'spatiality of adherence' based on an 'internal linkage' between the child's body and the mother's expression in which their intentional encroachments and emotional apprehension overlap. This, of course, was a topic Sartre would later investigate in depth in his study of Flaubert.

Vibrant matter

> [I]t is not dead but lives. For in it and conforming to its outer and inner organs, a thousand living, manifold forces are at work. The more we learn about matter, the more forces we discover in it, so that the empty conception of a dead extension completely disappears.
>
> (Johann von Herder, 'God: Some Conversations')

Although poststructuralism showed how social constructs can take on a negative life of their own, by placing everything inside the text some forms of poststructuralism have taken a retrograde step by ignoring matter. This is not true, however, of all poststructuralists. In his essay 'Theatrum Philosophicum', for instance, Foucault discusses the 'incorporeal' dimension of bodies. He recalls the Epicurean idea of simulacra, the thin sheet of atoms continually being shed from the thicker and slower compound of atoms. These filmy sheathes are the stimuli to human perception, mobile floaters that hit our sense apparatus and give us notice of an outside. For Foucault (1977: 169–70), they are a strange kind of matter, all surface and no depth – 'emissions' that rise like 'the wisps of a fog', a materiality that 'dissipate[s] the density of matter'.

They are incorporeal in that they are not quite a discrete body or substantial corpus but a kind of mobile activity that remains immanent to matter and incorporeality. Taking their lead from Spinoza's distinction between *natura naturata* (passive matter organized into an order of Creation) and *natura naturans* (the uncaused causality that constantly generates new forms), Deleuze and Guattari conceive nature as generativity, a productive power or 'continuous stream of occurrence' suspended and quenched in its products. Unlike Bergson's *élan vital*, matter needs no animating accessory since it is figured as itself animate, the 'active principle'. Nature is 'an immense abstract machine' of productivity, whose pieces 'are the various assemblages and individuals, each of which groups together an infinity of particles entering into an infinity of more or less interconnected relations' (1987: 254). As in Nietzschean and Sartrean ontology, this operates not for a pregiven end but for the sake of the process in itself and also expresses itself as a pluralistic monism: 'ontologically one, formally diverse' (Deleuze 1992: 67). Deleuze's and Guattari's (1987: 449) notion of active and expressive 'matter-movement' or 'matter-energy' that 'enters assemblages and leaves them' reveals the positive or productive power of things to draw other bodies near and conjoin powers: 'Each phylum has its own singularities and operations . . . the flow of matter in continuous variation, conveying singularities and traits of expression' (1987: 454). Just as Sartre describes the affectivity of objects as 'a game of back and forth' of constant enrichment between feeling and object to the extent that 'each affective quality is so deeply incorporated in the object that it is impossible to distinguish between what is felt and what is perceived' (IM 139), Deleuze notes in *Cinema 1* how affectivity is a quality of things as well as people: 'And why is expression not available to things? . . . The Stoics showed that things themselves were bearers of ideal events which did not exactly coincide with their properties, their actions and reactions' (1986: 118).

Nietzsche's will to power and Sartre's 'protean connectionism'[32] do justice both to systems and things, acknowledging the stubborn reality of individuation and the distributive quality of their affectivity. This was a point acknowledged by Deleuze who interpreted Nietzsche's will to power as a 'monistic differential of forces' and viewed Sartre's thought as a call to 'make its totalities anew, like a power that is at once collective and private'. 'This is why', he concludes, 'Sartre remains my teacher' (1987: 79). In this respect, we can trace a lineage from Nietzsche and Sartre to recent posthumanist theory, such as philosophical posthumanism, vibrant materialism and object-oriented ontology.[33] In Bennett's vibrant materialism, for instance, bodies enhance their power as a heterogeneous assemblage. Agency is distributed across an ontologically heterogeneous field rather than being localized in a single or collective human body, 'an animal-vegetable-mineral-sonority cluster with a particular degree and duration of power' (2010: 23). As in Nietzsche's idea of 'multiplicity-as-unity' and Sartre's notion of a 'detotalized totality', assemblages are not governed by any central head. No one materiality can determine consistently the trajectory or the impact of the group because each member-actant has an energetic pulse slightly off from that of the assemblage. An assemblage is never a static block but an open-ended collective, a 'non-totalizable sum', with a history of formation and finite lifespan (2010: 24). As a process of Nietzschean dissipative systems, the universe 'is a turbulent, immanent field in which various and variable materialities collide, congeal, morph, evolve and disintegrate'.

Within this field of 'events', an actant is a human or non-human source of action which has efficacy and can produce effects – 'any entity . . . modifies another entity' – although some things are proto-actants in the sense that their performances or energies are too small or fast to be 'things' (2010: xi). Alongside and inside singular human agents, there exists a heterogeneous series of actants with partial, overlapping and conflicting degrees of power and effect. Causality is *emergent* rather than efficient, arising from the process where 'the new effects become *infused* into the very . . . organization of the second level . . . such . . . that the cause cannot be said to be fully different from the effect engendered' (2010: 33). Bennett uses the concept of *shi* to describe this: '*Shi* is the style, energy, propensity, trajectory, or élan inherent to a specific arrangement of things . . . the dynamic force emanating from a spatio-temporal configuration rather than from any particular element within it' (2010: 35). The *shi* of an assemblage is vibratory: 'it is the mood or style of an open whole in which both the membership changes over time and the members themselves undergo internal alteration.' As in Deleuze's idea of 'adsorbsion', each individual possesses emergent qualities that are capable of independent variation and therefore the possibility of being in phase or out of phase with one another. This is a gathering of elements in a way that both forms a coalition, or an 'excess' irreducible to the particular bodies involved, and yet preserves something of the agential impetus of each element (2010: 35).

In Bennett's (2010: 30) view, vibrant materialism 'continues the radical displacement of the human subject' that phenomenology had installed (though she credits Merleau-Ponty with moving in this direction in his unfinished *Visible and Invisible*). But, as we have seen, this is also true of Sartre whose phenomenology 'is absolutely distinct from the idealist return to consciousness' (Merleau-Ponty 1962: x) and, as Deleuze (2004) noted, a genuine attempt, within a philosophy of immanence, to get back 'to the things themselves' as Husserl had defined as phenomenology's true purpose. As we saw in Chapter 3, Sartre's valorization of 'pre-reflectivity' and Nietzsche's championing of 'instinct' connect with Bennett's (2010: 127) contention that there are many forms of feeling or thought intermediate between the purely physical stage and the stage of conscious intellectual operations. Nietzschean and Sartrean philosophy both point to the need to maintain an 'open, pluralistic image of thought' and avoid the mistake of rigorously dividing sapience from sentience and consigning everything that is not purely rational and abstract into the category of causal deterministic mechanisms. As their ontology of forces show, most interactions between entities involve no conscious knowledge at all when we are touched or affected by things without necessarily understanding them. This finds expression in Nietzsche's 'sensism' that goes beyond ocularcentric/anthropocentric conceptions of 'knowledge' to a more synaesthetic conception of 'comprehension'.[34] In line with vital materialism, Nietzsche and Sartre propose a notion of freedom not tied to the emergence of reason, the phonocentric capacity for reflection or to some inherent quality of the human but situate it in the world of affective transfer.

In some ways in opposition to Deleuzian assemblages, but in agreement with its posthumanist standpoint, *object-oriented ontologists* have been attracted to Heidegger's focus in his later essays on the object's negative power, its persistent incalculability and withdrawal from any attempt to know it. Although they turn to

Heidegger, they could just have easily have plundered Sartre's literary phenomenology for inspiration. In Meillassoux's (2008: 63) view, we need to break our correlationist habit where we superimpose our own concepts on 'the great outdoors, the eternal in-itself, whose being is indifferent to whether or not it is thought'. Instead, we need to appreciate 'the strangeness of things', including the things we have made ourselves which possess 'their own bizarre and independent existence'. Harman argues that an object can never be equated with, or reduced to, our knowledge of it: 'Let's imagine that we were able to gain exhaustive knowledge of all properties of a tree. . . . It should go without saying that even such knowledge *would not itself be a tree*. Our knowledge would not grow roots or bear fruit or shed leaves, at least not in a literal sense' (2010: 788).[35] Thus, an object cannot touch or know another object completely: 'one object never affects another directly, since the cotton and fire both fail to exhaust one another's reality' (2005: 188). When something fails to function then its excess of being is revealed to us. There is 'an uprising of distinct elements . . . a surge of minerals and battle flags and tropical cats into the field of life, where each object bears a certain demeanor and seduces us in a specific way, bombarding us with its energies like a miniature neutron star' (2002: 47). Harman calls this the 'allure' of objects, the sense of an object's existence apart from and over and above its own qualities in which it 'invites us toward another level of reality'. Such an encounter alters the parameters of the world, tearing apart 'the contextual of meaning' (2005: 179).

Although objects are withdrawn epistemologically from others and are never exhausted by our knowledge of them, they are not 'barricaded behind firewalls' (2005: 188) and are ontologically, aesthetically and sensually intertwined with others through allure or vicarious causation. Allure means that one object calls to another from a distance. A 'fusion' takes place but one that 'remains only partial, encrusted with residual accidents'. In this indirect way, 'two objects . . . touch without touching' (2007: 204) with the effect that we are emotionally moved by objects (through affect) even if we cannot cognize them. This is not the 'efficient causation' described by physical science (2007: 174) but is a vicarious process that involves a kind of substitution, translation or transfer from a distance, a kind of occult influence. Contact is never literal but a metaphor, a 'transfer' or 'carrying across' (2005: 124), and causation is 'strangely akin to the allure of aesthetic experience', an occult process of influence, a sort of touching that involves 'a secret content that is never presentable' (2005: 124). Arguing against human exceptionalism and in line with Nietzsche's and Sartre's idea of the doubleness of privacy and relation as a condition of all entities in the universe, Harman (2007: 189) contends that 'intentionality is not a special human property at all, but an ontological feature of objects in general'.

A pair of posthumanist humanists

I teach you the superman. Man is something that should be overcome.
(Nietzsche, *Zarathustra* P3)

Nietzsche's relation to humanism is not straightforward, swinging between a Lutheran anti-humanist contempt and the Renaissance promissory faith in human perfectibility, of a Goethian god-in-the-making. Deflating human conceit and arrogance, he conceives of humanity as both an unfortunate aberration of nature and as a creature of unparalleled possibilities and becomings. He forges an ambiguous humanism that stresses our continuation with the rest of nature while both lamenting and celebrating our distancing ourselves from it as an emergent evolutionary bundle of values, experiments and self-overcoming. This conveys a certain love–hate relationship, a mixture of adulation and contempt that mirrors his self-relationship as one of affirmation and denial.[36] The danger of metaphysical thinking as religion, state or science is always ever ready to deform humanity and turn its will to power into a reactive force against itself and others. Turned against its animal instincts and drives, 'the human is *the* sick animal' (GM 3.13) tormented by its own self-consciousness. Even its finest notions, such as reason, are 'a mere idiosyncrasy of a certain species of animal, and one among many' (WP 515). For Nietzsche, '[r]eligion has debased the concept 'human' by placing all that is good in the realm of God' (WP 136). This has diminished the human condition for '[t]here is not enough love and goodness in the world for us to be permitted to give any of it away to imaginary things' (HH 129).

However, Nietzsche holds the comfort that 'above the steam and filth of human lowlands there is a *higher, brighter humanity*' (WP 993). To replace the humanism of the 'last man' who has learnt 'to perceive all diversity as immoral', Nietzsche proposes a 'radical humanism' in which the *Übermensch* 'radicalizes humanist principles' and avoids nihilistic cul-de-sacs (Manschot 2021: 145). This is to think the human but also to think beyond the human – from the inside and the outside – within a theory of action and responsibility that crosses the human–non-human divide. Throughout his writings, he offers several paragons to fit this 'radical' or 'posthumanist' humanism – 'musical Socrates' (BT 15), a productive synthesis of Dionysian art and science, the 'free spirit' wandering lonely beyond statist thought and boundaries, Zarathustra, connected and true to the Earth, the 'Genius of culture' who 'is a centaur, half animal, half human, and even has angel's wings on his head' (HH 241), Dionysus the god of masks, intoxication, rapture and wholeness, and the *Übermensch*, the re-evaluator of all values no longer bound by restrictive social mores and resentment who drags humanity by the coat-tails into a new dawn.

Like Nietzsche's moments of contempt, Sartre's early work is also liberally laced with anti-humanist sentiment. Roquentin dryly lists the many types of humanists he has known – the radical humanist, the Communist humanist, Catholic humanist among them who all hate each other 'as individuals, naturally, not as men' (N 117). He voices his 'theoretical opposition to humanism' (WD 87) and warns against the idea of a human nature or essence as a universalized 'species' 'whose destiny is to conquer and order the world. . . . The religion of man conceived as a natural species: the error of 1848, the worst error, the humanitarian error . . . . The notion of human species has made incredible ravages' (WD 21-2). In *Mallarmé*, he describes humanity poetically as no more than '[a] volatile illusion flittering over matter in movement' (1988: 135). Like Nietzsche, Sartre's antipathy towards humanism stems from its tendency to homogenize human plurality and ignore individuality, evident in his early Nietzschean celebration of the 'lone hero'. As Beauvoir (1983: 433) recounts, however, after the war she and Sartre renounced their individualistic anti-humanism and 'learned the value of solidarity'. During this period, Sartre alludes to a number of possible radical humanisms that might replace the abstract humanism of Enlightenment thinking[37] and give the term a 'modern meaning' (WD 25). He refers variously to a 'humanism of work', a 'humanism of need' and, in his final years, to a 'flourishing humanity' while simultaneously rejecting bourgeois humanism since 'humanism is shit' (EM 32): '[h]umanity *is not* and corresponds diachronically to no concept' (IF 3:346). In Merleau-Ponty's (2016: 239) view, Sartre's thinking shifted from the anti-humanism on display in *Nausea* to a 'difficult' humanism[38] in his subsequent writings and it is true that, like Nietzsche, he displays some ambivalence on the topic, lamenting what humanity has made of itself in its present historical condition but holding on to the promise of what it can become under a different system of values and collective existential orientation. In plain terms, for Sartre humanity is as humanity *does*: 'We experience humanism only as what is best in us, in other words, our striving to live beyond ourselves in a society of human beings. We can prefigure people in that way through our best acts' (HN 69). Like Nietzsche's 'Yes and No', Sartre conceives ethics as simultaneously creative and destructive: 'man chooses to illuminate what is, in the light of what is not' (NE 464). The essential question is, what sort of human shall we choose to project and invent in a world already historically constructed by humans? Each person is an individual adventure in the dimension of the universal shot through with possibilities: '[b]ut my destiny is me coming to myself as an image. What is more, humanity is an individual adventure that takes place in the dimension of the universal. The individual coming to himself in terms of the features of the universal, this is humanity's destiny' (NE 422). In his ethical vision of 'a flourishing humanity', he equates moral growth with intersubjectivity and reciprocity (NE 407). In *Hope Now*, he considers a 'post-humanist view of society':

> We are struggling to establish human relations and arrive at a definition of what is human. At this moment we are in the thick of the battle, and no doubt it will go on for many years. But one must define the battle: we are seeking to live together like human beings, and to be human beings so it's by means of searching for this definition in this action of a truly humankind – beyond humanism, of course – that we will be able to consider our effort and our end. In other words, our goal is to arrive at a genuinely constituent body in which each person would be a human being and collectives would be equally human. (HN 67)

Although a dialectical thinker, Sartre leaves the dialectic open and recognizes, along with Nietzsche, that '[i]f the world had a goal, it must have been reached' (WP 1062), but 'there is no final state' (WP 1064). Ethics is bound up with the possibility of failure, circumscribed by material and factitious limitations and the potential lapse into bad faith: 'Tomorrow, after my death, some may decide to set up Fascism, and the others may be cowardly and muddled enough to let them do it. Fascism will then be the human reality, so much the worse for us' (EH 31). There is 'a hidden immorality of the world' (hidden by the cover of respectability) just as there is a 'hidden irrationality of nature' in the form of cyclones, floods and tsunami (NE 13). Moreover, society generally prefers the familiar to the unfamiliar and order to disorder: 'Society as a whole is suspicious about creation. For it quickly appears as an overturning and negation of what is' (NE 511). In the *Critique*, Sartre leaves history as a series of 'broken sequences', each in relation dialectically to the prior ones, leaving open the possibility that history might end badly.

In broad terms, we can characterize Nietzsche and Sartre as 'posthumanist humanists' (Butterfield 2012). Extending their sublimating logic, they walk a *via media* between anti-humanism and humanism, establishing a 'progressive-regressive' perspective that moves from inside to outside and back again, identifying the 'distinctly human' in scalar or modal terms with the rest of nature. While it is possible to identify some humanist/metaphysical residues in their thinking, as we have seen, these generally run against the grain of their overall philosophical perspective and do not bring down the structure. In Ally's (2017: 385) words, '[t]he building still stands and can be further improved'. Unlike Foucault whose 'Death of Man' hypothesis was caesural, Derrida, for instance, believes humanism cannot simply be erased or avoided. A complete break is impossible since 'the end of Man' is bound to be written in the language of Man. There is no pure outside to which 'we' can leap for to oppose humanism by claiming to have left it behind is to overlook the very way that opposition is articulated (Badmington 2000: 9). It does not follow, however, that this means confirming the status quo, for Derrida's work repeatedly shows how systems are always self-contradictory, forever deconstructing themselves *from within*. Nietzsche and Sartre do not erase human agency but deconstruct its onto-epistemological primacy and present it in a relational form. They present the *human*, not as something to be taken for a static notion, but to 'be accessed as a process and as a verb (humanizing), for its dynamic, and also reiterative and performative, modes of proceeding' (Ferrando 2020: 52). It therefore points towards what it will become as *praxis*. This gives us a conception of posthumanity no longer as the rational species but as a 'transversal entity encompassing the human, our genetic neighbours the animals and the earth as a whole' (Braidotti 2013: 82) since, in Sartre's words, '[e]verything is always revealed as united to everything' (CDR 360). As we will see further in the next chapter when examining their views on religion, while recognizing the ultimate 'necessity of contingency', they propose an affirmation of existence and earthly-becoming (conceived as 'will to power' or as 'totalizing praxis') that celebrates nature in a bid to overcome passive nihilism.

7

Lebensphilosophie

The product of the philosopher is his life (first, before his works). *That is his work of art.*

(Nietzsche, KSW 7.712)

There is 'nothing whatever impersonal' about the philosopher (BGE 6), as Nietzsche wrote, or, as Sartre contended, you have to take into account the life of people who write as 'it is projected in the writing in one way or another' (1979: 26). Both philosophers stand as exemplars of the intertwining of philosophy and life, a *Lebensphilosophie* in which comprehension, experimentation and praxis go hand in hand. Nietzsche proposes an experimental type of critique (UM 3.8) and describes the philosopher of the future as a 'critic in body and soul' (BGE 210). His later work is generally disparaging towards academic scholars, viewing scholarship as an extension of industry (BGE 58), and the ascetic ideal (GM 3.23). Overly specialized and cramped into a little 'corner' (GS 366), scholars are generally unable to grasp the whole and provide a comprehensive view (BGE 204). What both philosophers lament more than all is the separation of life and philosophy, the detached view of the 'pure, will-less, painless, timeless knowing subject' who supposedly sees a faithful 'mirror' of events (GM 3.26).

Philosophy aside, when you delve beneath the surface, there are a surprising number of incidental biographical similarities in the lives of these two philosophers. Both men were brought up without a father; were sickly children visually impaired from a young age; suffered from chronic ill health throughout their adulthood; were itinerant writers who lived propertyless with few material possessions in a succession of rented rooms and apartments (but whose books enriched others materially); both were unmarried and childless (though Sartre adopted Arlette Elkaïm-Sartre later in life) despite proposing marriage to Mathilde Trampedach and Lou Salomé (Nietzsche) and Simone de Beauvoir (Sartre); both were independent philosophers not beholden to institutions and institutional thinking; both served two stints in the army (though they could probably have avoided this due to their poor eyesight); finally, both were beset by melancholia at several stages of their lives, ending their days in the throes of madness and dementia cared for and tended by female hands.

Perhaps the major difference between them, however, was the lack of partnership in Nietzsche's life and a feeling of solitude that burns through the pages of his books. Whereas Sartre had Beauvoir (and his extended 'family'), whose thinking he wove indelibly into his own and who propelled him towards a more collectivist perspective, Nietzsche was, after abandoning his professorship at Basel, a solitary philosopher cut adrift in his thoughts (apart from his epistolary communications with friends). In a letter to Overbeck in March 1882, complaining about his failing eyesight and a defective typewriter, he wrote: 'I need a young person around me who is intelligent and educated enough to be able to work with me' (KSB 6.180). Four months later, he wrote in anticipation in a letter to Malwida von Meysenbug that with Salomé he had forged a 'fast friendship' and viewed her as a possible 'disciple . . . heir and successor' (KSB 6.223). After Salomé had broken free of him and abandoned him, however, his hope of an intellectual and amorous partnership soon evaporated, leading him to declare in despair to Overbeck: 'Now I am facing my task all alone. . . . I need a bulwark against the unendurable' (KSB 6.306).

In this final chapter, I set out to connect the thinking of Nietzsche and Sartre to its biographical moorings, showing, in certain facets of their lives, how these two thinkers lived out their contradictions of self and Other as 'a play of instincts that conflict powerfully . . . but are controlled' (WP 966), and how these became fertile points of overcoming in their thinking in relation to four key areas that were significant in their life trajectories: *religion*, *feminism*, *music* and *madness*.

Religious atheists

There are no philosophers more readily associated with a diehard atheism than Nietzsche and Sartre.[1] '[U]nconditional honest atheism', the German philosopher wrote, is 'the only air we breathe' (GM 3.27). Above all, they both viewed the existence of a Christian God as incompatible with a creative ethics, human freedom and the fundamental contingency of the world. And yet, as several scholars have attested, their atheism is not entirely uncomplicated and beyond ambiguity, for if we survey their writings, we see that they are replete with biblical imagery and bristling with religious themes. On the evidence of this explicit religiosity, Nietzsche and Sartre have been described as 'secret', 'crypto' or 'closet' Christians.[2] However, though influenced by biblical themes, assigning a Christian orientation to Nietzsche and Sartre is, I suggest, a false move. Their religiosity, as their writings attest, is conceived firmly within an ethico-political 'terrasophical' framework and not a transcendental, other-worldly Christian one. The 'new religion' they espouse to escape moral nihilism is, to all intents and purposes, a *pagan* one that is consistent with the main facets of their philosophical thinking, including their *pluralistic* ethics and politics, their physiological aesthetics of *rapture*, their phenomenology of affect and their Heraclitean ontology of *relationality* and *becoming*.

Nietzsche's pagan Gods

> *Pagan-Christian. The affirmation of the natural, the sense of innocence in the natural, 'naturalness', is pagan. The denial of the natural, the sense of degradation in the natural, unnaturalness, is Christian.*
>
> (Nietzsche, *The Will to Power* 147)

Incense – Buddha said: 'Do not flatter your benefactor!' Repeat this saying in a Christian church – and it at once purifies the air of everything Christian.
(Nietzsche, *The Gay Science* 142)

There is a poignant irony about Nietzsche's funeral. Interred on 25 August 1900 next to his father in the pastoral village of Röcken, the author of *Der Antichrist* was buried in a coffin embossed with an ornate silver cross to the sound of church bells and the village choir singing Christian hymns. One might have expected a pagan ceremony with the choral chanting of dithyrambs and dancing full of excess led by the flute of Dionysus, but by this time his sister had gained full autonomy over her brother's destiny. Solemn Christian respectability was now the prescribed order of the day and there would no sybaritic indulgence or Zarathustrian celebration. Nietzsche, 'the little pastor' and 'a plant, born near the churchyard' (as he described himself, aged twelve), was returned to the earth with full Christian rites and august sobriety where he had playfully taken his first steps fifty years or so previously.[3]

It is true to say that he had some difficulty forsaking his God, but once disturbed, the sediments of Nietzsche's pious religious inculcation would from then on settle into the alternative image of a pagan God, Dionysus, a persona he repeatedly invoked in his work and supplanted only in his final writings by that of the Antichrist. Nietzsche's apostasy from Christianity is probably best viewed as a steady erosion or gradual weaning beginning in earnest at school, aged seventeen, when he read and was deeply influenced by the writings of Emerson and later, Lange's *History of Materialism* which precipitated his 'naturalist turn'.[4] Whereas in his autobiography of 1858, for instance, he had written, 'God has led me safely through it all as does a father his weak little child' (KGW 1.1.310), he strikes a more naturalist note in 1863, remarking that '*events* have up to now led me along like a child' (KGW 1.3.193 – my emphasis). In a similar turn away from theological horizons, in 1861 he abandoned the composition of an oratorio dealing with the birth of Christ and worked instead on a composition 'Pain is the keynote of nature'. It was clear that from now on religion was just one competing voice among many and had lost its primacy. After graduating from Pforta, at first he acceded to his mother's wishes to become a pastor in his father's footsteps but broke off his study of theology at the University of Bonn after a single term and moved over to the exclusive study of classical philology. This was a symbolic move away from Christianity into the pagan world of the Ancient Greeks, exchanging the study of monotheistic theological texts for the philological analysis of classical ones populated by many gods. When he returned to Naumburg in 1865 during the first-semester break, Franziska was horrified to see her son demonstratively refusing to take communion. In a declaration of his growing dissatisfaction with Christianity, he wrote to his sister on 11 June of that year: 'If you want to attain peace of mind and happiness, then you should have faith; if you want to be a disciple of truth, then you should probe' (KSB 2.61).

Once the doubts had crept in, there was no placating them for the once-pious Nietzsche and, as his life progressed, his writings became increasingly scarifying towards the metaphysical and moral claims of Christianity, reaching fever pitch in his final works, particularly *The Antichrist: A Curse on Christianity* (1888). He condemned

Christianity chiefly for its devaluation of existence and hatred of the body (*odium corporis*), for being 'a monstrous mode of valuation' that has produced an '*ascetic planet*', a 'nook of disgruntled, arrogant, and offensive creatures filled with a profound disgust at themselves, at the earth, at all life, who inflict as much pain on themselves as they possibly can out of pleasure of inflicting pain' (GM 3.11). Christianity is bound up with tradition, slavish morality and *ressentiment* against life: 'the individual is tied to them almost automatically and moves with the regularity of a pendulum' (HH 111). Moreover, it introduced a new Platonic dualism between Good and Evil into our understanding of the world: 'It was Christianity which first painted the Devil on the world's walls; it was Christianity which first brought sin into the world' (WS 78). He ranks Christianity as among the most pernicious of all religions: 'The Christian idea of God – God as a god of the sick, God as spider, God as spirit – is one of the most corrupt conceptions of God the world has ever seen' (A 18).

However, it should be noted that within his vitriol, it is only *certain forms* of Christianity that Nietzsche excoriates. His sympathetic attitude towards Jesus is very different, for instance, than his critical view of Paul. Jesus, who 'could be called a "free spirit", using the phrase somewhat loosely' (A 32), is included in his examples of the 'higher type' of humanity who provide prophetic imitations of what might be. Nietzsche makes a strong connection between the mythmaking projects of Jesus and Zarathustra (A 32), praising Jesus, above all, for his rejection of two key features of nihilism – transcendence and *ressentiment*. By bringing heaven down to earth, Jesus demonstrates how '[t]he "kingdom of heaven" is a state of the heart – not something lying "above the earth" or coming "after death"' (A 34). The crucifixion represents 'the exemplary character of dying in this way, the freedom, the superiority *over* every feeling of *ressentiment*' (A 40). Nietzsche's only objection against Jesus was that he wanted people to follow his example rather than creating their own. Unfortunately, Jesus' 'good news' died on the cross and was corrupted into a creed of slavish morality by his followers: '*there have never been any Christians*' (A 39). Paul was 'the genius in hatred' (A 42) and 'the greatest of all apostles of revenge' (A 45) who reversed Jesus' message by choosing a slave morality in revenge against the strong. Pauline Christianity preached a pernicious anti-naturalism and inaugurated a hatred of the body and sensuality (A 21).[5]

Despite his searing attacks on Christianity for its life-denying metaphysics, its 'ontology of decline', its slave morality and its other-worldly illusions, the idea that Nietzsche should be read as a religious thinker goes back to the earliest years of his reception. In Salomé's (1988: 24) view, '[o]f all [Nietzsche's] great intellectual dispositions, none is bound more profoundly and unremittingly to his whole intellectual being than his religious genius'. The existentialist theologian Paul Tillich (1886–1965) remarked in a similar vein that 'Friedrich Nietzsche, the famous atheist and ardent enemy of religion and Christianity, knew more about the power of the idea of God than many faithful Christians' (2001: 174). For Tillich, the *Übermensch* resurrects Nietzsche's belief in God in secular form, reconfiguring God as a figure of ethical concern. Other religious existentialist theologians, such as Karl Barth (1886–1968) and Martin Buber (1878–1965), also took inspiration from Nietzsche while seeking to overcome some of the shortcomings of his thinking as they perceived it. Nietzsche's distinction between slave morality and master morality was a clear influence on Buber's typology of 'I-It' relations (slave morality that relates to others as objects to be manipulated) and 'I-Thou' relations (reciprocal relation of self-actualization through respect and dialogue that belong to master morality).[6] Nietzsche, in Megill's (1985: 315) view, exhibits 'a post-Christian rather than an anti-Christian' viewpoint, drawing heavily on the Christian notions of radical creativity, apocalypse and crisis (the City of Man giving way to the City of God). Apollo and Dionysus are insufficient to embrace Nietzsche's perspective: 'On the contrary, the pastor's son tries to save Christianity even as he destroys it, imputing to the Overman those qualities that he is no longer willing to see embodied in the Godhead' (1985: 347). Despite his avowed celebration of the materiality of the earth, the real direction of his thought is often the sky and ascent.[7]

But while it may be right to identify Nietzsche as 'deeply religious by temperament ... terrified of where nihilism could lead' (Hayman 1982: 8), and point to the prevalence of quasi-religious images and invocations in his work, he looks to the future for a source of spirituality or 'new religion' to *replace* Christianity rather than *resurrect* it. Indeed, if we are to look into the past, others view Nietzsche's spirituality as aligning much closer to Eastern thought (e.g. Taoism and Buddhism) than it does to Western Christianity.[8] Parkes (1996: 373), for instance, emphasizes Nietzsche's ontology of impermanence and becoming, his anti-metaphysical and atheistic tendencies, his denial of any substantial self or ego viewed as a conventional unity of 'energy-aggregates' and his celebration of the 'lived body'. In *The Antichrist*, Nietzsche describes Buddhism as 'a hundred times more realistic than Christianity' (A 20), while in *Twilight of the Idols* he follows the Buddhist notion that the individual is an error: 'he is nothing in himself, not an atom, not a "link in the chain", not something merely inherited from the past – he is the entire chain of humanity all the way up to himself' (TI 9.33). As we saw in Chapters 5 and 6, Nietzschean wholeness and intersubjectivity are often overlooked by attributing to him an undialectical and dichotomous view of self and Other, individual and group. One easily forgets Zarathustra's 'great love' for his fellow human beings, which only comes if one loves and despises oneself first. Zarathustra's almost fatal nausea at the prospect of the eternal recurrence of the rabble, as Parkes (1996: 375) observes, is thus 'prompted as much by the rabble within his own most comprehensive soul as by the "other"'. Like the Japanese Nietzscheans, such as Keiji Nishitani, who emphasized the religious aspect of Nietzsche, viewing it as embodying a form of Dionysian pantheism in a fully creative affirmation of life, others align Nietzsche with a strongly pantheistic viewpoint.[9] Nietzsche's affirmation of life, as Richardson (2020: 363) argues, brings him 'into harmony with certain mysticisms and pantheisms'. The Dionysian is, as Nietzsche describes it, 'the great pantheistic sharing of joy and suffering that calls good and sanctifies even the most terrible and questionable qualities of life' (WP 1050), a rapturous 'religious affirmation of life, life whole and not denied or in part' (WP 1052). It is a 'deification' (WP 534), 'sanctification' (WP 539), 'an ecstatic affirmation of the total character of life' (WP 539) that 'replenishes and gilds . . . life' (WP 534), enabling us to grasp the constitutive links between individual and whole and recognize that 'there is no thing without other things' (WP 557).

Nietzsche's pantheism is most evident in *Zarathustra* that proclaims in poetic form his erotic love of life and the living vitality of the earth. In Zarathustra's two 'dance-songs' (Z 2.10, Z 3.15), life is personified as a woman whom he loves in a sexual way, culminating in Zarathustra's marriage to life with the ring of eternal return. As Richardson (2020: 483) notes, there is an ambiguity in Zarathustra's atheism – '[h]e seems on the whole quite anti-god' and yet the book's overall view of gods is 'complex and ambiguous'. In the Third book, he pronounces 'God is dead' (Z 3.5) and, in the Fourth, embraces the title 'Zarathustra, the godless' (Z 4.6), having declared in the First, 'I would only believe in a god that knew how to dance' and his feeling of possession in which 'a god dances through me' (Z 1.7).[10] This possession is marked by the power of affect or rapture, a bodily condition of excitement, intoxication and transient joy in which one feels the presence of eternal harmony. Erotic love is an affirmation of life that 'reshapes and elevates the beloved' and provides a 'tremendous energy of greatness' that allows us 'not to perish of the suffering one creates' (WP 506). Through his emphasis on religious pathos and the feeling of rapture, Nietzsche hopes to *aestheticize* religion. Gods are now the imaginary or fictive objects of an aesthetic play: '[t]he wealth of religious feeling, grown to a torrent, breaks out ever again and wants to conquer new realms' (HH 150). His highly damning condemnations of religion are interlaced with an embrace of his own god, Dionysus, and with a favourable view of religious sentiment based on the primacy of affectivity. In turn, his main concepts – eternal return, *amor fati* and the Universal Yes – carry an emotional weight and strong religious force as forms of an ethical imaginary.[11]

Gods exist for Nietzsche as 'metaphor' for love, affective possession and spiritual power: 'The only possibility of maintaining a meaning for the concept of "god" would be: god not as driving force but as *maximal state*' (WP 639). As the creation of an aesthetic and ethical imaginary, they multiply the feeling of the greatest heightening of power through the inspiration of an indwelling, collaborating god. This is a terrestrial religion of affectivity and pathos, the inexplicable surplus of divine communication or attunement. It is a pantheistic religion that embraces and participates in the universal joy of becoming and the Heraclitean play of forces, leading to the elevation of power: 'What is essential in such *Rausch* is the feeling of increased strength and fullness' (TI 9.8). To fill the spiritual and ethical void left by the death of the Christian God,[12] 'everything will be divine' (Richardson 2020: 495). This expresses in religious form Nietzsche's ontological schema of pluralistic monism that all is connected as one, expressing itself differently in the many. This in turn lends itself to a pluralistic ethical and political imaginary. As 'the last disciple and initiate of the god Dionysus' (BGE 296), the deity of many masks, Nietzsche pluralizes the divine, condemning Christianity for its monotheism and praising the Greeks' relation of 'free-spiritedness' towards their many gods. Unlike monotheism's 'rage for generalization' and edicts of a universalizing morality to impose a single worldview (BGE 202), he favours Roman tolerance and pagan plurality (BGE 46):

> Polytheism was a prefiguration of free-spiritedness and multi-spiritedness: the power to create new and personal eyes for oneself and again and again new and even more personal ones: so that for man alone of all the animals there is no eternally fixed horizon and perspectives. (GS 143)

Atheism (akin to nihilism) is viewed by Nietzsche as a transitional stage – in itself, it is ascetic in its will to truth (GM 3.27). Although he abandons belief in a transcendent God that he views as a forward step culturally (D 96), he modifies atheism with his commitment to the Dionysian ideal (BGE 295). The free spirit is not identified with atheism per se since atheism is a kind of dead negation blissfully unaware of the implications of the death of God (GS 125). For Nietzsche, the fact that the Christian God is such a bad communicator (Z 4.6, BGE 53) has led to scepticism and atheism. Monotheism crushed the concept of humanity underneath an impossible ideal and caused the 'premature stagnation' of human development (GS 143, TI 3.1). By contrast, the Greek gods were an 'artistic middle world' developed to both view and veil the horrors of existence – they were the 'ideal image' of the Greek way of life (BT 3). Nietzsche disavows founding a religion (EH 4.1, D 542) but proposes a form of piety towards an ideal that satiates the religious instinct without a theism (BGE 53). Indeed, holiness is a constant theme Nietzsche employs to describe a powerful and healthy will to power (Z 1.20). Free spirits, he advises, can use religion for ethical ends in order to serve the development of humanity (BGE 61).

Nietzsche's 'new religion' is that of Dionysus (BGE 295, EH P2), a god who is inside the world and changing rather than outside it: 'Even the gods philosophise' (BGE 295). Raised in a cave by nymphs, represented as kind and generous, though cruel to his enemies, Dionysus is in some tales torn apart and then reborn. He has a strong association with natural and mythic animals, with the wearing of different masks, and is presented as a mythic god or personification who tempts or seduces humanity to growth and health in the future. Above all, it is Dionysus' association with joy, ecstasy, wholeness and the release from care that attracts Nietzsche. The Dionysian state is a total stimulation of the affective system, transforming itself through and into those affects and constituting a movement to 'redeem reality' by immersion in and identification with it (TI 9.10). Religious fervour is identified by Nietzsche as a kind of delirium (*folie circulaire*), an alternation of feelings between ecstatic redemption and severe penitence (EH 4.8, A 51). It is Dionysus who captures the feeling of ecstatic redemption or rapturous intoxication[13] in which 'I am the eternally creative primordial mother' and, 'by the mystical triumphant cry of Dionysus the spell of individuation is broken, and the way lies open to the Mothers of Being, to the innermost heart of things' (BT 16).

Sartre, the voodoo child

Like Nietzsche, as a child Sartre was steeped in Christianity but soon threw off its conceptual shackles while remaining aware of the power of religious faith and iconography to inspire and communicate. The philosopher, who infamously followed the 'consequences of a coherent atheistic position' (EH 51), casually describes the genesis of his atheism; when aged twelve, he encountered a sudden loss of faith in God while standing on the street waiting for friends:

> One morning, in 1917, at La Rochelle, I was waiting for some companions who were supposed to accompany me to the *lycée*; they were late. Soon I could think of

nothing more to distract myself, and I decided to think about the Almighty. He at once tumbled down into the blue sky and vanished without explanation: He does not exist, I said to myself, in polite astonishment, and I thought the matter was settled. In one sense it was, because I have never since had the least temptation to revive Him. But the Other, the Invisible, the Holy Ghost, he who guaranteed my mandate and dominated my life through great, anonymous, and sacred forces, he remained. (W 155–6)

God was 'an old flame' that took root and then died in his heart: 'I needed God, he was given to me, and I received him without understanding what I was looking for. Unable to take root in my heart, he vegetated in me for a while and then died' (W 65).

From then on, he would devote his childhood instead to the 'religion of letters' of his grandfather, searching for salvation through writing rather than prayer or religious observance. He began to harbour a dislike for Christianity when his relatives, split between the dual traditions of Catholicism and Protestantism, would argue at the dinner table. According to Sartre, 'I was the prey of two opposing mystical theologies, but I adapted myself very well to their contradictions' (W 108). As a 'weed on the compost of Catholicity, my roots sucked up its juices and I changed them into sap' (W 157). Unlike Beauvoir, whose hostility to her Catholic upbringing became a generalized rejection of all religion, Sartre's atheism was directed at a particular model of the Christian deity and should not be construed, as Charmé (1999: 302) warns, as 'an automatic rejection of alternative models of the divine or religious symbolism in general'.[14] Despite his youthful rejection of God, his autobiography makes clear the affinities between his own thought and religion. Just as Nietzsche's work bore the stigmata of Christianity's influence even as he sought to cleanse himself from its markings, Sartre imbued his atheism with a deep focus on the divine, regularly invoking religious themes and imagery in his plays, novels and philosophical works. As he wrote:

> God is dead but man has not, for all that, become atheistic. Today, as yesterday, this silence of the transcendent, combined with modern man's enduring religious need, is the great question of the age. (2010: 235)

For Gillespie (2013: 83, 85), Sartre's 'exultant atheism' is, at the same time, a 'limited' one. For Sartre, '[the existence of] God is, paradoxically both absent and present' – his writings 'both reject it and incorporate it'. Citing Dostoevsky's dictum that '[i]f God didn't exist, everything would be permitted' and presenting it as 'existentialism's starting point' (EH 22), God's absence poses a problem for Sartre's moral concerns. Although philosophically he had no time for Christianity as a body of metaphysical thought and doctrine, like Kierkegaard and Nietzsche, he glimpsed the existential power of religious faith.[15] While a prisoner of war in 1940, he wrote and produced the first of his eleven plays, *Bariona*, and described the experience of performing it as a moment of religious discovery: 'As I addressed my comrades across the footlights . . . I realized what theatre ought to be: a great, collective, religious phenomenon . . . a theatre of myths' (1992a: 63–4).

Along with Gillespie (2013, 2014), other scholars highlight the importance of religious themes in Sartre's philosophy, running through his early philosophy in *Being and Nothingness*, his expression of the messianic role and qualities of the writer in *What Is Literature?*, to his final thoughts about Judaism and eschatology in *Hope Now*. For Howells (1981: 550), for instance, 'the parallels between the mystical conception of God and the transcendent *néant* of Sartrean consciousness are striking'. In Richmond's (2018: xlviii) view, Sartre's frequent use of theological vocabulary – incarnation, deliverance, salvation, emanation, grace and passion – reveals his Christian framework of understanding in spite of his professed atheism and relates to the fact that 'for Sartre the concept of God is philosophically necessary, even if He does not exist'. Kirkpatrick (2017a: 1) reiterates Sartre's connection to Christian thinking, arguing that his early philosophy retained a recognizable inheritance from the Christian doctrine of original sin. In his discussion of shame, Sartre explicitly refers to *Genesis* and introduces the theological idiom of sin into his phenomenology (BN 312, 431) linking it to the theme of physical 'nakedness' (BN 392). For Kirkpatrick (2017a: 13, 188), *Being and Nothingness* can be read as an anti-theodicy and presents a 'hermeneutics of despair': 'The conclusion of *Being and Nothingness* – for all its promises of an ethics – is bleak.' Sartre's atheism is thus ambiguous or, even, 'duplicitous' for advancing sublimated theological ideas at the same time that he professes the death of God (2017a: 4, 8).

While scholars are right in identifying Sartre's 'theological horizons', there is a significant difference between following a religion and being fascinated by its images, themes and metaphors as a body of intellectual interest. Like Nietzsche, Sartre had no time for Western Christianity in philosophical terms or, indeed, as an ethical system of values: 'liberty is freedom *without* God' (EM 558). God's absence is a golden gift: '*God's absence* is no longer closure: it is an opening out to the infinite. *God's absence* is greater and more divine than God' (1983: 40). God is a *non-sequitur* of existential freedom since the road to freedom and authenticity 'leads from the belief in God to atheism, from an abstract morality divorced from time and time to concrete commitment' (1976: 228). He also investigates the idea of God as creator as a myth of inversion for it is God who is dependent on humankind to create Him. He describes God as an old-fashioned concept (EM 776) and a human construct – 'God is an image prefabricated by man' (EM 559) – and engages with the concept of God by initially equating belief in a personal God and the attempt to gain his favour with self-centredness: 'Morality should surpass itself towards a goal that is not . . . . It should be a choice of the world, not of oneself' (NE 11). Like Nietzsche's 'superhumanity', it is 'integral humanity' that can fill God's absence: 'I don't need God to love my neighbour' (EM 558).

Sartre's final encounter with theism in *Hope Now* is part of his long-term engagement with the divine, but although Sartre does not become a theist at the end, his position both rejects and incorporates a sense of divinity. Just as Nietzsche viewed atheism as potentially a dead negation leading to passive nihilism, Sartre describes it as a 'cruel, long-term business' (W 157). He complains that materialistic atheism is hard to sustain as an existential creed: 'I don't feel myself to be like a speck of dust that has appeared in the world, but a being who is expected, provoked, prefigured' (EM 551). The figure of God furnishes us with a vague sense of destiny without which it is easy to succumb to the nausea of superfluity, of being simply *de trop*. Sartre also notes the link between God and Absolute morality. Even without God, moral activity must be, in some sense, 'an absolute in the relative' (EM 552). Like Nietzsche, he displaces this moral imperative onto humanity, holding an affirmative view of fraternity as the culmination of the evolution of humanity towards achieving the best in humanity. Sartre takes the force of the divine and transposes it onto the group in the *Critique* which can be 'heavenly' when it is fusing and autonomous but 'hellish' when serialized or subordinated. In answer to the question of Sartre's purported deathbed conversion to Judaism, it is clear that, even though there are parallels between a Jewish messianic resurrection and his eschatological approach to ethics, he does not accept the ethical laws of the Torah or Christian metaphysical schema. Instead, it is distinctly a secular morality that he advocates as capable of launching revolutionary change. Above all, Sartre recognized that religious images and themes emerge from a certain historical situation. He presents Greco-Roman religion (as depicted in *The Flies* and *The Trojan Woman*) as a religion of conquest and oppression. Zeus/Jupiter is a vengeful and cruel God who terrorizes humanity and keeps them in ignorance. Submission to such gods can only take place as an act of bad faith, and Orestes heroically expresses his freedom by acting against their repressive values and customs.

So then, where does Sartre sense the divine, one might ask, if not in Christianity or classical antiquity? For a religion to be viable as an ethical scaffold for Sartre, it would have to be 'committed' and contain the same perspective that he found appealing as a messianic theme in Judaism, envisioning a new social order to replace the existing apparatus of oppression. Moreover, it must be a terrestrial religion, like Nietzsche's, that dispenses with 'the illusion of backworlds' (BN 2) and forms of slavish morality. Scanning through his writings, Sartre's strongest overtures of warm embrace towards religion can be found in two pieces – in his essay 'Black Orpheus' (1964) and in a journalistic interview 'Haiti vu par J.- P. Sartre' (1949). In 'Black Orpheus', Sartre raises his interest in *African spirituality*. He warns that European civilization had developed a purely technological and mechanical relation towards nature that had become lifeless. The white man, consequently, is alienated from nature and remains only on the surface of things, like an engineer, 'unaware of life' (1964: 38). The black man, by contrast, understands nature as a creative power, a kind of Mother Goddess, 'an enormous perpetual birth; the world is flesh and the son of flesh; on the sea and in the sky, on the dunes, on the rocks in the wind, the Negro finds the softness of human skin, he rubs himself against the sand's belly, against the sky's loins' (1964: 40). This, Sartre argues, demonstrates a vital, carnal and androgynous connection to nature: 'the dynamic feeling of being an erect phallus, and the more deaf, more patient, more feminine one of being a growing plant' (1964: 40). He pays homage to black spiritual poetry for its deconstructive, transgressive qualities that challenges the binary hierarchies of dualistic Christian thinking, using negritude as a means of positing 'a secret blackness in white, a secret whiteness in black' (1964: 28). These insights build upon Sartre's observations on the voodoo religion of Haiti in an interview with Georges Altman in 1949 in which he expresses a great fascination with '*Envoutement vaudou*' (voodoo bewitchment). Driven by the rhythm of the voodoo drum, like the one he had imagined as a child (W 79), Sartre was impressed how the religious devotees became entranced in a 'religion of possession' centred on the expressive dance of the body.

In this form of rapturous spirituality, he recognized the possibility of a completely different cosmology and ontology, 'a certain affective attitude toward the world' (1964: 36) that forms the imaginary of a terrestrial religion which can be counterposed to the Christian 'Seriousness' of the white man.

As Neppi (1995: 16) comments, for Sartre, 'man and nature are not opposed in an irreducible manner. Their separation is not an ontological structure, but only a moment in the process of being.' Like Nietzsche's, Sartre's thinking evinces a form of pantheism expressed through his affective dialectic, his views on animal consciousness and his ontological relationality. Although he continued to look forward into the future for the realization of a new society based on a new form of morality (much as the biblical prophets did), he turned back to a pagan prebiblical period, to a tribal view of totemism for a model of human interconnection by recapturing the sense of the Mother Goddess as a totem: 'When I see man, I think: he has the same origin as myself, like me he comes from Mother Humanity, let's say, Mother Earth as Socrates says, Mother' (HN 90). From this shared belonging, he develops an idea of 'fraternity':[16]

> To belong to the same species is, in a way, to have the same parents. In that sense we are brothers... the great concept of the clan, its womb-like unity – starting with an animal, for example, that is supposed to have engendered them all – is what we must rediscover today, for that was true fraternity. In a sense it was a myth, no doubt about it, but it was also a truth. (HN 87–8)

These passages reveal a 'proud pagan' Sartre[17] whose interest in mysticism and Dionysian religious experience runs from his earliest writings, resurfaces sporadically in his middle period and climaxes in his final thinking. Thus, despite attempts to read them as inveterate atheists or as closet Christians, it is fairer to say that, though strongly atheistic in terms of metaphysical speculation, Sartre and Nietzsche were really neither. Instead, both openly embraced a form of 'imaginative divinity', a 'new religion' of the earth based on an affective spirituality of existence, Being and becoming, in order to fill the void of nihilism that circumscribes the modern condition of humankind following the death of what they saw as a defunct Christian God: 'Inaccessible to the sacred, I adored magic' (W 77). This should be viewed as a quintessentially posthumanist religion that signals the transition beyond the 'political theology' (Shapiro 2016: 79) of Christianity. Broadly speaking, Nietzschean and Sartrean divinity display a ternary deconstructive logic of inversion and displacement. They invert the life-denying metaphysics of Christianity with a 'cruel atheism' that ultimately leads to a displaced third orientation that attempts to fill the ethical void 'where everything is permissible if God does not exist' (EH 22). This is a life-affirming celebration of existence and 'new religion', expressing the plurality found in the diversity of nature and human individuality. Sartrean and Nietzschean ethics represent the search for a new earthly Good and Bad based on the dynamic dialectical interplay of self and Other, a form of 'an absolute in the relative' (EM 552). This engenders, in a mythic terrestrial form, a spiritual replacement for the Christian God that captures their aesthetic-ethical, pluralistic imaginary. Sartre's religious (re)turn towards mysticism and Mother Earth propels him towards a feminine economy, which, as we will see in the next section, becomes a dominant theme of his later thinking.[18]

Gentle Nietzsche and feminine Sartre

> *I want to proceed as Raphael did and never paint another image of torture. There are enough sublime things so that one does not have to look for the sublime where it dwells in sisterly association with cruelty; and my ambition also could never find satisfaction if I became a sublime assistant at torture.*
>
> (Nietzsche, *The Gay Science* 313)

Were Nietzsche and Sartre guilty of an anti-feminist bias or does their thinking lend itself to the philosophical promotion of the feminine, as in their valorization of 'the eternally creative primordial mother' (BT 16) and 'Mother Earth' (HN 90)? Scholars are divided over the relationship of their philosophy to feminism and to the depictions of 'the feminine' in their work, taking the attitude of either a rejectionist, refusalist or retrievalist approach.[19] In this section, I take a retrievalist route, looking at some of the contradictions in their writings, but demonstrating how, in the wider arc of their thinking, they move towards a multiplying or sublimating logic that, through the category of the *androgynous*, challenges the bivalent logic of man and woman as a dualistic metaphysical category.

Lost and found: Nietzsche's 'missing' mother

> *The good fortune of my existence, its uniqueness perhaps, lies in its fatality: I am, to express it in the form of a riddle, already dead as my father, while as my mother I am still living and becoming old.*
>
> (Nietzsche, *Ecce Homo* 1.1)

After the death of his father, young 'Fritz' fell firmly under the influence of the women who controlled his household, in particular, his mother Franziska, his grandmother Erdmuthe and his aunt Rosalie. He was known for being pedantic in his inordinate following of rules, including 'the Fourth Commandment' – do as Franziska wished.[20] His main adult male influence was his grandfather David Oehler who introduced the precocious young bibliophile to his library (with a range and depth of books far wider than the narrow selection of religious texts belonging to Erdmuthe back home in Naumburg) when Franziska visited her family at Pobles. At school, Nietzsche was propelled into a ring of male hierarchy and violence, teased and bullied by his schoolmates at the *Gymnasium* for his seriousness and his withdrawn character, as well as for his zealous following of rules. At the age of fourteen, he left the family home in Naumburg for the elite boarding school Pforta which was a conservative factory of masculine values, 'a fusion of monastic austerity and Prussian militarism' (Blue 2016: 100). Nietzsche's 'toughening up' continued into his university years. He competed in a fraternity duelling contest while at the University of Bonn (despite his athletic deficiencies) from which he subsequently bore a small scar on his nose. After conscription into the army in 1867 for military service, he learnt how to fire canons and ride horses but was disbanded a year later after a serious riding accident. 'My career as warrior', he wrote with some chagrin, 'has not set the stage on fire' (KSB 2.292).[21] Despite this masculine and pugilistic posturing, however, he was well known for his gentleness and effeminacy (a fact that Wagner liked to spread through gossip and scandalizing as Nietzsche found out with some annoyance after the composer's death).

This same mixture of the masculine and feminine can also be found in Nietzsche's writings. Displaying the contours of a 'divided self', even within the same text, he is apt to present divergent perspectives. It is hard to decide when reading *Ecce Homo*, for instance, whether he wishes to present himself as a hawk or a dove (or just a confusing farrago of warring and peaceful instincts). Juxtaposing his professed bellicosity as an 'annihilator' (EH 4.2) near the beginning of the book – 'I am warlike by nature. Attacking is one of my instincts' (EH 1.7) – with his peaceful declaration towards the end – 'It is part of my nature to be gentle and benevolent toward everybody' (EH 3.10.4), we are left with a Nietzsche wrought with opposing tendencies and conflicting drives. Solomon (2003: 7) picks up on this paradox of war and peace in his life and work, contrasting the 'Nasty Nietzsche' – the immoralist and Antichrist, the 'mad-dog foaming at the moustache' – with the 'Gentle Nietzsche' – a 'quite respectable and house-trained lapdog, a defender of Good Things and an advocate of, among other things, self-reliance, intellectual courage and honesty, creativity, democracy, feminism, animal rights, naturalism, the scientific method, aesthetic appreciation, wit and irony, hermeneutics, pragmatism, humanism and a good night's sleep'. The same man who was a 'literary megalomaniac' and who took some pride in a review that spoke of his attempt 'to abolish all decent feelings' was also a decent human being disposed to politeness who exuded feminine gentleness.

Thus, underneath Nietzsche's hard Stoic skin lies a soft Epicurean underbelly, revealing contradictory impulses and directions in his ethics. Despite his professed 'pathos of distance' from others and disdain of the world,[22] his attacks on pity and compassion are inconsistent. As Safranski (2003: 167) notes, Nietzsche's compassionate disposition caused him to suffer: 'The philosopher who later assailed the morality of compassion displayed an almost osmotic sympathy . . . he could not be as nearly as ruthless as he demanded from his *Übermensch*'. It could be argued in this vein that his warlike instincts are often overemphasized above his peaceful ones. In *Beyond Good and Evil*, for instance, he includes sympathy (*Mitgefühl*) as a basic virtue: 'Courage, insight, sympathy, solitude' (BGE 284). In *Daybreak*, his list of virtues is anything but hawkish: '[h]onesty, courage, generosity, politeness' (D 556). Even in his final works, he suggests we have a duty to help the weak and unfortunate in an Aristotelian ('the great-souled man') rather than Kantian sense (as a universal mandate of reason): 'When the exceptional human being treats the mediocre more tenderly than himself and his peers, this is not mere courtesy of the heart – it is simply his duty'

(A 57). Indeed, benevolence is considered by Nietzsche to be a key virtue. He praises small acts of kindness that people show (HH 49) and the way they contribute to a collective well-being (HH 111). In *Ecce Homo*, he proposes the virtues of magnanimity and veneration (EH 3.10.4). He makes it clear that social power does not necessarily dictate whether one adopts master or slave morality, and he warns time and again against confusing political power with strength and misfortune with weakness: 'I have found strength where one does not look for it; in simple, mild and pleasant people, without the least desire to rule – and, conversely, the desire to rule has often appeared to me as a sign of inner weakness' (D 413).

For Safranski (2003: 99), what lies at the heart of Nietzsche 'is a mixture of contempt and helplessness in the face of both suffering and compassion'. The philosopher 'whose last fully conscious action was embracing a dumb animal to keep it from being beaten was deeply troubled both by the weakness of others and his own weakness'. Love is a concept not readily associated with Nietzsche but plays a significant part in his ethics. He employs the concept of love as an attitude or mode of being responsible for creativity and the growth of the human since in love I joyously affirm the existence of someone who is not me. This extends to a social program of justice as 'love with seeing eyes' (Z 1.19). He hopes that someday 'we will no longer have the heart for the logical sin that lies concealed in anger and punishment, whether practiced individually or socially' (WS 183). Although it is important not to sanitize Nietzsche and efface all traces of Stoicism or 'hardness' within his thinking, it is equally important not to overemphasize them. While he advocates a pathos of distance (BGE 257, TI 9.37) and argues that a certain form of cruelty is indispensable in which greatness means the ability to inflict great pain (GS 325) – life means 'being cruel ... toward anything that is growing old and weak in us' (GS 26) – he recognizes that some cruelties are 'anti-life'. Nietzsche may sometimes identify with Roman stoicism – brave tough, resilient, insensitive – but he shows only a 'qualified admiration' for it, ridiculing Stoic metaphysics regarding the rationality of nature (BGE 9) and more readily aligning himself with Epicureanism (GS 306). Symbolically, the fourth book of *Zarathustra* ends with the appearance of a laughing lion among a flock of doves. In a note of 1883, Nietzsche discusses this symbol as combining strength and power with gentleness (KSW 21.2), and it is this dialectical tension between the two that he attempts to sublimate in his apparent contradictory thinking.

Nietzsche's ambivalence towards women is common knowledge. The philosopher who advocated taking the whip to women (Z 1.18)[23] was the same person who throughout his life was always gentle, polite and respectful to them. The 'man of dynamite', as Diethe (2006: 302) remarks, 'was nothing if not a gentleman'. In July 1874, while a professor, he voted for the admission of women or female students into the doctoral programme at Basel. It may be the case that three unsuccessful marriage proposals (and his sister's intrusive involvement with his relationship to Lou Salomé) soured his views on women over time, and particularly those of his family. His ambivalence towards the women in his family surfaces in *Ecce Homo* where, after stating 'as my father I am already dead and as my mother I am still alive and growing old' (EH 1.1), he goes on later in the suppressed (by Peter Gast and Elisabeth) part of the chapter (EH 'Wise' 3) to refer to his mother and sister as 'rabble' and a 'hell-machine'. Indeed, he went on to add caustically 'the deepest objection against the "eternal recurrence", my genuine abysmal thought, is always [my] mother and sister' (in Oliver 1995: 140). Previously, in March 1883, he had declared, 'I do not like my mother, and hearing my sister's voice annoys me. I always fell ill when I was with them' (cited in Safranski 2003: 366).

His confrontational literary style, as Richardson (2020: 111–12) remarks, is framed 'in the swaggeringly male persona he often adopts', a sublimation for his sexual energy that finds expression in his 'writerly voice'. It is in this masculine voice that, in the view of some feminists, Nietzsche repeats the masculine bias of Western philosophy. In Irigaray's (1981: 43) view, he negatively associates woman with water, the element that he most feared, the open seas of groundlessness and the abyss that we must brave following the death of God. His concept of the eternal return, as an economy of the same, appropriates and synthesizes all otherness, including the feminine. Oliver (1995: xi) argues that although Nietzsche has opened up philosophy to its others – the body, unconscious, untruth, contingency – he has excluded the 'feminine other', specifically the maternal other, as a possible subject position. His misogyny can be seen in this light as an aberrant psychosexual symptom exhibiting what psychoanalysts call abjection. This is a feeling of disgust or nausea in the face of things that threaten clear distinctions between borders, especially between self and other relating to bodily wastes, such as faeces and vomit, that elide the distinction between inside and outside the body, as well as to our mother's body when we were inside and not distinct from it. Nietzsche's 'misplaced abjection' was a severe and demanding 'imaginary father figure', many of whom, such as Julius Caesar and Alexander the Great, populate his texts. Through his idea of the *Übermensch* who self-creates, Nietzsche subsumes creativity in the masculine while the maternal remains an object of hostility displaced onto all women (1995: 154).[24] While his idea of the decentred, non-essential historical self supports a positive mode of resistance to social domination and normalization, his anti-feminism is not so much inconsistent but symptomatic of his own *ressentiment*.

Kofman and Derrida are two philosophers who have grappled directly with Nietzsche's depiction of the feminine, presenting his work as a melting pot of both positive and negative interpretations. For Kofman (1998: 40), there is no essentialist idea of woman in Nietzsche. Instead, what we find are 'Nietzsche's many heterogeneous texts on woman' (1998: 46) in which some women are given a higher value as more life-affirmative than some men. His first nihilistic image of woman is associated with the Greek goddess Circe as a goddess of seduction, magic and trickery who in Homer's *Odyssey* attempts to fatally entrap Odysseus and his men: 'morality has shown itself to be the greatest of all mistresses of seduction . . . the actual *Circe of philosophers*' (in 1998: 26). By contrast, in the preface to the second edition of *The Gay Science* (1887), Nietzsche uses the Greek female demon Baubô, a minor Greek goddess associated with Demeter (the 'female Dionysus'), as a symbol for 'truth' as she is subversively associated with female fertility, fecundity, perspectivism and creation. Where Dionysus appears naked, however, Baubô is veiled with skirts: 'The figure of Baubô indicates that a simple logic could never understand that life is neither depth nor surface, that behind the veil, there is another veil, behind a layer of paint, another layer' (1998: 44). By identifying wisdom of life with Baubô, Nietzsche celebrates 'the female sexual organ . . . [as] a guarantee of regeneration and eternal return of all things' (1998: 197).

In Derrida's (1979) view, although Nietzsche's texts are 'littered with misogynistic remarks', they also deconstruct their own phallocentric pretensions through a celebration of woman as a metaphor representing the creative forces of life. Nietzsche's writings purposively yield multiple interpretations that give rise to heterogeneity and allow for difference. In *Spurs*, Derrida articulates three versions of the Nietzschean woman. First, woman is condemned as a figure of falsehood – the man 'offers truth and his phallus as his own proper credentials' (1979: 97). This is why woman 'compromises herself' when she attempts to seek enlightenment (BGE 232). Second, woman is condemned as a figure of truth when she attempts a Christian-Platonic representation of it but is more liberated when she becomes the 'phallic woman', performing the truths of woman and manipulating them to her own ends within a phallogocentric economy (1979: 67). In this second position, she does not believe in truth of woman as such but enacts feminine seductive power in her interest (1979: 67). She exhibits the positive characteristics of the actor: 'falseness with a good conscience; the delight in simulation exploding as a power that pushes aside one's so-called "character", flooding it and at times extinguishing it; the inner craving for a role and mask, for appearance; an excess of the capacity for all kinds of adaptation' (GS 361). Derrida sees this as a form of self-mastery in women. By using her 'seductive power', she 'rules over dogmatism, and disorients and routs those credulous men, the philosophers' (1979: 67). As an appropriator, she upsets the binary divisions between possessed and possessor, master and slave: 'Would a woman be able to hold us (or, as they say, "enthral us") if we did not consider it quite possible that under certain circumstances she could wield a dagger (any kind of dagger) against us? Or against herself – which in certain cases would be crueller revenge' (GS 69). Third, as represented by Baubô, Nietzsche conceives women as an active source of creativity 'recognized and affirmed as an affirmative power, a dissimulatress, an artist, a dionysiac' (1979: 97).

While applauding the fact 'feminine behaviour is celebrated and even coveted' by Nietzsche and Derrida, Verkerk notes how both are critical of feminists that attempt to become like men and inculcate masculine values of rationality and logical thinking (BGE 232, Derrida 1979: 65). This is conceived as a loss to women's feminine artistry and style and reveals in their thinking 'a double gendered position . . . open to men but not to women' (2020: 155–6). Although Nietzsche uses the notion of pregnancy to explain creativity in general, he makes spiritual pregnancy exclusive to men (GS 72). Consequently, he closes the doors of his Epicurean Garden to women. Unlike 'free spirits' 'who think differently from . . . the dominant views of the age' (HH 225), women are ideologically enslaved and socialized to be subservient to social authority more than men (HH 435).[25] Verkerk (2020: 154) thus both welcomes and questions the attempt by Nietzsche and Derrida to write in the hand of a woman and 'bear witness to her *abduction*' (Derrida 1979: 41).[26] Neither philosopher escapes their own fetishizations of the concept of woman, but they do proliferate these fetishizations and thus lay the groundwork for others to exceed them. Although Nietzsche disputes the coherence of the concept of woman through revealing her phallogocentric genealogy and also by abducting her as a performative fiction (as both a male mother and a phallic woman), he does so without releasing her from the 'straitjacket of misogyny' (2020: 164). For Oliver (1988: 25), 'dressing up like woman' to write as her, Nietzsche writes women out of their own self-articulation – he not only wants to become woman but also to possess her and shape her to his own ends.

If we look closely at the denouement of the feminine in Nietzsche's thinking, it is possible to discern a sublimating dialectic of the feminine and masculine at play. Arguably, he valorizes the feminine over the masculine (in the form of an 'inverted Platonism') but seeks like a 'noble individual' to lessen 'the deadly hatred between the sexes' (EH 3.5) and elide/synthesize/multiply binary divisions. Alongside his agonistic conception of human relations runs a parallel (feminine) economy of gift-giving. The virtues of giving and bestowing are constant themes in Nietzsche and integral to his ideal of healthy friendship. The abundance of gifts is a feature of the Dionysian where 'freely nature offers her gifts' (BT 1). Wagner's 'true music' is also a gift (UM 4.6), and *Zarathustra* is Nietzsche's 'greatest gift' (EH P4). '[T]o *give* is more blessed than *to have*' (Z 2.9), he maintains, a form of giving that does not shame either giver or receiver, without gratitude or debt (BGE 265). Life presented as a woman is itself a gift: '*Vita feminina*' – 'But perhaps that is the strongest magic of life: a gold-worked veil of beautiful possibilities lies over it, promising, resisting, bashful, mocking, pitying, seductive. Yes, life is a woman!' (GS 339). He criticizes Christianity 'with its unfathomable meanness' for debasing women and praises the Laws of Manu (a Hindu text) for a more positive conception of the female:

> I do not know any book that says as many kind and delicate things to females as the law book of Manu. . . . 'The mouth of a woman', it says at one point, 'the breasts of a girl, the prayer of a child, the smoke of a sacrifice is always pure'. (A 56)

Valuing women for their artistry – 'woman is so artistic' (GS 361) – Nietzsche theorizes gender as performative. Women take up their previous articulations and failures and then enact new ones, putting on masks even when they appear to be revealing something about themselves (GS 361). The feminine art of seduction can lead astray in a negative way, like Wagner, Christianity or Circe (WC 3, A 44, Z 4.15), but is also positive attracting by 'another ideal' (GS 382) rather than compelling or forcing, just like Dionysus 'the pied piper of consciences' (BGE 295).

For Nietzsche, Ariadne is representative of the mythic feminine. She becomes the lover of Dionysus after her abandonment by Theseus, which is viewed as humanity abandoning its possibilities for growth and health in favour of a turn towards European modernity and misplaced masculine values (BT 7, Z 2.13). He praises Goethe for expressing the idea of the 'eternal feminine' as divine, not in a transcendent sense but as anticipated in the physical workings of the earth in which 'everything is redeemed in the whole' (TI 9.49). While he often values the feminine, Nietzsche's wider purpose is to move beyond binary divisions. Dionysus is venerated as the experimenting or tempting god who *integrates* masculine and feminine principles (EH 3.6).[27] What is most important about these two drives is their interaction and reciprocity. The feminine without the masculine is simply 'weak' (GS 24) while the masculine without the feminine is simply 'strong' (BGE 241) – neither on its own is healthy or productive (TI 9.38). Alongside the positive connotations of masculinity as exemplified by Napoleon (GS 362), Nietzsche is careful to distinguish between greatness and strength (BGE 241), arguing that the masculine values of the Germans make them 'stupid' (TI 8.1). Likewise, woman's artistry is applauded by Nietzsche (GS 361) at the same time as too much artistry or performance in social roles is seen to make women incapable of the independence required of the free spirit (HH 435). *Zarathustra* is symbolic of his 'feminine-masculine' dynamic. The violent scenes of Z 3.2, for instance, are followed by the calm and peacefulness of Z 3.3, repeated again at Z 4.2.9 and Z 4.10 following their synthesis in the form of the child at Z1.1.[28] Zarathustra is accompanied at all times by the eagle as the masculine Greek and the snake as the feminine Judaic (BT 9). Indeed, *Zarathustra* itself, the work Nietzsche most esteemed, can be viewed as a 'feminine-masculine' synthesis, an amalgam of poetry and philosophy that combines both his 'feminine hand' (Derrida 1979) and his masculine 'writerly voice' (Richardson 2020; Oliver 1995).[29]

Reading Nietzsche in a retrievalist way, his ambiguous/polysemous writings on femininity and masculinity can be viewed productively as a deconstructive manoeuvre for overcoming binarisms. Safranski (2003: 245) views this as leading Nietzsche towards an economy of the *androgynous* or ('feminine-masculine') that pluralizes rather than binarizes sexuality and gender. Significantly, Nietzsche himself, a synthesis of effeminacy and machismo, entitled the fourth book of *The Gay Science* 'Sanctus Janarius', paying homage to the martyred saint known in Naples as San Gennaro who was known for his striking feminine characteristics, soft beauty and his period bleeding. Considered both man and woman, he is the patron saint of androgyny, a beautiful synthesis of the masculine and feminine who challenges the coherence of the bivalent logic of man and woman as a dualistic metaphysical category.[30]

Sartre and Mother Earth

Like Nietzsche, Sartre was brought up fatherless and lived for periods of his adult life with his mother. When Jean-Baptiste Sartre died in 1906, young 'Poulou' was only fifteen months old. Describing himself as a 'fatherless orphan' (W 70) and the 'son of a dead man' (W 12), he viewed this event positively in retrospect since it 'gave me my freedom' (W 14) and allowed him to be his 'own cause' (W 71). When his mother remarried, this was far from a happy occasion for the young Sartre since it broke the close intimacy he shared with Anne-Marie and subjected him to his stepfather's patriarchal law: 'I sensed his desire through Anne-Marie; through her, I learned to scent the male, to fear and loathe him' (W 137).[31] Sartre's 'hardening up' came, as Nietzsche's had done, at the hand of other boys at school. The violence and bullying he suffered at La Rochelle made him take that violence into himself and implement 'a physically confrontational masculinity' as one 'who can endure hard blows' (1995: 175). Alongside learning how to box, his masculine sense of self was built around his heroic project of writing: 'For a long while I treated my pen as a sword' (W 157). Although friendship with other males (Mahieu, Nizan, Merleau-Ponty, Camus, Cau) was an abiding feature of his life, these were built on philosophical allegiances rather than any kind of shared intimacy and, when these alliances split, the friendship ended in a bout of masculinist adversarialism. As he later confessed, 'I can't imagine tenderness in my relation with men' (1995: 277). Continuing the filial intimacy Sartre felt from a young age with Anne-Marie, close female relationships dominated his life. In his *War Diaries*, Sartre declared that for the first time in his life he felt 'humble and disarmed' in Beauvoir's company and credits her with 'forcing' him to renounce his early theory of salvation through art (WD 78, 88). Beauvoir, along with his adopted daughter, Arlette, would be a philosophical partner until his final years.[32]

Feminist criticisms of Sartre often focus upon certain passages in *Being and Nothingness*, particularly his discussion of viscosity and 'the obscenity of the feminine sex' towards the end of the book:

The viscous . . . is a revenge . . . a sickly-sweet and feminine revenge. (BN 789)

the obscenity of the feminine sex organ is that of all *gaping* things; it is a call for being, as all holes are, moreover; in herself, the woman is calling for a foreign flesh which, penetrating and diluting her, must transform her into a plenitude of being. . . . Doubtless the sex organ is a mouth, and a voracious mouth which swallows the penis. (BN 794)

Many feminists, however, take a reconstructive approach to Sartre's philosophy. Mui (1999: 32) characterizes Sartre as a 'grumbling misogynist' that shows through as an integral component in his ontology in *Being and Nothingness* but contends 'woman nevertheless prevails as a full-fledged consciousness in [his] ontology'. Similarly, although the passages above 'are clearly demeaning to women', according to Sutton Morris (1999: 70), Sartre is not as guilty of anti-feminism as some suppose. While he symbolizes the viscous with a repugnant moral quality, his analysis isn't necessarily hopelessly sexist, for he also states 'the viscous is *me*' (BN 789) and doesn't restrict it to the feminine. Indeed, his idea of holes-to-be filled symbolizes a general human tendency to desire the 'spherical plenitude, of Parmenidean being' (BN 794) and, in using it, 'he had more general symbols in mind' (1999: 71).[33] Another complaint levied against Sartre is his characterization of love as objectification and domination of the Other in *Being and Nothingness* as exercised through 'the look'. However, this is not the only mode of love Sartre describes in *Being and Nothingness* and elsewhere. His description of the process of sexual caress, for instance, involves a '*twofold reciprocal incarnation*' (BN 516) and a form of mutual becoming and enrichment. In the *War Diaries*, he displays a certain ambiguity over love, seduction and mutual recognition, stating at one point, 'nothing is dearer to me than the freedom of those I love . . . but the fact is, this freedom is dear to me provided I don't respect it at all. It's a question not of suppressing it, but of actually violating it' (WD 256). But, a few pages later, he adds, '[t]he love that wants freedom in others only so that it can violate it – that form of love is utterly inauthentic. There are other ways of loving' (WD 258). He points to the necessary role of (non-dominative) objectification in reflective self-knowledge as an affirmation and recognition of our singularized material embodiment and our individual consciousness, a form of mutually fulfilling recognition unfolding 'in the dimension of otherness' (NE 280).

In the view of Lacoste (1999: 272, 292), as Sartre's thought matures it moves towards a Cixousian 'feminine economy of reciprocal abandon' that reverses his earlier masculine economy and ontology of sadism and masochism in *Being and Nothingness*. The hostile look of independent consciousnesses is replaced by the 'fraternity' of 'people bound to each other in feeling and action' (HN 91). This involves a form of abandon as not a negative purely passive thing but as an activity of 'de-selfing' or 'de-egoisation' that lends itself to an ethics of 'gift-giving'. For Cixous (1994: 133), there are two different criteria that mark masculine and feminine economies – the relation to pleasure and the attitude towards giving. She explains the relation to pleasure through the story of the Apple and Eve and the quest for the Holy Grail. On one side is the law 'which is absolute, verbal, invisible' and which is not and, on the other, 'the apple which is, is, is'. Perceval (who seeks the Holy Grail) is a mother's son with no father on the side of innocence and happiness, but after he is educated, he becomes 'phallicized' and falls prey to the law which is 'anti-pleasure' (1994: 135). One's path in life and participation in either or both economies is not determined by anatomical sex but is determined by history, by 'the cultural schema and the way the individual negotiates with these schema . . . adapts to them and reproduces them, or else . . . goes beyond them' (1994: 135). In many respects, Nietzsche and Sartre were two archetypal Percevals, raised by feminine hands on the side of 'innocence and happiness', 'phallicized' by institutions and male violence, but eventually negotiating a path out of this. In philosophical terms, this is represented through their proposed economy of the gift. In his 'Essai sur le don', Sartre very much anticipates Cixous (and Derrida) in his distinction between authentic giving and the subjugating gift where the former 'presupposes a reciprocity of recognition' (NE 369) in contrast to the Potlatch ceremony which involves debt and the alienation of freedom bound up with proprietorship or mastery and other where '[t]he act of gift-giving installs my freedom in the other as a subjective limit to the other's freedom' (NE 376). Sartre extends his notion of deep recognition to love where '[t]he ego exists to lose itself. It is the gift' (NE 418). Love is not an appropriation but an unveiling or creating: 'In pure generosity, I assume myself as losing myself, so that the fragility and finitude of the other exists absolutely as revealed within the world' (NE 507). As Lacoste (1999: 285) comments, in 'a tone at once Zen and Derridean', here Sartre is 'deconstructing himself, three decades before Jacques Derrida would begin his own deconstruction'. He did not return to the themes of gifting and authentic love until the interviews of the 1970s, but in *Saint Genet* he gives a strong Cixousian conception of love that involves a total acceptance of the loved one, including the most contingent dimensions of the body. Genet loves Decarnin unprovisionally in even the body lice he receives from him. '[O]ne loves nothing, if one does not love everything' (SG 532) since love is 'the acceptance of the total person, including his viscera' (in 1999: 286).

In understanding Sartre, Lacoste (1999: 273) and Boulé (2005: 196) both make a strong connection between *bios* and mind, between the personal and political. In the interviews that took place with Beauvoir in 1974, Sartre mentions his fear of abandon (to his body and to others) throughout his life and how he tried to exorcize this through aggressive war games that symbolized mastery over the external world. 'Appropriating women' represented a magical means of forgetting about his own perceived ugliness and recapturing feelings he had long suppressed like tenderness.[34] In confronting his 'neurosis' and fear of abandon to the women in his relationships, he admits that he performed the active, objective part of the act but left out the passive, subjective aspect that would have involved self-abandon and *jouissance*. This led to a *coupure* or split between what he would give and receive since he was pure activity, 'the active principle' (1981b: 400, 415). For Lacoste (1999: 282), this mirrors the masculine economy of *Being and Nothingness* where Sartre expresses his fear of self-abandon, of receptivity, of *jouissance* and of openness to the other by the creation of two antagonistic categories, the in-itself, 'which like Cixous' apple *is, is, is*', and the for-itself, which, like Cixous' law, 'is abstract and is not'.[35]

In Boulé's (2005: 198) view, Sartre's progression beyond a divided masculine and feminine side occurred in the 1970s when, due to his blindness and the fact that he was no longer able to write, he began a process of psychic and social reintegration of his self, replacing the divided and split selves he had inhabited with a more inclusive sense of self that involves 'the closer relationship to the m/other, the body and hence to love' (Cixous 1986: 17). A key factor in this transition was his intellectual partnership with Lévy, a collaboration that split Sartre from his 'family' at *Les Temps Modernes*, including, of course, Beauvoir. As the Beauvoir interviews took place, Sartre soon became occupied fully with the Lévy interviews because they were not primarily about his past life as the Beauvoir interviews were but about his future philosophical orientation and the formulation of a new social philosophy that he had been grappling with for several years. The Beauvoir interviews can be seen in many respects as a domesticated construction of Sartre as a thinker for whom nothing had really changed in the topography of his thought from his early days, yielding no 'unexpected revelations' (1984: 163).[36] Sartre's ability to form an intimate relation with a man (Lévy), based not on violence but on partnership and reciprocity, allowed him to experience those things he had relegated to a footnote in *Being and Nothingness*, such as maternal love, pity and kindness. It was not until May 1968 and his collaboration with Lévy that he was able to finally experience the solidarity and fraternity that he longed for which was vitalizing for Sartre. They both criticize and modify each other, helping to shed their 'grandiose selves' in a dialogue of mutual support. He defines their work as 'plural thought', revealing a transformed Sartre open to criticism, negotiation and critical reflexivity.[37] This transition is reflected in his shift in the idea of violence. In the notion of an 'authentic appeal' that reaches consciously beyond all inequalities 'toward a human world where any appeal of anyone to anyone will always be possible' (NE 285), Sartre does not legitimize the violence of the slave and views it as a dead end (NE 399–404). In the *Critique*, however, he turns away from the feminine economy in the essential role he gives to violence. He finds solidarity in the notion of fraternity but views the 'links of reciprocity' in the 'fraternity' of the fusing group as ambivalent and unstable in that it is only a 'resemblant solidarity' (CDR 437). The notion of 'fraternity' in the *Critique*, as Lacoste (1999: 290) comments, is 'violent through and through', a union in violence based on the initial violence against those perceived as oppressors. Discussing the Algerian war of independence, for instance, Sartre argues, 'the only possible way out was to confront the total negation with total negation, violence with equal violence' (CDR 733). The 'violence of the rebel' was 'the violence of the colonialist' (CDR 433), a message he reinforced even stronger in his preface to Fanon's *The Wretched of the Earth*.

In his later thinking, however, Sartre reconfigures the notion of *fraternity* as no longer the 'fraternity-terror' of the *Critique* but as 'necessarily linked to and often is even engendered by the presence of another' (HN 71). To consider ourselves as a 'self for the other' (HN 71) means positing transparency as a new intersubjective ideal. This is a 'feeling' for the gift, for a notion of 'open' fraternity that extends beyond closed groups to include all of humanity. He articulates (against Lévy's pressing) a new ideal of non-violence and fraternity based on the birth from a common Mother (HN 87) or 'le matriciel' (mother-matrix). He tells Lévy that woman has 'the womb that gives life, the breasts that nourish and the back that carries', establishing a relationship where 'the motivations for an act come from the affective realm' (HN 89).[38] In an interview in 1965, he aligns himself openly with a feminine economy of thinking: 'But when the day comes, of course, the special qualities of [sensitivity] for which I prefer the company of women will be due purely to chance... They'll cease to be a feminine prerogative.'[39] Ten years later, he tells Beauvoir that there was a sort of woman inside him (1976a: 116). In his final years, he fulfils the project articulated in *Notebooks for an Ethics* in 1947–8 of 'getting rid of one's ego', reaffirming and reinforcing the notion of reciprocal giving: 'Tenderness one receives, tenderness one gives, the two are linked and there exists only a general tenderness, both given and received' (1977b: 81).

As was the case with Nietzsche, the trajectory of Sartre's thinking gravitates towards the feminine within a deconstructive logic of inversion and displacement that follows the 'dialectical development . . . [of] the feminine and masculine poles of the world' (BN 779). As Lacoste (1999: 292) argues, Sartre's last personal philosophy belongs to an economy that aims at gender-free distinctions (active and passive/masculine and feminine) where abandon is deconstructed and where it is 'not negative, not mindless, nor even passive' but a positive form of 'de-selfing'. To avoid essentialism, Sartre's thinking follows Cixous' (1994: 197–205) ideal of bisexuality or 'the presence of both sexes' within each of us, two economies within an individual. On a personal level, he follows Nietzsche in identifying himself as *androgynous*. Referring to Flaubert's 'androgynous nature', he states, 'I'm certainly androgynous myself, which is not a flaw' (1979b: 37). In another interview (1977b), he attributes sensitivity and subjectivity to women and rationality and objectivity to men but states that there are some 'men-women' (*homes-femmes*) who have more subjectivity, a point of androgyny with which he himself identifies: 'I was to have the sex of angels, indeterminate but feminine around the edges' (in Hayman 1986: 23). Despite his professed ugliness, he views himself as an '*homme-femme*' and declares his attraction for androgyny in men, that is, those who have not split their masculine and feminine sides.[40]

Playful pianists

Everything seems dead to me when I don't hear music.

(Nietzsche, KSB 1.238)

Accounts of Nietzsche and Sartre often exclude or marginalize their deepest love – music, the province of the female Muses Euterpe, Erato and Terpsichore – and one that embodies the cardinal elements of their existentialist philosophy. The piano was for both philosophers a meeting place where their aesthetics, pre-reflective freedom, ethics of play and creation, affective phenomenology and Dionysianism coalesce, forming a composite chord of harmonic resonances, sonorities and parallel wavelengths. Moreover, the piano signified a perfect expression of their feminine sociality, encompassing a type of 'Racinian love', 'sororal Eros' or 'amorous disposition' along the lines of a shared horizon (Noudelmann 2012: 151).[41] 'Making music', Nietzsche wrote, 'is another way of making children' (WP 421). Reading *The Birth of Tragedy* and *Nausea*, we might say that the idea of *salvation through music* is the most dreamily metaphysical or starry-eyed that Nietzsche and Sartre ever get in their terrestrial philosophizing.

Nietzsche, the aspiring composer

Without music, life would be a mistake.

(Nietzsche, *Twilight of the Idols* 1.33)

In a letter to his friend Erwin Rohde following a Wagner concert in Mannheim in 1871, Nietzsche declared, '[e]verything that . . . cannot be understood in relation to music engenders . . . downright aversion and disgust in me' (KSB 3.257). He began his study of the piano aged nine and soon developed a passion for Bach, Haydn and Mozart. In 1857, he began to compose music, encouraged by his mother who passed on her skill and arranged for piano lessons. In 1861, at Pforta, he started to experiment in his musical tastes, leaving Beethoven and Haydn to one side and becoming entranced with the music of Schumann. He also at this time embarked on an intense spree of composition, including a piece he entitled 'Satan rises out of Hell', which he eventually abandoned for not being able 'to strike the exact Satanic tone' (KGW 1.3.3).[42] In 1874, he wrote a piano piece for four hands *Hymn to Friendship* that he adapted to Salomé's poem *Prayer for Life* in 1882, an intimate expression of their love which they could play together without Paul Rée sitting between them. His childhood friend Paul Deussen described how, when taken by a guide in Cologne to a brothel (instead of his request for a restaurant), Nietzsche confessed to him in a letter that he was 'speechless' when surrounded 'by a half dozen apparitions in tinsel', whereupon he went instinctively to the piano and struck several chords before hurrying outside. In line with this, in 1877 he devised a hierarchy of things according to the pleasure they afforded with musical improvisation at the pinnacle followed by Wagnerian music and then lust. Losing himself to the world and his playing, he would play piano for hours on end, experiencing a sustained form of rapture in which '[e]very fibre and nerve of my being is tingling' (KSB 2.332).[43] He had strong aspirations to become a professional composer that was mortally deflated when in 1872 he sent his *Manfred Meditation* to Hans von Bülow who was far from impressed, stating that 'you persistently defy every rule of tonal connection' and display 'a frenzied imagination'.⁴⁴ Nietzsche's playing, as Noudelmann (2012: 54) remarks, was akin to his writing – 'powerful', 'brutal', 'sweeping and polyphonic', letting the piano resonate fully and sonorously.

Although he was infatuated for a period by Wagner and Bizet, Chopin was Nietzsche's firm companion, a composer he never denied his passion for. He listened to Chopin's *Barcarole* over and over again, associating it with his love for Italy and Mediterranean culture. He connected his own Polish origins to Chopin's 'princely nobility', imagining himself as a brother to the composer. One of his youthful compositions, a Mazurka, reproduces many elements of Chopin's *Mazurka op.7, no.1*.⁴⁵ Wagner was at first the great redeemer who embodied the Romantic aspect of Schopenhauerian 'great art', but Nietzsche eventually tired of him and, as his estimation of Wagner deteriorated, he reached the point where he had nothing but deep contempt for Wagnerian theatre. Expecting an art of cultural regeneration, on visiting Bayreuth in 1876, he found instead an extortionate, soulless circus with Wagner in the middle as the great showman and egomaniac: 'It was not just that the complete indifference and illusion of the Wagnerian "ideal" was palpably evident to me at that time . . . the pitiful assemblage of patrons and little patronesses. . . . The entire idle dregs of Europe coming together, and every prince racing in and out of Wagner's house as though it were more of a sporting event' (KSW 14.492). The final straw for Nietzsche was Wagner's *Parsifal*, a work that expressed anti-Semitic sentiment and projected Christian ideals (EH 2.5–6).⁴⁶

Nietzsche's approximately seventy works (*lieder*, symphonies, choral works, piano pieces) cannot be reduced to a mere hobby divorced from his philosophical writings but, as Noudelmann (2012: 50) suggests, 'lie at the very heart of his thinking'. Rhythm and tempo are key features of his writing (he often referred to his books in terms of musical scores) and denote a certain style connected to the cycles of life and the flux of feelings (BGE 28, EH Z3), sometimes slow and cautious (D P5) and sometimes quick and lively (BGE 213, GS 381). His philosophical conception of music runs in parallel with the three phases of his thinking. His early work champions the idea of *art as salvation*, viewing the 'Dionysian wisdom' of music as the highest and most profound of all artistic expression that articulates the 'gospel of universal harmony', not as religion or morality but as purely aesthetic (BT 22). True art is both token and salvation of a unified culture, employs myths that unify a people (BT 23, UM 4.8) and conceives tragedy as a means for glimpsing and resolving psychological and metaphysical realities. After his turn away from Schopenhauer and Wagner towards naturalism and science in his middle period, he sets art and science in a different order of priority (D 433), viewing art as a dangerous narcotic (HH 108, 148), as 'degenerate' (HH 158) or as a form of deception involving the positing of metaphysical illusions or falsehoods (HH 220, 222). In turn, he is somewhat more circumspect about noumenal pronouncements ('as though the innermost abyss of things were speaking imperceptibly' (BT 21)), dismissing the idea that music could ever be objective – 'we do not make contact with the "essence of the world in itself" and only "fancy" that a colossal power speaks through music' (HH 10). It is not a 'direct language of feeling', he now states, but merely 'empty noise' into which we project memories, associations and physical responses (HH 216). From *The Gay Science* onwards, however, in his final phase of thinking his perspective is more nuanced, establishing a distinction between true art and degraded art (Wagner is presented as a sorcerer in *Zarathustra*).⁴⁷ He returns enthusiastically to his former ideal of art as a means to a new ideal, urging us to live as a work of art (GS 78, 299) and to pursue an 'art of life' (A 56) associated with overfullness and perfection as a tool for combating asceticism (GM 3.5). In *Zarathustra*, he associates artistic creation with procreation and pregnancy (Z 2.2) and revisits his earlier recognition of music's special powers, beckoning us to 'Sing! Speak no more!' (Z 3.16.7) and contrasting music's revelatory disclosure of Dionysian insight with the regime of words and concepts that obscure the reality of things: 'Speech is a beautiful foolery; with it man dances over all things' (Z 3.13.2).

Central to Nietzsche's distinction between true and degraded art is the role of the body, hence the importance of rhythm in his thinking that he describes as the imposition of form upon the real establishing order in terms of measurable space and time through a form of compelling (GS 84). He links music and thought in general with the metaphor of dancing – thinking is 'being able to dance with the feet, with concepts, with words' (TI 8.7). In his physiological conception of art, rapture is the basic aesthetic state: 'What is essential in rapture is the feeling of enhancement of force and plenitude' (TI 9.8).⁴⁸ Rapture is not an 'inner feeling' but, in Heidegger's words, 'a mode of the embodying, attuned stance towards beings as a whole' (1987: 1:105).⁴⁹ All art 'exercises the power of suggestion over the muscles and senses, which in the artistic temperament are originally active' (WP 809). Lying at the very heart of his Dionysian aesthetics and philosophical thinking, music embodies the quintessential expression of his ethics of play and pre-reflective freedom: 'It is the music in our conscience, the dance in our spirit that makes all the puritanical litanies, all the philistinism and moral sermons sound so dissonant' (BGE 216). 'In *relation to music*', he writes, 'all communication through *words* is shameless; the word dilutes and makes stupid' (WP 810). Music is the superior language of Nietzsche's Dionysian imaginary and one he would speak when words could no longer convey the inner drives of his *Lebensphilosophie*.

Sartre, the aspiring jazz singer

Sartre's early writings are honed around the Schopenhauerian claims of art's redemptive qualities in a meaningless world full of suffering and pain. In his story *Er the Armenian*, Apollo exclaims, '[a]n ethics, what foolishness! But guard the desire to create a work of art', and yet warns against the aesthete who merely consumes art. *Nausea* is often viewed as both a symptom and antidote of the faith in art as an aesthetic cure for an ontological sickness in which Roquentin can cleanse himself of 'the sin of existing' (N 251) and 'look back on his life without repugnance' (N 252). This ambivalence towards aestheticism is repeated in *Existentialism Is a Humanism* where he defends existentialism against the charge of aestheticism or *l'art pour l'art* (which he also criticizes in *What Is Literature?* and *The Family Idiot*) and yet draws a strong parallel between ethical invention and the creation of works of art as they both originate in the imagination.⁵⁰

Sartre had an interest in many of the arts. Alongside his interest in literature and drama, as early as 1924 he had written an 'Apologie pour le cinéma' (EJ 388–404) in which he describes the beauty of the union of image and motion in art form: 'The film is the poem of modern life' (EJ 392). He also defends its anti-elitist spirit and its advocacy of moral values that are often implicit but easily discernible. The Fine Arts also captured his imagination. He had a lifelong interest in painting and sculpture, writing essays on studies of Titian, Tintoretto, Mason, Giacometti and Calder and commented in a letter to Beauvoir that he was thinking of developing a system of aesthetics based on cinematic art and a theory about the function of image in the arts (1981: 27). Despite the variety of his interests, however, music was his prime love and childhood choice:

> I resolved to dispense with speech and live through music. . . . Taken in huge doses, the music would at last begin to work. Like a voodoo drum, the piano would impose its rhythm on me. The *Fantaisie Impromptu* would oust my soul, dwell in me, endow me with an unknown past, a brilliant, deadly future. I was possessed; the devil had seized me and shaken me like a plum-tree. (W 79)

In Chopin, Sartre shared a favourite composer with Nietzsche. He would play the Polish composer assiduously, again and again, and 'steep myself in the passionate melancholy of Chopin' (W 80). His mother's playing of Chopin's *Funeral March* moistened his eyes with tears while her renditions of Chopin's *Ballades* would inspire him to act out his adventures as a child (W 78–9). While at the ENS he gave piano lessons and, by all accounts, had a fine baritone voice. During the years of his greatest political interventionism in the late 1960s, he still maintained an almost daily regime of playing the piano.[51] He rarely risked writing his own music down, but he did compose a sonata in the style of Debussy that he described as a simple private exercise.[52] Apart from a preface to René Liebowitz's *The Artist and His Conscience*, however, Sartre wrote very little on the subject of music. In an interview with *Obliques-Arts*, he expresses his preference for classical music over the avant-garde, for an art of sounds over an art of noise. He was not opposed to new creative forms (like serial music and aleatoric music) but wondered where the beauty lies in such art forms: 'I no longer know what this new beauty is; do they even care about it any more?'[53]

When Sartre poses the question of art's salvation in *Nausea*, it is through music and, more specifically, a jazz song. The 'sweetish sickness' of Roquentin's nausea abates when he hears a record 'Some of These Days' playing in a café. It begins with a piano intro, which segues into the singer's warm voice. For the next few minutes, all is right with Roquentin's world for he is '*in* the music' (N 38). Each note in the melody leads to the next with a necessity that bestows necessity on his existence too. For once, everything is poised and smooth. His movements flow with ease and grace as if he were dancing, until the song ends and everything goes to pieces again. Roquentin's compulsive listening to 'Some of These Days', as Noudelmann (2012: 40) argues, is a complex and contradictory exercise in which Sartre 'mixes the search for a pure essence of music with the supposed impurity of jazz'. The sound of the saxophone and the musical progression of the notes momentarily quell the nausea he feels and sublimate his disenchantment. But pure style, pure art and pure form evince a modernist Kantian logic that goes against both the practice of jazz and Sartre's own relation to Romantic music. The record of 'Some of These Days' privileges the imagination and enables the scene of a man alone who can project himself into the role of the musician: 'And that is where, without doubt, Sartre's interior theater reveals itself: The ideal of musical purity dissolves in favor of role-playing' (2012: 42). The necessity Sartre describes is not an ontological necessity but a phenomenological one of constructing fixity for transient forms that is temporally felt and which dissipates once the record ends. Sartre is viewed by Noudelmann in this light as 'a jazzman manqué' (2012: 42). According to Hayman (1986: 42), the young Sartre dreamt of being a jazz singer and jazz, 'the music of the future' as he once described it, is the musical genre that best represents freedom-as-praxis for him.[54] Jazz functions within *Nausea*, first, to espouse Sartre's opposition to the distinction between high and vernacular art and, second, as an exotic Other to represent *la mentalité primitive* in an increasingly industrialized and depersonalized modern world.[55] We may view this as an extension of the Dionysian in Sartre's thinking and a connection to the Nietzschean emphasis on 'physiological art' centred on the body, rhythm, affect and rapture.

For Nietzsche and Sartre, the piano represented a necessity of life, an active retreat and the singular affirmation of a self who cannot be summarized into History. Improvising Chopin transported them 'to worlds without power', taking them out of the general linearity of time and loosening their engagement with their own situation, offering a privileged time for subjectification within an activity of *Kinderspiel*.[56] For Sartre, playing the piano signified the harmonious fusion of *pour-soi* and *en-soi*, a body of desire and glory without want, remainder or approximation, involving the fluttering and subtle movement of temporalities. At the piano, the artist becomes one with his body: 'the pianist is his hand, and even that he is entirely in his hand' (Noudelmann 2012: 18). This creates a sensual dialogue 'between the ivory shelf and the cushion of the skin', revealing chiasmic and recursive effects where, by touching the keys, the performer is in turn touched, 'unleashing a sound that enters him'. Rhythm creates movement and engagement, a corporeal scene in which the body is engaged to move, vibrate and perform as a musical organism 'mixed together with the musical materiality in a flowing reciprocity' (2012; 136, 140).

In sketching out the subjective scene of their emotions and feelings at the piano, their playing became an expression of the Dionysian freedom their work argued passionately for. As Barthes observed, music facilitates 'the freedom to be delirious (*mainomai*: I am lost, I am in love)',[57] a form of pre-reflective praxis that is not a psychotic delirium but one which allows one to follow one's unchartered paths. For Nietzsche, the piano became his last means of communication and subjectification as he wandered ever further down the path of mute insanity in his final years. After being committed to a psychiatric clinic in Jena, he spoke rarely but still played every day, improvising and performing on the upright piano in the cafeteria. On visiting him in 1890, his friend Peter Gast was taken aback with the contrast between the loquaciousness and precision of his piano playing and the vague sparseness of his words: 'Not one wrong note! Interweaving tones of Tristan-like sensitivity . . . Beethoven-like profundity and jubilant songs rising above it. Then again reveries and dreams.'[58]

Madness and epiphany: Turin and Billancourt

Ah give me madness, you heavenly powers! Madness, that I may at last believe in myself! Give deliriums and convulsions, sudden lights and darkness, terrify me with frost and fire such as no mortal has ever felt, with deafening din and prowling figures, make me howl and whine and crawl like a beast: so that I may only come to believe in myself!

(Nietzsche, *Daybreak* 14)

As Howells (2011: 20–1) complains, theories of modern philosophy tend not to focus on the subject's disintegration, weakness and ultimate dissolution in 'the radical alterity of death'. Conceptions of subjectivity that manifest the vulnerability and fragility of the subject are demoted in favour of those that express autonomy, rationality and transcendence. In this section, I look at the final years of Nietzsche and Sartre and how these have been perceived by some scholars as aberrations or 'breakdowns' in their thinking, symbolized dramatically by Nietzsche's 'Turin Event' of 1889 and Sartre's 'Billancourt Episode' of 1970. Against this standard view, I argue for the importance of their final years as exemplifying key elements of their living philosophy and providing a window into the nuances and evolution of their thinking.

Nietzsche's mysterious madness

There is a certain mystery and mystique that surrounds Nietzsche's madness and some disagreement as to what caused it. Was it congenital encephalitis, acquired syphilis, a flight of the untrammelled imagination, a social conduct or mask, a performative self-configuration or just, as Salomé suggested, the Dionysian terminus of self-dispersal towards which his *Lebensphilosphie* was always bound? Was it, one could additionally ask, a desperate affliction or a saintly gift? A descent into the bowels of despair or an ascent into the mystic? *Pharmakon*, both disease and cure? Or, simply, all these things in combination, embodying an intersectional manifestation of the three ecologies of the decentred self working together to a point of disintegration? Ironically, in *Twilight of the Idols* Nietzsche had roundly condemned the invalid he became: 'Society should only have a profound contempt for the man who survives like a vegetable in cowardly dependence on doctors and medicine after he has lost the meaning of his life, the right to live' (TI 9.36). Yet it was only as a 'vegetable' and 'museum exhibit' of Elisabeth after the onset of insanity in the 1890s that Nietzsche finally began to achieve the literary fame and renown he had craved for in his earlier, 'fully sentient' years.

Nietzsche's psychological and physiological infirmity ran from a young age when, as a sickly child, he was prone to chronic headaches and eye pain. There was always a strong connection between his physical condition, mental health and social environment. When, after the death of his grandfather in 1859, he fell ill and spent long periods in the school infirmary, those around him wondered whether there might be a 'psychogenic dimension' to his illness.[59] His family and friends often expressed doubts about his insanity in regard to both his writing and his personal behaviour. In 1877, an entry in Ida Overbeck's diary records how his sister lists a few reasons 'that would probably land her brother in a mental institution'. In Bayreuth, Nietzsche's doctor, Eiser, suggested that his most recent writings indicated 'the onset of the softening of the brain'.[60] Two years later, after a violent and sustained migraine attack in Basel which led to his release from the university on a pension, he conducted what he referred to as 'a daily battle against headache', suffering a 'laughable diversity' of ailments. A few years later, he visited Gottfried Keller in Zurich who declared, 'I think that this fellow is crazy'. After an onslaught of depression in 1888, Nietzsche felt the same depths of melancholia (that would afflict Sartre in the 1930s), lamenting, '[t]here are nights in which I can no longer endure myself' (KSB 8.231). Along with the lows, however, he also felt the highs, feeling intense periods of sudden euphoria, often dancing naked in his room (as his landlady reported), singing and making 'strange noises', wandering into distant futures and 'into hotter souths than any artist ever dreamed of; there, where dancing gods are ashamed of all clothing' (Z 3.12.2).

On 3 January 1889, Nietzsche left his apartment and caught sight of a carriage driver beating his horse on the Piazza Carlo Alberto in Turin. Weeping, he threw himself around the horse's neck to protect it and collapsed in compassion with the animal. Soon after, he was taken to a psychiatric unit and diagnosed with 'paralysis progressiva'. At the clinic in Jena, he suffered delusions of grandeur believing himself to be the Duke of Cumberland or the Kaiser. He spoke only to the other patients in French and engaged in periodic bouts of violence, smashing windows and throwing objects.[61] In early 1890, his friend Gast went for long walks with Nietzsche whom he suspected did not want to be cured: 'it seemed – horrible though this is – as if Nietzsche were merely feigning madness, as if he were glad for it to have ended this way'. This tallies with Franz Overbeck's impression who, after spending time with Nietzsche, wrote, 'I cannot escape the ghastly suspicion . . . that his madness is simulated.'[62] Those who visited him during the 1890s tell of his physical degeneration and laconic utterances but commented on 'the power of his glance' (Gabriele Reuter) and the 'unfathomable exultation' (Rudolf Steiner) of his facial expression.[63] Salomé recorded that, during his period of madness, 'his physiognomy, his entire exterior, appeared to be most characteristically formed' (1988: 9). When Horneffer visited Nietzsche in the final months of his life, he described him in beatific terms: 'Although his eyes were vacant and his features slack, and although the poor man lay there with crooked limbs, more helpless than a child, a sense of magic radiated from his personality, and his appearance revealed a majesty that I would never experience again with any human being.'[64]

In Safranski's (2003: 318–19) view, throughout his adult life Nietzsche had dared to conceive the inconceivable and 'fell victim to the colossal dimensions of life'. His *Lebensphilosophie* was 'a departure to far-off shores', signalling 'a plethora of forms, a wealth of invention, and an ocean of possibilities so incalculable and adventurous that no "beyond" would be required'. This was a culmination of a process of Dionysian dispersal that brings both great terror and joy (BT 2). As Nietzsche describes the realm of the Dionysian in his notebooks:

> [It is] a drive towards unity, reaching beyond personality, the quotidian, society, reality, across the chasm of transitoriness: an impassioned and painful overflowing into darker, fuller, more buoyant states; an ecstatic affirmation of the totality of life as what remains constant – not less potent, not less ecstatic – throughout all fluctuation; the great pantheistic sharing of joy and distress which blesses and endorses even the ghastliest, the most questionable elements in life; the eternal will for regeneration, fruitfulness, recurrence; the awareness that creation and destruction are inseparable. (WP 1050)

Of course, as he debunked and profaned the idea of reason throughout his writings, it is little surprise that he should succumb to its antipode. Madness was signalled in his writings as fault lines that become ever more and more pronounced in his undertaking as 'the last disciple of Dionysus' (TI 10.5). Like the naked Nietzsche cavorting in his room, Zarathustra walks like a dancer (Z P2) and 'must yet become a child and without shame' (Z 2.22). Reverence for the body and earth makes naked Dionysus the ideal of a being without shame (BGE 295) since the gods require other masks than clothes (BGE 40, GS 77). It is dance that prevents the 'spirit of gravity' (Z 2.10), and Dionysus is the dancing god. In madness, as in dance, one has the sense of being possessed by a higher power in order to throw off the yoke of custom (D 14). As the sine qua non for moral evolution, madness produces innovation and creativity where moral innovators had to feign madness or induce it by means of asceticism. To project his saintly persona, Nietzsche follows the path of the Jewish prophets, the medicine man of the Indians, the Christian saints, the Greenland angekok and the Brazilian Pajee who created new moral ideals through 'ecstasy or mental derangements' (D 14). In a note of 1882/3, he foretells all signs of the *Übermensch* will appear as signs of madness or illness to the human herd (KSW 10.217): 'Where is the madness, with which you should be cleansed? Behold, I teach you the Superman: he is the lightning, he is this madness!' (Z P3). Those who cannot stand their ground above the law and moral conformity must find another law or seek refuge in insanity (D 14). Nietzsche associates madness with far-reaching insights, such as 'the madman with the lantern' (GS 125) who casts light on things others don't see and madness as the serum 'with which you must be inoculated' (ZP 3) to protect against the incursion of social norms. However, he views madness as manifesting in different forms since social norms carry their own force of madness, warning us to protect against the insanity of groups who have deviated from health and alignment to the world as will to power (BGE 156). Similarly, he urges us to guard against the 'madhouse air' of those whose shepherd is the ascetic priest (GM 3.14) and those whose 'bad conscience' leads them to posit a transcendent god as their judge and executioner of their guilt (GM 2.22). Zarathustra also preaches against the madness of pessimism and nihilism conceived as an end state rather than as a transitional phase (Z 2.20).

As evidenced by Nietzsche's sporadic fits of violence in his final years where, along with smashing the odd window he would also kick the odd dog while out walking with Franziska, his madness also bore some terror presaged in his final works and notes of the late 1880s as his aristocratic radicalism took firm hold. Klossowski (1997: 256, 234) reads Nietzsche's final writings in the light of a new revolutionary 'grand politics' modelled in part on the violence of the French Revolution which would 'break the history of humanity into two'. Extolling the virtues of war and revolution that he had spoken disparagingly of in his middle period, he proposed heavy artillery, dynamite and explosive terror. In a letter to August Strindberg in December 1888, he declared, 'I mean to have the young emperor shot', and to Overbeck in 1889 he extended this to haters of the Jewish people: 'I am just having all anti-semites shot' (1969: 344, 346). His demand for the *Übermensch* may be seen in this light as a form of self-conquest in which his madness and delusions made him solipsistic enough to identify humanity with the part of himself that he wanted to conquer. It was, of course, Nietzsche's journeying to the other side of reason and the subversive Dionysian wisdom and terror that his writings contained that were later celebrated by Bataille and Deleuze and taken up in earnest as a subject of inquiry by Foucault (*Madness and Civilization*) and Derrida (*Writing and Difference*).

Sartre's crabs

Sartre's madness is less documented and was less dramatic than Nietzsche's, but a certain imprint of insanity and melancholia and a flight towards imagination were regular elements of his *Lebensphilosophie*. Grabbed by the voodoo music at a young age (W 79), Sartre always held a deep fascination for Dionysian experience from his early intellectual interest in mystics like Teresa de Avila to his later admiration for the bodily rapture and intoxication of African spirituality. As a boy, he felt more at home among his books than in the big wide world: 'I found ideas more real than things' (W 34). He was wrapped not in the serious world of adults but in the imaginary world of the swashbuckling heroes of the comic books he read that fed his fertile imagination: 'Everything took place in my head; an imaginary child, I projected myself through the imagination' (W 71). He also recounts his childhood fears – 'I was afraid of water, of crabs, and of trees' (W 96) – three things of the world outside that would reappear as grotesque recurring elements in his novels, plays and psychological infirmities. He was always in danger of sliding into the world of the imaginary in a heroic flight against the world. He relates that, when aged nine, he was beset by a certain schizophrenia that created a divided self within him: 'It began with an anonymous flow of chatter in my head. . . . I thought I had two voices; one – which hardly belonged to me and was not dependent on my will – was dictating to the other what to say. I decided that I was dual' (W 136).

With lack of success as a writer and disenchantment with his job as a teacher, deep depression took hold of Sartre in his twenties. Boulé (2005: 77) attributes the catalyst for this to have been his conscription for military service in the meteorological corps at Tours from 1929 to 1931 when he recorded: 'I know that the same thought will recur, the same hope and despair and all the schizophrenic fabrications which I notice I'm trusting more and more. Thus I sink into the condition of all who are sequestered' (1983a: 33). This fed into his private life where he felt himself catapulting towards delirium, describing his relationship with Olga Kosakiewicz as 'passion and madness' in which he was transformed from a pitiable neurotic into a dramatic buffoon. Fascinated by the anomalies of perception which he was analysing in his study on the imagination, in 1935 he asked his friend Dr Daniel Lagache to inject him with mescaline, an experiment that would have a long-lasting effect on the young philosopher, both philosophically and psychologically. After the injection, he lay down on a bed in a barely lit room while, as Beauvoir (1983: 209) recorded, 'just past the corner of his eye, swarmed crabs'. The hallucinatory patterns did not pass and Sartre mentions in a letter to Louise Védrine in August 1939 of being in fear when swimming alone of the Beast who lives under the water. In the aftermath of his psychedelic experiment, Sartre never quite saw the world in the same way again. He told Gerassi decades later that, for days after, he saw crabs in the street 'trotting along behind him': 'I started seeing crabs around me all the time. They followed me in the streets, into class ... and they would be there, around my desk, absolutely still, until the bell rang' (2009: 62–3). It was only writing and socializing with his friends that 'protected him from [these] crabs and similar monsters' (1983: 211).[65] His faculties, as Beauvoir (1983: 210) reported, were distorted for weeks: 'Houses had leering faces, all eyes and jaws, and he couldn't help looking at every clockface he passed, expecting it to display the features of an owl.' He told her while walking by the Seine in Rouen that he was 'on the edge of a chronic hallucinatory psychosis' but she downplayed this, thinking that his only madness was thinking he was mad and believing his anxieties and psychoses to be the result of a deep emotional malaise in which he was unable to confront growing into full adulthood and manhood.[66]

Unsurprisingly, the subject of madness and psychological bewitchment surfaced in Sartre's writings around this period. Crabs emerge twice in *Nausea*, firstly in Roquentin's sexual encounter with the restaurant proprietor. When he is caressing her thigh, he begins to dream and suddenly finds himself in a garden full of insects and 'even more horrible animals' which 'were walking sideways with crab-like legs' (N 89). After that, he is wandering by the docks and looks down at the water to see a cork floating on the speckled surface. He wonders 'what could be *under* the water? . . . A monster? A huge carapace, half embedded in the mud? A dozen pairs of claws slowly furrow the slime. The monster raises itself a little, every now and then' (N 116). Crustaceans reappear in his last original play *The Condemned of Altona* in which the protagonist is hauled before a condemnatory court of crabs as creatures of the thirtieth century who are aware of the entire history of humanity.[67] Also in the late 1930s, in *The Wall* (*Le Mur*), a collection of five short stories published in 1939, Sartre directly explored the question of madness in literary form. In the third story, *The Room*, Monsieur and Madame Dabedat think that their son-in-law Pierre is insane and should be placed in an asylum. However, their daughter Eve accepts her husband in his deteriorating condition and seeks to accommodate and understand his delirium in contrast to those who want to lock his madness away. Sartre shows in this short story, as Vasey (2020: 432) points out, how the madman's abnormality is but a manifestation of our contingency: 'we are not all the same, we are not all normal, but we all experience the burden of being ourselves nonetheless. To be rid of him is to be rid of a window into our contingency.'

Sartre pursued this further in philosophical form in *The Imaginary* (1940) where he sets about effacing the strict Cartesian boundaries of madness and reason. The act of imagination, he argues, 'is a magical act' (IM 125). Imagination and perception are 'the two great irreducible attitudes of consciousness' (IM 120) and they are coextensive – there is no real without the irreal and *vice versa*. Consciousness in the world is always 'pregnant with the imaginary' and is constantly presented as 'a surpassing of the real' (IM 186). The imaging consciousness is described as 'magical' by Sartre as it is a spontaneous creation of consciousness that does not obey causal laws and, in certain cases (artistic creation, dreams, madness), it can captivate itself so much that the real can be completely suspended, transfigured or corrupted. This culminates in the phenomenon of possession where the imaginary saturates the world in 'every concrete and real situation' through a form of magical hypercaptivation (IM 186). Extreme cases can fragment consciousness and suspend the real attitude for long periods or even for the rest of one's life. For Sartre, hallucinations and visions are like waking dreams (IM 152) when imaginary consciousness is completely captive to itself (IM 164) and when one is 'isolated from the real world, enclosed in the imaginary'. The psyche becomes a 'closed consciousness' that has 'lost the very notion of reality' (IM 165), immersed within a 'spellbinding fiction' divorced from the real (IM 175). In madness, 'the distinction between subjective and objective' (IM 158) collapses where one enters a 'twilight life' (IM 157) in which 'spontaneities, wholly unforeseeable and fragmentary as they are, can be charged little by little with a certain ideo-affective material' (IM 159). In psychosis, 'spasms of consciousness' (IM 154) precipitate a progressive 'disintegration' (IM 155) and fragmentation. As Sartre demonstrates, 'partial systems' develop to the extreme whereby one's magical creations take over and persecute the mind that gave birth to them (IM 155).

In later life, madness revisited Sartre. As his health deteriorated in the 1970s, in the spring of 1973 on holiday in the South of France, he was beset by symptoms of vascular dementia, mistaking one person for another and believing that fictional characters were real like in his childhood. Mirroring symptoms of delusion and confusion displayed by Nietzsche in the 1890s, his imagination took over as he expected the arrival of Hercule Poirot and regularly confused Arlette with Beauvoir when they met up in Avignon.[68] This was presaged in Sartre's 'Turin moment' of October 1970 when he was scheduled to appear as a witness in the trial of a Maoist, Alain Geismar, but chose instead to stand on an oil drum and address workers at a Renault factory in Billancourt in order to break with the role of the 'classical intellectual' and forge a new union between workers and intellectuals in which the intellectual is not to give advice to the people but to help the masses take on a new shape (1974c: 66). Like Nietzsche's event in Turin, Sartre's Billancourt incident has splintered perception of their final years, between those who view these events as catalysts and symptoms of their impending madness and downward spiral and others who see them as epiphanies of their self-overcoming and reinvention. There is something quite poignant and powerful about this Renault episode which, as Cox (2016: 268) notes, represents 'a key element in the folklore of the later Sartre, a crucial piece of the Sartre jigsaw'. Was Sartre losing it, becoming a caricature of himself – the spokesman of a generation standing undignified on an oil barrel, being ignored in a factory car park? Or was it '[a] Socrates moment, maybe even a Jesus moment' (2016: 268), a symbolic expression of his spiritual and philosophical growth? Or even a 'Zarathustra experience' whose philosophical imploring in the marketplace also fell on deaf ears?

Sartre's physical deterioration and the 'philosophical turn' of his last decade have been viewed differently by separate factions of the 'Sartrean family' and continue to stimulate debate. The struggle between Elisabeth Förster-Nietzsche and Lou Salomé for what Nietzsche truly thought as he was still drawing breath in his armchair was re-enacted in type between the 'old Sarteans' (Beauvoir, Lanzmann, Bost and Pouillon) and 'New Sartreans' (Lévy and Arlette) who squabbled over Sartre's sanity as he sat there listening. Lévy was appointed as Sartre's secretary in September 1973, but this was something Beauvoir would soon regret. She regarded the Lévy interviews (which were assembled by Lévy as *Hope Now* in 1991) with horror, calling them the 'abduction of an old man' by his young secretary and countered them with a publication of her own interviews conducted in 1974 which she included in her last book, *Adieux: A Farewell to Sartre* (1984). Despite attempts by the old Sartreans to block its publication, *Le Nouvel Observateur* published the interviews as *Hope Now* in three consecutive weeks. In Beauvoir's eyes, Lévy steered Sartre towards Jewish Messianism and was 'cajoled' to be dismissive of old Sartrism, rejecting the meaning of literature and political engagement which had been lifelong Sartrean concerns. Following a decision not to publish a piece by Lévy and Sartre in *Le Nouvel Observateur* on the peace movement in Israel (Beauvoir and Bost persuaded Sartre not to), Lévy stormed out of the meeting calling Beauvoir and the editors 'putrefied corpses' and referring to them disparagingly from then on as 'old Sartreans'.[69]

Against those who believed Sartre's 'addled brain' was being manipulated, the editor Jean Daniel related how clear-headed and lucid Sartre was just prior to the interviews and how well he knew the text in his head. Sartre resisted the view of the interviews as a dynamic of subordination but viewed the interviews as a collaborative project or co-creative effort representing 'something new, a thought created by two people' (HN 73). Nonetheless, he insisted that he maintained control of the ideas they developed, being the essential voice of the conversation and transforming Lévy's understanding of freedom and political equality. Responding to the old Sartreans, Sartre insisted '[t]he itinerary of my thought eludes them all, including Simone de Beauvoir' (in Solal 1991: 514). One of the charges levelled against Sartre in *Hope Now* is that his pugnacious spirit is no longer there. Raymond Aron finds him unrecognizable because he is strangely reasonable, something he hasn't encountered in Sartre before – 'Sartre's work has never been sensible' for he is 'an excessively delirious man'. Edward Said described Sartre at a meeting a year before his death where he was largely silent and despondent, 'a haunted version of his earlier self'. In his final months, Jean Pouillon, Sartre's friend from *Les Temps Modernes*, advised Peter Caws not to interview Sartre for he was such 'a wreck of his former self' that it would be 'an embarrassment all around'.[70] In Boulé's (2005: 194) view, however, Sartre's later period was not the abduction of an old man by a young pretender but a mark of Sartre's own transformation into a new kind of intellectual and self. He has realized he 'does not have to carry on boxing; he can retire from the ring'. In his final years, Sartre finally fulfils the project he articulated in *Notebooks for an Ethics* of 'getting rid of one's ego'.[71] Whereas he could simply have rested on his laurels and his notoriety, he still accepts being challenged past his retirement age, questions himself and is prepared to change.[72] In trying to fix Sartre's meaning once and for all when he told Daniel that the new trajectory of his thought had eluded them, it could be more a case that that old Sartreans had become the old guard and his psycho-social evolution had simply continued to evolve beyond their expectations.[73]

In the work of his later years, Sartre revisited the question of madness in *The Family Idiot* via his analysis of the imaginary which he presents as a complex interplay between freedom and the unconscious. Analysing Flaubert's crisis and epileptic seizure at the Pont-l'Évêque in January 1844 (Nietzsche's 'Turin Event' of 1889?), Sartre construes this as a form of autosuggestion or 'Pithiatism' where the ill bear some sort of responsibility for their maladies. This illness allowed Flaubert to abandon his law exams and become an artist. His neurosis was in this sense 'chosen' as a purposive manoeuvre: 'To imagine is at once to produce an imaginary object and to become imaginary' (FI 912). As Flynn (2014: 404) notes, Sartre distinguishes pre-reflective from irreflective consciousness in this context to arrive at a middle level or dimension between pre-reflective (common awareness that precedes reflective knowledge) and reflective, introducing a 'somatic aspect' that was present in emotional consciousness in magical bodily incantations that acts as the operative intentionality of the unthought. Gustave's understanding

> is a silent adjunct to live experience, a familiarity of the subjective experience with itself, a way of putting components and moments in perspective but without explanation; it is an obscure grasp of the meaning of a process beyond its significations. . . . Intermediary between nonthetic consciousness and reflexive thematization, it is the dawning of a reflection, but when it surges up with its verbal tools it frequently falsifies what is 'understood'. (FI 3:429)

In cases of autosuggestion, Sartre writes, 'it all happens *unbeknownst* to the pithiatic subject', but it must be understood that this unknowingness is not unaware: 'it is an intentional unknowingness that is *play-acted* as the necessary condition of the process.' In the depths of this reflective intimacy, 'meditative thought *conceals itself* and by the same token *senses* that it is *suffered*, that without the body's docility it would remain imaginary, that it finds its *seriousness* and its reality in the way the organism receives it and by conforming to it, gives it a dimension of *nonthought*' (FI 3:628). This is akin to Nietzsche's idea of intentionality as '[s]omething that does not will and is unconscious' yet purposive (WP 675).

In line with their philosophy of the pre-reflective, the aesthetic and the performative self, it is important to embrace the final years (and madness) of Nietzsche and Sartre as a vital and revelatory window into the evolution of their thinking and the complex, ambiguous freedom they embraced, displaying the reconfirmation of youthful impulses, a form of innocent child's play and a new becoming that enfolded their contingency. Sartre links his 'madness', as Nietzsche did, to a germinal political vision and creative ethics: 'What I like about my madness is that it has safeguarded me, from the very first, against the blandishments of the elite' (W 158). It is ironic, but also perhaps inevitable, that the two philosophical/psychological therapists who devoted their minds to exposing and dissolving the bewitchments of human consciousness in the form of 'purifying reflection' should fall prey to insanity and the wild flight of the imagination. After all, both philosophers, experimenters for the future, showed how madness infects groups, as well as individuals, implying not only disintegration and dispersal but also freedom and a subversive wisdom. Although Sartre is left out of the debate around madness, his writings very much inform it. As early as 1939, he displays a sensitivity to the other side of reason in *The Room*, a theme, as Hayman (1986: 442) notes, he presaged in Derrida and Foucault 'to listen more sympathetically to the "insane" discourse of those who might formerly have been dismissed as incapable of communicating with us'. As Sartre remarks in *Words*, for instance: 'A madman's ravings, for example, are absurd in relation to the situation in which he finds himself, but not in relation to his madness' (N 185). Like Derrida, for whom a 'madness must watch over thinking' (1995: 342–5), and for Lacan, for whom 'madness is the permanent virtuality of a gap opened up in [our] essence . . . [and] is freedom's most faithful companion, following its every move like a shadow' (2018: 262), and, of course, Nietzsche before them, Sartre's writings attest to reverse Cartesian separation and deconstruct the firm dualistic boundary between reason and madness in search of a sublimating logic.

Conclusion

Twin ternary thinkers

> *Revaluation of all values: that is my formula for an act of supreme self-examination on the part of humanity, become flesh and genius in me.*
>
> (Nietzsche, *Ecce Homo* 4.1)

In analysing the Nietzsche–Sartre connection, my conclusion in this book has been firmly *associative*. Sartre's philosophy is unthinkable without its Nietzschean influences but utilizes, develops and expands those insights significantly, particularly in the area of intersubjectivity and social ensembles. When we filter out the noise and distortion that has plagued the broadcasting of their thinking, we find true harmonic resonance between them right across their philosophy in the areas of the self, ethics, ontology, aesthetics and even politics. In this study, I have attempted to open up the vault of the Nietzsche–Sartre connection and survey the objects within, but there are other treasures of comparison to intrigue that I have left untouched, such as their shared Hebreophilia and their love of travel (in Italy in particular), more evidence of their pluralist defence of the 'Otherized' and their 'spiritual nomadism'. My hope is that this book will stimulate others to look more closely at the fecundities of their thinking and find other objects of parallel interest. As 'prey for the living' (BN 706), I have tried to view these parallel philosophers with fresh eyes (in terms of the 'New Nietzsche' and the 'New Sartre') in a bid to alter the future perception of them as well as to rethink the twentieth-century triangulation of Nietzsche-existentialism-poststructuralism which, through the distortions of Heidegger, Derrida, Foucault and a cohort of interpreters, has misled many into thinking them as adversaries.

Given the prescience and ingenuity of their thinking, it is easy to label both of these thinkers as 'philosophical geniuses', but if so, then we must follow their own advice and do so non-metaphysically since both conceive of the genius as much more of a 'serious worker' than divinely inspired. There is, Nietzsche argues, no fundamental difference between the activity of the genius and that of 'the inventor of machines, the scholar of astronomy or history, the master of tactics. . . . Genius too does nothing except learn first how to lay bricks then how to build. . . . Every activity of man is amazingly complicated, not only that of the genius: but none is a "miracle"' (HH 162). Genius is something we acquire through *praxis* alone:

> Do not talk about giftedness, inborn talents! One can name great men of all kinds who were very little gifted. They acquired greatness, became 'geniuses' (as we put

it), through qualities the lack of which no one who knew what they were would boast of: they all possessed that seriousness of the efficient workman which first learns to construct the parts properly before it ventures to fashion a great whole; they allowed themselves time for it, because they took more pleasure in making the little, secondary things well than in the effect of a dazzling whole. (HH 163)

Sartre concurs wholeheartedly on this point, agreeing that genius is as genius *does*: 'The genius of Proust is the totality of the works of Proust; the genius of Racine is the series of his tragedies, outside of which there is nothing' (EH 32–3). He describes in his autobiography how his own works are more the result of perspiration than inspiration as they 'reek of sweat and effort' (W 103).

'Each individual', according to Sartre, 'moves History forward by recommencing it, as well as by prefiguring within himself new beginnings yet to come' (1974: 166). Alongside their cultivated genius, I have set out also to expose some of their all-too-human prejudices, such as Nietzsche's aristocratism and *ressentiment* and Sartre's residual anthropocentrism/exclusivism, showing that, as Nietzsche said, despite our spirals of self-overcoming, 'we remain under the sway of that world we receive as a legacy from our youth'.[1] But breaking through the logic of modernity (even if they couldn't completely erase it in their thinking), both philosophers, as 'posthuman progenitors' and 'inverted Platonists', supplied a philosophical groundwork for, among other things, the deconstructed self; a relational ontology of interconnectedness; an enchanted, magical view of nature as a sympoietic aesthetic assemblage; a pluralist ethico-political vision that goes beyond the antinomies of modernist thinking in eliciting vital forms of subjectivity and collectivity; a Dionysian ethic of musical intoxication and play; a concept of affectivity and vicarious causation; an androgynous conception of gender; and a deconstructionist method of inversion and displacement.

Prefiguring Derridean deconstruction, their 'inverted Platonism' does not exclude subordinated terms, however, but sublimates them into a 'mediated' or 'modified' Third, evidenced, for example, in Sartre's concept of 'lived experience' as an amalgam of 'unconscious-conscious'. Although Nietzsche disparages the dialectic (TI 2.6, WP 431), he employs a form of non-Hegelian dialectical thinking that Sartre expands and elucidates brilliantly in the *Critique*, a 'decapitated dialectic' that incorporates openness, sublimation, contingency and emergence. Embracing ambiguity dialectically without metaphysical consolations or analytical closure, they confront the problem of freedom and existential meaning in a contingent universe without extrinsic purpose or design. Like a dice game, even the origin of those things we take to be necessary (our mental categories, knowledge, reason) are the products of chance and historical circumstance (Z 1.16). In Z 1.1 Zarathustra celebrates this contingency. The struggle against the dragon is for chaos against a fixed order since 'one must have chaos within one still, in order to give birth to a dancing star' (Z P5). And yet, amidst this contingency, both thinkers impose an existential and ethical imperative. For Nietzsche, humans must be liberated from chance as from priests (EH 3D2), from the diversion of the aimless and incidental (D 150, A 58) or from the rule of chance in human evolution (HH 24). Great culture must will some underlying necessity so that it becomes a willed achievement. There is an intimate relation between culture and the artist (BGE 62, Z 3.1) such that, for instance, Wagner could not have come about by chance (UM 4.5–6). Nietzsche also views self-overcoming as a necessity not an accident by imposing a single taste or self-imposed law on the multiplicity of drives (GS 290, GS 277, Z 2.20). In the stage of higher spiritual liberation, 'one should replace everything that is contingent-natural in relation to life with something that is chosen-necessary' (KSW 8.23, 8.426). Freedom and necessity are thus not opposites that exclude each other but implicated in one another as dialectical coordinates. Knowledge of necessity becomes a form of freedom (Z 3.12.2, BGE 213), allowing us '*to seize hold of chance by the forelock!*' (BGE 274) and so avoid the impasses of nihilism.

Viewed from the outside, Nietzsche and Sartre were stuck in the paradox of meaning that their philosophy laid bare. We are inescapably condemned to meaning in an objectively meaningless universe. In such a Heraclitean universe of becoming and passing away and in the quantum reality of dissipative systems without cosmic or moral purpose, the notion of progress seems a spurious concept since 'becoming aims at *nothing* and achieves *nothing*' (WP 12A).[2] However, such a 'view from above' ignores the phenomenological perspective of the philosopher, the intentional and existential view 'from the inside', and the counter-cry of active nihilism that is the enduring hallmark of their ethical thinking. Curbed of metaphysical consolations and idealist illusions, they provide us with an earthly compass to navigate the twenty-first century and the age of the Anthropocene, responding to our present predicament in all its contingency by urging humanity on affirmatively 'as Diogenes did, by walking' (CDR 806).

Nietzsche defines the true philosopher as a 'liberator' (UM 3.1) and it is in this light that I present Sartre and Nietzsche – as twin thinkers of freedom, but not, of course, abstract freedom in the metaphysical sense that they relentlessly critiqued in their terrasophical thinking. In broad terms, both can be characterized as 'philosopher doctors' or 'spiritual physicians',[3] analysing patterns of thinking and opinions, spiritual and moral ailments or bewitchments 'which have so deranged mankind!' (D 563) and practising a form of 'existential psychoanalysis' directed towards the 'art and science of healing' (D 202). In asking what philosophers have previously lacked, Nietzsche suggests a three-pronged answer: '(a) an historical sense, (b) knowledge of physiology, (c) a goal in the future' (WP 408). Along with Sartre's, his philosophy represents a form of 'unveiling' or demystification, identifying patterns of philosophical befuddlement, bad faith and asceticism with a view to eliminating them and replacing them with a creative, playful, terrestrial and aesthetic eudaimonist ethics. In the precarious posthumanist/transhumanist crossroads of our present time, their parallel thinking as 'a totalization of knowledge, a method, a regulative Idea, an offensive weapon, and a community of language' (SM 6) is needed as a crucial vector for the future to go beyond ultra-humanism and the ravages of modernity more than ever. Consigning them to the nineteenth century, or indeed the twentieth century, is thus a serious mistake since, as I have set out to demonstrate, they clearly foreshadowed many of the dominant themes in contemporary posthumanist thinking. As Negri said of Marx, the same is also true of these two extraordinary existentialists – just as we feel that we are over them and have got beyond them, we are forever discovering that they were already there long before us.

Notes

Introduction

1. As Cox (2016: 76) writes: 'the moustache, for Sartre, became the emblem of the shallow, self-satisfied, respectable, reactionary middle-class gentleman that he despised even more than crustaceans.' According to Burnier, one of Sartre's self-professed most successful ventures was to deter a number of young men from growing moustaches (in Boulé 2005: 89). Roquentin, the protagonist of *Nausea*, leaves us in no doubt how he feels about moustaches: 'The fine gentleman exists Legion of Honour, exists moustache, that's all . . . he sees the two pointed ends of a moustache on both sides of the nose; I do not think therefore am moustache' (N 147).
2. See Daigle (2009: 57).
3. While at the Lycée Louis-le-Grand, for instance, Sartre and Nizan would occasionally refer to themselves as 'supermen'. One should also not take at face value Sartre's oft-quoted youthful remark about Nietzsche in the *Carnets Midi* – 'He is a poet who had the bad fortune to be taken for a philosopher' (EJ 471). In Aron's *Mémoires*, he reports that Sartre wrote an essay for one of Brunschvicg's seminars arguing firmly against this view that Brunschvicg himself espoused (see Flynn 2014: 28).
4. See Boulé (2005: 53). Boulé points out that Frédéric shares Sartre's own characteristics of being a prankster, looking awkward in fashionable clothes and feeling lonely even as the 'dominant male' at the epicentre of his group of friends. Noudelmann (2012: 46) suggests that Richard's sarcastic treatment from Sartre is a tacit swipe at his grandfather, Charles Schweitzer, describing, with a 'flagrant anti-German' tinge, for example, how his 'arrogance' comes to the fore when he sings with an exaggerated movement of the jaw, 'his lips ferociously revealing his teeth'.
5. See Flynn (2014: 38).
6. See Flynn (2014: 45).
7. There are three other references to Nietzsche in *Being and Nothingness*. The second (favourable) reference is to Nietzsche's 'become what you are' which he translates as 'become what I was' (BN 189), the third a casual reference, and the fourth an identification of the will to power with libido as a 'psychobiological residue' (BN 741) which he translates as *volonté de puissance*.
8. See Flynn (2014: 200).
9. See Woodward (2011: 42) and Churchill (2013: 47).
10. See also Contat and Rybalka (1981: 1663) and Boulé (2005: 86). I address this more fully in the next chapter.
11. For Solomon, Sartre is 'the ultimate individualist' (1988: 173), and 'the basic ontology Sartre accepts is . . . a Cartesian one' (1988: 179).

12 See Reynolds and Woodward (2011) for a succinct overview of these similarities. This is a case, as Webber (2018) advises, of 'rethinking existentialism' beyond common misconceptions and distortions.
13 See Ansell-Pearson (2011) who asks this question about Nietzsche and decides that he is both. Analysing the 'existential signatures' in Nietzsche, Bergoffen (2002: 84) concurs, stating that it should not be conceived as an 'either/or' choice.

Chapter 1

1 See Beauvoir (1981:165–6). Nietzsche also expresses an admiration for Stendhal – 'one of the most beautiful accidents of my life' who 'took away from me the best atheistical joke that precisely I might have made: "God's only excuse is that he does not exist"' (EH 2.3).
2 If, as Flynn notes (2014: 314), these two elements lived in creative tension in Sartre's work, the philosophical gene emerged as dominant in his later years after he bid his farewell to imaginative literature in *Words*.
3 See Charmé (2020: 258). Heldt (2020: 162–3) describes this process in the framing of the self as 'Memorial Totalization' wherein 'both aspects of the dialectical relationship between the subjective and the objective, between the psychic life of the individual and the world of which it is a part' are considered. The dynamics of 'memorial appropriation' refers to 'a particular facet of the unifying and multiplying activity of (self-)temporalization (and psychic spatialization) . . . [that] remains, in unreflective lived experience, predominantly *non-thetic*'. Nietzsche captures mnemotechnics with the following aphorism, giving full sense to Heldt's notion of 'memorial appropriation': '"I have done that", says my memory. "I cannot have done that", says my pride, and remains adamant. At last – memory yields' (BGE 68).
4 See Davis (2011: 140), Boulé (2005: 86) and Contat and Rybalka (1981: 1663) who warn against assimilating Sartre directly to his literary characters.
5 See Solomon (2003: 407) for a good account of Nietzsche's *ad hominem* method.
6 Sartre also recognizes the merits of the aphoristic or notebook form, which of course he utilized in his *War Diaries* and his *Notebooks from Youth*: 'this free and fragmented form isn't subject to prior ideas, you write each thing according to the moment and only take stock when you want to' (1983: 14).
7 As Catalano notes (2010: 203), in spite of Sartre's insistence in *The Family Idiot* on the 'Universal Singular' and the importance of Gustave's choice in determining his writing self, he hints in the concluding paragraph that a proper reading of the text will show how it was the 'objective spirit' of art for art's sake that prompted Flaubert to write rather than individual predilection or 'original choice'.
8 See Schrift (1990: 109).
9 See Mueller (2019: 46).
10 Nietzsche and Sartre were both fond of this exercise of overwriting original texts. As a young boy Sartre would directly base his stories in a plagiaristic way on those he had just read in comics and adventure books, overwriting odd sections or phrases. Given La Fontaine's *Fables* by his grandfather, he recounts how 'I decided to rewrite them in alexandrines' (W 90) and how making minor alterations to texts 'enabled me to blend memory and imagination' (W 91). Nietzsche took a similar approach to his piano playing, learning complex pieces by his favourite composers but never reproducing

them to the strict edicts of the written score, preferring instead to infuse them with his own extemporizations.
11 See Woodward (2011: 92).
12 In *Ecce Homo*, Nietzsche is much more disparaging of his 'German blood' and the 'German spirit', proposing the word 'German' as 'an international coinage for . . . psychological depravity' and as singularly 'lacking the idea of depth' (EH 3CW3).
13 Cf. HH 185 '*The paradoxes of an author*. The so-called paradoxes of an author, which a reader objects to, are often not at all in the author's book but rather in the reader's head' where he hints at such a sublimating logic.
14 *Words* is littered with accounts of Sartre's self-transfigurations enacted through the regular shifting of perspective: 'I never stopped creating myself; I was both giver and gift' (W 23); 'Above all, I had to renounce myself' (W 102); 'I have often written them against myself' (W 103); 'I came to think systematically against myself to the point of weighing the evidence for an idea by how much I disliked it' (W 156).
15 Characterizing Sartre as 'a play of temperamental opposites', Boulé (2005: 119) cites the testimony of Perrin, a priest in the Stalag where Sartre was held as a prisoner of war who described him as a 'steamroller' with 'the milk of human kindness'.
16 Also: 'I've changed like everyone: within a permanence' (cited in Flynn 2014: 377).
17 *Zarathustra* is often considered as a 'transitional' or 'bridge' text that links the middle texts to the late ones.
18 See Schrift (1990: 16).
19 See, for instance, Verkerk (2020: 11).
20 See, for instance, Betschart (2016), Boulé (2005), Lacoste (1999) and Murphy (2020).
21 See, for instance, Cumming (1981), Mirvish (1994), Remley (2020), Heldt (2020) and O'Shiel (2020).

Chapter 2

1 He speaks dismissively of the fabricated character of *The Will to Power*, 'the so-called major work' (1987: 3:10) that contains a 'mixing' of passages 'from many different periods' (1987: 3:13).
2 According to Beauvoir (1977: 288–9), the one occasion Sartre met Heidegger, Marcel's play (*La Dimension Florestan* which parodied Heidegger) was 'all they talked about'. Heidegger was unaccustomed to seeing himself in satire and Sartre politely apologized on behalf of his compatriot.
3 According to Richmond (2018: xxvii), Heidegger's influence pervades *Being and Nothingness*, though Sartre does not always acknowledge it, citing four main elements that derive from Heidegger: (i) his *Being and Time* might have inspired Sartre's title, (ii) his deployment of anguish as apprehension of freedom, (iii) his decision to make nothingness a central philosophical category and (iv) his emphasis on 'throwness', 'instrumentality' and authenticity. Kirkpatrick (2017a) and Baugh (2020) argue that the influence of the three 'Hs' (Hegel, Heidegger, Husserl) on Sartre is overemphasized at the expense of his French influences, such as the French Mystics and French interpreters of the three 'Hs'. In support of this second view, it should be noted that, in a letter to Marcel (1943), Sartre expresses gratitude to Marcel for being the primary inspiration for his theory of embodied consciousness and idea of 'situatedness' (which are often automatically attributed by scholars to Heidegger's influence).

4 See Perrin (2020: 264–6).
5 See Burnham (2017: 215) and Perrin (2020: 265–6).
6 See Warren (1991: 34–6) for an elaboration of this point.
7 See Schrift (1996: 336) and Woodward (2011: 337) for a good account of Derrida's use of Nietzsche.
8 As Schrift (1990: 14, 17, 52) remarks, Heidegger's Nietzsche may be more 'excellent Heidegger' than it is 'good Nietzsche', involving a wilful dogmatic reading of a text in accordance with a pre-existing schema of interpretation by 'overdetermining Nietzsche's philosophy as metaphysical'. This is a case of 'appropriation becoming *ex*propriation' that demonstrates the kind of 'incapacity for philology' Nietzsche criticizes in A 52.
9 It is said that Foucault's editor at Gallimard insisted on the removal of many anti-Sartrean remarks from the manuscript of *The Order of Things* before its publication. In riposte to Foucault, Sartre argued that what Foucault offers is not an *archaeology* of human thought but a *geology* of successive levels: 'But Foucault doesn't tell us what would be the most interesting, namely, how each thought is constructed from these conditions or how men move from one thought to another. For that he would have to allow praxis and thus history to intervene, and that is precisely what he refuses to do. To be sure, his perspective remains historical. He distinguishes epochs, a before and after. But he replaces the movie with the magic lantern, movement with a succession of immobilities' (1966: 87).
10 During the 1960s, Sartre exchanged some lively arguments with Lacan concerning freedom, the self, language and the unconscious (see Sartre 1966). Several scholars, however, detect a strong Sartrean influence on Lacan's (early) thinking on subjectivity – see, for example, Charbonneau (1999) and Richards (2019). Perhaps the most vitriolic attack on Sartre came from Althusser who wrote in graphic terms in February 1964: 'He has to be shaken out of his happy psychosis and only a whip will do it.' Referring to *Words*, Althusser states, 'when you think that such a theoretical mess . . . serves as thought – or saves the bother of thinking – for so many men . . . I can see only the whip across the face as a way to silence him or send him back to literature' (1998: 518). In November of the same year, however, he also wrote 'about Sartre: did I tell you I have always recognized in him an incomparable genius' (1998: 580).
11 See Howells (1992, 1999), Davis and Davis (2019), Davis (2011), Baugh (1999), Chambers (2019), Martinot (1999), Sawyer (2015) and Reynolds (2006).
12 He does criticize Sartre, however, for confining this to 'the "Look"' in *Being and Nothingness* and falling back on a subject/object distinction. Deleuze was also critical of Sartre's *Existentialism Is a Humanism* which he felt repeated Kantian tropes of humanist and universalist thinking (as did Sartre himself).
13 Cited in Young et al. (2013: 271).
14 See, for instance, Daigle (2009, 2011), Tubert (2018), Richardson (2009), Safranski (2003), Solomon (2003), Haar (1988) and Megill (1985).
15 As we will see in the next chapter, Sartre's 'pre-reflective' (*Being and Nothingness*) or 'irreflective' (*The Family Idiot*) cogito is far removed from the transparency and detachment of the Cartesian cogito and much closer in nature (though not identical) to Freud's Unconscious.
16 See Ally (2017) and Flynn (2014) for a clear analysis of Sartre's abiding phenomenological method of doing philosophy.
17 See Tubert (2018: 223–5) for an overview and critique of this view.

18 Nietzsche also extends this phenomenological approach in our relation to other people as a form of analogical introjection or transference into a first-person perspective: 'To understand another person, that is, *to imitate his feelings in ourselves*' (D 142).
19 This phrase is Merleau-Ponty's (1968: 69).

Chapter 3

1 According to Gardner (2009: 1), this shows an irresolvable tension in Nietzsche since 'there is a striking lack of fit between the . . . conception of the self that is presupposed by his practical philosophy' and the theoretical self that he dissolves. He posits the self as a fictive entity while requiring a substantive notion of selfhood for his normative project. What Gardner misses here is that Nietzsche's 'revisionary self' (Riccardi 2018: 187) and 'new version of the soul hypothesis' are altogether different from the fictive egoic substantial self that he critiques. Not *all* conceptions of selfhood are 'fictive', for Nietzsche, although they are emergent, transitory and derivative from pre-reflective consciousness or 'herd-consciousness' as I argue below.
2 See Warnock (1989: 135) and Solomon (2003: 225).
3 See Ure (2015) and Cannon (2013) who view Nietzsche and Sartre primarily as *therapists* whose aim is to cure psychological and philosophical bewitchments that lead to ascetic morality and tropes of bad faith.
4 Cited in Manschot (2021: 30).
5 As Ferrando (2020: 126) notes, Nietzsche's Lamarckism should not be read deterministically or metaphysically as an 'either/or', for Lamarck posited an internal force in organisms where individuals in a species 'willed' themselves to change. This connects to the science of 'epigenetics' in which the effect of environmental factors on the genetic make-up of an organism demonstrates the irreducible intra-actions and intra-changes between things – a 'link between nature and nurture'.
6 See Manschot (2021: 88).
7 Beauvoir (1984: 288) relates that, as an adult, Sartre felt people were often unfriendly to him as a result of his ugliness. As he remarked: 'if you are ugly, then asking the way to the Rue de Rome means inflicting a disagreeable presence on the person you ask.'
8 See Boulé (2005: 182).
9 See HH 543 where Nietzsche also illustrates such a unity: '*Embodiment of the spirit.* When a man thinks much and cleverly, not only his face, but also his body takes on a clever look.'
10 See Howells (2011: 32), Sutton Morris (1999: 84) and Morris (2020: 235).
11 For instance, 'the truest caress consists in the contact made by the most carnal parts of the two bodies' (BN 522), also in *The Family Idiot*, 'woman making herself flesh in order to nourish, nurture, and caress the flesh of her flesh' (IF 1:47).
12 Howells (2011: 40) quotes Sartre himself who was critical of his own position on the body in *Being and Nothingness*, exclaiming in an interview in 1970: 'It's incredible: I really believed it.'
13 As Burnham (2015: 339) notes, Nietzsche thinks of heaviness as a burden that prevents ascension and flight, like the camel at Z 1.1, and is associated with the 'spirit of gravity' (Z 1.7, Z 3.11) characterized by seriousness, deliberation in thought

and action rather than by instinct (TI 6.2). In his middle works, he links heaviness with adherence to rules or structures imposed externally (moral laws from God or nature).
14. At Z 2.7, Zarathustra states that the unfulfilled moral feeling of the parent is regularly acted out by the children: 'What the father kept silent, that comes in the son to be spoken and often I found the son to be the father's unveiled secret.'
15. Although Nietzsche presents individuality as deriving from the herd requirement to be able to make promises and form a moral conscience in order to follow social rules, he shows how in older historical times: 'To be a self and to esteem oneself according to one's own weight and measure – that offended taste [in the past] . . . There is no point on which we have learned to think and feel more differently' (GS 117).
16. See Charmé (2020: 262).
17. See Martinot (1999: 50).
18. See Solomon (2003: 180).
19. See Solomon (2003: 207) who argues that Nietzsche's ideas of *amor fati* and eternal recurrence of the same are best read not as fatalism but as 'basically a form of compatibilism'.
20. Hayman (1982: 28) records how Nietzsche put a handful of lit matches onto his palm at Pforta in imitation of the Roman soldier, Gaius Mucius Scaevola, who had put his hand into a fire to demonstrate his indifference to pain. In his time at Pforta, '[h]is desire for self-mastery made him willing to accept a stringent discipline, while his submissiveness was fortified by fanatical piety'. Safranski (2003: 45) also notes how Nietzsche practised asceticism on himself. In Leipzig between 1866 and 1868, for instance, in order to gain mastery over himself, he imposed a strict regime of minimal sleep, a restricted prescribed diet and long periods of solitude.
21. See Richardson (2020: 187).
22. In Verkerk's (2020: 93) words, 'consciousness and the activation of the intellectual conscience brings Apollonian structure and semblance to the Dionysian will to power and allows for the human to emerge as a creative being that employs its reflective and communicative skills to sublimate the drive into something new'.
23. Plank (1998: 375) is one of the few to notice the similarity between the 'terrible joy' of the Dionysian and the nausea felt by Roquentin as he loses his individuality and becomes totally enmeshed in Nature in apprehending the brute existence of the chestnut tree.
24. Richardson refers to this as '*self out of multiple parts*' and the '*self out of enveloping other*' (2020: 419, 424).
25. See Richardson (2020: 419).
26. See Howells (1979: 1–2).
27. See Flynn (2014: 68).
28. Sartre locates this in the pre-reflective cogito where 'any conscious existence exists as the consciousness of existing' (BN 12).
29. As Solomon (2003: 79) rightly observes, Sartre's development of emotion as 'a different way of eluding a difficulty, a particular way of escape, a special trick' (STE 25) overlaps with Nietzsche who showed how passions are not just physiological disturbances but also involve an emotional intelligence and an element of strategic agency. For Nietzsche, pity is an expression of egoism and fear (HH 103), magnanimity is cloaked egoism and revenge (GS 49), neighbourly love is a way to avoid self-reflection rather than a concern for others (Z 1), generosity is motivated

by a desire to rule over others (Z 3), humility is 'timid baseness' (GM 1.14), a means to gain moral superiority, and erotic love is a form of possessive greed (GS 14).

30 As Boulé (2005: 113) notes, Sartre himself was apt (along with others) to over-rationalize his self and his work. When he submitted himself to a Rorschach test in 1960, he was surprised to find out that, according to Denise Pouillon, it revealed a creativity springing from affects rather than from logic or rational reflection. '[I]t was obvious', she recorded, 'that for Sartre emotions were not a temporary state but the very fabric of his life.'

31 As Burnham (2015: 8–9) notes, despite his valorization of play, Nietzsche is ambivalent about acting. The actor is often used pejoratively as vain and fake (UM 1.10) or as a sorcerer (Wagner in Z4 5.2). He bemoans the use of actors in the Greek chorus to represent mythic figures (BT 5, 12) and views acting as forming a pretence that is bred in certain classes or groups as a requirement of constant adaptation (D 306, GS 356). However, Nietzsche praises Odysseus' self-possession by wearing masks without having any faith in them (D 306), and, of course, he identifies himself with Dionysus, the god of masks. Nietzsche's pejorative remarks are directed towards forms of *Schauspiel* that involve bad faith or 'metaphysical consolation'.

32 See Sawyer (2015: 46).

33 Although some read the conclusions of *Being and Nothingness* as 'bleak' and 'pessimistic', we misunderstand Sartre if we ignore this progression of his analysis in which he weaves the ontic facts of our current existence into the more generalized ontological structures of existence (see Webber 2011: 182). Sartre's discussion of interpersonal relations, for instance, cannot be arguing for the pessimistic view that human interaction is necessarily (ontologically) conflictual but is rather intended to show that such alienating relationships are inevitable within patterns and projects of bad faith. Bad faith is endemic in capitalist society but it is contingent and not necessitated by the basic structures of human existence: 'bad faith is the corruption from which authenticity is recovery' (Webber 2011: 187).

34 Simont (1992: 193) describes Sartre's ideal of authenticity as one of the 'aesthetic attitude' in which he links generosity and gift-giving to the work of art. According to Wittmann (2009: 19–20), '[o]ne can accuse Sartre of many mistakes, but he never questioned the connection between art and freedom, which he regarded as indissoluble'. In Sartre's aesthetics, art is given a particular function. It points the way into the future and anticipates something 'by revealing what a human being can one day make of himself, of his life or of his work and even of the world'.

35 In Sutton Morris' (1997) view, Foucault emphasizes conscious self-control and fashioning more than Sartre whose freedom is more pre-reflective, involving the conscious relation of self to itself through the writing of diaries and meditational practices more than the agent engaged practically in the world as a 'lived body'.

36 See Howells (1992, 1999), Baugh (1999), Sawyer (2015) and Chambers (2019).

37 The poststructuralist advocacy of 'transgressive practices' and 'limit experiences' echoes the importance given to the experience of 'extreme' or 'boundary' situations in existentialist philosophy. 'In these situations', as Mitchell (2020: 6, 22) writes, 'one is no longer be governed by internalized norms and is thus free to invent oneself'. Jolted into sharp relief by the dramatic presentation of extreme situations, authenticity can be attained when one's experience reveals the pre-reflective self behind the masks and disguises that no longer function. Authenticity thus cannot be achieved simply by reflecting deeply on the events of our lives for it involves

the pursuit of, and openness to, exceptional and boundary experiences as well as a continual awareness of, and resistance to, social and existential structures that inhibit it.

Chapter 4

1. See Schrift (1995: 257–63).
2. As Woodward (2011: 74) notes, the poststructuralist relation to Hegel is akin to the one with structuralism – more of a critical transformation than outright rejection, more 'post' Hegel than 'anti' Hegel. Reynolds (2006: 165) suggests deconstruction was perhaps influenced and pre-empted by Merleau-Ponty's 'hyper-dialectic' articulated in *Visible and Invisible* (which is similar in turn to Sartre's 'decapitated dialectic' in the *Critique*).
3. See Richardson (2020: 367).
4. Nietzsche especially denies *being dualism* where things are grounded in distinct ontological realms and 'the things of the highest value must have another, peculiar origin – they cannot be derived from this transitory, seductive, deceptive, paltry world' (BGE 2). He also rejects both sides of Cartesian duality – there's no 'merely material body' (as conceived by Descartes) just as there is no incorporeal body.
5. See Siemens (2015: 97–8).
6. In philosophical posthumanism, *relata* do not precede relations, but relations do not precede *relata* either: 'relata and relations generate out of co-constitutive, embodied, agential processes, situated in specific spatio-temporal environments', therefore neither is primary (Ferrando 2020: 165).
7. To grasp Sartre's 'Cartesianism' in *Being and Nothingness*, it is essential *ab initio* to note the distinction between Cartesian philosophy (the rationalistic analysis of the structures of individual existence) and the philosophy of Descartes (dualism, *ego-cogitans*). Sartre doubtlessly inherited the influence of the former (largely through the philosophy of his 'Mentor', Husserl) but not the latter, and it is perhaps the failure to recognize this that leads certain scholars to conclude erroneously that '*Being and Nothingness* is actually an essay in Cartesian dualism' (McCann 2011: 202). If Sartre *inherited* a Cartesian framework of understanding from Husserl, he *bequeathed* a distinctly anti-Cartesian schema, one that is evident even in his early work.
8. According to Flynn (2014: 317), Sartre's dialectical thinking begins in his early phenomenology with his correction of Husserl and Descartes by granting ontological priority to pre-reflective consciousness above the reflective cogito.
9. For a critical review of this new translation and a list of the ways in which it improves upon Barnes' original translation in clarifying Sartre's philosophy, see Eshleman (2020b) and van den Hoven (2020).
10. Beauvoir recounted how Sartre was always reluctant to be cornered into sharp dichotomies when pressed by Aron's analytic approach into either/or choices – 'as there was more imagination than logic in his mental processes, he had his work cut out' (1983: 33).
11. Eshleman (2020a: 150) also posits a vertical axis of explanation, consisting of five different levels of analysis within which Sartre moves seamlessly but unpredictably – phenomenological, inferential, ontological, epistemological and metaphysical.

Phenomenological descriptions supply the evidentiary basis that leads to an inferential strategy that establish or justify ontological claims that in turn supply onto-ontological conditions that motivate speculative metaphysics.

12 See Ally (2017: 98).
13 See Eshleman (2011: 43) and Webber (2011: 182).
14 See Ally (2017: 128). Boxing, of course, is an apt metaphor for Sartre. As a young adult, the 'masculinist' Sartre boxed regularly and later he used the theme of boxing centrally in the *Critique* to explain the dynamic of the class struggle.
15 See Flynn (2014: 316).
16 See, for instance, Solomon (1988: 173) and Dobson (1993: 186).
17 See Perna (2007: 38) who draws firm parallels between Sartre's ontology of the group and Hardt's and Negri's (2005) concept of the 'multitude'.
18 The intermezzo, as Deleuze and Guattari theorize it, is the space of the ampersand, the conjunctive and 'included middle' in which we are able to 'pass between the traditional dualisms' (1987: 277). This consists, as Deleuze writes, of a 'set of these enveloping and enveloped intensities, of these individuating and individual differences which endlessly penetrate each other' (2004: 327). Rozehgy (2002: 117) argues that the category of 'the outside' and 'open space' that circulates in Deleuze's and Guattari's idea of smooth space is rooted firmly in the ontology of *Being and Nothingness* in which consciousness must constantly realize its being outside of itself, both temporally and spatially.
19 See Braidotti (1991: 67) who argues that Deleuze employs a modified dialectic. Aligning with Sartre's 'dialectic with holes' (NE 449), one might term this a 'dialectic with folds'.
20 In *The Antichrist*, he declares his allegiance towards science and truth against Christianity which has cleansed our culture of the scientific advances and understanding of the Ancient world (A 59).
21 It is said that Plato burned the works of Democritus.
22 See Ally (2017: 164, 174).
23 As Ally (2017: 180) notes, this also links Sartrean dialectics to the Niche-Construction Theory that emphasizes the capacity of organisms to modify their environment (and thereby natural selection) and act as co-directors of their own and other species' evolution.
24 Ally (2017: 332) and Farrell Fox (2020: 492–3) are exceptions to this but are suggestive rather than systematic. Plank (1998) provides an in-depth analysis of the relation between Nietzsche's will to power and quantum mechanics in *The Quantum Nietzsche*.
25 See Zohar (1991: 107).
26 See Zohar (1991: 95, 66) who states in Bose-Einstein condensates the many parts that make up an ordered system not only behave as a whole but also become a whole: 'their identities merge or overlap in a way that they lose their individuality – like individual voices in a chorus which become "one voice" at certain levels of vibration or harmony.'
27 Cited in Zohar (1991: 115, 155). Interestingly, Zohar's (1994: 106) analogical model for quantum interaction as an emergent collective reality is a free jazz jam session. Rhoad (2009: 167) argues exactly the same for Sartre's social ontology, proposing improvised jazz as illustrative of the intersubjective ethic of *Hope Now*. Unfortunately, Zohar is oblivious to Sartre's dialectical ontology in her brief allusions to his philosophy, accusing him erroneously of 'liv[ing] in the shadow of Descartes' isolated *cogito* and Newton's impenetrable billiard balls' (1991: 113).

28 This quantum penetration is evident in Sartre's own 'twinship transference' (Boulé 2005: 130) with Beauvoir, who, in Beauvoir's words, fused together '[l]ooking at the world in unison and sharing its enchantment' (1983: 259). In his letters to 'the beaver', Sartre describes her variously as 'my dear little you who are me' (1983b: 501), 'my little self' (1983b: 169), 'my little moral consciousness' (1983b: 180) and 'little paragon' (1983b: 95). He states that '[w]hatever I thought, it seemed as though I was saying it to you or rather that you were thinking it with me', that '[y]ou seem to have a surer sense of me than I do' and that 'I haven't stopped feeling that there's an internal link between us. [. . .] I had the feeling of two consciousnesses melted into one' (1983b: 417, 157). In his very earliest recollection of fusion, Sartre recalls in his youth running down the Place du Panthéon with his friends, playing ball and shouting in glee: 'I felt like steel, freed at last from the sin of existing . . . I was indispensable' (W 139).
29 See Mirvish (1996: 65, 69).
30 Just as Sartre devotes much space to his description of the 'viscous' in *Being and Nothingness* when illustrating the ontological continuity of *pour-soi/en-soi*, quantum biologists gave much of their early research to looking at the quantum properties of 'warm and sticky' phenomena, such as the brain, yeast cells and bacteria. See Zohar (1991: 77).
31 Following Haraway, Ferrando (2020: 140–1) prefers the term 'sympoiesis' which unfurls and extends autopoiesis to describe the fundamental exchanges between organism and environment since no system is self-producing or organizing.
32 According to Randall (2005: 83), the 'materialization' of matter occurs like the strings on a musical instrument. On a subatomic level, matter is not static and fixed but constantly vibrating, composed of tiny vibrating loops of energy, defined as strings. As the vibrations of strings produce different sounds, the vibrations of energy strings produce different kinds of particles and different modes of existence. There are no fundamental particles or atoms since '[e]ach and every particle corresponds to the vibrations of an underlying string, and the character of those vibrations determines the particle's properties. Because of the many ways in which strings can vibrate, a single string can give rise to many particles.' This is a musical conception of nature that resonates sonorously, as we will see in Chapter 7, with Nietzsche's and Sartre's Dionysian and ontogenetic view of art and music.

Chapter 5

1 Cf. Nietzsche – 'Fundamental thought: the new values must first be created – we shall not be *spared* this task!' (WP 979) and Sartre – 'You are free, so choose; in other words, invent' (EH 28) and 'What art and ethics have in common is that we have creation and invention in both cases' (EH 43).
2 There is a significant field of literature on this topic, but some of the most prominent advocates are Hatab (1995), Warren (1991), Siemens (2015), Connolly (1988) and Patton (2015). Additionally, Shapiro (2016), Lemm (2020) and Manschot (2021) give Nietzsche's democratic ethos a strong ecological inflection.
3 As Sartre was still working on the study in his later years, it would have been fascinating to view his analysis of Nietzsche's ethics in the light of the 'New Nietzsche' as presented by the French poststructuralists in the 1960s and 1970s.

4 This, it must be said, creates a certain tension in his thinking between his historical and naturalistic approaches (which we saw at play in his theorization of the self) that intensifies in his final period where he tends to replace psychological explanations with physiological ones. Megill (1985: 30), for instance, takes Nietzsche's morality to be anti-naturalistic to the extent that 'for any culture that is sufficiently self-conscious about its behaviour, the idea of naturalness has become so distant as to be useless, except as propaganda'. Richardson (2020), by contrast, posits Nietzsche as a thoroughly naturalistic philosopher. Reading Nietzsche dialectically, we can say that this opposition is sublimated within his concept of 'transfigured physis' (UM 2) as a 'nature-culture continuum'. As biological organisms we have natural drives but these are elastic in the sense that they are recursively affected by the cultural forms they take.

5 Richardson (2020: 355) refers to Nietzsche's value monism as a 'surprising, more radical analogue to [his] ontological monism'. In his attack on opposite values, he denies the opposition and strict separation of good and bad.

6 Elsewhere he posits honesty (BGE 227), scepticism/the abandonment of certainty (GS 347), the destruction of habituated beliefs (HH 225) and the pursuit of one's 'own experience' (HH 292) as the defining features and values of the 'free spirit'.

7 This is a view also taken by Linsenbard (2020: 291), Remley (2020: 277), Perna (2007: 47) and Mirvish (1996: 67).

8 See Webber (2018: 96–109) for a lucid commentary on the deeper ethical message of *Huis Clos*.

9 Although (contra Sartre) Nietzsche dismisses the idea of reciprocity as 'a piece of gross vulgarity' that assumes something I do can be done by another (WP 926), his concept of friendship (and the bad friend Zarathustra identifies who is like a leech) implies some form of reciprocity.

10 Flynn (2014: 361) refers to Sartre in this context as 'the moralist of paradox'.

11 Although *groupe-en-fusion* is often translated as 'fused group', 'fusing group' better captures Sartre's sense of fusion as an ongoing totalization rather than as fixed or static.

12 See Ansell-Pearson (1994: 3). Strong (1996: 132) asks whether Nietzsche really has a 'real' political doctrine. If so, he makes no attempt in finding an intersubjective standard by which policy can be judged and 'appears to make political action impossible, pointless or without standards'.

13 As Blue (2016: 146) observes, Nietzsche's time at Pforta was characterized by the conflicting desires of conformity and a growing rebellious individualism inspired by Schopenhauer. Despite his conservative upbringing, in 1861 he was drawn to the Hungarian poet Sándor Petőfi, a radical who had been a ringleader in the Revolution of 1848. As late as December 1864, he composed six songs based on Petőfi's texts and also gave expression to other revolutionary sentiments. In reaction to Wagner's essay 'Art and Revolution' of 1848, he exclaimed, for example, '[d]own with all art that does not by its very nature urge on to the revolution of society and the renewal and unity of the people!' (KSW 8.218).

14 See Ansell-Pearson (1994: 162, 96).

15 It should be noted that Nietzsche's aristocratism is not based on a simple class or economic distinction between the base rabble and the educated elites: 'there might still be a greater *relative* nobility of taste and tactfulness of respect within a people these days, within a lower sort of people, namely within the peasantry, than among the newspaper-reading *demimonde* of the spirit, the educated' (BGE 263).

16 See Verkerk (2020: 88) and Aydin (2007: 31).

17 Also, EH 4.1: 'And with all this there is nothing in me of the religion-founder – religions are mob-affairs. . . . I never speak to masses.'
18 See Zamosc (2018: 176–7).
19 According to Plank (1998: 128–30, 389), Nietzsche proposes a cosmology that subsumes the mental-physical and the scientific-moral, making possible 'a coherent Darwinian-evolutionary ethics in which the epigenetic has equal reality with the genetic'. Individuality (in the form of genetic diversity and variation) is essential for the biological integrity of the species since rigid encodement is evolutionarily degenerate just as it is for the moral integrity and advance of humankind.
20 See Richardson (2020: 237).
21 Also: '*Collective mind*. A good writer possesses not only his own mind but also the mind of his friends' (HH 180).
22 Nietzsche distinguishes between higher and lower forms of friendship based on the main criterion of reciprocity/non-reciprocity. Some people have nothing to bestow or offer in a friendship, suffering from greed or weakness, acting like secret thieves who manipulate situations for their own ends: 'With the eye of a thief it looks at everything that shines; with the greed of hunger it measures him who has plenty to eat; and it is always skulking around the table of those who bestow' (Z 1.22.1). Zarathustra's first friend is the corpse who weighs heavily on his shoulders and drags him down. His second is the jester, a companion who ridicules and pokes fun, ready to deceive at any moment.
23 This is not to say some of Nietzsche's insights cannot be used in turn to supplement Sartre's theory of mediations and ensembles. As Diers (1999: 254) notes, friendship is a topic to which Sartre granted very little attention. This deficiency can be seen as a weakness of the social theory that Sartre develops in the *Critique* since he stays on the 'historical' level of explanation and neglects the 'local' level where friendships develop and emerge. Ideally, Diers (1999: 255, 263) avers, we need to build a bridge between the two levels in order to explore friendship as 'a source of revolutionary praxis'.
24 See Boulé (2005: 76).
25 In March 1940, he writes that in the camp he seeks Grener's esteem because he is a worker despite the fact that he 'belches, farts, spits in constant floods' (1983a: 119).
26 Danto (1980: 12), for instance, describes Nietzsche as 'a critic of concepts and a word-tormenting anarchist'.
27 See Manschot (2021: 48).
28 Also, WP 744: 'An old Chinese said he had heard that when empires were doomed they had many laws.'
29 Although there is evidence to support mutually inconsistent ideologies (anarchist, totalitarian, classical liberal, radical liberal), in Hunt's (1993: 184, 65) view, Nietzsche's political orientation 'is clearly an instance of "individualist anarchism"' which he describes earlier as a 'liberalism with teeth'.
30 See Eshleman (2020), Heter (2020), Remley (2018), Betschart (2016), Farrell Fox (2003) and McBride (1991) for characterizations of Sartre as 'a deeply anarchistic thinker' (Heter 2020: 528) of a 'unique but unfinished version of democratic anarcho-socialism' (Eshleman 2020a: 20).
31 See Remley (2018: 206) and Heter (2020: 533) who reject common associations of Sartre's anarchism with Stirner's individualism.
32 See Betschart (2016) for a salient overview of Sartre's pluralistic politics.
33 See Heter (2020: 535).

34 Deleuze and Guattari both credit Sartre with inspiring their notion of the 'subject-group' as a basis for the production of richer modes of subjectivity (this they later modified to the 'collective assemblage of enunciation'). See Young et al. (2013: 148).

Chapter 6

1. The Anthropocene, also referred to as 'Anthrobscene', 'Capitalocene', 'Plantationocene' and 'Chthulucene' (Ferrando 2020: 105), describes the period of catastrophic environmental damage done to the Earth since the Industrial Revolution, and, in general, to describe the recognition of the intimate symbiotic connection between the actions of humans and the well-being of the planet. Most see the Anthropocene beginning with the Industrial Revolution, but others (e.g. Shapiro 2016: 202) view it as a process beginning with urban life and agriculture starting around 8,000–10,000 BCE.
2. See Woodward (2011: 187).
3. This exhortation is repeated when Zarathustra praises the tightrope walker for making danger his vocation (ZP 4) and talks about courage and seeking danger as main characteristics of the growth of the human (Z 4.15).
4. In Plank's (1998) view, both the evolutionary and juridical models work together in tandem in terms of the 'goal' of promoting plurality and singularity.
5. See Richardson (2020: 480).
6. See also (Verkerk 2020: 58) who argues that Nietzsche's aim 'is to eclipse the metaphysical faith of Christianity with a *post-metaphysical* approach to life'.
7. In the passage 'On Redemption', Zarathustra declares to a gathering of cripples who surround him that the redemption we should seek are opportunities to transform our experiences of earthly time rather than try to escape from it or reverse its marks.
8. See Ferrando (2020: 135).
9. See O' Shiel (2019: 113) for a good discussion of how the 'magic of experience' can, through modes of impure reflection, become 'dark forms' that lead to bad faith, addiction, madness and prejudice.
10. This is a point illustrated by E. M. Forster in *The Machine Stops* where Vashti contemplates the 'imponderable bloom' of real things compared to their impoverished digitally generated simulacra: 'she fancied that he looked sad. She could not be sure, for the Machine did not transmit *nuances* of expression. It only gave a general idea of people – an idea that was good enough for practical purposes. . . . The imponderable bloom, declared by a discredited philosophy to be the actual essence of intercourse, was rightly ignored by the Machine, just as the imponderable bloom of the grape was ignored by the manufacturers of artificial fruit' (2011: 5). Nietzsche makes a similar point in HH 218 when he speaks of the '*desensualization of higher art*' as leading to a 'coarsening of the senses'.
11. See, for instance, Deleuze (1977), Mellamphy (2015), Shapiro (2016) and Manschot (2021).
12. See Blue (2016: 59).
13. See Shapiro (2016: 13).
14. See Manschot (2021: 83, 151, 22).
15. For Nietzsche there is a productive tension in nature between the garden and the volcano wherein volcanoes are not only threats but also sources of nourishment for gardens. This is why we should '[b]uild our cities on the slopes of Vesuvius!' (GS 283).

16 See Manschot (2021: x).
17 Also, WP 540: 'There are many kinds of eyes. Even the sphinx has eyes – and consequently there are many kinds of "truths", and consequently there is no truth.'
18 See Richardson (2020: 161).
19 They describe *scenopoetes dentirostris*, a bird in the Australian rainforest, as 'a complete artist' (1994: 189).
20 See Ansell-Pearson (1997: 138, 124).
21 This is consistent with *The Transcendence of the Ego* where Sartre ascribes qualities and characters to things: 'It is a *property* of this Japanese mask to be terrible, an inexhaustible, irreducible property belonging to its very nature – and not the sum of our reactions to a piece of sculpted wood' (TE 89).
22 See Gorz (1966), McBride (1991) and Farrell Fox (2003), for instance.
23 Here I concur with Ally (2017: 39) who disagrees with McBride (1991: 74) that 'the early Sartre is of little use for the more positive task of constructing a suitable ecological ethic'. His early phenomenology of the affective dialectic between consciousness and world, as I have argued, contributes much to a Sartrean 'socioecological imaginary'.
24 As Ally (2017: 396–7) notes, this matter is not helped by Barnes' misleading translation of 'une rubrique categorielle' as '*the* rubric of a category'. This is also the case with Sheridan-Smith's translation of praxis in the *Critique* that leads us to think praxis is the *sole* or *primary* relation to matter rather than the first relation. Furthermore, Sartre's relentless use of qualifiers and modifiers in his texts are sometimes omitted in Sheridan-Smith's translation, giving us a sense of analytical closure in place of an open-ended integrative approach.
25 In a footnote in her translation to *Search for a Method*, for instance, Barnes writes, '[a]s Sartre uses it, praxis refers to any purposeful human activity' (SM 5).
26 It is as if, as Ally (2017: 370) remarks, we can find two Sartres in the same work (and breath) – the assertive Sartre of the text (where he makes bold exclusivist claims) and the querying Sartre of the footnote (where he questions them and suggests alternatives). We have less to learn from the assertive Sartre of the text, in Ally's view, than we do from the parenthetical Sartre who 'wears his [ecological] secrets on his sleeves'.
27 On this point I have to disagree with Reynolds' (2006: 164–5) statement – 'while Derrida's later interest in the question of animality can be seen to undermine aspects of Sartre's philosophy, animals were an ongoing concern of Merleau-Ponty's from the 1930s'. This is a slight oversight on Reynolds' part as elsewhere (2006, 2013) he writes with some perspicuity on the similarities between (Sartre's) existentialism and poststructuralism but here doesn't consider Sartre's comments (1981c, 2014, CDR) when representing his view.
28 See Boulé (2005: 29).
29 See, for instance, Coole (2005) and Abram (1997).
30 Against the charge that Sartre doesn't supply a concept of 'objective possibility' as the negative dimension (1973: 122), this ignores Sartre's *The Communists and Peace* where he does prefigure a concept of counter-finality that he would develop further in the *Critique*. Also, his criticism that Sartre's thinking 'derive[s] from his philosophy . . . of consciousness' (1973: 105) ignores the concept of Sartrean praxis that he had articulated as a literature of praxis in *What Is Literature?*. See Flynn (2014: 320–1).
31 See Boulé (2005: 29).

32 This phrase is used by Connolly (2011) to describe the emergent and shifting reality of assemblages.
33 Although Baudrillard (2003: 3) indicates that the trajectory of his thought should be understood as an examination of the object in opposition to phenomenological and existentialist views of the subject, interestingly he cites Sartre's depiction of Roquentin's encounter with the tree in the park as his prime inspiration for his 'philosophy of the object'.
34 'Ideas are worse seductresses than our senses' (GS 372). As Plank (1998: 256, 352) points out, Nietzsche recognized that humans and animals use unconscious systems of difference to achieve individuation, for example, by pheromone. His will to power can be compared to Deleuze's 'autoproductive unconscious' in the sense that it generates desire below the level of reflective consciousness through a synthesizing fusion of all senses.
35 This, of course, is exactly what Roquentin's nausea of the chestnut tree in the municipal park in *Nausea* reveals.
36 Nietzsche is often scathing about our 'human, all-too human' features: '*Most ugly*. It is to be doubted whether a well-traveled man has found anywhere in the world regions more ugly than in the human face' (HH 320). Also: '*Lower than the animal*. When man howls with laughter, he surpasses all animals by his coarseness' (HH 544).
37 According to Heidegger (1993: 243) in his 'Letter on Humanism' (1947): 'The first humanism, Roman humanism, and every kind that has emerged from that time to the present, has presupposed the most universal "essence" of man to be obvious. Man is considered to be an *animal rationale*. This definition is not simply the Latin translation of the Greek *zoon logon echon* but rather a metaphysical interpretation of it.'
38 It is interesting to note that *Existentialism Is a Humanism*, a lecture hastily delivered to dispel the charge that existentialism was a philosophy of pessimism, quietism and despair, was left by Sartre in the interrogative in French '*l'existentialisme, est-il une humanisme?*'.

Chapter 7

1 As Bakewell (2016: 323) writes, for instance, 'Sartre was a profound atheist, and a humanist to his bones. He outdid even Nietzsche in his ability to live courageously and thoughtfully in the conviction that nothing lies beyond, and that no divine compensations will ever make up for anything on this earth.'
2 See, for instance, Megill (1985) and Kirkpatrick (2017b).
3 Of Nietzsche's many criticisms of Christianity, its torturous aesthetic was a not insignificant one: 'what a wretched place Christianity has managed to make of the earth, merely by erecting the crucifix everywhere, thereby branding the earth as the place "where the righteous are tortured to death"!' (D 77). Indeed, for Nietzsche, Wagner committed the unpardonable aesthetic sin in his last opera *Parsifal* – he became a Christian (EH 2.5–6).
4 See Blue (2016: 127).
5 Despite his admiration for Jesus, although Nietzsche viewed the Old Testament as one of the greatest pieces of literature (BGE 52, GM 3.22), he believed the New Testament (following Luther's translation) marked a catastrophic turn in European history (WP 186).

6 See Golomb (2004: 178).
7 'Life desires ascent, and in ascending it will overcome itself' (Z 2.7), the teacher of the overhuman is 'he who will teach human beings to fly' (Z 3.11.2). Nietzsche describes free spirits as 'astronomers of the ideal' (D 551) and *aeronauts of the spirit* (D 573). It is, of course, possible to interpret these passages in a naturalistic or 'terrasophical' way, as Manschot (2021) does, for instance, linking Nietzsche's love of heights and ascent to his love of mountains and climbing.
8 See Parkes (1996: 373) and Richardson (2020: 477). Nietzsche's new religion is close to Buddhism, in Richardson's view, as it dispenses with gods and affirms existence. He is, however, critical of Buddhism's renunciation of the will which he views as a form of passive nihilism (GM P5, WP 155, WP 220).
9 See Richardson (2020: 363–5) and Plank (1998: 406) who ascribe pantheism to Nietzsche. Plank describes him as 'a pantheist and mystic without God'.
10 Nietzsche states that 'Zarathustra himself indeed is merely an old atheist' – he could believe in a god that dances but will not (WP 1038).
11 See Richardson (2020: 476).
12 Nietzsche puts the *Übermensch* where God once was – 'Once one said "god" when one looked upon distant seas; but now I have taught you to say: superman' (Z 2.2), but there is still room, as Richardson (2020: 475) argues, for the existence of many fictive gods in the creation of his ethical imaginary.
13 Dionysian intoxication, Nietzsche warns, should not to be confused with 'narcotization' that acts like a sedative rather than stimulant, for example, Wagner's music (EH 3HH3).
14 Charmé (1999: 302) contrasts Sartre's interest in religious concepts with Beauvoir's disinterest: 'Where Beauvoir saw only stinking garbage in the "compost of religion", Sartre found nourishment for his own budding vision of reality.'
15 As he recounts in *Words*, '[t]he myth was a very simple one and I swallowed it without difficulty . . . a vast collective power had penetrated me; lodged in my heart, it was keeping watch, it was the Faith of others' (W 155).
16 This passage illustrates perfectly Sartre's residual metaphysics woven, as Derrida said, into the very language it uses to attack it, where 'the end of Man is bound to be written in the language of Man' (Badmington 2000: 9). Sartre continued to use 'man' and 'fraternity' even in his depiction of a 'feminine economy' of thinking in his later years.
17 Sartre refers to his *War Diaries* as a 'proud, pagan journal' (WD 69).
18 As Ferrando (2020: 207) notes, mysticism was the preserve of women, their only access for 'words to be heard' due to their exclusion from Christian religious orthodoxy.
19 See Ally (2017: 32–3).
20 See Blue (2016: 40).
21 He tried to redeem this (unsuccessfully) by pursuing attempts to become an officer. By contrast, from 1929 to 1931 Sartre did his compulsory military service and refused to become a military officer, preferring instead to mix with private soldiers rather than the officers.
22 See Alfano (2018: 122, 126).
23 For other remarks that display Nietzsche's 'misogynistic straitjacket' (Verkerk 2020: 164), see EH 3.5, BGE 144, 232, CW 3, HH 435.
24 This is evidenced by the fact that Nietzsche consistently downplayed his mother's role in his upbringing and development, stating, aged twenty-one, 'the main points of my upbringing were left to me' (KGW 1.5.52) despite the fact, for instance, that he only

took responsibility for his own laundry from Franziska in 1868, aged twenty-four. Although, of course, she would later exert her influence in dramatic (and unfortunate) ways, his sister Elisabeth had regularly acted since childhood as a kind of amanuensis for her brother, transcribing his early plays and as a university student helping him to compile and index material. See Blue (2016: 106, 296, 307).

25 See Verkerk (2020: 32).
26 In *Ecce Homo*, for example, Nietzsche wonders, 'Do I dare to suggest that I *know* women? This is part of my Dionysian dowry. Who knows? Perhaps I am the first psychologist of the eternal-feminine' (EH 3.5).
27 As Burnham (2015: 34) notes, it is likely Nietzsche was influenced by the work of Swiss anthropologist Johann Bachofen, a source of the Apollo/Dionysus account who argued that the Dionysian was a 'transitional phase' between matriarchal societies (Gaia and Demeter) and the patriarchal stage of the Apollonian which included the formation of states and the 'male lust for struggle' (BT 21).
28 See Burnham (2015: 133).
29 Irigaray identifies the Presocratics after whom a rupture between poetry (feminine) and philosophy (masculine) took place, that, through language, marked the problematic differentiation of the sexes and 'the point at which male identity constituted itself as patriarchal and phallocratic' (cited in Woodward 2011: 151).
30 It is worth remembering, of course, that the *Übermensch* is not gendered.
31 Like David Oehler had been for Nietzsche, Sartre's grandfather Charles Schweitzer was his main male adult influence as a young boy, introducing him to a large library of books and ideas.
32 Gordon (2020: 508) notes the 'glaring absence' of the recognition of Beauvoir's influence on Sartre's thought and expresses surprise at her 'Heloïse complex' in insisting that she did nothing original in philosophy and that her writings were applications of Sartre's philosophy as a mere acolyte. As is the case with Merleau-Ponty, it is perhaps most useful to see Sartre's intellectual relationship with Beauvoir in simple terms as one of 'reciprocal influence', as in his description of himself and *le castor* engendering 'the feeling of two consciousnesses melted into one' (1983b: 157).
33 According to Noudelmann (2012: 19–20), '[t]he jelly that remained stuck to the mind's finger in *Being and Nothingness*, or the pebbly mud that had made Roquentin's hand sticky in *Nausea*, speak to a Sartrean repugnance at feeling one's own body plunge into a suspect substance'. More a 'masturbator of women' than a 'penetrating Hussar', Sartre himself caressed both beings and things, staying at their surface. This, of course, has parallels with Oliver's diagnosis of Nietzsche's abjection.
34 See Boulé (2005: 57).
35 While Lacoste plots with some acuity Sartre's passage to a fully feminine economy of reciprocal gift-giving, I do think she overstates differences between Sartre's early and later thinking, viewing them caesurally rather than as a form of continuous enrichment. As I argued in Chapters 4 and 6, the elements of Sartre's smooth ontology in *Being and Nothingness* are often overlooked and therefore it is misleading to equate the *pour-soi* straightforwardly with an abstract 'imperialistic stance' to appropriate, control and master the world as Lacoste (1999: 282) does.
36 See Lacoste (1999: 274).
37 See Boulé (2005: 195–6).
38 See Lacoste (1999: 293–4).
39 In interview with Gobeil, cited in Boulé (2005: 5).

40 Speaking about Lévy, Sartre states, '[y]ou were a man, but a man with feminine qualities.' Boulé suggests this may partly account for the rift between Lévy and Beauvoir. Just as Beauvoir represented for Sartre someone who had integrated her feminine and masculine aspects, Lévy was 'the male equivalent of Beauvoir' (see 1977c: 10).
41 Sartre associated music with feminine company. He did not own a piano so would play at Arlette's place, or his mother's or at his grandmother's when he was younger. Similarly, Nietzsche would always associate piano playing with a shared intimacy, a union of solitude and communication. He played fourhanded Haydn sonatas with Franziska and later he often played piano duets with Sophie Ritschl (as a student in Leipzig) and Lou Salomé. Both found solace in feminine company that suspended the power relations that often alienate the male psyche. Tellingly, Nietzsche had a preference for playing duets on two pianos whereas Sartre preferred to play fourhanded pieces on the same piano (where he could *feel* as well as hear the other). See Noudelmann (2012: 20–1, 113).
42 See Blue (2016: 76, 229, 147).
43 See Safranski (2003: 20–1).
44 Cited in Danto (1980: 50).
45 See Noudelmann (2012: 55, 63).
46 According to Siemens (2018: 324–6), Nietzsche's criticisms of Wagner play upon this notion of measure where genius must learn to measure itself or limit its dominant discharge through 'creative restraint'. Wagner created powerful and beautiful illusions that energized cultural life but lacked self-restraint and so became a tyrannical force without measure or limits. The trauma of Wagner's megalomania is 'clearly visible in the "exclusivity" of genius in the modern sense and the loathing of one-man rule Nietzsche shares with the agonal Greeks'.
47 With Wagner 'music has been deprived of its world-transfiguring, affirmative character, that is *décadence* music and no longer the flute of Dionysus' (EH 3WC1).
48 Nietzsche wrote of his own extreme physiological response to music and how it became 'a total digestive experience', recounting how his compulsive listening to *Carmen* reduced him to tears after concerts. See Noudelmann (2012: 92).
49 Nietzsche argues music must be understood geographically, praising Bizet for having 'discovered a piece of the *southernness of music*' (BGE 254) in contrast to German music of the North that 'loves clouds and everything that is unclear, becoming, twilit, damp, and overcast' (BGE 244). Deleuze links this to Nietzsche's 'geophilosophy' and to the close relations between sonority and territory in nature. See Shapiro (2016: 92).
50 See Flynn (2014: 36).
51 See Noudelmann (2012: 35).
52 Noudelmann (2012: 132, 44) notes how in this composition Sartre took his inspiration more from Debussy than from Chopin, making some use of Debussy's innovative and extended spacings but ultimately sticking to the sonata form instead of trying, through Debussy, 'to use intervals capable of disrupting traditional forms'.
53 Cited in Flynn (2014: 388).
54 See Rhoad (2009: 167) who views improvised jazz as the perfect analogue of Sartre's social ethics in *Hope Now*. In *Being and Nothingness*, Sartre describes rhythm as a unifying bond that facilitates fusion between individuals: 'the rhythm that I generate comes into being jointly with me and laterally, as a collective rhythm; it is *my* rhythm

to the extent that it is their rhythm, and *vice versa*. That is precisely the basis of the experience of the we-subject: in the end, it is *our rhythm*' (BN 559).
55 See Carroll (2006: 406).
56 See Noudelmann (2012: 44, 31).
57 Cited in Noudelmann (2012: 143).
58 Cited in Hayman (1982: 341).
59 See Blue (2016: 112).
60 See Safranski (2003: 179).
61 See Safranski (2003: 339).
62 See Hayman (1982: 341).
63 Interestingly, it was only when he was mad in 1890 that he wrote a love letter to Cosima Wagner whom Nietzsche liked and admired more than any other woman. See Hayman (1982: 122).
64 See Safranski (2003: 371).
65 He sought out Jacques Lacan for help and together they concluded that the crabs represented his 'fear of being alone' (in Gerassi 2009: 62–3).
66 See Boulé (2005: 76).
67 'What crabs? Are you mad? What crabs? Ah! Yes' (*The Condemned of Altona*). In Lethbridge's view (2015: 75), the crabs are, for Sartre, 'the symbolic representation of a deep-rooted Oedipus complex and its attendant castration anxiety' conceived as strange creatures that lurk in the dark depths of the Unconscious, rising to the surface intermittently to pinch with their sharp pincers.
68 See Cox (2016: 283).
69 See Beauvoir (1984: 110–1) and Kirkpatrick (2019: 373).
70 See Murphy (2020: 321). Interestingly, Caws (1999) changes his view of *Hope Now* from his previous one of scepticism to one of a more positive consideration, symbolizing a general trend in Sartrean scholarship towards this more sympathetic viewpoint (see, for instance, Murphy (2020), Boulé (2005), Santoni (1998) and Lacoste (1999)). As Caws writes, 'I felt along with many Sartre scholars a cognitive dissonance between the philosopher we knew through his earlier writings and the apparently pliable old man who seemed to talk about whatever his handler wanted him to . . . [but] . . . it was a mistake on all our parts to consign Sartre to complaisance or enfeeblement, to dismiss him as an old man led by the nose, to regard him as, in effect, as good as dead' (1999: 24).
71 When they interviewed Sartre not long before his death, Le Bitoux and Barbadette of *Le Gai Pied* remarked on his 'stupefying freshness' and 'extraordinary kindness'. See Lacoste (1999: 295).
72 See Boulé (2005: 183). Throughout the interview, Sartre and Lévy address one another with the informal 'tu' as a move to dissolve distinctions of class perpetuated through linguistic convention as he had done with all of his Maoist friends for whom he was not a celebrity but just one of them. After 1968, he also changes his lifelong dress code of formal tie and suit in order to embrace informality and avoid rigid bourgeois convention.
73 Betschart (2016: 5–6) brings attention to the political rupture between Sartre and Beauvoir that had taken place during the second round of the presidential elections in1974. Whereas Sartre did not vote, Beauvoir supported Mitterrand and by that became a social democrat. When we read the interviews of the 1970s in the order they were actually taken and not published, according to Betschart, we clearly

recognize a high consistency in the development of Sartre's ethical and political thinking in them.

Conclusion

1 Cited in Hayman (1982: 104). On the importance of childhood, see Sartre's concession to Freudianism in *Words* – 'Every man has his natural place; its altitude is determined neither by pride nor value: childhood decides' (W 60) – in addition to numerous passages in *The Family Idiot* and *Search for a Method*.
2 Also, 'the nineteenth century does not represent progress over the sixteenth . . . . "Mankind" does not advance' (WP 90). Sartre also views the idea of progress as highly questionable – see CDR 2:409 and CDR 33: 'what was progress becomes proposed solution, that is, closed in on itself and problematic.'
3 See Ure (2015: 163).

Bibliography

Abram, D. *The Spell of the Sensuous*. New York: Vintage Books, 1997.
Alfano, M. 'A Schooling in Contempt: Emotions and the Pathos of Distance'. In *The Nietzschean Mind*, edited by P. Katsafanas, 121–39. London: Routledge, 2018.
Ally, M. C. *Ecology and Existence: Bringing Sartre to the Water's Edge*. Lanham: Lexington Books, 2017.
Ally, M. C. 'The Logics of the *Critique*'. In *The Sartrean Mind*, edited by M. Eshleman and C. Mui, 362–75. London: Routledge, 2020.
Althusser, L. *Lettres á Franca (1961–1973)*. Paris: Stock/Imec, 1998.
Ansell-Pearson, K. *An Introduction to Nietzsche as Political Thinker: The Perfect Nihilist*. Cambridge: Cambridge University Press, 1994.
Ansell-Pearson, K. *Viroid Life: Perspectives on Nietzsche and the Transhuman Condition*. London: Routledge, 1997.
Ansell-Pearson, K. 'New Directions: Nietzsche'. In *The Continuum Companion to Existentialism*, edited by F. Joseph, J. Reynolds and A. Woodward, 290–99. London: Continuum, 2011.
Aronson, R. 'Sartre and Marxism: A Double Retrospective'. *Sartre Studies International* 1, no. 1/2 (1995): 21–36.
Aydin, C. 'Nietzsche on Reality as Will to Power: Towards an "Organization- Struggle" Model'. *The Journal of Nietzsche Studies* 33 (2007): 25–48.
Badiou, A. *Pocket Pantheon: Figures of Postwar Philosophy*, trans. D. Macey. London: Verso, 2009.
Badmington, N., ed. *Posthumanism*. New York: Palgrave, 2000.
Bakewell, S. *At the Existentialist Café: Freedom, Being and Apricot Cocktails*. London: Vintage Books, 2016.
Barad, K. 'Posthumanist Performativity: Toward an Understanding of How Matter Comes To Matter'. *Signs: Journal of Women in Culture and Society* 28, no. 3 (2003): 801–31.
Baudrillard, J. *Passwords*, trans. C. Turner. London: Verso, 2003.
Baugh, B. '"Hello, Goodbye": Derrida and Sartre's Legacy'. *Sartre Studies International* 5, no. 2 (1999): 61–74.
Baugh, B. 'French Influences'. In *The Sartrean Mind*, edited by M. Eshleman and C. Mui, 25–37. London: Routledge, 2020.
Beam, C. 'Sartre vs. Nietzsche: Will to Power, Platonism and Pessimism'. 1998. http://www.pengkolan.net/ngelmu/filsafat/index.php?nomor=27
Beauvoir, S. de. 'Merleau-Ponty et le pseudo-Sartrisme'. *Les Temps Modernes*, June–July 1955.
Beauvoir, S. de. *Force of Circumstance: Hard Times*. New York: Harper & Row, 1977.
Beauvoir, S. de. *La Cérémonie des adieux, suivi de Entretiens avec Jean-Paul Sartre*. Paris: Gallimard, 1981.
Beauvoir, S. de. *Prime of Life*, trans. P. Green. London: Penguin, 1983.

Beauvoir, S. de. *Adieux: A Farewell to Sartre*, trans. P. O'Brian. New York: Random House, 1984.
Beauvoir, S. de. *The Ethics of Ambiguity*, trans. B. Frechtman. New York: Citadel, 2000.
Beauvoir, S. de. *Simone de Beauvoir: Philosophical Writings*, trans. M. Timmerman. Urbana: University of Illinois Press, 2004.
Bell, L. *Sartre's Ethics of Authenticity*. Tuscaloosa: University of Alabama Press, 1989.
Bennett, J. *Vibrant Matter: A Political Ecology of Things*. Durham: Duke University Press, 2010.
Bennett, J. 'Vibrant Matter'. In *The Posthuman Glossary*, edited by R. Braidotti and M. Hlavajova, 447–8. London: Bloomsbury, 2017.
Bergoffen, D. 'Nietzsche's Existential Signatures'. *International Studies in Philosophy* 34/3 (2002): 83–93.
Betschart, A. 'Sartre's Anarchist Political Philosophy: A Draft for a Diverse Society?'. Presented at the 22nd Meeting of the North American Sartre Society, University of North Carolina, 2016.
Betschart, A. 'An Overview of the International Reception of Existentialism: The Existentialist Tsunami'. In *Sartre and the International Impact of Existentialism*, edited by A. Betschart and J. Werner, 1–41. London: Palgrave Macmillan, 2020.
Blanchot, M. *Entretien infini*. Paris: Gallimard, 1969.
Blue, D. *The Making of Friedrich Nietzsche: The Quest for Identity, 1844–1869*. Cambridge: Cambridge University Press, 2016.
Böhme, G. *Atmosphere: Essays on the New Aesthetics*. Frankfurt: Suhrkamp, 1995.
Boulé, J-P. *Sartre, Self-Formation and Masculinities*. London: Berghahn, 2005.
Braidotti, R. *Patterns of Dissonance*, trans. E. Guild. Cambridge: Polity Press, 1991.
Braidotti, R. *The Posthuman*. Cambridge: Polity Press, 2013.
Burnham, D. *The Nietzsche Dictionary*. London: Bloomsbury, 2015.
Butterfield, E. *Sartre and Posthumanist Humanism*. Oxford: Peter Lang, 2012.
Caeymaex, F. and G. Cormann. 'Sartre and Merleau-Ponty'. In *The Sartrean Mind*, edited by M. Eshleman and C. Mui, 475–86. London: Routledge, 2020.
Cannon, B. 'Psychoanalysis and Existential Psychoanalysis'. In *Jean-Paul Sartre: Key Concepts*, edited by S. Churchill and J. Reynolds, 76–92. Durham: Acumen, 2013.
Carroll, M. '"It Is": Reflections on the Role of Music in Sartre's *La Nausée*'. *Music and Letters* 87, no. 3 (2006): 398–407.
Catalano, J. *Reading Sartre*. Cambridge: Cambridge University Press, 2010.
Caws, P. *Sartre*. London: Routledge & Kegan Paul, 1984.
Caws, P. 'The Curve of the Epoch: Sartre at the End of the Twentieth Century'. *Sartre Studies International* 5, no. 2 (1999): 15–32.
Chambers, P. 'Iterable Praxis: Theory and Sartre's Concept of the Practico-inert'. In *Freedom and the Subject of Theory: Essays in Honour of Christina Howells*, edited by C. Davis and O. Davis, 24–35. Oxford: Legenda, 2019.
Chancel, J. 'Radioscopie: Roland Barthes'. In *Radioscopie*, edited by J. Chancel, Vol. 4, 255–6. Paris: Robert Laffont, 1976.
Charbonneau, M.-A. 'An Encounter between Sartre and Lacan'. *Sartre Studies International* 5, no. 2 (1999): 33–44.
Charmé, S. Z. 'Sartre and the Links Between Patriarchal Atheism and Feminist Theology'. In *Feminist Interpretations of Jean-Paul Sartre*, edited by J. Murphy, 300–24. University Park: Pennsylvania State University Press, 1999.
Charmé, S. Z. 'Existential Psychoanalysis'. In *The Sartrean Mind*, edited by M. Eshleman and C. Mui, 251–63. London: Routledge, 2020.

Churchill, S. 'Contingency and Ego, Intentionality and Nausea'. In *Jean-Paul Sartre: Key Concepts*, edited by S. Churchill and J. Reynolds, 44–65. Durham: Acumen, 2013.
Churchill, S. and J. Reynolds. 'Sartre's Legacy'. In *Jean-Paul Sartre: Key Concepts*, edited by S. Churchill and J. Reynolds, 213–28. Durham: Acumen, 2013.
Cixous, H. *Hélène Cixous Reader*, ed. S. Sellers. New York: Routledge, 1994.
Cixous, H. and C. Clément. *The Newly Born Woman*, trans. B. Wing. Minneapolis: University of Minnesota Press, 1986.
Clark, M. 'Nietzsche Was No Lamarckian'. *The Journal of Nietzsche Studies* 44, no. 2 (2013): 282–96.
Cohen-Solal, A. *Sartre: A Life*. London: Heinemann, 1991.
Cohen-Solal, A. *Sartre 1905–1980*. Paris: Gallimard, 1999.
Cohen-Solal, A. *Une Renaissance sartrienne*. Paris: Gallimard, 2013.
Connolly, W. *Political Theory and Modernity*. Oxford: Blackwell, 1988.
Connolly, W. *Identity / Difference: Democratic Negotiations of Political Paradox*. Ithaca: Cornell University Press, 1991.
Connolly, W. *A World of Becoming*. Durham: Duke University Press, 2011.
Conway, D. 'Overcoming the *Übermensch*: Nietzsche's Revaluation of Values'. *Journal of the British Society for Phenomenology* 20 (1989): 211–24.
Coole, D. 'Rethinking Agency: A Phenomenological Approach to Embodiment and Agentic Capacities'. In *Political Studies* 53, no. 1 (2005): 124–42.
Cox, G. 'Life and Works'. In *Jean-Paul Sartre: Key Concepts*, edited by S. Churchill and J. Reynolds, 5–11. Durham: Acumen, 2013.
Cox, G. *Existentialism and Excess: The Life and Times of Jean-Paul Sartre*. London: Bloomsbury, 2016.
Cumming, R. 'To Understand Man'. In *The Philosophy of Jean-Paul Sartre*, edited by P. Schlipp, 55–85. La Salle: Open Court, 1981a.
Daigle, C. 'Sartre and Nietzsche: Brothers in Arms'. In *Sartre's Second Century*, edited by B. O' Donohoe and R. Elveton, 56–72. Newcastle: Cambridge Scholars Press, 2009.
Daigle, C. 'Nietzsche's Notion of Embodied Self: Proto-Phenomenology at Work?'. *Nietzsche-Studien* 40 (2011): 226–43.
Danto, A. *Nietzsche as Philosopher*. New York: Columbia University Press, 1980.
Davis, C. 'Existentialism and Literature'. In *The Continuum Companion to Existentialism*, edited by F. Joseph, J. Reynolds and A. Woodward, 138–54. London: Continuum, 2011.
Davis, C. and O. Davis. 'Introduction: Pathways to Freedom in the Work of Christina Howells'. In *Freedom and the Subject of Theory: Essays in Honour of Christina Howells*, edited by C. Davis and O. Davis, 1–9. Oxford: Legenda, 2019.
Deleuze, G. 'Il a été mon maître'. *Arts*, November (1964): 1207–27.
Deleuze, G. 'Nomad Thought'. In *The New Nietzsche*, edited by D. Allison, 142–9. New York: Delta, 1977.
Deleuze, G. *Nietzsche and Philosophy*, trans. H. Tomlinson. New York: Columbia University Press, 1983.
Deleuze, G. *Cinema 1: The Movement-Image*, trans. H. Tomlinson and B. Habberjam. Minneapolis: University of Minnesota Press, 1986.
Deleuze, G. *Dialogues* (with Claire Parnet), trans. H. Tomlinson and B. Habberjam. London: Athlone, 1987.
Deleuze, G. Expressionism in Philosophy: Spinoza, trans. M. Joughin. New York: Zone Books, 1992.
Deleuze, G. *Difference and Repetition*, trans. P. Patton. New York: Columbia University Press, 1994.

Deleuze, G. *Pure Immanence: Essays on A Life*, trans. A. Boyman. New York: Zone Books, 2001.
Deleuze, G. *The Logic of Sense*, trans. M. Lester. London: Continuum, 2004.
Deleuze, G. and F. Guattari. *A Thousand Plateaus*. Minneapolis: University of Minnesota Press, 1987.
Deleuze, G. and F. Guattari. *What is Philosophy?*, trans. H. Tomlinson and G. Burchell. New York: Columbia University Press, 1994.
Derrida, J. *Speech and Phenomena, And Other Essays on Husserl's Theory of Signs*, trans. D. Allison. Evanston: Northwestern University Press, 1973.
Derrida, J. *Writing and Difference*, trans. A. Bass. Chicago: University of Chicago Press, 1978.
Derrida, J. *Spurs: Nietzsche's Styles*, trans. B. Harlow. Chicago: University of Chicago Press, 1979.
Derrida, J. *Dissemination*, trans. B. Johnson. Chicago: University of Chicago Press, 1981.
Derrida, J. *Margins of Philosophy*, trans. A. Bass. Chicago: University of Chicago Press, 1982.
Derrida, J. *Glas*, trans. J. Leavey and R. Rand. London: University of Nebraska Press, 1986.
Derrida, J. *Spectres of Marx: The State of the Debt, the Work of Mourning and the New International*, trans. P. Kamuf. London: Routledge, 1994.
Derrida, J. *Points . . . Interviews, 1974–1994*, trans. P. Kamuf. Stanford: Stanford University Press, 1995.
Derrida, J. 'Il courait mort: Salut, salut, Notes pour un courrier aux Temps Modernes'. Les Temps Modernes 587 (1996): 7–54.
Derrida, J. *Of Grammatology*, trans. G. Spivak. Baltimore: John Hopkins University Press, 1998.
Derrida, J. *A Taste for the Secret*. Cambridge: Polity, 2001.
Diers, P. 'Friendship and Feminist Praxis: Insights from Sartre's *Critique of Dialectical Reason*'. In *Feminist Interpretations of Jean-Paul Sartre*, edited by J. Murphy, 253–71. University Park: Pennsylvania State University Press, 1999.
Diethe, C. *Historical Dictionary of Nietzscheanism*. Lanham: Scarecrow Press, 2006.
Dobson, A. *Jean-Paul Sartre and the Politics of Reason: A Theory of History*. Cambridge: Cambridge University Press, 1993.
Eshleman, M. 'What Is It Like To Be Free?'. In *Reading Sartre: On Phenomenology and Existentialism*, edited by J. Webber, 31–47. London: Routledge, 2011.
Eshleman, M. 'A Sketch of Sartre's Life'. In *The Sartrean Mind*, edited by M. Eshleman and C. Mui, 8–21. London: Routledge, 2020.
Eshleman, M. 'On the Structure and Method of *Being and Nothingness*'. In *The Sartrean Mind*, edited by M. Eshleman and C. Mui, 143–57. London: Routledge, 2020a.
Eshleman, M. 'In Praise of Sarah Richmond's Translation of *L'Être et le néant*'. Sartre Studies International 26, no. 1 (2020b): 1–15.
Farrell Fox, N. *The New Sartre: Explorations in Postmodernism*. London: Continuum, 2003.
Farrell Fox, N. 'The New Sartre: A Postmodern Progenitor?'. In *Sartre's Second Century*, edited by B. O' Donohoe and R. Elveton, 104–22. Newcastle: Cambridge Scholars Press, 2009.
Farrell Fox, N. 'Posthuman Horizons: Contemporary Responses to Sartre's Philosophy'. In *The Sartrean Mind*, edited by M. Eshleman and C. Mui, 487–500. London: Routledge, 2020.

Farrell Fox, N. 'Nietzsche and Sartre: Twin Philosophers of Paradox'. In *Nietzsche und der französische Existenzialismus*, edited by A. Betschart, U. Sommer and P. Stephan, 7–33. Berlin: Walter de Gruyter, 2022.

Ferrando, F. *Philosophical Posthumanism*. London: Bloomsbury, 2020.

Ferry, L. and A. Renaut, eds. *Why We Are Not Nietzscheans*, trans. R. de Loaiza. Chicago: University of Chicago Press, 1997.

ffrench, P. 'Catastrophe, Adherence, Proximity: Sartre (with Barthes) in the Cinema'. *Sartre Studies International* 19, no. 1 (2013): 35–54.

Fink, E. *Nietzsches Philosophie*. Stuttgart: W. Kohlhammer Verlag, 1960.

Flynn, T. 'Sartre and the Poetics of History'. In *The Cambridge Companion to Sartre*, edited by C. Howells, 213–60. Cambridge: University of Cambridge Press, 1992.

Flynn, T. 'Sartre and Foucault: A Cross-Generational Exchange'. *Sartre Studies International* 10, no. 2 (2004): 47–55.

Flynn, T. 'Sartre, Foucault and the Critique of (Dialectical) Reason'. *Sartre Studies International* 16, no. 2 (2010): 17–35.

Flynn, T. *Sartre: A Philosophical Biography*. Cambridge: University of Cambridge Press, 2014.

Forster, E. M. *The Machine Stops*. London: Penguin, 2011.

Foucault, M. *Madness and Civilization*, trans. R. Howard. New York: Pantheon, 1965.

Foucault, M. 'Répond á Sartre'. In *La Quinzaine Littéraire*, 46 (1968).

Foucault, M. *The Archaeology of Knowledge and Discourse on Language*, trans. A. Sheridan-Smith. New York: Pantheon, 1972.

Foucault, M. *The Order of Things: An Archaeology of the Human Sciences*, trans. A. Sheridan-Smith. New York: Random House, 1973.

Foucault, M. *Language, Counter-Memory, Practice: Selected Essays and Interviews*, ed. C. Gordon. Oxford: Blackwell, 1977.

Foucault, M. *Discipline and Punish: The Birth of the Prison*, trans. A. Sheridan. Harmondsworth: Penguin, 1977a.

Foucault, M. *Michel Foucault: Power, Truth, Strategy*, ed. M. Morris and P. Patton. Sydney: Feral Publications, 1979.

Foucault, M. 'How We Behave' (with H. Dreyfus and P. Rabinow) in Vanity Fair, (Nov) (1983).

Foucault, M. *The Foucault Reader*, ed. P. Rabinow. New York: Pantheon, 1984.

Foucault, M. *Philosophy, Politics, Culture: Interviews and Other Writings, 1977–84*, ed. L. Kritzman. London: Routledge, 1988.

Foucault, M. *Remarks on Marx: Conversations with Duccio Trombadori*, trans. R. Goldstein and J. Cascaito. New York: Semiotext(e), 1991.

Foucault, M. *Dits et écrits, vol. 1*, Paris: Gallimard, 2001.

Gardner, S. 'Nietzsche, the Self, and the Disunity of Philosophical Reason'. In *Nietzsche on Freedom and Autonomy*, edited by K. Gemes and S. May, 1–32. Oxford: Oxford University Press, 2009.

Gardner, S. *Sartre's Being and Nothingness: A Reader's Guide*. London: Continuum, 2009a.

Gerassi, J. *Talking with Sartre: Conversations and Debates*. New Haven: Yale University Press, 2009.

Gerhardt, V. 'The Body, the Self, the Ego'. In *A Companion to Nietzsche*, edited by K. Ansell-Pearson, 273–96.. Malden: Blackwell, 2006.

Gillespie, J. 'Sartre and God: A Spiritual Odyssey? Part 1'. *Sartre Studies International* 19, no. 1 (2013): 71–90.

Gillespie, J. 'Sartre and God: A Spiritual Odyssey? Part 2'. *Sartre Studies International* 20, no. 1 (2014): 45–56.
Golomb, J. *Nietzsche and Zion*. Ithaca: Cornell University Press, 2004.
Gordon, L. 'Sartre's Influence in Black Existentialism'. In *The Sartrean Mind*, edited by M. Eshleman and C. Mui, 501–14. London: Routledge, 2020.
Gorz, A. 'Sartre and Marx'. *New Left Review* 37 (1966).
Grene, M. 'The Aesthetic Dialogue of Sartre and Merleau-Ponty'. In *The Merleau-Ponty Aesthetics Reader*, edited by G. A. Johnson, 212–32. Evanston: Northwestern University Press, 1993.
Guattari, F. *The Three Ecologies*, trans. I. Pindar and P. Sutton. London: Athlone Press, 2000.
Haar, M. 'Heidegger and the Nietzschean Physiology of Art'. In *Exceedingly Nietzsche: Aspects of Contemporary Nietzsche Interpretation*, edited by D. F. Krell and D. Wood, 13–30. London: Routledge, 1988.
Hardt, M. and A. Negri. *Multitude: War and Democracy in the Age of Empire*. New York: Penguin, 2005.
Harman, G. *Tool-Being: Heidegger and the Metaphysics of Objects*. Chicago: Open Court, 2002.
Harman, G. *Guerilla Metaphysics: Phenomenology and the Carpentry of Things*. Chicago: Open Court, 2005.
Harman, G. 'On Vicarious Causation'. *Collapse: Philosophical Research and Harman, G. Development* 2 (2007): 171–205.
Harman, G. 'I Am Also of the Opinion That Materialism Must Be Destroyed'. *Environment and Planning D: Society and Space* 28, no. 5 (2010): 772–90.
Hatab, L. *A Nietzschean Defence of Democracy: An Experiment in Postmodern Politics*. Chicago: Open Court, 1995.
Hayman, R. *Nietzsche: A Critical Life*. London: Penguin Books, 1982.
Hayman, R. *Writing Against: A Biography of Sartre*. London: Weidenfeld and Nicolson, 1986.
Heidegger, M. *What is Called Thinking?*, trans. J. Gray. New York: Harper & Row, 1968.
Heidegger, M. *The Question Concerning Technology and Other Essays*, trans. W. Lovitt. New York: Harper & Row, 1977.
Heidegger, M. *Nietzsche, 4 Volumes*, trans. D. F. Krell, J. Stambaugh, F. Capuzzi. San Francisco: Harper Row, 1987.
Heidegger, M. 'Letter on Humanism'. In *Martin Heidegger: Basic Writings*, edited by D. Krell, 213–66 New York: Harper Collins, 1993.
Heldt, C. *Immanence and Illusion in Sartre's Ontology of Consciousness*. London: Palgrave Macmillan, 2020.
Heter, T. Storm. 'Sartre and Anarchism'. In *The Sartrean Mind*, edited by M. Eshleman and C. Mui, 528–40. London: Routledge, 2020.
Higgins, K. *Comic Relief: Nietzsche's Gay Science*. New York: Oxford University Press, 2000.
Hoven, A. van den. 'Sarah Richmond's Translation of Jean-Paul Sartre's *Being and Nothingness*'. *Sartre Studies International* 26, no. 1 (2020): 16–28.
Howells, C. *Sartre's Theory of Literature*. London: Modern Humanities Research Association, 1979.
Howells, C. 'Sartre and Negative Theology'. *Modern Language Review* 76, no. 3 (1981): 549–55.
Howells, C. '"Introduction" and "Sartre and the Deconstruction of the Subject"'. In *The Cambridge Companion to Sartre*, edited by C. Howells, 1–10, 318–52. Cambridge: Cambridge University Press, 1992.

Howells, C. *Derrida: Deconstruction from Phenomenology to Ethics*. Cambridge: Polity Press, 1999.
Howells, C. *Mortal Subjects: Passions of the Soul in Late Twentieth-Century French Thought*. Cambridge: Polity Press, 2011.
Hunt, L. *Nietzsche and the Origin of Virtue*. London: Routledge, 1993.
Hutter, H. *Shaping the Future: Nietzsche's New Regime of the Soul and Its Ascetic Practices*. Oxford: Lexington Books, 2006.
Hyppolite, J., 'Existence et dialectique dans la philosophie de Merleau- Ponty'. In *Figures de la pensée philosophique*, edited by J. Hyppolite, 685–730. Paris: PUF, 1991.
Inkpin, A. 'Sartre's Literary Phenomenology'. *Sartre Studies International* 23, no. 1 (2017): 1–21.
Ireland, J. 'Biography Good, Autobiography Bad: A Fundamental Sartrean Paradox?'. In *The Sartrean Mind*, edited by M. Eshleman and C. Mui, 450–60. London: Routledge, 2020.
Irigaray, L. *Le Corps-à-corps avec la mère*. Montrèal: Plein Lune, 1981.
Jameson, F. 'Preface'. In *Critique of Dialectical Reason: The Intelligibility of History, Vol. 2*, trans. A. Sheridan-Smith, , ix–xxiv., London: Verso, 1991.
Jameson, F. 'The Sartrean Origin'. *Sartre Studies International* 1, no. 1/2 (1995): 1–20.
Jaspers, K. *Nietzsche: An Introduction to the Understanding of his Philosophical Activity*, trans. C. Wallraff and F. Schmitz. Chicago: Gateway, 1966.
Katsafanas, P. 'The Antichrist as a Guide to Nietzsche's Mature Ethical Theory'. In *The Nietzschean Mind*, edited by P. Katsafanas, 83–101. London: Routledge, 2018.
Kaufmann, W. *Nietzsche: Philosopher, Psychologist, Antichrist*. Princeton: Princeton University Press, 1974.
Kirkpatrick, K. *Sartre and Theology*. London: Bloomsbury, 2017a.
Kirkpatrick, K. *Sartre on Sin: Between Being and Nothingness*. Oxford: Oxford University Press, 2017b.
Kirkpatrick, K. *Becoming Beauvoir*. London: Bloomsbury, 2019.
Kirsner, D. 'Sartre and the Collective Neurosis of Our Time'. In *Sartre After Sartre*, edited by F. Jameson, 206–25. Connecticut: Yale French Studies 68, 1985.
Klossowski, P. *Nietzsche and the Vicious Circle*, trans. D. Smith. Chicago: University of Chicago Press, 1997.
Kofman, S, 'Nietzsche and the Obscurity of Heraclitus', trans. F. Lionnet- McCumber, *Diacritics* 17, no. 3 (1987): 39–55.
Kofman, S, 'Baubô: Theological Perversion and Fetishism'. In *Feminist Interpretations of Friedrich Nietzsche*, trans. T. Strong, 21–49. University Park: Pennsylvania State University Press, 1998.
Kohák, E. *The Embers and the Stars: A Philosophical Inquiry into the Moral Sense of Nature*. Chicago: University of Chicago Press, 1984.
Lacan, J. *Alienation and Freedom*, ed. and trans. S. Corcoran. London: Bloomsbury, 2018.
Lacoste, G. de. 'The Beauvoir and Lévy Interviews: Towards a Feminine Economy'. In *Feminist Interpretations of Jean-Paul Sartre*, edited by J. Murphy, 272–98. University Park: Pennsylvania State University Press, 1999.
Lemm, V. *Homo Natura: Nietzsche, Philosophical Anthropology and Biopolitics*. Edinburgh: Edinburgh University Press, 2020.
Lethbridge, D. 'Sartre's Crabs'. *Sartre Studies International* 21, no. 1 (2015): 75–89.
Levins, R. and R. Lewontin *The Dialectical Biologist*. Cambridge: Harvard University Press, 1985.
Linsenbard, G. 'Ethics as Flourishing Humanity'. In *The Sartrean Mind*, edited by M. Eshleman and C. Mui, 288–99. London: Routledge, 2020.

Lyotard, J-F. 'A Success of Sartre's'. Foreword in *The Politics of Prose: Essay on Sartre*, D. Hollier. Minneapolis: University of Minnesota Press, 1986.

Magnus, B. and K. Higgins. 'Introduction'. In *The Cambridge Companion to Nietzsche*, edited by B. Magnus and K. Higgins, 1–20. Cambridge: Cambridge University Press, 1996.

Mann, T. 'Nietzsche's Philosophy in the Light of Recent History'. In *Last Essays*, trans. T. and J. Stern, 141–77. New York: Knopf, 1959.

Manschot, H. *Nietzsche and the Earth: Biography, Ecology, Politics*, trans. L. Waters. London: Bloomsbury, 2021.

Marcuse, H. *From Luther to Popper*, trans. J. de-Bres. London: Verso, 1983.

Martinot, S. 'The Site of Postmodernity in Sartre'. *Sartre Studies International* 5, no. 2 (1999): 45–60.

Massumi, B. 'The Supernormal Animal'. In *The Nonhuman Turn*, edited by R. Grusin. Minneapolis: University of Minnesota Press, 2015.

McBride, W. *Sartre's Political Theory*. Bloomington: Indiana University Press, 1991.

McCann, C. 'Existentialism, Authenticity and the Self'. In *The Continuum Companion to Existentialism*, edited by F. Joseph, J. Reynolds and A. Woodward, 198–214. London: Continuum, 2011.

Megill, A. *Prophets of Extremity: Nietzsche, Heidegger, Foucault, Derrida*. Berkeley: University of California Press, 1985.

Meillassoux, Q. *After Finitude: An Essay on the Necessity of Contingency*, trans. R. Brassier. New York: Continuum, 2008.

Mellamphy, N. 'Nietzsche and the Engine of Politics'. In *Nietzsche and Political Thought*, edited by K. Ansell-Pearson, 141–59. London: Bloomsbury, 2015.

Merleau-Ponty, M. *Phenomenology of Perception*. London: Routledge & Kegan Paul, 1962.

Merleau-Ponty, M. *Sense and Non-Sense*, trans. H. and P. Dreyfus. Evanston: Northwestern University Press, 1964a.

Merleau-Ponty, M. *Signs*, trans. R. McCleary. Evanston: Northwestern University Press, 1964b.

Merleau-Ponty, M. *The Visible and Invisible*, trans. A. Lingis. Evanston: Northwestern University Press, 1968.

Merleau-Ponty, M. *Adventures of the Dialectic*, trans. J. Bien. Evanston: Northwestern University Press, 1973.

Merleau-Ponty, M. *Parcours, 1935–1951*. Lagrasse: Verdier, 1997.

Merleau-Ponty, M. *The World of Perception*, trans. O. Davis. London: Routledge, 2004.

Merleau-Ponty, M. *Entretiens avec Georges Charbonnier*. Lagrasse: Verdier, 2016.

Mészáros, I. *The Work of Sartre: Search for Freedom*. Brighton: Harvester Press, 1979.

Meyer, M. 'Nietzsche's Ontic Structural Realism?'. In *The Nietzschean Mind*, edited by P. Katsafanas, 365–80. London: Routledge, 2018.

Mirvish, A. 'Sartre and the Problem of Other Embodied Minds'. *Sartre Studies International* 2, no. 2 (1996): 65–84.

Mitchell, D. *Sartre, Nietzsche and Non-Humanist Existentialism*. London: Palgrave Macmillan, 2020.

Moran, R. 'Foreword'. In *Being and Nothingness: An Essay on Phenomenological Ontology*, trans. S. Richmond, x–xvii. London: Routledge, 2018.

Morris, K. 'Sartre on the Body'. In *The Sartrean Mind*, edited by M. Eshleman and C. Mui, 225–38. London: Routledge, 2020.

Morris, P. Sutton. 'Self-Creating Selves: Sartre and Foucault'. *American Catholic Quarterly* 70, no. 4 (1997): 537–49.

Morris, P. Sutton. 'Sartre on Objectification: A Feminist Perspective'. In *Feminist Interpretations of Jean-Paul Sartre*, edited by J. Murphy, 64–89. University Park: Pennsylvania State University Press, 1999.

Mueller, M. 'Sartre and the (un-)Freedom of the Reading Subject'. In *Freedom and the Subject of Theory: Essays in Honour of Christina Howells*, edited by C. Davis and O. Davis, 36–47. Oxford: Legenda, 2019.

Mui, C. 'Sartre and Marcel on Embodiment: Reevaluating Traditional and Gynocentric Feminisms'. In *Feminist Interpretations of Jean-Paul Sartre*, edited by J. Murphy, 105–22. University Park: Pennsylvania State University Press, 1999.

Murdoch, I.. *Sartre: Romantic Rationalist*. London: Vintage, 1999.

Murphy, J. 'Hope Now'. In *The Sartrean Mind*, edited by M. Eshleman and C. Mui, 313–23. London: Routledge, 2020.

Mussett, S. 'Nature as Threat and Escape in the Philosophies of Sartre and Beauvoir'. In *The Sartrean Mind*, edited by M. Eshleman and C. Mui, 515–27. London: Routledge, 2020.

Neppi, E. *Le Babil et la caresse: Pensée du maternal chez Sartre*. New York: Peter Lang, 1995.

Noudelmann, F. *The Philosopher's Touch: Sartre, Nietzsche and Barthes at the Piano*, trans. B. Reilly. New York: Columbia University Press, 2012.

Noudelmann, F. *Un Tout Autre Sartre*. Paris: Gallimard, 2021.

O' Shiel, D. *Sartre and Magic: Being, Emotion and Philosophy*. London: Bloomsbury, 2019.

Olafson, F. 'Review of *Being and Nothingness*'. *Philosophical Review* 67, no. 2 (1958): 276–80.

Oliver, K. 'Nietzsche's Woman: The Poststructuralist Attempt to Do Away with Women'. *Radical Philosophy* 48 (1988): 25–9.

Oliver, K. *Womanizing Nietzsche: Philosophy's Relation to the "Feminine"*. London: Routledge, 1995.

Parkes, G. 'Nietzsche and East Asian Thought: Influences, Impacts and Resonances'. In *The Cambridge Companion to Nietzsche*, edited by B. Magnus and K. Higgins, 356–84. Cambridge: Cambridge University Press, 1996.

Patton, P. 'Nietzsche, Genealogy and Justice'. In *Nietzsche and Political Thought*, edited by K. Ansell-Pearson, 7–22. London: Bloomsbury, 2015.

Perna, M. 'Spinozean Multitude Radical Italian Thought vis-à-vis Sartrean Existential Marxism'. *Sartre Studies International* 13, no. 1 (2007): 35–61.

Perrin, C., 'Ontology and Metaphysics', trans. A van den Hoven. In *The Sartrean Mind*, edited by M. Eshleman and C. Mui, 264–74. London: Routledge, 2020.

Picard, M. *La Lecture comme jeu*. Paris: Minuit, 1986.

Plank, W. *The Quantum Nietzsche: The Will to Power and the Nature of Dissipative Systems*. Lincoln: Writers Club Press, 1998.

Randall, L. *Warped Passages: Unraveling the Mysteries of the Universe's Hidden Dimensions*. New York: Harper Collins, 2005.

Raulet, G. 'Structuralism and Post-Structuralism: An Interview with Michel Foucault', trans. J. Harding, *Telos* 55 (Spring) (1983): 195–211.

Redeker, R. 'La dernière peau philosophique de Michel Foucault'. *Critique* (2002): 660.

Remley, W. *Jean-Paul Sartre's Anarchist Philosophy*. London: Bloomsbury, 2018.

Remley, W. 'Ethics of Authenticity'. In *The Sartrean Mind*, edited by M. Eshleman and C. Mui, 277–87. London: Routledge, 2020.

Reynolds, J. *Understanding Existentialism*. Chesham: Acumen, 2006.

Reynolds, J. and A. Woodward. 'Existentialism and Poststructuralism: Some Unfashionable Observations'. In *The Continuum Companion to Existentialism*, edited by F. Joseph, J. Reynolds and A. Woodward, 260–81. London: Continuum, 2011.

Rhoad, I. 'Destabilizing Identities and Distinctions: The Literary- Philosophical Experience of *Hope Now*'. In *Sartre's Second Century*, edited by B. O' Donohoe and R. Elveton, 155–72. Newcastle: Cambridge Scholars Press, 2009.

Riccardi, M. 'A Tale of Two Selves: Nietzsche and the Contemporary Debates on the Self'. In *The Nietzschean Mind*, edited by P. Katsafanas, 186–200. London: Routledge, 2018.

Richards, S. 'Sartre and Lacan: Reading *Qui Perd Gagne* alongside *Les Non- Dupes Errent*'. In *Freedom and the Subject of Theory: Essays in Honour of Christina Howells*, edited by C. Davis and O. Davis, 48–59. Oxford: Legenda, 2019.

Richardson, J. 'Nietzsche's Freedoms'. In *Nietzsche on Freedom and Autonomy*, edited by K. Gemes and S. May, 127–50. Oxford: Oxford University Press, 2009.

Richardson, J. *Nietzsche's Values*. Oxford: Oxford University Press, 2020.

Richmond, S. 'Magic in Sartre's Early Philosophy'. In *Reading Sartre: On Phenomenology and Existentialism*, edited by J. Webber, 145–60. London: Routledge, 2011.

Richmond, S. 'Nothingness and Negation'. In *Jean-Paul Sartre: Key Concepts*, edited by S. Churchill and J. Reynolds, 93–105. Durham: Acumen, 2013.

Richmond, S. 'Translator's Introduction'. In *Being and Nothingness: An Essay on Phenomenological Ontology*, trans. S. Richmond, xix–xxxvii. London: Routledge, 2018.

Rozehgy, M. 'Hitting the Slopes with Sartre and Deleuze and Guattari'. *Sartre Studies International* 8, no. 2 (2002): 112–26.

Safranski, R. *Nietzsche: A Philosophical Biography*, trans. S. Frisch. London: Granta Books, 2003.

Saint-Aubert, E. de. 'Merleau-Ponty face à Husserl et Heidegger'. *Revue Germanique International* 13 (2011): 59–73.

Salomé, L. *Nietzsche*, trans. S. Mandel. Redding Ridge: Black Swan Books, 1988.

Santoni, R. 'In Defence of Lévy and *Hope Now*: A Minority View'. *Sartre Studies International* 4, no. 2 (1998): 61–8.

Sawyer, D. 'Playing Seriously with Bad Faith: A Derridean Intersection'. *Sartre Studies International* 21, no. 1 (2015): 34–52.

Schacht, R. 'Nietzsche's Kind of Philosophy'. In *The Cambridge Companion to Nietzsche*, edited by B. Magnus and K. Higgins, 151–79. Cambridge: Cambridge University Press, 1996.

Schrift, A. *Nietzsche and the Question of Interpretation: Between Hermeneutics and Deconstruction*. London: Routledge 1990.

Schrift, A. 'Putting Nietzsche to Work: Deleuze'. In *Nietzsche: A Critical Reader*, edited by P. Sedgwick, 250–75. Oxford: Blackwell, 1995.

Schrift, A. 'Nietzsche's French Legacy'. In *The Cambridge Companion to Nietzsche*, edited by B. Magnus and K. Higgins, 323–55. Cambridge: Cambridge University Press, 1996.

Shapiro, G. 'Kairos and Chronos: Nietzsche and the Time of the Multitude'. In *Nietzsche and Political Thought*, edited by K. Ansell-Pearson, 123–40. London: Bloomsbury, 2015.

Shapiro, G. *Nietzsche's Earth: Great Events, Great Politics*. London: University of Chicago Press, 2016.

Siemens, H. 'Reassessing Radical Democratic Theory in the Light of Nietzsche's Ontology of Conflict'. In *Nietzsche and Political Thought*, edited by K. Ansell-Pearson, 83–105. London: Bloomsbury, 2015.

Siemens, H. 'Nietzsche's Agon'. In *The Nietzschean Mind*, edited by P. Katsafanas, 314–33. London: Routledge, 2018.

Simont, J. 'Sartrean Ethics'. In *The Cambridge Companion to Sartre*, edited by C. Howells, 178–210. Cambridge: Cambridge University Press, 1992.

Solomon, R. *From Hegel to Existentialism*. Oxford: Oxford University Press, 1987.
Solomon, R. *Continental Philosophy since 1750: The Rise and Fall of the Self*. Oxford: Oxford University Press, 1988.
Solomon, R. *Living with Nietzsche: What the Great 'Immoralist' Has to Teach Us*. Oxford: Oxford University Press, 2003.
Sorgner, S. 'Nietzsche, the Overman and Transhumanism'. *Journal of Evolution & Technology* 20 (2009): 29–42.
Stauth, G. and B. Turner. *Nietzsche's Dance: Resentment, Reciprocity and Resistance in Social Life*. Oxford: Blackwell, 1988.
Stiegler, B. *La Société automatique, 1: L'Avenir du travail*. Paris: Fayard, 2015.
Strong, T. 'Nietzsche's Political Misappropriation'. In *The Cambridge Companion to Nietzsche*, edited by B. Magnus and K. Higgins, 119–50. Cambridge: Cambridge University Press, 1996.
Thody, P. *Jean-Paul Sartre*. London: Macmillan, 1992.
Tillich, P. 'The Escape from God'. In *Nietzsche and the Gods*, edited by W. Santaniello, 173–80. New York: SUNY Press, 2001.
Tönnies, F. *Der Nietzsche Kultus*. Leipzig, 1987.
Trottignon, P. 'Le dernier métaphysicien'. *L'Arc* 30 (1966): 27–32.
Tubert, A. 'Nietzsche and Self-Constitution'. In *The Nietzschean Mind*, edited by P. Katsafanas, 218–30. London: Routledge, 2018.
Ure, M. 'Nietzsche's Political Therapy'. In *Nietzsche and Political Thought*, edited by K. Ansell-Pearson, 161–78. London: Bloomsbury, 2015.
Vasey, C. 'Sartre's Fiction'. In *The Sartrean Mind*, edited by M. Eshleman and C. Mui, 429–39. London: Routledge, 2020.
Verkerk, W. *Nietzsche and Friendship*. London: Bloomsbury, 2020.
Visker, R. 'Was Existentialism Truly a Humanism?'. *Sartre Studies International* 13, no. 1 (2007): 3–15.
Warnock, M. *Existentialism*. Oxford: Oxford University Press, 1989.
Warren, M. *Nietzsche and Political Thought*. London: MIT Press, 1991.
Webber, J. 'Bad Faith and the Other'. In *Reading Sartre: On Phenomenology and Existentialism*, edited by J. Webber, 180–94. London: Routledge, 2011.
Webber, J. *Rethinking Existentialism*. Oxford: Oxford University Press, 2018.
Wittmann, H. *Aesthetics in Sartre and Camus: The Challenge of Freedom*, trans. C. Atkinson. Frankfurt: Peter Lang, 2009.
Woodward, A. *Understanding Nietzscheanism*. Durham: Acumen, 2011.
Young, E., G. Genosko and J. Watson. *The Deleuze and Guattari Dictionary*. London: Bloomsbury, 2013.
Zamosc, G. 'Nietzschean Wholeness'. In *The Nietzschean Mind*, edited by P. Katsafanas, 169–85. London: Routledge, 2018.
Zohar, D. *The Quantum Self*. London: Flamingo, 1991.
Zohar, D. and I. Marshall. *The Quantum Society: Mind, Physics, and a New Social Vision*. New York: Quill, 1994.

Nietzsche

'The Greek State'. In *The Complete Works of Friedrich Nietzsche, Vol. 2*, edited by O. Levy, trans. M. Mügge. London: T.A. Foulis, 1911. **[G.S]**

'Philosophy in the Tragic Age of the Greeks'. In *The Complete Works of Friedrich Nietzsche, Vol. 2*, edited by O. Levy, trans. M. Mügge. London: T.A. Foulis, 1911. [**PTAG**]
The Birth of Tragedy and The Case of Wagner, trans. W. Kaufmann. New York: Vintage, 1967. [**BT**], [**CW**]
On the Genealogy of Morals, trans. R. J. Hollingdale and W. Kaufmann. New York: Random House, 1967. [**GM**]
Ecce Homo, trans. W. Kaufmann. New York: Random House, 1967. [**EH**]
The Will to Power, trans. R. J. Hollingdale and W. Kaufmann. New York: Random House, 1967. [**WP**]
Twilight of the Idols, trans. R. J. Hollingdale. Middlesex: Penguin, 1968. [**TI**]
The Antichrist, trans. R. J. Hollingdale. Middlesex: Penguin, 1968. [**A**]
Thus Spoke Zarathustra, trans. R. J. Hollingdale. Middlesex: Penguin, 1969. [**Z**]
Selected Letters of Friedrich Nietzsche, ed. and trans. C. Middleton. Chicago: University of Chicago Press, 1969.
Beyond Good and Evil, trans. R. J. Hollingdale. Middlesex: Penguin, 1973. [**BGE**]
The Gay Science, trans. W. Kaufmann. New York: Random House, 1974. [**GS**]
Sämtliche Werke, Kritische Studienausgabe, 15 vols, ed. G. Colli and M. Montinari. Berlin: Walter de Gruyter, 1980. [**KSW**]
Daybreak, trans. R. J. Hollingdale. Cambridge: Cambridge University Press, 1982. [**D**]
Untimely Meditations, 4 Vols., trans. R. J. Hollingdale. Cambridge: Cambridge University Press, 1983. [**UM**]
The Wanderer and his Shadow, trans. R. J. Hollingdale. Cambridge: Cambridge University Press, 1986. [**WS**]
Human, All Too Human, trans. R. J. Hollingdale. Cambridge: Cambridge University Press, 1986. [**HH**]
Sämtliche Briefe, Kritische Studienausgabe, 8 vols., ed. G. Colli and M. Montinari. Berlin: Walter de Gruyter, 1986. [**KSB**]
The Pre-Platonic Philosophers, ed. and trans. G. Whitlock. Champaign: University of Illnois Press, 2000. [**PP**]
Writings from the Late Notebooks, trans. K. Sturge. Cambridge: Cambridge University Press, 2003. [**LN**]

Sartre

Le Sursis. Paris: Gallimard, 1945.
'Haïti vu par J.-P. Sartre' (with Georges Altman) in *Franc-Tireur*, 21.10.1949 (1949).
The Transcendence of the Ego, trans. F. Williams and R. Kirkpatrick. New York: Noonday Press. 1957 [**TE**]
'Merleau-Ponty vivant'. *Les Temps Modernes* 184–5 (1961): 304–76.
'Black Orpheus'. *Massachusetts Review* 6 (1964a): 13–52.
Situations IV. Paris: Gallimard, 1964b.
Nausea, trans. R. Baldick. Harmondsworth: Penguin, 1965. [**N**]
What is Literature?, trans. B. Frechtman. New York: Harper & Row, 1965. [**WL**]
'Jean-Paul Sartre répond'. *L'Arc* 30 (1966): 87–96.
Words, trans. B. Frechtman. London: Penguin, 1967. [**W**]
Search for a Method, trans. H. Barnes. New York: Vintage Books, 1968. [**SM**]
The Communists and Peace, trans. M. Fletcher and P. Beak. New York: Braziller, 1968.

'Intentionality: A Fundamental Idea of Husserl's Phenomenology'. trans. J. Fell, *Journal of the British Society for Phenomenology* 1, no. 2 (1970): 4–5.
L'Idiot de la famille: Gustave Flaubert de 1821 à 1857, tome III. Paris: Gallimard, 1972. [**IF 3**]
Between Existentialism and Marxism, trans. J. Mathews. New York: Pantheon, 1974a.
The Writings of Jean-Paul Sartre, Vol. 2, ed. M. Contat and M. Rybalka. Evanston: Northwestern University Press, 1974b.
On a raison de se révolter, with P. Victor and P. Gavi. Paris: Gallimard, 1974c.
'Sartre at Seventy: An Interview'. (with M. Contat), trans. P. Auster and L. Davis, *New York Review of Books*, 1975 (July 8).
Critique of Dialectical Reason: Theory of Practical Ensembles, Vol. 1, trans. A. Sheridan-Smith. London: New Left Books, 1976. [**CDR**]
Sartre on Theater. New York: Pantheon Books, 1976.
Situations X: Politique et Autobiographie. Paris: Gallimard, 1976a.
Situations, Vols. 1–10. Paris: Gallimard, 1977.
Life / Situations: Essays Written and Spoken, trans. P. Auster and L. Davis. New York: Pantheon, 1977a.
'Sartre et les femmes' (interview with Catherine Chaine) in *Le Nouvel Observateur* (31 January 1977b).
'Pouvoir et liberté: actualité de Sartre' (dialogue avec Pierre Victor). *Libération* January 6 (1977c): 10–11.
'L'écriture et la publication' (interview with Michel Sicard) in *Obliques* 18–19 (1979): 9–29.
'La Gauche, désespoir, et l'espoir' (interview with Catherine Clément) in *Le Matin* (10 November 1979a).
'Entretien avec Jean-Paul Sartre' (with Catherine Clément & Bernard Pingaud) in *L'Arc* (1979b) (Nov): 33–7.
'An Interview with Jean-Paul Sartre' (with Leo Fretz) in *Jean-Paul Sartre: Contemporary Approaches to his Philosophy*, edited by H. Silverman and F. Elliston. Pittsburgh: Duquesne University Press, 1980.
The Family Idiot: Gustave Flaubert 1821–1857, vol. 1, trans. C. Cosman. Chicago: University of Chicago Press, 1981a. [**FI**]
Oeuvres Romanesques, ed. M. Contat and M. Rybalka. Paris: Gallimard, 1981b.
The Philosophy of Jean-Paul Sartre, ed. P. Schlipp. Illnois: Open Court, 1981c.
Lettres au Castor et á quelques autres, 1926–1939. Paris: Gallimard, 1983a.
Lettres au Castor et á quelques autres, 1940–1963. Paris: Gallimard, 1983b.
Cahiers pour une morale, ed. A. Elkaïm-Sartre. Paris: Gallimard, 1983c.
The War Diaries of Jean-Paul Sartre, November 1939–March 1940, trans. Q. Hoare. New York: Pantheon, 1984. [**WD**]
Existentialism and Human Emotions, trans. B. Frechtman. New York: Citadel Press, 1985. [**EH**]
The Family Idiot: Gustave Flaubert 1821–1857, vol. 2, trans. C. Cosman. Chicago: University of Chicago Press, 1987. [**FI 2**]
Mallarmé, or the Poet of Nothingness, trans. E. Sturm. University Park: Pennsylvania State University Press, 1988.
Being and Nothingness: An Essay on Phenomenological Ontology, trans. H. Barnes. New York: Routledge, 1989.
Ecrits de jeunesse, ed. M. Contat and M. Rybalka. Paris: Gallimard, 1990. [**EJ**]
Critique of Dialectical Reason: The Intelligibility of History, Vol. 2, trans. A. Sheridan-Smith. London: Verso, 1991. [**CDR 2**]

L'espoir maintenant: les entretiens de 1980. Paris: Verdier, 1991. [**EM**]
Notebooks for an Ethics, trans. D. Pellauer. Chicago: University of Chicago Press, 1992. [**NE**]
Un Théâtre de situations. Paris: Gallimard, 1992.
Literary and Philosophical Essays. New York: Criterion Books, 1995.
Hope Now: The 1980 Interviews (with B.-H. Levy), trans. A. van den Hoven. Chicago: University of Chicago Press, 1996. [**HN**]
Sketch for a Theory of the Emotions, trans. P. Mairet. London: Routledge, 2002. [**STE**]
The Imaginary: A Phenomenological Psychology of the Imagination, trans. J. Webber. London: Routledge, 2004. [**IM**]
'A New Mystic'. In *Critical Essays*, trans. C. Turner. London: Seagull Books, 2010.
The Imagination, trans. K. Williford and D. Rudrauf. New York: Routledge, 2012. [**I**]
Saint Genet: Actor and Martyr, trans. B. Frechtman. Minneapolis: University of Minnesota Press, 2012. [**SG**]
'Lettre à Gabriel Marcel de Jean-Paul Sartre'. *BNF Revue* 248 (2014). Paris [1943].
Being and Nothingness: An Essay on Phenomenological Ontology, trans. S. Richmond. London: Routledge, 2018. [**BN**]

Index

abjection 189, 231
affect 6–8, 26, 50–2, 58–65, 77–82, 111–13, 136–7, 149, 155, 157–60, 168–71, 180–1, 201, 212, 221
affirmation 5, 16, 21, 29, 45–6, 63, 75–7, 86, 120, 134–6, 172–4, 179–80, 204
agonism 35, 115, 128–32, 134–5, 142
Alain 25
Alcibiades 63
Alexander the Great 189
Althusser, L. 218
amor fati 180, 220
anarchism 115, 138–46, 226
androgyny 184, 186, 192, 196, 212
anguish 60, 217
animal(s) 77, 104, 136, 149, 153–9, 162–4, 172, 174, 181, 185, 187, 203, 228–9
Anthropocene, the 25, 147, 153, 164–5, 213, 227
anthropocentrism 30, 46, 147–9, 158, 161, 165, 170, 212
Antichrist, the 16, 133, 153, 187
aphorism 2, 14–15, 20, 28, 33, 216
Apollo/nian 77, 79, 82, 87, 94, 105, 125, 128, 132, 151, 179, 199, 220, 231
Argos 52
Ariadne 19, 191
Aristocratism 2, 5, 30, 33–4, 115, 117–18, 121, 125–7, 132, 136, 141–2, 204, 212, 225
Aristotle 42, 95, 187
Aron, R. 208, 215, 222
art 6, 34–5, 40, 52–3, 63–4, 71, 75–6, 78, 80, 85–7, 93, 105, 122, 125, 128, 134, 142, 151, 158, 172, 193, 198–201, 213, 216, 224–5
asceticism 44, 56, 64, 75–6, 103, 116, 149, 175, 181, 199, 204, 213, 219–20
assemblage 61, 96, 107, 112–13, 144, 165, 169–70, 198, 212, 227, 229

assimilation 62, 79, 96, 110–12, 129–31, 152
atheism 4, 127, 176–85, 216, 229–30
authenticity 4–6, 26, 30, 41, 49, 74, 79–80, 82, 84–6, 89, 117, 121–3, 130–1, 144, 183, 194–5, 217, 221
autopoiesis 108, 111, 158, 224
Avila, T. de 25, 205

Bachofen, J. 231
bad faith 4–5, 36, 68, 81, 84–6, 122–3, 138, 166, 173, 184, 213, 219, 221, 227
Badiou, A. 99
Bakunin, M. 138
Barth, K. 178
Barthes, R. 31, 201
Bataille, G. 20–1, 46, 116, 205
Baubô 189–90
Baudelaire, C. 15, 80
Baudrillard, J. 229
Beaufret, J. 41
Beauvoir, S. de 3–4, 10, 15, 26, 36, 41, 64, 66, 105, 115, 136, 143, 159, 166–7, 173, 175, 182, 193–6, 200, 206–8, 217, 219, 222, 224, 230–3
becoming 4, 6–8, 18, 28, 30, 40, 45, 48, 50, 55, 60–1, 75, 80, 84, 89, 92–3, 100–1, 113, 117, 128–31, 135, 138, 149–50, 153, 156, 158, 172, 174, 176, 179–80, 185, 193, 209, 213
Beethoven, L. von 197, 201
Being and Nothingness 4, 7, 26, 31, 36, 41–2, 48–9, 51–2, 55–6, 66, 69–70, 81, 84–5, 89, 91, 106, 109, 131, 145, 162, 165–6, 183, 193–5, 215, 217–18, 221, 223–4, 231–2
  and Cartesianism 9, 23–4, 64–5, 222
  new translation of 24, 222
  pour-soi/en-soi 98–9, 102
  Sartre on 37, 80, 97, 121–2, 136, 167, 219
  structure of 56, 98, 161, 222

Bergson, H.   25, 169
Binswanger, L.   50
Bizet, G.   133, 198, 232
Blanchot, M.   28, 46
body, the   20–1, 26, 30, 40, 55, 61–7, 71–2, 76, 78–9, 82, 87, 90–1, 98, 105, 110, 112, 137, 148–50, 157, 159–61, 166, 168–9, 178–9, 184, 189, 194–5, 199, 201, 204, 219, 222, 231
Boscovich, R.   95
Brunschvicg, L.   215
Buber, M.   178–9
Buddhism   62, 179, 230

Caesar, Julius   29, 63, 141, 189
Camus, A.   192
capitalism   142, 149–51
caress, the   65–6, 69, 168, 193, 219
Chancel, J.   31
Chopin, F.   27, 198, 200–1, 232
Christian/ity   25, 43, 63, 77, 83, 94, 121–2, 131, 149, 155, 157, 176–85, 190–1, 198, 204, 223, 227, 229–30
cinema   137, 199–200
Circe   189, 191
Cixous, H.   194–6
cogito
 Cartesian   40, 68, 223
 irreflective   218
 pre-reflective   50, 81, 166–7, 220, 222
communism   138
compatibilism   7, 55–6, 220
consciousness   7, 11, 17, 22, 26, 40, 51–2, 55–66, 68–9, 76–8, 80–2, 86, 88–9, 94, 98, 101, 108–10, 113, 117, 130, 152, 155, 160, 164, 167, 170, 172, 183, 185, 193–4, 207, 209, 217, 219–20, 222–4, 228–9, 231
contingency   3–5, 8, 10, 21, 24, 40, 44, 60, 65, 83–4, 88–9, 100, 104–5, 128–9, 149, 161, 165, 167, 174, 176, 189, 206, 209, 212–13
contradiction   12–13, 27–32, 34, 46, 48, 55–6, 79, 85, 93, 97, 99–100, 156, 164, 174
 law of (non-)   3, 21, 94–5, 186–8
Copernicus, N.   27
Corbin, H.   46
counterfinality   73, 112

dancing   34, 84, 180, 184, 199–200, 203–4, 230
Darwin, C.   30, 104, 148, 155–6, 226
Death of God, the   2, 22, 44, 115–16, 120, 180–1, 183, 185, 189
Death of Man, the   22, 44, 47, 174
Debussy, C.   200, 232
deconstruction   7, 9–10, 13, 22–3, 25, 30, 32, 43, 45, 47–8, 55, 73, 78, 83, 86, 89, 113, 115, 127, 147, 161, 174, 184–5, 190, 192, 194, 196, 210, 212, 222
de-egoization   49, 77, 82, 87, 124, 145, 194–6, 208
Deleuze, G.   9, 13–14, 19–22, 24, 36, 44–6, 48, 50, 69, 79, 89, 91–2, 94, 102, 112, 136, 139, 143–4, 146, 154, 158, 164, 169–70, 205, 218, 227, 229, 232
Demeter   189, 231
democracy   5, 33–4, 115, 117, 121, 125–30, 134–9, 141–5, 187, 224, 226
Democritus   104, 223
Derrida, J.   7–9, 16, 18–20, 22, 24, 36, 39, 41–53, 86–9, 112, 116, 146, 164, 174, 189–90, 192, 194, 205, 210–11, 218, 228, 230
Descartes, R.   23, 42, 48, 50–1, 57–8, 62, 222–3
determinism   7, 30, 55–6
dialectic/al   9, 36–7, 42, 49–50, 56, 60, 76, 78, 82, 91, 94, 112–13, 115, 123, 128, 131–8, 160–4, 173–4, 185, 188, 191, 196, 216, 222, 225, 228
 circularity   67, 70–3
 comprehension   31–2, 99–102
 distortion of   92
 Hegelian   21, 24
 'with holes'   96–7, 212–13, 223
 of nature   105–8
 nominalism   24, 28
difference   21–2, 24, 87–9, 92, 96, 128–30, 141–2, 148–9, 190
Dionysus/Dionysian   5–6, 16, 20, 29–30, 33–5, 45, 61, 63–4, 75–9, 82, 87, 91, 94, 105, 128, 132, 134, 136, 151, 160, 164, 172, 179–81, 185, 189–91, 197–205, 212, 220–1, 224, 230–2

dissipative systems   96, 105, 109, 169, 213
Dostoevsky, F.   182
drives   14, 40, 51–2, 55, 58, 63, 65,
   74–9, 94, 96, 105, 119, 129,
   149–50, 153, 155–7, 172, 187,
   191, 213, 220, 225
dualism   9, 43, 63, 65, 92–4, 97–102,
   113, 147, 178, 184, 186, 192, 210,
   222–3
Durkheim, E.   25

Ecce Homo   2, 16, 27, 30, 34–5, 74, 77,
   148, 187–8, 217, 231
École Normale Supérieure (ENS)   1, 165
ecology   113, 153, 161–5
ego, the   11, 26, 40, 42, 56–61, 69, 74, 76,
   81–2, 89, 134, 179, 219, 222
egoism   125, 128–9, 133–5, 143, 198, 220
eliminativism   55–6, 74
emergence   44, 53, 61, 68, 76, 96,
   102, 115, 137, 167, 172, 212, 219,
   223, 229
emergent interactionism   100–1, 107–9,
   144–5
Emerson, R. W.   151–2, 154, 177
emotion   7, 26, 51, 59–64, 75, 78–9,
   81, 91, 111, 168, 171, 201, 209,
   220–1
Engels, F.   106, 163
Enlightenment, the   121, 127, 148,
   155, 173
Epicureanism   64, 75, 118–19, 151, 154,
   168, 187–8, 190
eternal return of the same   2, 13, 21, 28,
   34, 40–1, 44–5, 127, 153, 179–80,
   189–90, 220
eudaimonia   119
exclusivism   156, 161, 163, 212
existentialism   10, 23, 26, 30, 36,
   41, 46, 48–9, 84, 87, 97, 182,
   211, 216, 229
Existentialism is a Humanism   6, 35–6,
   41, 199, 218, 229

facticity   42, 65–6, 84, 86, 88, 97, 167
fascism   127, 173
feminine, the   7, 36, 64, 92, 186–97,
   230–2
Fink, E.   44–5

Flaubert, G.   12, 15, 71–2, 82, 89, 168,
   196, 209, 216
Foerster, H. von   109
Forster, E.M.   227
Foucault, M.   7–9, 13, 16, 20–4, 36,
   39, 42, 44, 46–7, 49–50, 86–7,
   146–7, 168, 174, 205, 210–11,
   218, 221
fraternity   47, 123–4, 145, 184–5, 187,
   194–6, 230
free spirit, the   16, 29, 52, 56, 75, 78,
   118–20, 133, 135, 151–4, 172, 178,
   180–1, 192, 225, 230
Freud, S.   20, 70–1, 81–2, 218, 234
Friedrich, Caspar D.   151
friendship   27, 129, 131, 134–6, 191–3,
   225–6
fusion   86, 102, 109, 111, 123, 134, 138,
   145, 151, 171, 201, 224–5, 232

Gaia   108, 154, 231
garden/s   118–19, 151–4, 190, 227
genealogy   21–2, 39, 43–4, 77, 79, 113,
   115, 117, 127–8, 158, 190
Genet, J.   15, 72, 80, 194
geophilosophy   143, 154, 232
gift, the   29, 121–4, 129, 135, 191, 194,
   196, 221, 231
Goethe, J.W. von   76, 148, 172, 191
groups   49, 70, 77, 79, 99–101, 109,
   123–4, 127, 133–8, 142–6, 154,
   179, 184, 195–6, 204, 221, 223,
   225, 227
Guattari, F.   8–9, 46, 49, 56, 61, 79,
   89–92, 94, 102, 112, 143, 146, 150,
   154, 158, 169, 223, 227

Haydn, J.   197, 232
health   14, 62–4, 76, 118–19, 124, 140,
   153, 175, 192, 204
Hegel, G.   20–1, 24–5, 43, 45–6, 91–2,
   99–100, 102, 125, 144, 149, 212,
   217, 222
Heidegger, M.   6–8, 13, 18, 20, 22,
   25–6, 35, 39–46, 62, 78, 98,
   154, 156, 170–1, 199, 211,
   217–18, 229
'hell is other people'   9, 12, 23
Helmholtz, H. von   95

Heraclitus 4, 6, 28, 44–5, 92–3, 95, 104–5, 120, 128, 155, 176, 180, 213
herd, the 1, 27, 58, 62, 68, 115, 117, 128, 132–6, 138, 140–3, 204, 219–20
holism 24, 91, 98, 105
humanism 9–10, 15, 22–4, 31, 39–41, 43–4, 46–7, 116–17, 151, 156–7, 162–3, 171–4, 187, 213, 218, 229
Hume, D. 42, 78
Husserl, E. 20, 25–6, 39, 46–8, 50, 58, 69, 98, 106, 170, 217, 222
Huston, J. 81

idealism 42, 50, 58, 165
imagination, the 18, 26, 36, 68, 80, 87, 110, 124, 145, 150, 199, 201, 205–7, 222
incorporation 62–3, 69, 96, 111, 129–31, 152
individualism 23–4, 34–6, 109, 123, 129, 144, 150, 173, 215, 225–6
  ethical 7, 117–18, 131–3, 135–6
  methodological 10, 91, 101–2
institution, the 13, 61, 69, 71–2, 135, 137–8, 175, 194
instrumentalism 161–2, 217
intellectual conscience, the 61, 77–81
interconnectedness 100, 102, 109, 212
intermezzo, the 102, 223
intersubjectivity 12, 70, 101, 108, 122, 132–6, 145, 166–7, 173, 179, 211
Irigaray, L. 189, 231

Jaspers, K. 28, 33, 35
jazz 199–201, 223, 232
Jesus Christ 178, 207, 229
justice 125–6, 140–1, 144, 155, 188

Kant, I. 7, 15, 23, 29, 36, 43, 51–2, 55, 57–8, 69, 187, 200, 218
katharsis 82
Kierkegaard, S. 99, 182
Klossowski, P. 20–1, 204
Kofman, S. 20, 44, 189
Kropotkin, P. 138

Lacan, J. 24, 39, 73, 210, 218, 233
Laing, R.D. 50
Lamarck, J.B. 62, 68, 104, 219

Lange, F.A. 104, 177
language 16–17, 24, 28, 43–4, 50, 60, 67–8, 72–3, 86, 112, 218, 230–1
La Rochefoucauld, F. 43
last man, the 44, 116, 120, 150, 153, 172
Laws of Manu 118, 191
Lebensphilosophie 31, 175, 199, 202–3, 205
Lefebvre, H. 25
Leibniz, G.W 42–3
Les Temps Modernes 36, 47–8, 143, 165, 195
Levinas, E. 25–6
Lévy, B. 36, 195–6, 208, 232–3
Lévy-Bruhl, L. 25
Lewin, K. 110
liberalism 127, 226
Liebowitz, R. 200
look, the 36, 50, 166, 193–4, 218
love 14, 71, 78, 129–31, 134, 145, 172, 179–80, 183, 188, 193–5, 220–1
Lyotard, J.-F. 36, 39, 73

Machiavellianism 126–7
madness 19, 34, 42–3, 50, 52, 90, 127, 175, 203–10, 227
magic 25–6, 58–61, 64, 81, 111–13, 150, 164, 185, 203, 206–7, 209, 212, 227
Mallarmé, S. 80, 172
Mann, T. 34–5
Marcel, G. 10, 217
Marx, K./Marxism 20, 23, 25, 33, 36, 41, 46, 138, 141, 143–4, 150, 213
masks 15–16, 28, 30, 84, 150, 172, 180–1, 191, 204, 221
materialism 24, 42, 56, 102, 111, 165, 169–70, 183
matriciel, le 36, 167, 196
Mauss, M. 25
Menge, die 142–3
mereology 107, 113
Merleau-Ponty, M. 10, 26, 46, 65–6, 164–8, 170, 173, 192, 219, 222, 228, 231
metaphysics 16, 21, 24, 31, 33, 40–3, 45–7, 89, 94, 102, 105, 178, 185, 188, 223, 230

mnemotechnics 11, 74, 216
monism 28, 51, 91–2, 94–5, 98, 101–2, 113, 163, 169, 180, 225
Montaigne, M. de 16, 43
Mozart, W. 197
multiplicity 17–18, 52, 55, 61–2, 76–9, 89–92, 96–7, 100–1, 145, 157, 159, 169, 213
music 5, 64, 105, 125, 151, 158, 191, 196–201, 205, 212, 224, 230, 232
myth 28, 33–4, 67, 128, 139, 151, 178, 181–3, 185, 191, 198, 221, 230

Nachlass, the 13, 34–5, 76, 91, 127, 148, 156
naturalism 104, 178, 198
nature 3, 6–7, 34, 51, 69, 79, 104, 106–8, 112–13, 121, 148–54, 157–69, 172, 174, 184–5, 189, 212, 219, 224–5, 227, 232
nausea 5, 60, 75, 160, 179, 183, 189, 200, 220, 229
Nazism 2, 20, 22, 44, 127
Negri, A. 143, 184, 213, 223
Newton, I. 104, 107, 109, 223
Niche Construction Theory 223
Nietzsche, Elisabeth Förster 19, 127, 189, 202, 208, 231
Nietzsche, Franziska 177, 186, 189, 204, 231–2
nihilism 2, 5–6, 21, 23, 39–40, 43–5, 62, 83, 103–5, 116–17, 120–1, 138, 149, 172, 174, 176, 178–9, 181, 183, 185, 204, 213, 230
nomad/ism 14, 89, 92, 139, 143–4, 152, 154, 158, 211

objective spirit 67, 69–70, 167
Odysseus 158, 189, 221
Oehler, D. 186, 231
O-O-O (object-oriented ontology) 111, 169–71
Orestes 4, 184

pagan/ism 153, 164, 176–7, 180, 185, 225, 230
pan-Europeanism 126, 128, 133, 153

pantheism 179–80, 185, 204, 230
paradox 7, 9, 13, 15, 20–1, 27–33, 55, 66, 84, 100, 122, 131, 182, 187, 213, 217, 225
Pardaillan 64, 84
Parmenides 95
Paul, St. 178
perspectivism 17, 29–30, 50–3, 55, 112, 142, 156, 167, 189
Petőfi, S. 225
Pforta 104, 177, 186, 197, 220, 225
pharmakon 116, 157, 202
phenomenology 5–6, 11, 25–6, 48–53, 60, 66, 69, 80, 99, 111, 122, 160, 164–6, 170–1, 176, 183, 197, 222, 228
philology 13, 15, 18–19, 22, 44, 177, 218
Picard, M. 18, 33
Pithiatism 209
Plato/nism 3–4, 6–7, 39–43, 45, 51, 62–3, 78, 93, 104, 116, 121, 149, 178, 190–1, 212, 223
play 5–6, 8, 11, 16–19, 22, 28, 31, 44–6, 82–6, 93, 104, 118, 151, 154, 180, 197–201, 212, 221
pluralism 10, 18, 46, 79, 91–2, 96, 101–2, 112–13, 115, 118, 121–2, 126, 128, 138–9, 141–4, 154, 156, 169–70, 172, 176, 180, 185, 192, 211–12, 226–7
polytheism 180
Ponge, F. 46
posthumanism 9, 19, 26, 31, 35, 53, 86, 96, 111–13, 147–51, 158, 164, 169–74, 185, 212–13
postmodernism 8–10, 23–5, 31, 91, 112, 148
practico-inert 70, 72–3, 80, 100, 107, 112, 123, 137, 150, 167
praxis 9, 18, 30, 66–7, 70, 79–82, 85, 90, 99–102, 106–8, 112–13, 123, 131, 137, 145, 162–3, 174–5, 201, 211, 218, 226, 228
precautionary principle 150
pre-reflective 25, 52, 58–9, 61, 63, 78, 80–2, 130, 164, 166–7, 170, 197, 199, 201, 209, 218–22
progress 30, 127, 148–9, 213, 234

progressive-regressive method   32, 51, 174
psychoanalysis   23, 46, 50, 71, 106, 189, 213
psychology   14, 28, 34, 51, 60–3, 77, 81, 85–7, 90, 103, 105, 120, 167, 198, 202, 219, 225, 231

quantum physics   104–5, 108–10, 113, 213, 223–4

rapture   6, 64, 76–8, 86, 90, 134, 161, 172, 176, 180, 197, 199, 201, 205
reason   4, 7, 23, 40, 42–3, 52, 60, 62–3, 76–9, 84, 89, 91, 101–4, 106–7, 150, 156, 170, 172, 187, 204–6, 210, 212
reflection   6, 12, 44, 57–9, 61, 78, 80–2, 85, 87, 133, 166–7, 170, 209, 221, 227
relationality   94–6, 100, 162, 176, 185
rhizomatic   90, 92, 158
Roquentin, A.   2, 4–6, 11–12, 159–161, 172, 199–200, 206, 215, 220 231
Rousseau, J.-J.   29, 125

Salomé, L.   14, 20, 33–4, 175–6, 178, 188, 197, 202–3, 208, 232
Sanctus Janarius   192
Sartre, Anne-Marie   64, 143, 192–3, 232
Sartre, Arlette Elkaïm   175, 193, 207–8, 232
Saussure, F. de   89
Schopenhauer, A.   6, 13, 27, 33, 43, 74, 125, 157, 198–9, 225
Schweitzer, C.   215, 231
science   3, 27, 29, 33, 93, 95, 102–8, 111, 142, 148, 151, 171–2, 198, 213, 219, 223
Selbst   62–3, 78
selfishness   62, 134
self-overcoming   29, 74–5, 77–8, 86, 116, 119, 129, 172, 207, 212–13
sensism   154, 170
seriality   49, 68, 79, 109, 112, 124, 135, 137–8, 144, 184, 200
seriousness, the spirit of   83–6, 103, 118, 145, 185, 219

socialism   125–6, 130, 138, 141, 144, 226
socius   61, 63, 67, 90
Socrates   52, 93, 103–5, 151, 167, 172, 185, 207
space   5, 69, 91, 110–11, 130, 135, 137, 143, 152–3, 166, 168, 199, 223
Spinoza, B.   11, 42, 91, 101–2, 113, 143, 169
Stalinism   138, 143
state, the   29, 121, 125, 128, 130, 133, 138–45, 154, 172, 231
Stendhal   11, 133, 216
Stirner, M.   144, 226
Stoicism   64, 75–6, 78, 118, 120–1, 169, 187–8
style   20, 28, 30, 46, 64, 74–5, 78, 83, 87, 154
sublimation   32, 77–9, 82, 87, 94, 96, 117, 131, 145, 189, 212

Taoism   179
ternary   9, 25, 91, 96, 100, 113, 117, 185, 211
terrasophy   154, 176, 213, 230
theatre   137, 182, 198
Theseus   191
Tillich, P.   178
Tönnies, F. de   34
totality   20, 48, 59, 88, 92, 96, 98–101, 109, 133, 144, 168–9
totalization   10, 24, 66–7, 70, 72, 80–1, 97, 99–102, 107–8, 112–13, 123, 163, 174, 216, 225
transcendence   40, 60, 65–6, 70, 84, 86, 88, 97, 100, 116, 149, 178, 202
transhumanism   147–50, 213
truth   4, 6, 23, 27, 32, 34, 40, 42, 45, 49–50, 83, 94, 103, 105, 113, 121, 141–2, 152, 164, 181, 189–90, 223, 228

Übermensch   2, 5, 13, 21, 29–30, 34, 40, 44, 75, 77, 83, 92, 117, 120–1, 128, 132, 136, 148–50, 155, 157, 172, 178, 187, 189, 204–5, 230–1
Uexküll. J. von   158
unconscious, the   10, 20, 73–4, 78–9, 81–2, 189, 209, 212, 218, 229, 233

undecidability   22, 48, 86, 89, 150
Universal Singular   9, 67, 72, 99, 216

vécu, le   81
vicarious causation   171, 212
virtues   7, 117, 119, 127, 132, 135, 152, 155, 187–8, 191, 205
viscous, the   61, 111, 193, 224
Voltaire   43
voodoo   181, 184, 200, 205

Wagner, Cosima   3, 233
Wagner, Richard   3, 13, 27, 33, 35, 78, 103, 125, 138, 187, 191, 197–9, 213, 221, 225, 229–30, 232
Wahl, J.   25
wholeness   76, 79, 132–3, 148, 172, 179, 181

will to power   2–3, 5–7, 9, 13, 21–2, 28–9, 34, 40–1, 57, 79, 92, 95–6, 104–5, 108, 116, 127, 136, 139, 148, 152, 154–7, 160, 169, 172, 174, 181, 204, 215, 220, 223, 229
Will to Power, The   20, 35, 217
Words   17, 73, 89, 164, 210, 216–18, 230, 234
writing   11–17, 19, 43, 45, 64, 72, 122, 174–5, 182–3, 189, 191–2, 195, 198, 206, 216–17, 221, 226

Zarathustra   1, 4, 16, 27, 34, 40, 62, 75, 83, 94, 120, 132–3, 135–6, 140–1, 148, 151, 153–5, 157, 172, 178–80, 192, 204, 207, 212, 220, 225–7, 230
Zeus   120, 184

www.ingramcontent.com/pod-product-compliance
Lightning Source LLC
Chambersburg PA
CBHW062128300426
44115CB00012BA/1857